THE CERTIFICATION SERIES

US SAILING®

Basic Keelboat

The national standard for quality sailing instruction

Published by the UNITED STATES SAILING ASSOCIATION Copyright © 1998 by the UNITED STATES SAILING ASSOCIATION
All rights reserved. No part of this publication may be reproduced, stored in a retrieval system, or transmitted, in any form or by
any means, electronic, mechanical, photocopying, recording, or otherwise without prior written permission from the UNITED
STATES SAILING ASSOCIATION.   ISBN 1-882502-21-3.   Printed in the United States of America
UNITED STATES SAILING ASSOCIATION   P.O. Box 1260, 15 Maritime Drive, Portsmouth, RI 02871-6015

Acknowledgments

The US SAILING Keelboat Certification System and this book are the result of many people working together as a team. But without the initial and ongoing support of Robert H. Hobbs, James P. Muldoon, John Bonds, the Board of Directors of US SAILING, the Commercial Sailing Committee, the Training Committee and Sail America, this program would not have been launched. In addition, representatives from various sailing schools, charter companies and the boating industry have shared their invaluable input and advice. Assisting the creative team for this book has been a privilege and an adventure for Tim Broderick and Timmy Larr who have put in many long hours. We would also like to John Rousmaniere, author of *The Annapolis Book of Seamanship*, who along with Designer/Editor Mark Smith originally developed a number of presentation concepts adapted for use in this book.

Mark Smith
Designer/Editor
A lifelong sailor, graphic designer, editor and illustrator, Mark is currently Creative Director for North Sails. Mark was editorial and art director for *Yacht Racing/Cruising* magazine (now *Sailing World*) from 1970-83, editor and publisher of *Sailor* magazine from 1984-86, and editor and art director of *American Sailor* from 1987-89. His works include design and illustration for the *Annapolis Book of Seamanship*, authored by John Rousmaniere and published by Simon and Schuster. Mark lives in Rowayton, CT with his wife Tina and daughters Stephanie, Natalie and Cristina.

Monk Henry
Writer
Several years ago Monk became involved with sailing on San Francisco Bay as he approached retirement from a career in television as director and producer. He is currently preparing for his next career as he fulfills his lifelong ambition to sail to parts unknown on his 36-foot ketch.

Kim Downing
Illustrator
Kim grew up in the Mid-West doing two things, sailing and drawing, so it's only natural that his two favorite pastimes should come together in the production of this book. Kim is the proprietor of MAGAZINE ART and provides technical illustrations to magazine and book publishers. He recently helped his father complete the building of a custom 30-foot sailboat and enjoys racing and daysailing his own boat with his wife and two children.

Rob Eckhardt
Illustrator
A graphic design professional, Rob is currently on the staff of *SAIL* Magazine and has many years of experience as a designer for advertising agencies, publications and his own business clients. He is a graduate of the Rochester Institute of Technology, Rochester, NY. Rob began sailing dinghies as a youngster and currently enjoys one-design racing and coastal cruising.

James Chen
Photographer
James' work has been featured in numerous publications and corporate marketing promotional pieces. He is the recipient of many national and international photographic awards. James is a graduate of the Brooks Institute of Photography, Santa Barbara, CA, and enjoys occasional daysailing from his home in Santa Barbara, CA.

Foreword

Once you have spent time under sail, you will notice that people on sailboats tend to wave at each other. For many, sailing is a passion to be enjoyed for a lifetime. Ours is a sport that brings people together. A larger reward is often the places you go and the people you meet.

But sailing is challenging. And, in fact, at times can be dangerous. Therefore, safety at sea is of paramount importance.

To maximize your enjoyment on the water, you must have confidence in yourself, your boat, equipment and crew. *Basic Keelboat*, published by US SAILING, helps you learn to sail with all the skills required for safety at sea. For newcomers, careful study and practice is essential. When you're prepared, life under sail is more enjoyable.

For me, racing has been my primary focus. More recently, cruising, daysailing as well as racing boats of all sizes from Lasers to maxis, have blended together in a rewarding lifestyle. The lessons learned in *Basic Keelboat* will provide a strong foundation to help you build your skills for the future.

Gary Jobson

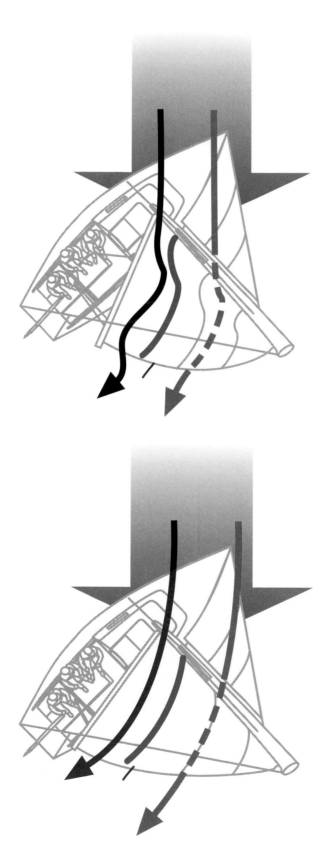

Part 1: Sailing Concepts

Part 2: Sailing Preparation

Part 3: Your First Sail

Part 4: After the First Sail

Part 5: The Sailing Environment

Part 6: Safety and Emergencies

Appendix

Parts of the Boat

Let's begin by learning some of the important parts on a boat and their names. Knowing some of these sailing terms will allow you to communicate better when on board the boat. Here's a quick overview.

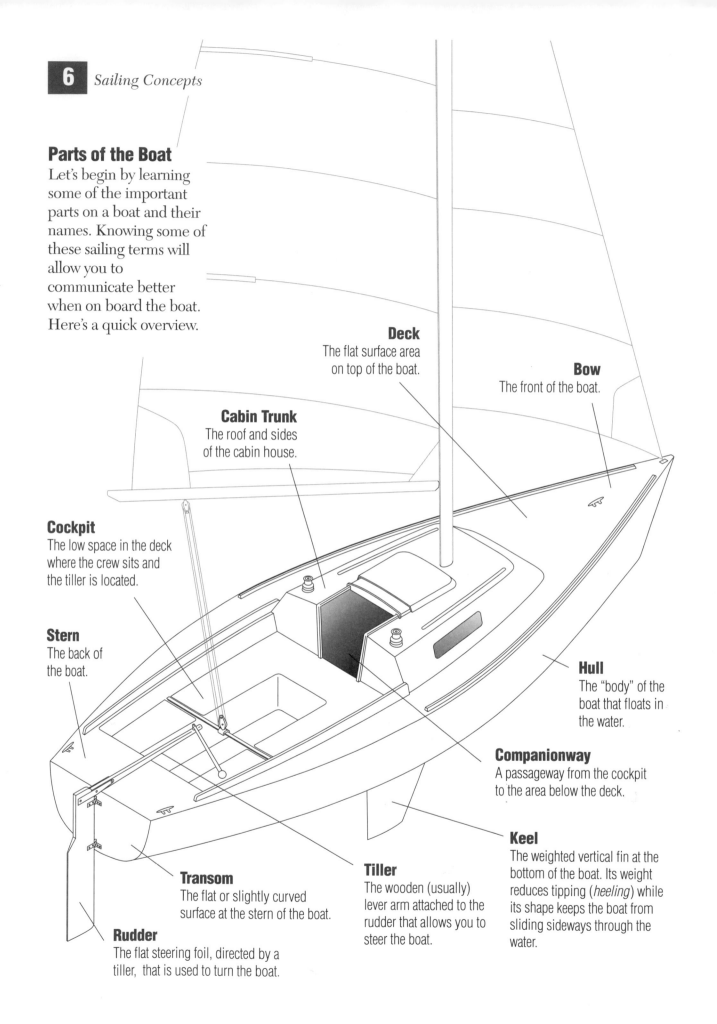

Deck
The flat surface area on top of the boat.

Bow
The front of the boat.

Cabin Trunk
The roof and sides of the cabin house.

Cockpit
The low space in the deck where the crew sits and the tiller is located.

Stern
The back of the boat.

Hull
The "body" of the boat that floats in the water.

Companionway
A passageway from the cockpit to the area below the deck.

Keel
The weighted vertical fin at the bottom of the boat. Its weight reduces tipping (*heeling*) while its shape keeps the boat from sliding sideways through the water.

Transom
The flat or slightly curved surface at the stern of the boat.

Tiller
The wooden (usually) lever arm attached to the rudder that allows you to steer the boat.

Rudder
The flat steering foil, directed by a tiller, that is used to turn the boat.

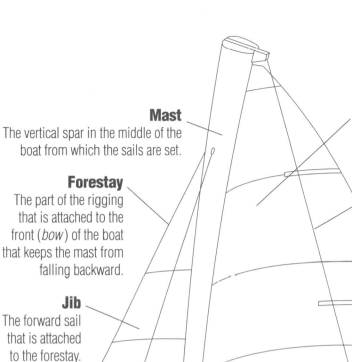

Mast
The vertical spar in the middle of the boat from which the sails are set.

Forestay
The part of the rigging that is attached to the front (*bow*) of the boat that keeps the mast from falling backward.

Jib
The forward sail that is attached to the forestay.

Mainsail
The sail hoisted on the back side of the mast and attached to the boom.

Backstay
The part of the rigging, attached from the top of the mast to the back (*stern*) of the boat, that keeps the mast from falling forward.

Batten
A slat of fiberglass, plastic or wood inserted into a pocket in the sail to help it hold its shape.

Spreader
Struts that extend from the side of the mast that keep it from bending sideways.

Parts of the Rig

Now that you know your way around the deck, it's time to look up. The *rig* includes sails (*mainsail* and *jib*), spars (*mast* and *boom*), supporting wires (*standing rigging*) and sail controls (*running rigging*).

Shrouds
Rigging wires extending up from the sides of the boat to the mast that keep the mast from falling to either side.

Boom
The horizontal spar extending back from the mast. The bottom (*foot*) of the mainsail is attached to it.

How a Sail Works

Sails are a boat's engine, and they produce power in one of two ways. When the wind is coming from the side of the boat, it flows around both sides of the sail (like an airplane wing), creating *lift* which "pulls" the boat forward. When the wind is coming from behind the boat, it "pushes" against the sail and simply shoves the boat forward.

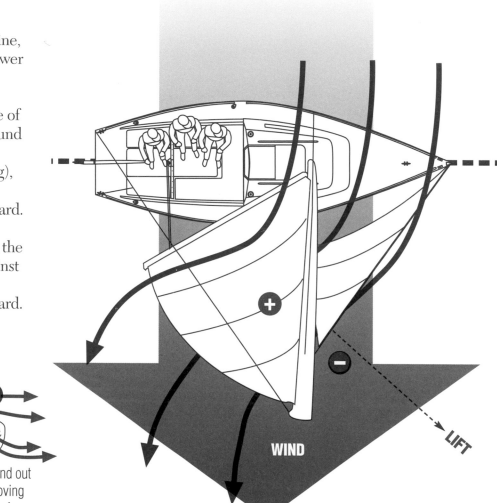

LIFT

If you hold your hand out the window of a moving car, you can feel the force of the wind lifting your hand. This is the same force that "pulls" a sailboat forward when the wind comes over the side of the boat.

WIND

LIFT

PULL MODE

Your sail is much more efficient at using the wind than your hand. It is shaped to bend the wind as it flows by, creating higher pressure on the inside of the sail ➕ and lower pressure on the outside ➖, thus creating lift. The lift the sail creates "pulls" the boat forward and sideways. The boat's *keel* (underwater fin) keeps the boat from being pulled sideways through the water.

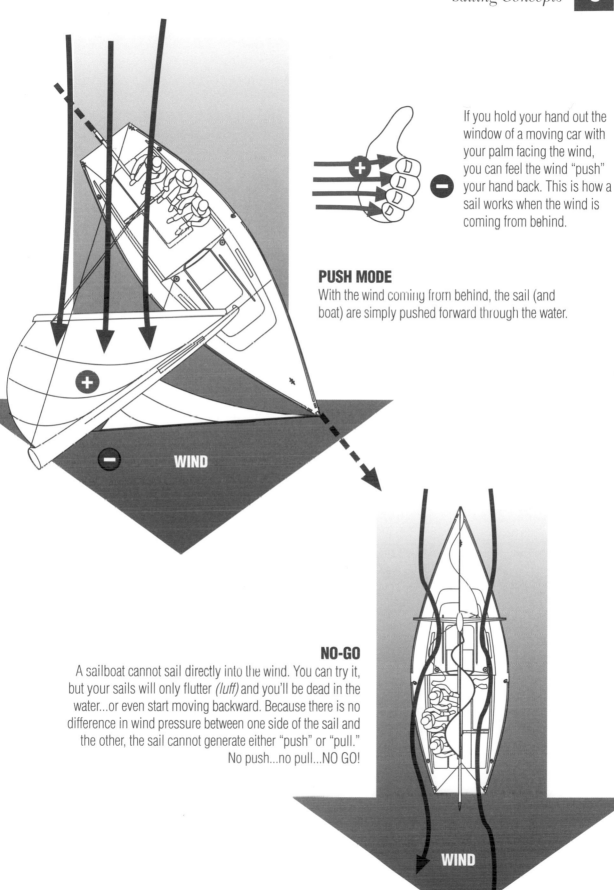

If you hold your hand out the window of a moving car with your palm facing the wind, you can feel the wind "push" your hand back. This is how a sail works when the wind is coming from behind.

PUSH MODE
With the wind coming from behind, the sail (and boat) are simply pushed forward through the water.

NO-GO
A sailboat cannot sail directly into the wind. You can try it, but your sails will only flutter *(luff)* and you'll be dead in the water...or even start moving backward. Because there is no difference in wind pressure between one side of the sail and the other, the sail cannot generate either "push" or "pull." No push...no pull...NO GO!

WIND

WIND

Trimming a Sail

Many sailors view a boat's mainsheet and jib sheet as they would the accelerator on a car...the more they sheet in (*trim*), the faster they go. This is true to a certain extent, but not completely. As we described on the previous spread, a sail creates power (*lift*) by redirecting wind *flow*. If the wind flows smoothly past the sails, optimum power will be achieved as well as maximum boat speed. If the sails are sheeted in or out too much, turbulent flow will result, reducing power and slowing the boat.

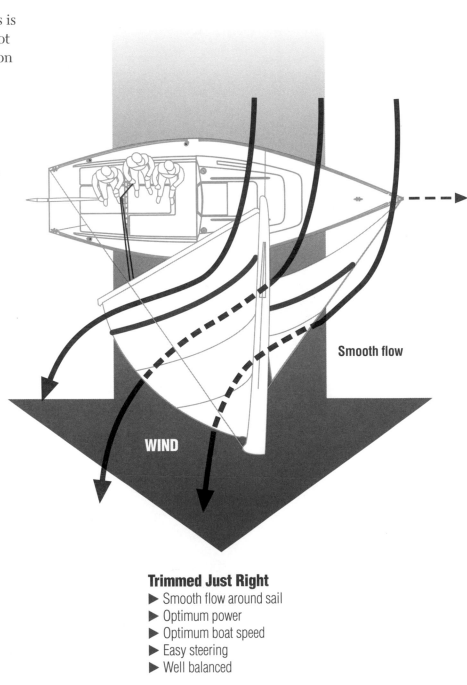

Smooth flow

WIND

Trimmed Just Right
▶ Smooth flow around sail
▶ Optimum power
▶ Optimum boat speed
▶ Easy steering
▶ Well balanced

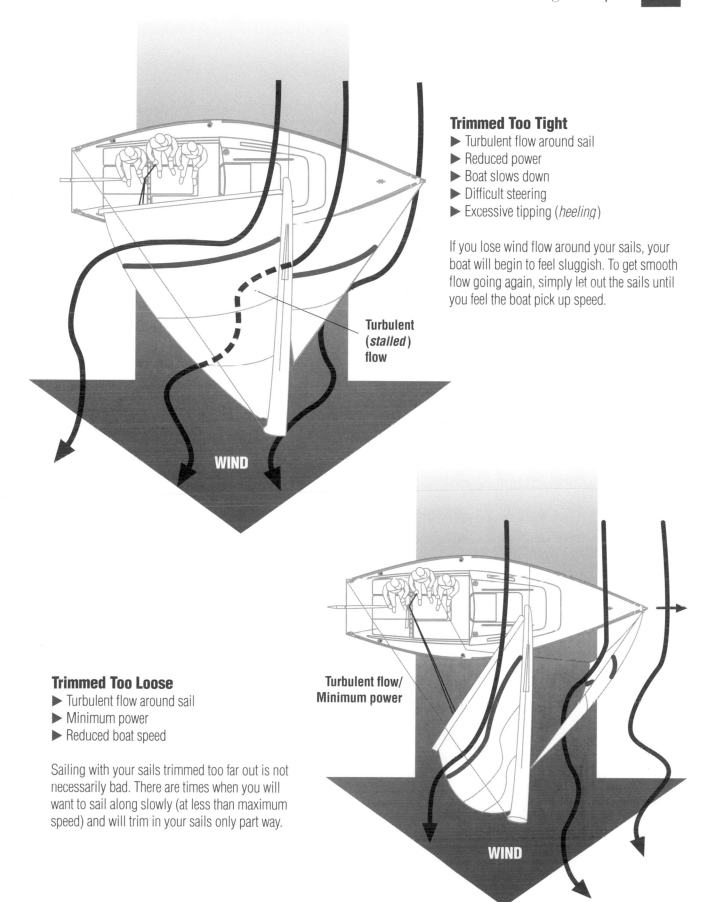

Trimmed Too Tight

▶ Turbulent flow around sail
▶ Reduced power
▶ Boat slows down
▶ Difficult steering
▶ Excessive tipping (*heeling*)

If you lose wind flow around your sails, your boat will begin to feel sluggish. To get smooth flow going again, simply let out the sails until you feel the boat pick up speed.

Turbulent (*stalled*) flow

WIND

Trimmed Too Loose

▶ Turbulent flow around sail
▶ Minimum power
▶ Reduced boat speed

Sailing with your sails trimmed too far out is not necessarily bad. There are times when you will want to sail along slowly (at less than maximum speed) and will trim in your sails only part way.

Turbulent flow/ Minimum power

WIND

Sailing Across the Wind

Sailing across the wind, with the wind perpendicular to the side of the boat, is a fast and easy way to sail — certainly easier than sailing upwind. In your first lesson, you will spend a lot of time sailing across the wind, learning how to steer and trim the sails.

Checklist

▶ Feel the wind coming across the boat.

▶ Sheet the sails about halfway out.

▶ Steer toward an objective or landmark. Adjust the sails to changes in the boat's direction or changes in wind direction.

These boats are sailing perpendicular to the wind with the wind coming over the side of the boat. This is called a *beam reach*.

WIND

Sailing across the wind (*reaching*) is easy, fun, and lively. There's a slight tip (*heel*) to the boat, the sails are about half-way out, and it's easy to steer straight ahead or to the left or right.

Sailing Upwind

Although a boat cannot sail directly into the wind, it can sail *upwind*, or close to where the wind is coming from. Sailing about 45 degrees from the direction of the wind is about the closest a boat can sail to the wind (although some high performance boats can sail as close as 30 to 35 degrees).

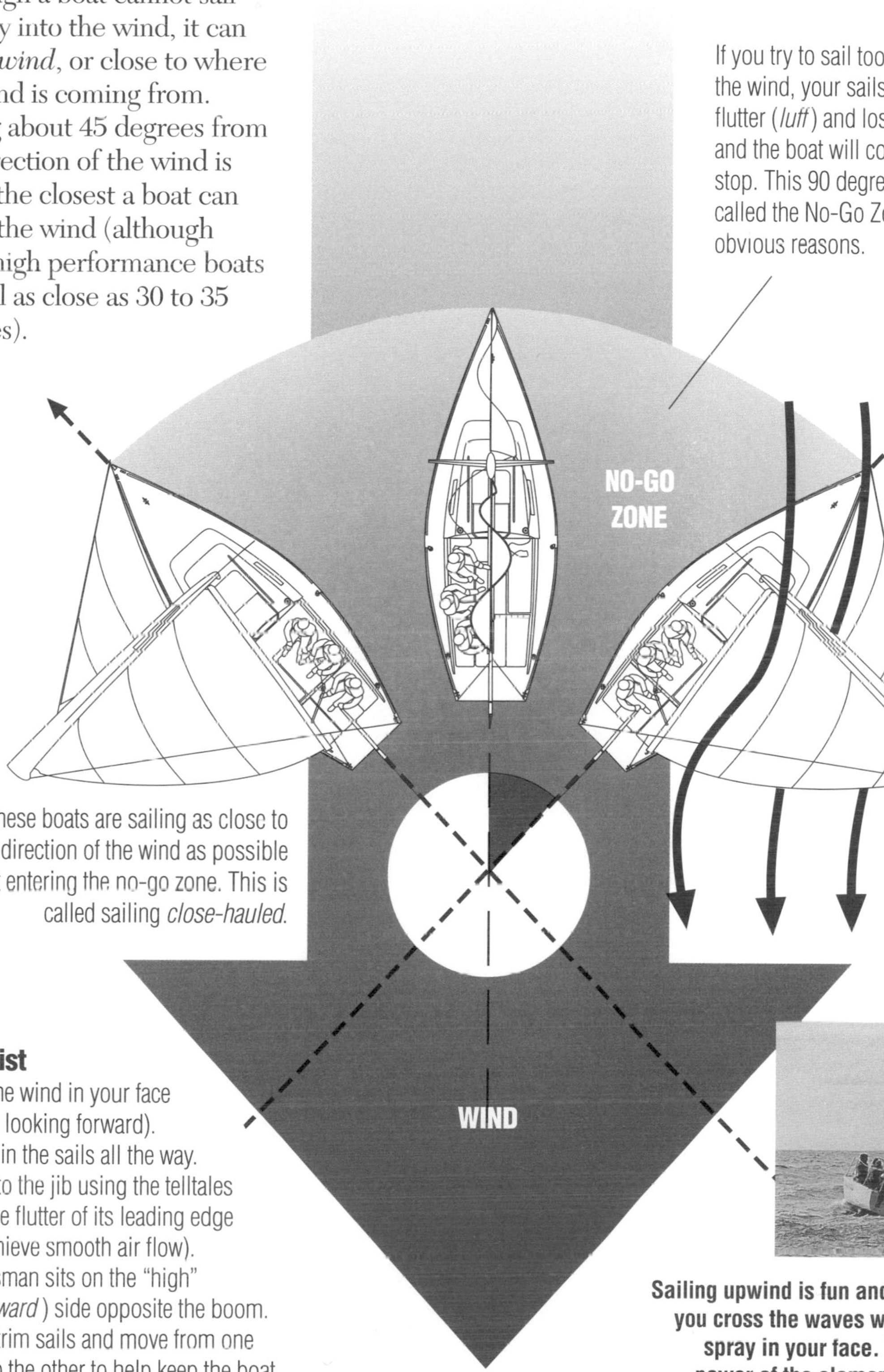

If you try to sail too close to the wind, your sails will flutter (*luff*) and lose power, and the boat will come to a stop. This 90 degree area is called the No-Go Zone for obvious reasons.

NO-GO ZONE

Two of these boats are sailing as close to the direction of the wind as possible without entering the no-go zone. This is called sailing *close-hauled*.

WIND

Checklist

► Feel the wind in your face (when looking forward).
► Sheet in the sails all the way.
► Steer to the jib using the telltales and the flutter of its leading edge (to achieve smooth air flow).
► Helmsman sits on the "high" (*windward*) side opposite the boom.
► Crew trim sails and move from one side to the other to help keep the boat from tipping (*heeling*) too much or too little.

Sailing upwind is fun and exhilarating as you cross the waves with the wind and spray in your face. You can feel the power of the elements of nature and know that you are using only this power to move through the water.

Sailing Downwind

Sailing downwind, with the wind coming over the back end of the boat, is the most comfortable and relaxing point of sail. The wind and the waves are following you, the ride is smooth, and the boat stays upright. Sailing at an angle to the wind is faster, safer, and easier than sailing with the wind coming directly behind the boat (*dead downwind*) because there is less chance for the boom to accidentally fly across the boat.

Sailing downwind is a very relaxing, "take it easy" way to sail with the wind at your back, your sails let out, and no spray to wet you.

Checklist

▶ Feel the wind on the back of your neck (when facing forward).

▶ Sheet out the sails so they're almost perpendicular to the wind.

▶ Steer toward an objective or landmark.

▶ Adjust the sails to changes in boat or wind direction.

▶ Watch the jib as an early warning for an accidental jibe where the boom suddenly comes flying across the boat. If the jib goes limp and starts to cross the boat, push the tiller toward the boom until the jib returns and fills with wind again.

These boats are sailing away from the wind, but at an angle to it. The wind is blowing over the back corner of the boat and the sails are sheeted perpendicular to the wind. This is called a *broad reach*.

WIND

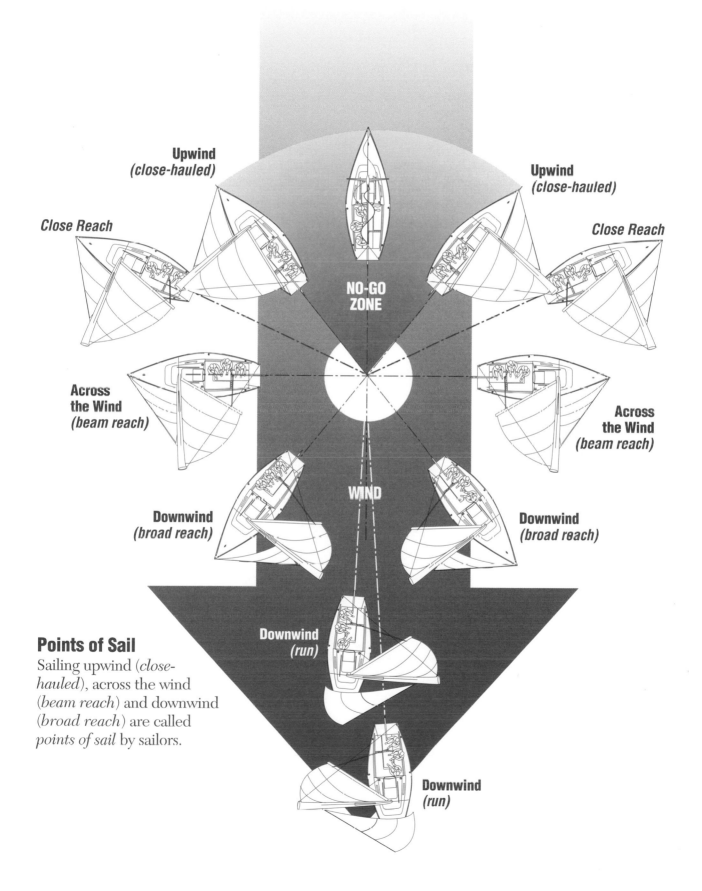

Upwind
(close-hauled)

Upwind
(close-hauled)

Close Reach

Close Reach

**NO-GO
ZONE**

**Across
the Wind**
(beam reach)

**Across
the Wind**
(beam reach)

WIND

Downwind
(broad reach)

Downwind
(broad reach)

Downwind
(run)

Downwind
(run)

Points of Sail

Sailing upwind (*close-hauled*), across the wind (*beam reach*) and downwind (*broad reach*) are called *points of sail* by sailors.

Heading Up and Down

Whenever a boat turns to change direction either to the left or right, it is also turning relative to the wind—either toward (*heading up*) or away from the wind (*heading down*). There are two key points to remember:

▶ To turn the boat, the tiller is pushed or pulled in the opposite direction that you want to turn.

▶ Whenever a boat changes direction, both the mainsail and jib should be sheeted in or out.

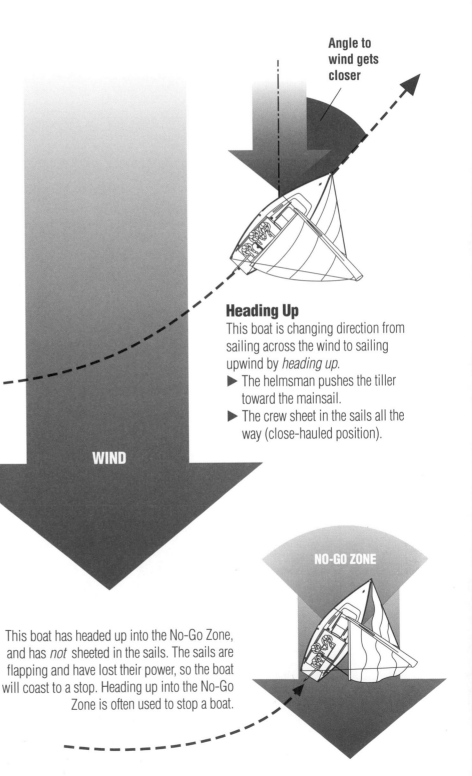

Angle to wind gets closer

WIND

Heading Up

This boat is changing direction from sailing across the wind to sailing upwind by *heading up*.

▶ The helmsman pushes the tiller toward the mainsail.

▶ The crew sheet in the sails all the way (close-hauled position).

NO-GO ZONE

This boat has headed up into the No-Go Zone, and has *not* sheeted in the sails. The sails are flapping and have lost their power, so the boat will coast to a stop. Heading up into the No-Go Zone is often used to stop a boat.

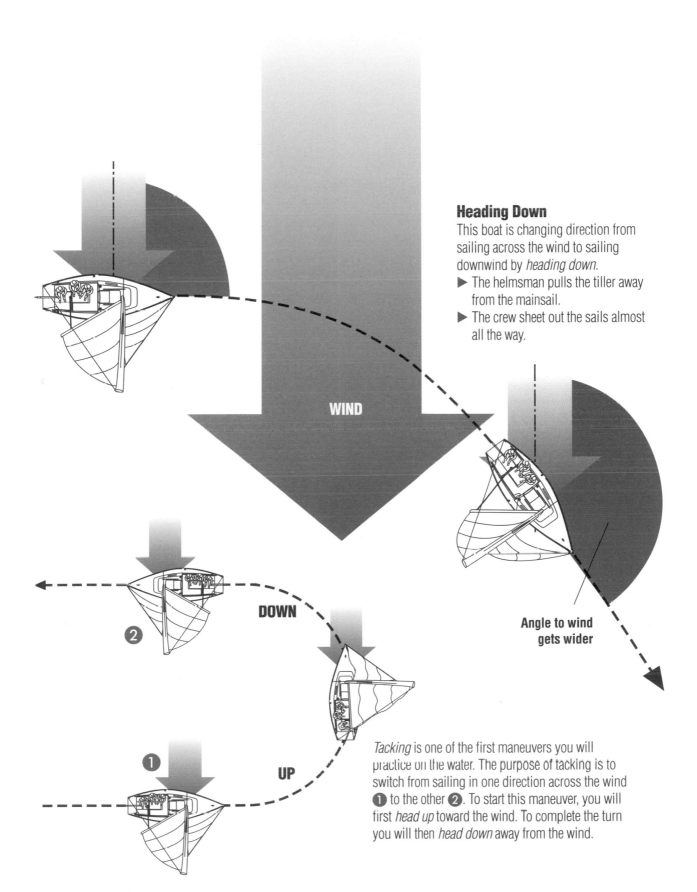

Heading Down
This boat is changing direction from sailing across the wind to sailing downwind by *heading down*.
▶ The helmsman pulls the tiller away from the mainsail.
▶ The crew sheet out the sails almost all the way.

WIND

DOWN

Angle to wind gets wider

❷

UP

❶

Tacking is one of the first maneuvers you will practice on the water. The purpose of tacking is to switch from sailing in one direction across the wind ❶ to the other ❷. To start this maneuver, you will first *head up* toward the wind. To complete the turn you will then *head down* away from the wind.

Tacking

A sailboat cannot sail directly into the wind. To make progress toward the wind, then, it must sail a zig-zag course, much as you would use a series of angular switch-backs to reach the top of a steep hill. When a sailboat switches from a "zig" to a "zag," it is called a *tack*. A tack or *tacking* is turning the front (*bow*) of a boat through the wind from one side of the No-Go Zone to the other. When a boat crosses the No-Go Zone, the sails will cross from one side of the boat to the other.

At the beginning of the tack ❶, the sailors are sailing close-hauled with the wind coming over the left or *port* side of the boat. In the middle of the tack ❷, the boat crosses the wind and No-Go Zone, and the sails lose all their power. In the final part of the tack ❸, their boat is again picking up speed, this time with the wind coming over the right (*starboard*) side of the boat. The boat's direction changed about 90°.

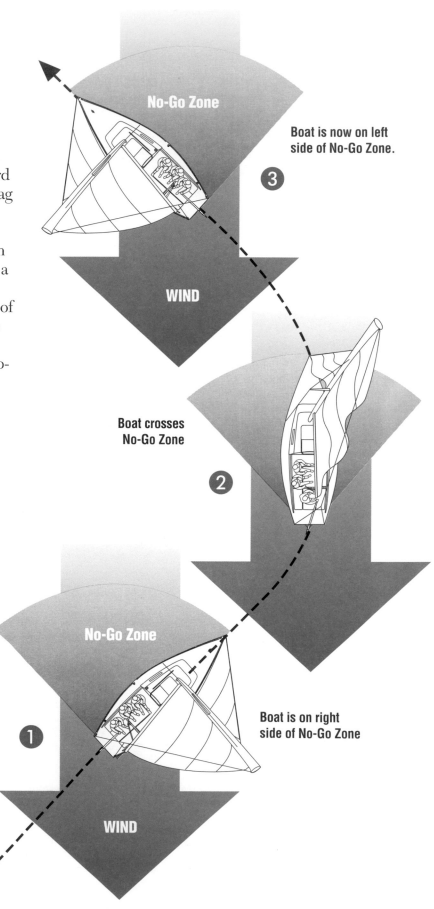

Boat is now on left side of No-Go Zone.

No-Go Zone

WIND

Boat crosses No-Go Zone

No-Go Zone

Boat is on right side of No-Go Zone

WIND

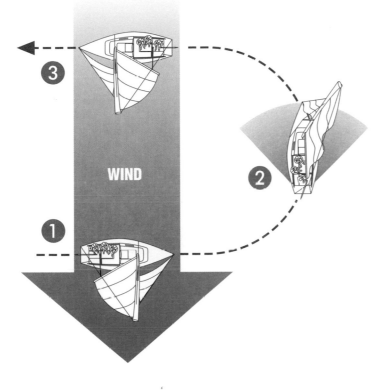

Tacking from Reach to Reach

Tacking doesn't only happen when you are trying to sail toward the wind. Any time you switch the wind from one side of the boat to the other by sailing through the No-Go Zone, you are performing a tack. In the sequence to the left, the boat is sailing across the wind (*reaching*) with the wind coming over the left (*port*) side ❶, then sailing through the No-Go Zone ❷ and finally sailing back across the wind (*reaching*) with the wind coming over the right (*starboard*) side ❸.

Getting Out of Irons

At some point while you are learning to sail, you will tack the boat too slowly through the wind and get stuck in the No-Go Zone. You are now *in irons*. It's a helpless feeling, but easily correctable. Here's how:

❶ Sheet in one of the jib sheets (in this case the one on the left side) until the wind blowing over the bow makes the sail billow back toward you. This will push the boat backward and also push the bow off to one side. When the boat starts to move backward, push the tiller in the same direction as the bow is turning (in this case to the right side) to help the boat turn more quickly. When the wind is coming over the side of the boat ❷, release the jib sheet and sheet in on the other side. Then straighten the tiller, sheet in the mainsail, and off you go!

In Irons

The boat is pointed directly into the wind, both sails are flapping, the boat has come to a dead stop, and the rudder and tiller don't work (water has to be flowing past the rudder for it to steer the boat).

Jibing

Another basic maneuver in sailing is the jibe. Like a tack, a jibe is a change in boat direction through the wind with the sails crossing from one side of the boat to the other. During a tack, you steer the front end (*bow*) through the wind (No-Go Zone). During a jibe, the wind crosses over the back of the boat (*stern*).

At the beginning of the jibe ❶ the sails are let out almost all the way with the wind coming over the right (*starboard*) side of the boat. In the middle of the jibe ❷, the back (*stern*) of the boat crosses the wind and the sail swings over from one side to the other. In the final part of the jibe ❸ the mainsail is let back out almost all the way and the boat continues on with the wind coming over the left (*port*) side of the boat.

NOTE: In a tack the boom crosses the cockpit relatively slowly. But in a jibe, the boom can whip across quickly as the sail swings from one side to the other. A "controlled" jibe (more on controlling the jibe later) helps minimize the speed of the boom crossing over. An uncontrolled or *accidental jibe* (see opposite page) should be avoided.

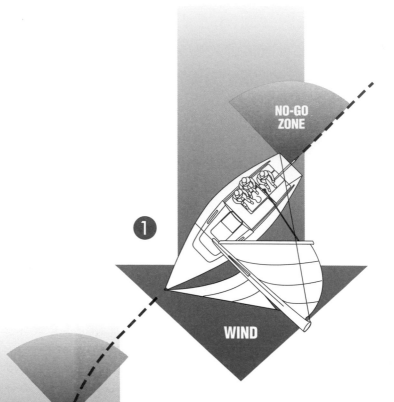

A key to controlling the mainsail as it crosses over during a jibe is to sheet it in to the center of the boat before the stern crosses the wind. After the boom flops over, the mainsheet is let out quickly. Remember: *KEEP YOUR HEAD LOW AS THE BOOM SWINGS OVER!*

Dangerous Accidental Jibes!

The boat in this illustration is going through a jibe, but has forgotten to sheet in the mainsail. The result is an uncontrolled, or *accidental jibe*. The force of the boom rapidly swinging across can break rigging or hit a crew member. In ❷ and ❸ it is still possible to avoid the accidental jibe, if the helmsman steers back onto the original course ❶. The key thing to remember if the accidental jibe occurs ❹ is to quickly duck under the boom's path. *The alert sailor should shout out a warning!*

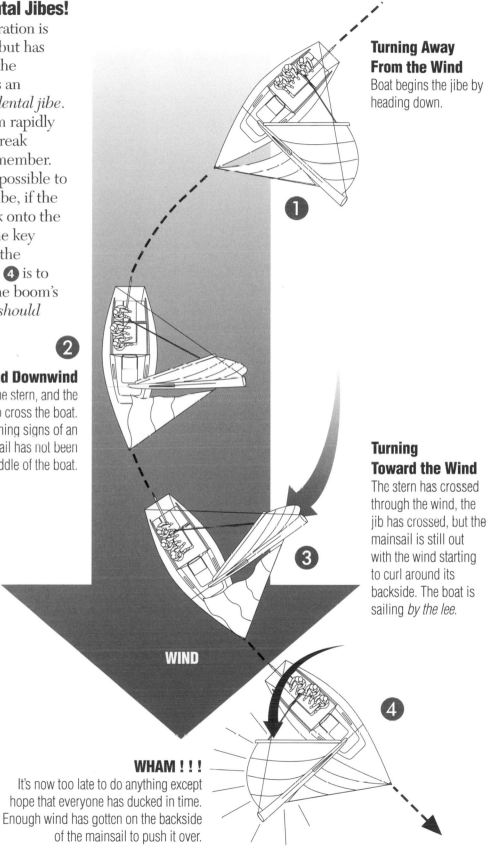

Turning Away From the Wind
Boat begins the jibe by heading down.

Dead Downwind
Wind is directly behind the stern, and the jib is limp and starts to cross the boat. These are the warning signs of an impending jibe. The mainsail has not been sheeted in to the middle of the boat.

Turning Toward the Wind
The stern has crossed through the wind, the jib has crossed, but the mainsail is still out with the wind starting to curl around its backside. The boat is sailing *by the lee*.

WIND

WHAM ! ! !
It's now too late to do anything except hope that everyone has ducked in time. Enough wind has gotten on the backside of the mainsail to push it over.

Getting There and Returning

Now, we will take what you have just learned about sailing upwind, across the wind and downwind and put them all together. Let's start by sailing toward the wind (*upwind*) to a buoy with a series of zig-zags called *tacks*. Then, we'll sail across the wind to another buoy. After rounding the buoy, we'll sail downwind using another series of zig-zags called *jibes*. Tacks are usually made at 90 degree angles. Jibes can be made at just about any angle.

Whether you are sailing upwind, across the wind or downwind, the wind will be blowing over one side of the boat or the other. If the wind is blowing over the right (*starboard*) side, you are sailing on *starboard tack*. If the wind is blowing over the left (*port*) side, you are sailing on *port tack*.

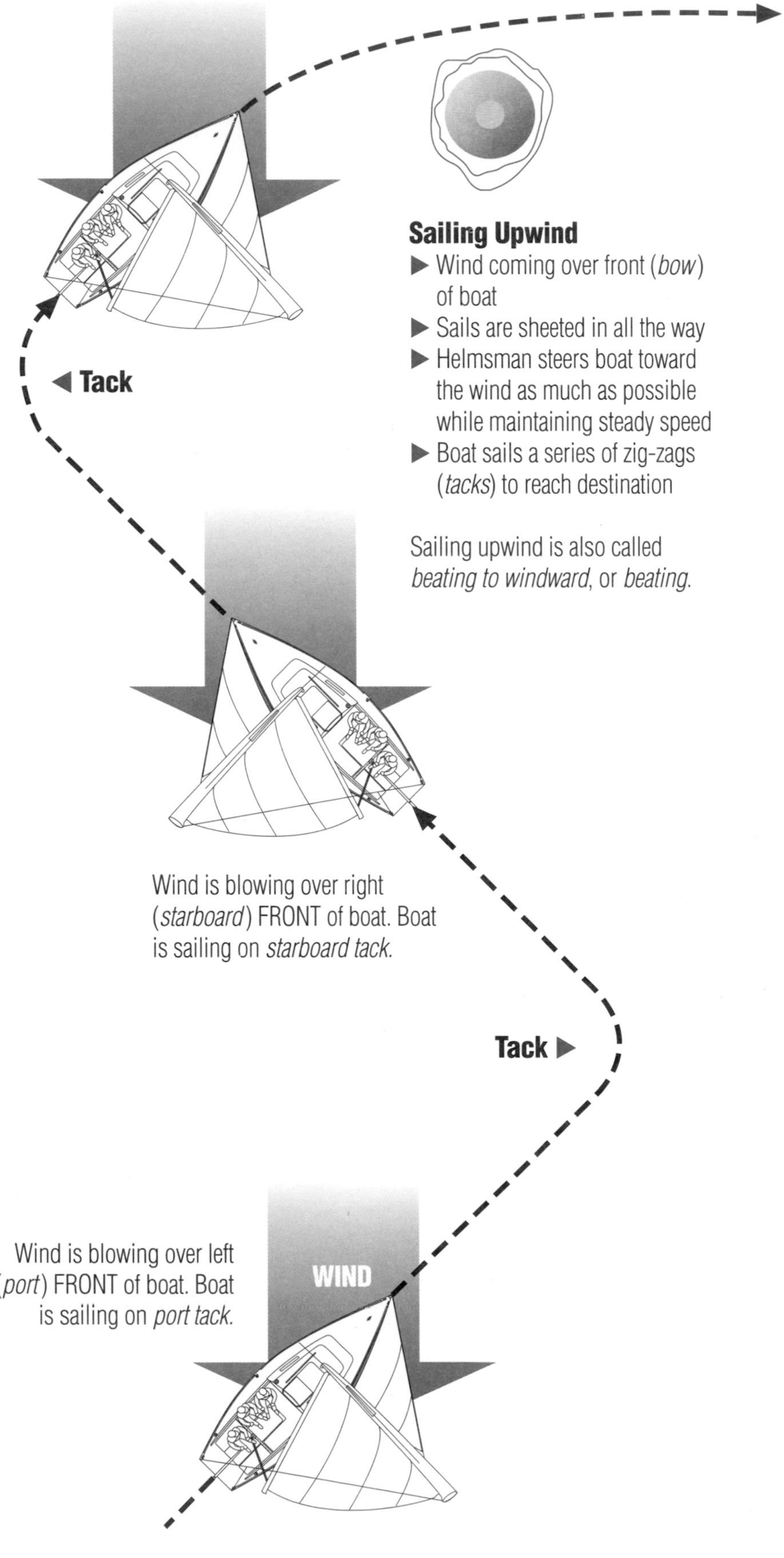

◀ **Tack**

Sailing Upwind
▶ Wind coming over front (*bow*) of boat
▶ Sails are sheeted in all the way
▶ Helmsman steers boat toward the wind as much as possible while maintaining steady speed
▶ Boat sails a series of zig-zags (*tacks*) to reach destination

Sailing upwind is also called *beating to windward*, or *beating*.

Wind is blowing over right (*starboard*) FRONT of boat. Boat is sailing on *starboard tack*.

Tack ▶

Wind is blowing over left (*port*) FRONT of boat. Boat is sailing on *port tack*.

WIND

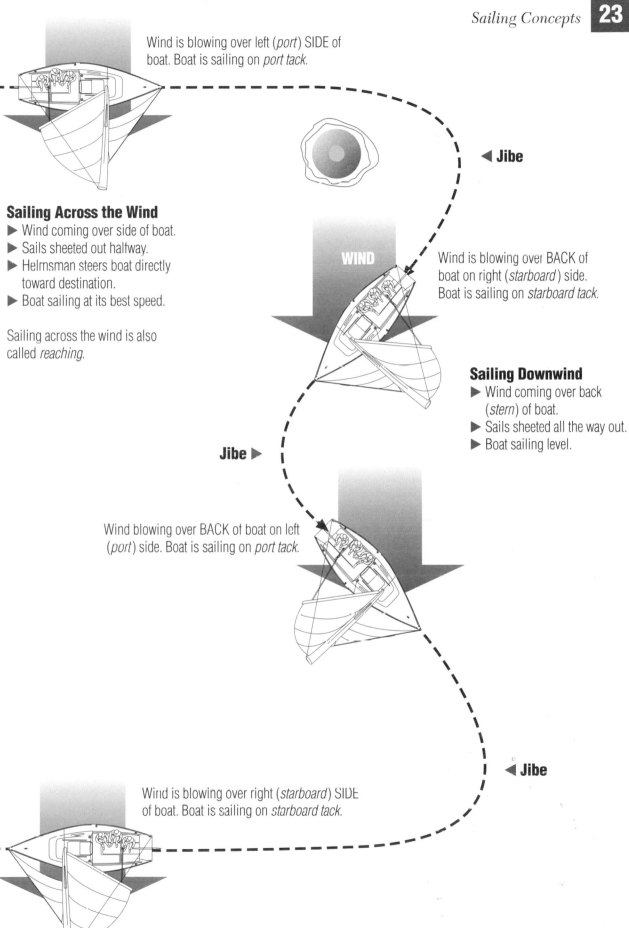

Wind is blowing over left (*port*) SIDE of boat. Boat is sailing on *port tack*.

◀ Jibe

Sailing Across the Wind
▶ Wind coming over side of boat.
▶ Sails sheeted out halfway.
▶ Helmsman steers boat directly toward destination.
▶ Boat sailing at its best speed.

Sailing across the wind is also called *reaching*.

WIND

Wind is blowing over BACK of boat on right (*starboard*) side. Boat is sailing on *starboard tack*.

Sailing Downwind
▶ Wind coming over back (*stern*) of boat.
▶ Sails sheeted all the way out.
▶ Boat sailing level.

Jibe ▶

Wind blowing over BACK of boat on left (*port*) side. Boat is sailing on *port tack*.

Wind is blowing over right (*starboard*) SIDE of boat. Boat is sailing on *starboard tack*.

◀ Jibe

Warm Weather Dressing

If you want to enjoy sailing, you've got to be comfortable. Preparation is the key, so put together a sailing gear bag for yourself with clothing and gear that will protect you and make you feel at ease in all weather conditions. Whether it's cloudy or sunny, protect yourself with sunscreen, using Sun Protection Factor (SPF) 15 or higher. You can get burned even on a cloudy day, especially with the sun's rays reflecting off the water.

Life jackets, known as **Personal Flotation Devices** or PFDs in Coast Guard vocabulary, are essential. They must be carried on all boats, and US SAILING recommends they be worn during classes, and especially on cold windy days.

Type I PFD   **Type II PFD**   **Type III PFD**

The Offshore Life Jacket, or **Type I PFD**, is very buoyant, but bulky. It is designed for moderately heavy seas and will keep an unconscious person's head face up. The Near-Shore Buoyant Vest, or **Type II PFD**, is less bulky but not as buoyant as the Type I. Common to many boats, the Type II turns some unconscious people to a face-up position. The vest type, or **Type III PFD**, is more comfortable and easier to swim in than the other two, but is not designed to keep a person's face out of the water.

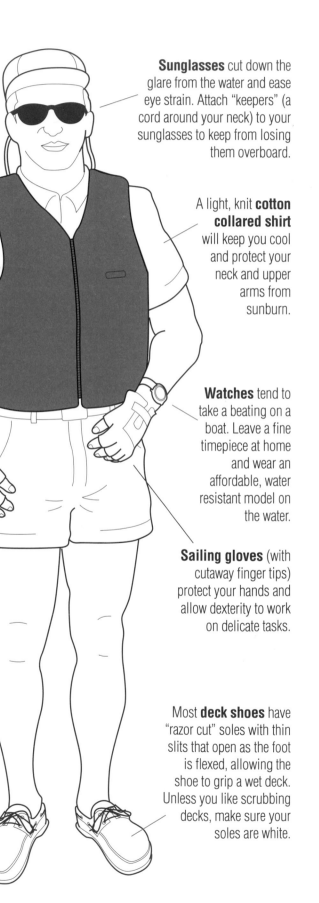

Sunglasses cut down the glare from the water and ease eye strain. Attach "keepers" (a cord around your neck) to your sunglasses to keep from losing them overboard.

A light, knit **cotton collared shirt** will keep you cool and protect your neck and upper arms from sunburn.

Watches tend to take a beating on a boat. Leave a fine timepiece at home and wear an affordable, water resistant model on the water.

Sailing gloves (with cutaway finger tips) protect your hands and allow dexterity to work on delicate tasks.

Most **deck shoes** have "razor cut" soles with thin slits that open as the foot is flexed, allowing the shoe to grip a wet deck. Unless you like scrubbing decks, make sure your soles are white.

Body heat escapes from the top of the head. A weather-proof hat will help keep you dry. Tie it on so it doesn't get lost overboard. **A knit ski cap** under the hood of your foul-weather jacket will keep you both warm and dry.

A **nylon-fleece jacket** with a tall collar will keep you warm and protect your neck from wind and spray. When worn over a turtleneck and sweater, you will be warm enough for most sailing situations.

Full-fingered **sailing gloves** make it easier to hold onto *lines* (ropes) and tiller on a chilly day.

Loose-fitting long pants over long underwear is usually enough to keep most people's legs warm. If you're still cold, you can wear your foul-weather gear pants on top. Loose pants also allow easier movement.

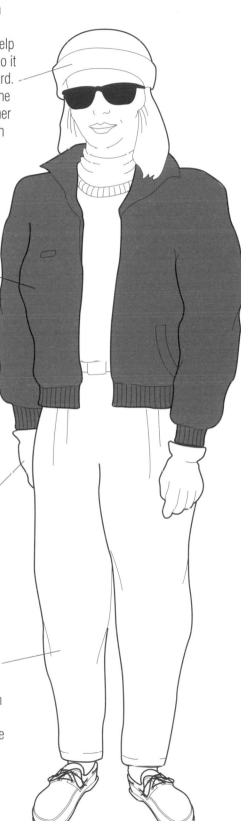

Cool Weather Dressing

Cold, wet weather offers more challenges to staying comfortable. Remember, just because a day looks dry and warm in the morning doesn't mean it's going to stay that way. Be prepared for a change in the weather, and carry your gear with you. The best defense against cold weather is a layered approach, from long underwear to a long-sleeved shirt and pants to a sweater or sweatshirt to an insulated jacket to foul-weather gear. Keeping your hands, feet, and head warm with gloves, wool socks, and a hat is essential for comfort.

The protection provided by the **foul-weather gear** keeps sailing pleasurable even in wet conditions. Two-piece foul-weather gear (pants and a jacket) is more versatile than a one-piece jump-suit. You will find weather conditions when you will want to wear only the jacket or only the pants. In selecting gear, make sure it:
▶ fits comfortably with enough room for movement and for extra clothes underneath;
▶ has flaps covering zippers and pockets;
▶ has velcro or elastic closures at the ankles and wrists;
▶ has abundant pockets;
▶ has a hood.

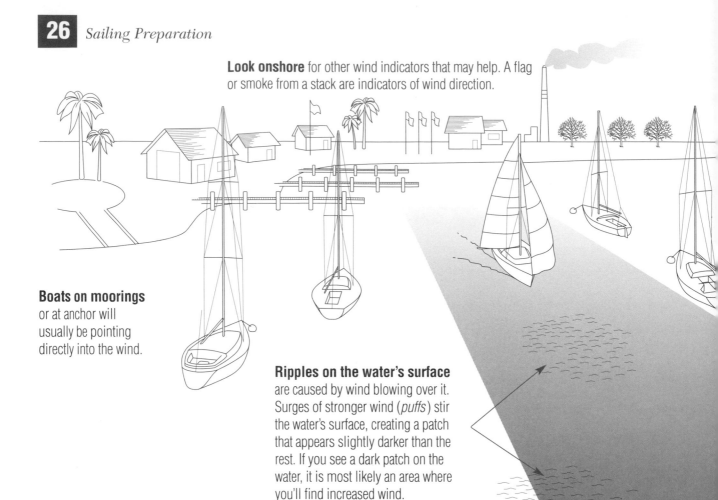

Look onshore for other wind indicators that may help. A flag or smoke from a stack are indicators of wind direction.

Boats on moorings or at anchor will usually be pointing directly into the wind.

Ripples on the water's surface are caused by wind blowing over it. Surges of stronger wind (*puffs*) stir the water's surface, creating a patch that appears slightly darker than the rest. If you see a dark patch on the water, it is most likely an area where you'll find increased wind.

"Reading" the Wind

Obviously you need wind to sail. You also need to know the direction of the wind. Out on the water you might have a nice breeze blowing, but if you don't know its direction, you won't know how to set your sails or steer your course. There are many clues, both on land and water, which you can use to tell which way the wind is blowing.

Your ears and your face are your own built-in wind indicators. After awhile they will become sensitized to the wind and you'll be able to sense wind direction quite accurately without relying as much on other references.

A masthead fly at the top of the mast is a helpful indicator of wind direction.

Look at other sailboats and how they have their sails trimmed. If you see a boat sailing *close-hauled*, you know that it is heading about 45° off the wind. A boat with its mainsail eased all the way out is pointing in the opposite direction to the wind.

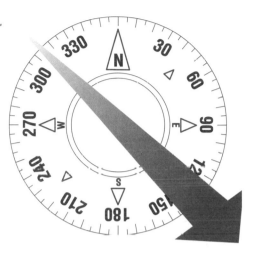

Wind direction is described by the direction it is coming *FROM*. A westerly wind is one that comes out of the west and blows toward the east. The wind on this *compass rose* is coming from a direction between north and west. It would be called a northwest wind (or *northwester*).

To determine the direction of the wind, head up directly into the wind so the sails are flapping (*luffing*) like a flag and the boom is on the boat's centerline. The front (*bow*) of the boat is now pointing directly into the wind.

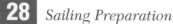

Parts of a Sail

Sails on modern sailboats are triangular, and the three corners and the three edges of the sail all have different names. Sails are raised by a line called a *halyard* attached to the top corner.

Edges of a Sail

▶ The bottom edge of a sail is called the **foot**. The foot of a mainsail is attached to the *boom*, while the *foot* of a jib is unattached.

▶ The forward edge of a sail is called the **luff**. On the jib the *luff* is attached (usually by *hanks*) to the forestay. The *luff* of the mainsail is attached to the *mast*.

▶ The back (*after*) edge of each of the sails is called the **leech**. It is not attached to the rig.

Halyards

Halyards are used to raise and lower the sails, and are often led inside the mast.

▶ The **jib halyard** runs over an internal pulley (*sheave*) in the front of the mast.

▶ The **main halyard** runs over the *sheave* on the back side of the top of the mast.

Corners of a Sail

▶ Both jib and mainsail are attached to the rig at their lower forward corners. This corner of the sail is called the **tack**.

▶ The lower back corner of each sail is called the **clew**. The *jib sheets* are attached to the clew of the jib, and the *outhaul* is attached to the clew of the mainsail.

▶ The top corner of the sails is called the **head**, and is attached to the *halyard*. The head is the corner with the smallest angle of the three corners.

HEAD

HEAD

LEECH

LUFF

LEECH

LUFF

CLEW

TACK

CLEW

TACK

FOOT

FOOT

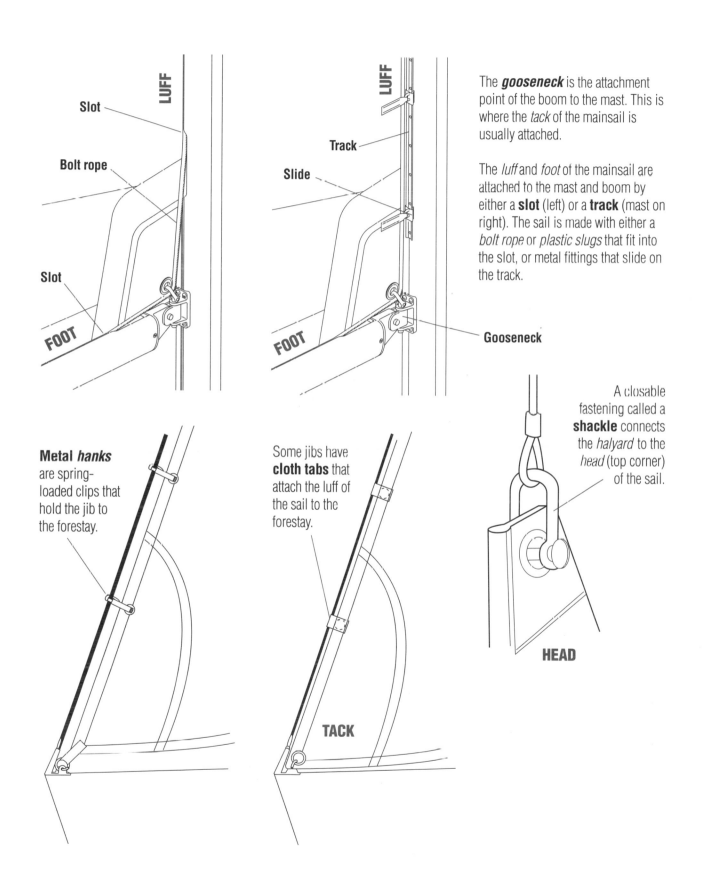

LUFF

Slot

Bolt rope

Slot

FOOT

LUFF

Track

Slide

FOOT

Gooseneck

The **gooseneck** is the attachment point of the boom to the mast. This is where the *tack* of the mainsail is usually attached.

The *luff* and *foot* of the mainsail are attached to the mast and boom by either a **slot** (left) or a **track** (mast on right). The sail is made with either a *bolt rope* or *plastic slugs* that fit into the slot, or metal fittings that slide on the track.

Metal *hanks* are spring-loaded clips that hold the jib to the forestay.

Some jibs have **cloth tabs** that attach the luff of the sail to the forestay.

A closable fastening called a **shackle** connects the *halyard* to the *head* (top corner) of the sail.

HEAD

TACK

Rigging the Sails

Before leaving the dock the sails must be properly attached and raised. To rig the mainsail, first ease the *outhaul* and *cunningham* lines and unfold the sail, then follow the recommended sequence on this page.

Make sure all halyard shackles are fastened securely.

Rigging the Jib:

❶ Fasten the *tack* of the jib to the proper fitting at the bow.

❷ Starting with the bottom fastener, attach the *luff* of the jib onto the *forestay*.

❸ After assuring that you have the proper line, attach the *jib halyard shackle* to the head of the jib. Check that the *halyard* is not wrapped around the forestay.

❹ Secure the jib sheets to the *clew* of the jib using *bowline knots*. Jib sheets usually pass inside the *shrouds*, through the *fairleads*, and to the cockpit. Tie a stopper knot (usually a *figure-8 knot*) into the ends of the sheets in the cockpit.

Tie jib sheets into the clew with bowline knots (see p.58).

Rigging the Mainsail:

❶ Attach the *foot* to the boom by inserting the *clew* of the sail into the forward end of the boom slot, pulling it along the boom, and attaching the *outhaul*.

❷ Attach the *tack* of the sail to the *gooseneck*.

❸ Connect the *cunningham*.

❹ Tighten the outhaul to tighten the foot of the main (your instructor will show you how tight it should be). Secure the outhaul line.

❺ Attach the luff to the mast, making sure it's not twisted (your instructor will show you how to avoid twists). If it is connected by metal or fiberglass slides, feed them onto the track, and make sure they are all attached. If it uses a *bolt rope*, slide the head into the slot on the mast.

❻ Attach the *main halyard shackle* and remove any slack to keep it from snagging a spreader and prevent the head from slipping out of the slot.

❼ If *battens* have been removed, insert them before raising the sail. The more flexible end, usually thinner or tapered, should be inserted into the pocket first.

Before you hoist the mainsail, remove slack from the halyard to keep it from snagging the rigging.

WIND

Hoisting the Sails

Before hoisting your sails, the boat should be pointed into the wind. Hoist the mainsail first, as it will help keep the boat's *bow* into the wind (and No-Go Zone) until you are ready to cast off.

Feeding the mainsail *luff* into the slot of the mast as it is raised helps keep the sail from jamming in the slot.

Hoisting the Mainsail:

❶ Tighten the outhaul.
❷ Loosen the cunningham and/or downhaul.
❸ Loosen the mainsheet and any reefing lines and remove any sail ties.
❹ Tighten the traveler controls.
❺ Release the boom vang.
❻ Check the halyard to make sure it's clear, then hoist away.

Snug up your *outhaul* before raising the sail. It's harder to do once the mainsail is hoisted and the boom is moving in the wind.

❼ Look up the mast to check that the sail is going up smoothly.
❽ Allow the sail to *luff* so it will go up more easily.
❾ Wrap the halyard around a *winch* if it becomes difficult to hold — be very careful about using a winch handle as it's easy to break something.

Hoisting the Jib:

❶ Everyone should clear the foredeck so they are not hit by the sail as it flaps in the wind.
❷ Make sure both the halyard and the jib sheets are clear and untangled.
❸ Make sure the sheets are in the cockpit and free to run.
❹ Raise the sail with the jib halyard. Finish hoisting by using a winch to tighten the luff if necessary.
❺ Secure and coil the halyard.

Make sure the mainsheet and jib sheets are loose and free to run. This allows the sails to move freely in the wind so the boat doesn't start sailing at the dock!

You should now have both sails up and luffing with the boat aimed directly into the wind. The boat is still secured to the dock.

WIND

Sail Controls

The sail controls of a sailboat (*running rigging*) allow you to adjust the position and shape of the sails in response to changes in course, wind direction and wind strength. Each sail adjustment involves a system of components. For example, trimming the jib involves using the jib sheet, the fairleads, and winches. Let's take a quick look at the sail control components found on most sailboats.

The **cunningham** is a line that is used to tighten the front (*luff*) of the mainsail along the mast. On some boats, a *downhaul* serves the same purpose.

The **boom vang** is used to keep the boom from rising up when wind hits the mainsail.

Jib sheets control the jib. They run from the bottom corner of the jib back to the cockpit. They are pulled in (*trimmed*) or let out (*eased*) to change the shape and angle of the jib.

Jib sheets run through **fairleads**. These pulleys (*blocks*) are usually attached to an adjustable track on the deck or to a rail (*toe rail*) on the side of the deck. The fairlead is moved forward and backward on the track to accommodate different sized jibs and jib trimming angles.

The **outhaul** is a line used to tighten the bottom (*foot*) of the mainsail.

The **mainsheet** controls the angle and shape of the mainsail. It runs through a series of pulleys (*blocks*) which give the crew mechanical advantage while they pull in (*trim*) or let out (*ease*) the sail.

A rope (*line*) is secured to a *cleat*. The most common is a **horn cleat**, which is secure and easy (but slow) to release under heavy load. A line that will be left unattended, such as a docking line, should be secured with a cleat hitch (shown).

The **traveler** controls the position of the boom across the boat.

A **cam cleat** ❶ has jaws with "teeth" that are spring loaded so they press and grip a line snugly. To release the line, pull and lift. Cam cleats can be difficult to release under heavy load.

A **clam cleat** ❷ is very easy to use...simply pull the line through it and let go. To release the line, pull and lift it out (this can be a difficult task under a heavy load).

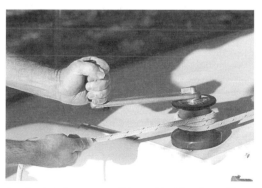

A **winch** helps you pull in and hold a sheet. The friction of wrapping a sheet around the winch drum reduces the pull needed to hold the sheet in. A winch handle can be inserted into the top of the winch to provide additional power for pulling in the sheet.

Leaving the Dock

Like learning how to park a car, learning how to leave or return to a dock can make beginning sailors nervous. With a little forethought and only basic sailing skills you can leave and return to a dock without risk. Boats and docks are large objects, however, and the safety of your crew should be foremost when departing or arriving at a dock.

First decide how you will leave the dock, then explain your departure plan to the crew members and make sure everyone knows what they should do and when. In both examples shown here, the boat is pointed into the wind (*No-Go Zone*) and must be turned out of the zone to sail away from the dock. In the example above, there is an open sailing area to the left of the dock. In the bottom example the boat will have to be backed out of the slip before it can be turned out of the *No-Go Zone*.

In preparation for leaving the dock, make sure the fenders are positioned to protect the boat while leaving the dock.

❶ Your sails are up and luffing as you are tied to the dock pointed into the wind. A crew member is on the dock to handle the docklines, and will release the bow line first, and then step aboard at the shrouds or stern helping to push the boat away from the dock.

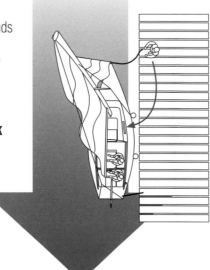

Leaving a Dock

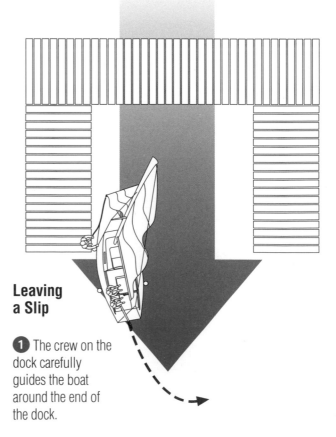

Leaving a Slip

❶ The crew on the dock carefully guides the boat around the end of the dock.

2 Sheet in the jib on the dock (right) side until the sail becomes backwinded and the boat slowly rotates out of the No-Go Zone. Then release the stern line either from a position on the boat or dock. Your instructor will show you the preferred method, depending on your boat and conditions. If the stern line is released from the boat, you will also be shown how to double the line back to the boat so it can be released.

3 Finally, sheet in the jib on the other side, and trim the mainsail, to propel you forward. Enjoy your sail!

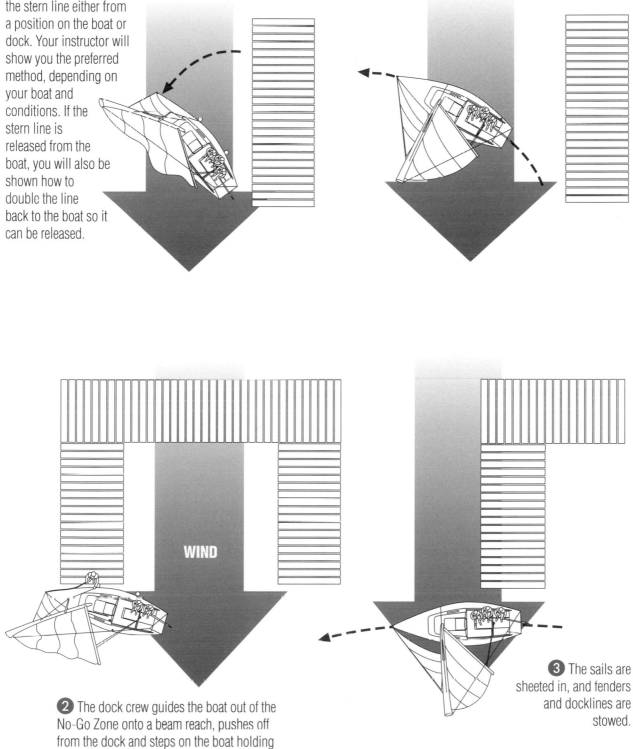

WIND

2 The dock crew guides the boat out of the No-Go Zone onto a beam reach, pushes off from the dock and steps on the boat holding onto the shrouds.

3 The sails are sheeted in, and fenders and docklines are stowed.

Crew Position

Small sailboats are relatively light, so the positioning of a helmsman and crew is critical to how the boat handles. The crew not only trim sails, but also help to balance the boat. Note how everyone is positioned on the high (*windward*) side of the boat. When the crew sit farther out on the side (*rail*), their weight helps counteract the boat's tendency to "tip" (*heel*) when the wind pushes against the sails. This is important, because excessive *heel* slows the boat and makes it harder to steer.

Crew Responsibilities

The crew are in charge of trimming and releasing the jib sheet and mainsheet. They will be the first to cross the cockpit during a *tack*, and will snug up the sheet not being used (*lazy sheet*) so it will be ready to trim for the next tack.

Helmsman Responsibilities

The helmsman should be seated near the after end of the cockpit holding the tiller with the hand farthest aft. On a two-person boat, he or she holds the mainsheet in the other hand and adjusts sail trim or course as needed. In a three-person crew, the middle crew usually handles the mainsheet and the helmsman only steers.

During tacks and jibes, the boom crosses over the cockpit. The helmsman and crew must first duck under the boom and cross over to the other side of the boat.

Steering

Using a tiller to steer the boat is simple. A common rule of thumb when you begin sailing is to push or pull the tiller away from the direction you want to turn. If you want to turn left, push or pull the tiller right, and vice versa. After a short while, using a tiller will become automatic.

❸ STRAIGHT AHEAD
Here the helmsman has centered the tiller and is sailing a straight course.

NOTE:
It is important to know that the boat must be moving for you to steer. The *rudder* (the pivoting underwater foil at the back of the boat) redirects the flow of water to create a steering force. *NO MOVEMENT...NO FLOW...NO STEERING FORCE!* Try to keep steering motion firm, but smooth. Herky, jerky tiller movements can disrupt water flow around the rudder and reduce its effectiveness.

❷ RIGHT TURN
The helmsman pulls the tiller to the left (*port*) side, and the boat turns right (to *starboard*) and back on course.

❶ LEFT TURN
The helmsman pushes the tiller right (to starboard) and the boat turns left.

Starting and Stopping

A sailboat can be started and stopped by using its sails, much like using the accelerator on your car. Sheeting in a sail to proper trim is like stepping on the accelerator. Sheeting the sail out and letting it flap (*luff*) is like taking your foot off the gas. With the sails luffing, the boat will coast to a stop.

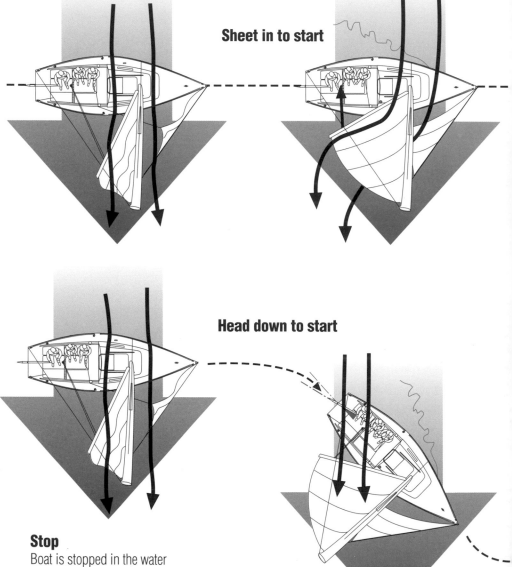

Stop
Boat is stopped in the water with its sheets eased out and its sails flapping (*luffing*).

Start
Sheeting in the sails to their proper trim gets the boat moving.

Sheet in to start

Head down to start

Stop
Boat is stopped in the water with its sheets eased out and its sails flapping (*luffing*).

Start
In this case, the mainsail is sheeted in slightly to get the boat moving, then the helmsman heads the boat away from the wind (tiller *away* from mainsail) onto a broad reach where the sails are now properly trimmed.

Stop

To stop the boat the mainsail is sheeted out so the sails flap (*luff*). The boat then coasts to a stop.

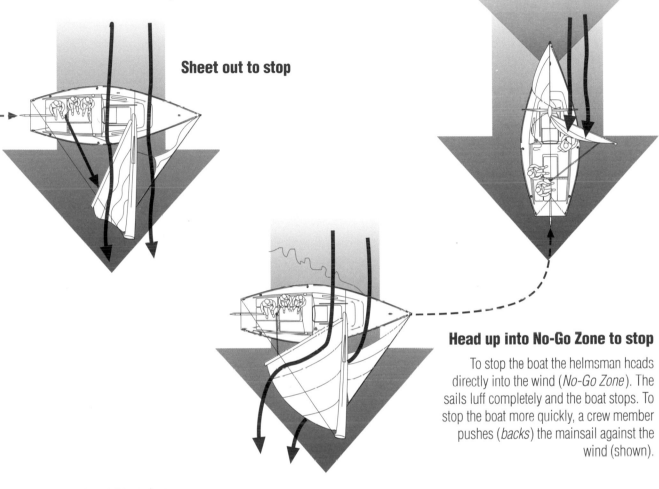

Sheet out to stop

Head up into No-Go Zone to stop

To stop the boat the helmsman hcads directly into the wind (*No-Go Zone*). The sails luff completely and the boat stops. To stop the boat more quickly, a crew member pushes (*backs*) the mainsail against the wind (shown).

Head up to stop

Stop

In order to stop the boat, the helmsman heads back toward the wind (tiller *toward* the mainsail) until the sails luff again, and the boat coasts to a stop.

Jib and Mainsail Trim

Sail trim is one of the most important skills in sailing, but because the wind is invisible, it can sometimes be difficult to judge whether your sail is trimmed properly. A very helpful way to detect wind flow around your sails (and adjust your sails or change course accordingly) is with *telltales*.

How Telltales Work

Telltales are pieces of yarn or sail cloth attached near the front edge (*luff*) of the sail. Here's how they work:

▶ If both telltales stream straight back, it means the wind is flowing smoothly over both sides of the sail.

▶ If a telltale is fluttering, there is turbulence on that side of the sail, and the sail needs to be adjusted. An easy way to remember how to adjust the sail is to *move the sail toward the fluttering telltales*.

▶ If the *leeward* (farthest away from the wind's direction) telltale is fluttering, sheet out the sail toward the telltale or turn the boat away from the telltale until it flows smoothly.

▶ If the *windward* (closest to the direction from which the wind is coming) telltale is fluttering, either sheet in the jib toward the telltale or turn the boat away from the telltale until it stops fluttering and flows smoothly.

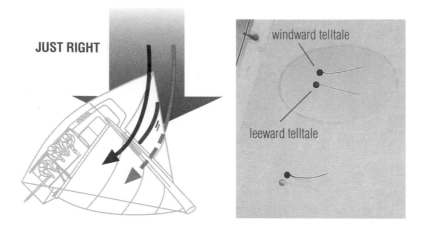

Air flow is smooth on both sides of the jib, and the telltales are both streaming back.

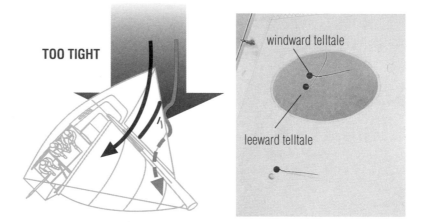

This jib is sheeted in too tight, air flow is turbulent on the outside (*leeward*) side of the sail as indicated by the fluttering telltale. Ease the jib sheet out to get smooth air flow.

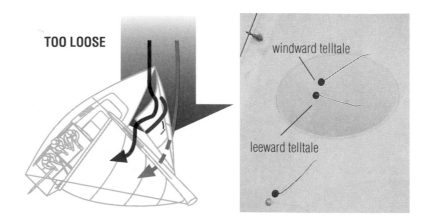

The *windward* telltale (on side closest to the wind) is fluttering, indicating turbulence on that side of the sail. Sheet in the jib until the telltale stops fluttering.

JUST RIGHT

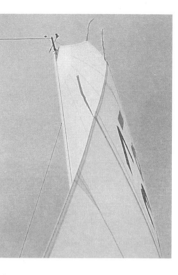

This mainsail is sheeted just right. The air flow is smooth on both sides of the sail, and the telltale at the back end (*leech*) is streaming back.

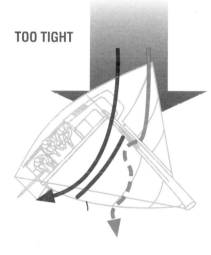

TOO TIGHT

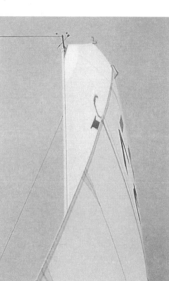

This mainsail is sheeted in too tightly. Air flow is turbulent on the outside (*leeward* side) of the sail as indicated by the fluttering telltale. Ease the mainsheet out to get smooth air flow. Many beginning sailors tend to trim mainsails too tight. Remember the saying, "When in doubt, let it out!"

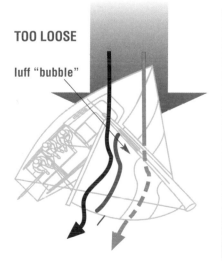

TOO LOOSE

luff "bubble"

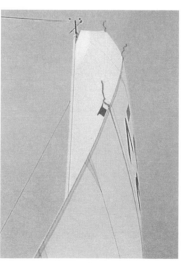

The mainsail here is trimmed too loose. Turbulent flow is indicated by a backing on the forward edge of the mainsail (luff "bubble").

Sailing in the Groove

As you learn to sail close to the wind, you will develop a technique called "sailing in the groove." The *groove* is an invisible sailing angle where your boat is making progress toward the wind (*to windward*), but also moving smoothly and steadily through the water and tipping (*heeling*) a comfortable amount. Finding the groove and staying there can be a bit of a challenge at first, but sailors soon learn how to "feel it" when their boat is in the groove. Some call this "sailing by the seat of their pants." The best references are your boat's speed, how much it tips (*angle of heel*) and the telltales on the jib.

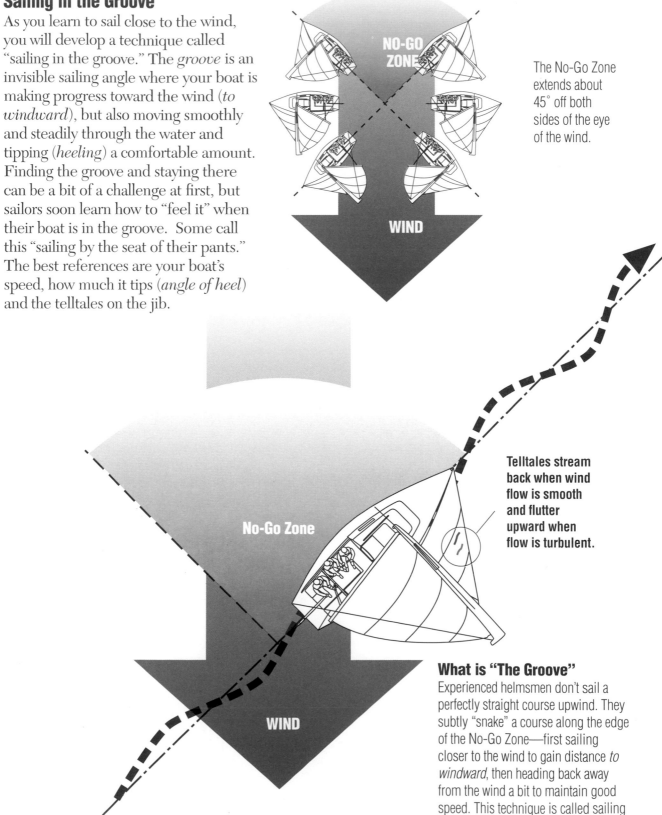

The No-Go Zone extends about 45° off both sides of the eye of the wind.

Telltales stream back when wind flow is smooth and flutter upward when flow is turbulent.

What is "The Groove"

Experienced helmsmen don't sail a perfectly straight course upwind. They subtly "snake" a course along the edge of the No-Go Zone—first sailing closer to the wind to gain distance *to windward*, then heading back away from the wind a bit to maintain good speed. This technique is called sailing in the groove.

Here's how to do it:

With sails trimmed in, sail as high toward the wind as you can while maintaining steady speed **1**. *The windward telltale will be flowing back.* You are on the edge of the No-Go Zone. Now, carefully steer the boat a bit more toward the wind until you see the jib start to flutter (*luff*) and feel the boat start to slow down **2**. You'll also feel the boat straighten up because there is less power from the sails. *The windward telltale is now fluttering.* At this point, smoothly steer back down away from the wind until the jib stops luffing and you feel your boat speed pick up again. That's it! Now repeat the process. NOTE: If you sail too far away from the wind **3**, you'll feel the boat tipping (*heeling*) too much and your boat speed will drop. Too much heel slows the boat's movement through the water. Simply edge back up toward the wind again.

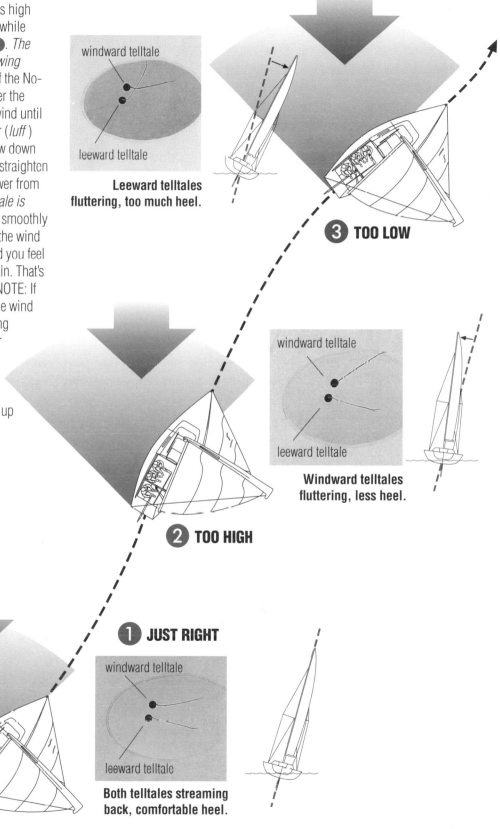

windward telltale

leeward telltale

Leeward telltales fluttering, too much heel.

3 TOO LOW

windward telltale

leeward telltale

Windward telltales fluttering, less heel.

2 TOO HIGH

WIND

No-Go Zone

1 JUST RIGHT

windward telltale

leeward telltale

Both telltales streaming back, comfortable heel.

Tacking Step-by-Step

You've already learned that tacking is changing a boat's direction by first turning the bow toward the wind (*heading up*), then through the wind and No-Go Zone, and away from the wind (*heading down*) to a new direction. Also you've learned that whenever the bow turns through the wind, the sails will cross from one side to the other. Now you'll learn how to tack.

In sailing always remember that preparation and communication are key to the safety of your crew and enjoyment of your sail. These two factors are essential in all phases of the sport, including leaving the dock, anchoring, responding to emergencies, and tacking and jibing. Know what you are going to do and how you are going to do it. Talk to your crew…and listen.

WIND

❹ Tack Is Completed

Once the tack is completed the helmsman centers the tiller and steers for the reference picked at the beginning of the tack. The crew adjust the mainsail and jib for the new direction. The jib sheets are then coiled and readied for the next tack.

"Ready!"

"Ready!"

"Ready about!"

❶ Preparing to Tack

The boat is on a beam reach with the wind coming over the left (*port*) side of the boat. Helmsman checks for anything that might be in the way, selects a reference point to steer for after completion of the tack, and then calls out, "*Ready about!*" The crew checks to make sure the jib sheets are clear and ready to run out, then uncleats and holds the working jib sheet and gets ready to sheet in the lazy jib sheet before responding, "*Ready!*"

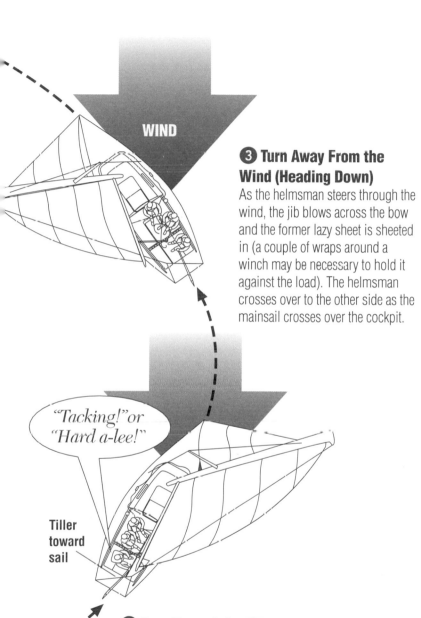

WIND

❸ Turn Away From the Wind (Heading Down)

As the helmsman steers through the wind, the jib blows across the bow and the former lazy sheet is sheeted in (a couple of wraps around a winch may be necessary to hold it against the load). The helmsman crosses over to the other side as the mainsail crosses over the cockpit.

"Tacking!" or "Hard a-lee!"

Tiller toward sail

❷ Turn Toward the Wind (Heading Up)

After the crew have announced they are ready, the helmsman calls out, *"Tacking!"* or the more traditional *"Hard a-lee!"* to announce the beginning of the tack, and starts to turn the boat into the wind (tiller *toward* sail). As the boat turns into the wind the sails begin to luff. When the forward edge of the jib is luffing, the crew releases the working jib sheet so the jib can cross over to the other side.

Heaving-to

If you want or need to stop sailing for awhile, for instance to check a chart, or relax for lunch, the best way is to heave-to. This holds your position with the sails and rudder countering each other as the boat drifts forward and to leeward (*downwind*). Always check that you have plenty of room to drift downwind before heaving-to.

❶ To heave-to, steer your boat so it is sailing close to the wind with the jib sheeted tightly.

❷ Tack the boat, but do not uncleat the jib sheet so the jib will become "backed."

❸ Move the tiller toward the mainsail and, after the boat has settled down, secure the tiller to leeward.

❹ Trim the mainsail so the boat lies at an upwind angle.

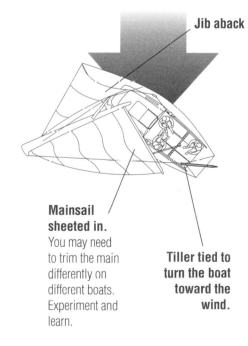

Jib aback

Mainsail sheeted in.
You may need to trim the main differently on different boats. Experiment and learn.

Tiller tied to turn the boat toward the wind.

Jibing Step-by-Step

As you have already learned, jibing is changing the direction of the boat while passing the stern through the wind. Again, preparing and communicating with your crew is essential for a smooth, controlled, and safe maneuver.

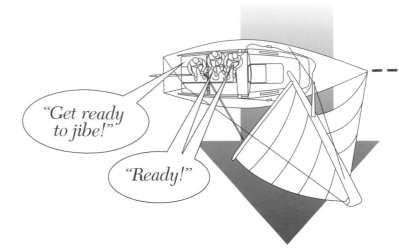

① Preparing to Jibe

Helmsman checks wind direction and selects reference to steer for after completion of jibe, and then calls out, "*Get ready to jibe!*" The crew check the sheets to make sure they are ready to run out, and uncleat the working jib sheet and mainsheet before responding, "*Ready!*"

It is important to be aware of the boom crossing the boat and to keep your head down!

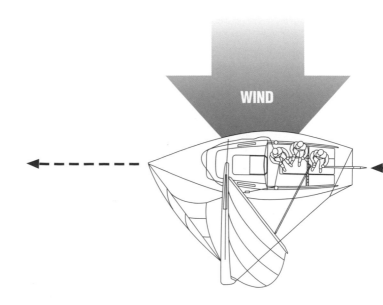

"Jibing!" or "Jibe-ho!"

WIND

❷ Turn Away from the Wind (Heading Down)

After the crew respond, *"Ready!"* the helmsman calls out *"Jibing!"* or *"Jibe-ho!"* and slowly turns the boat away from the wind (tiller away from sail). The crew members ease the working jib sheet and start to sheet in the mainsail.

❸ Turn Stern Through the Wind

Helmsman continues to turn the boat, and the main is shooted into the center. As the stern crosses the wind, the jib crosses over to the other side, and the former working jib sheet is released. Just before the boom flops across, the helmsman calls out *"Jibing!"* or the more traditional *"Jibe-ho!"* as a warning that the boom is coming across. In lighter winds the crew may simply grab the mainsheet or the boom and throw the sail to the other side of the boat. As the main crosses the center, the helmsman briefly steers against the turn.

▶ *EVERYONE KEEPS HIS OR HER HEAD SAFELY DOWN AS THE BOOM CROSSES THE COCKPIT!*

❹ Turn Toward the Wind (Heading Up)

As soon as the boom has crossed the cockpit the crew let the mainsail run out to keep the boat from rounding up (turning too much) and sheet in the former lazy jib sheet. The helmsman heads up the boat toward the wind and steers for the reference, while the crew adjust the sails.

Returning to the Dock

When returning to the dock, BE PREPARED! Have the fenders hung at the right height to safeguard the hull. Have the docklines attached properly to the boat and strung under the lifelines so they are ready to be used. Once you are ready to approach the dock, do it carefully.

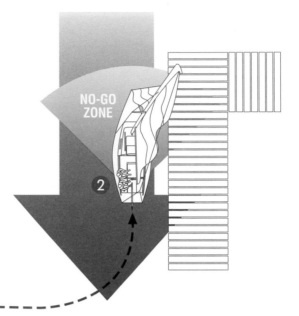

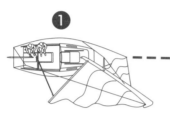

When nearing a side dock, ease out your sails on your approach to slow the boat ❶. As you come closer, steer up into the wind, letting the sails luff. Coast to a stop along the dock ❷. If the dock is short or has limited space you will want to make your approach more slowly.

In making an approach to an upwind slip, ease the sails to slow your speed. Further decrease your speed, if necessary, by wiggling the boat back and forth on its course ❶. Once you are sure your speed is correct (fast enough to get you into the slip, but not fast enough to bang your bow), head into the slip ❷. If your speed is slightly high going into the slip, push the boom out to backwind the mainsail to help stop the boat. (Your instructor will show you how).

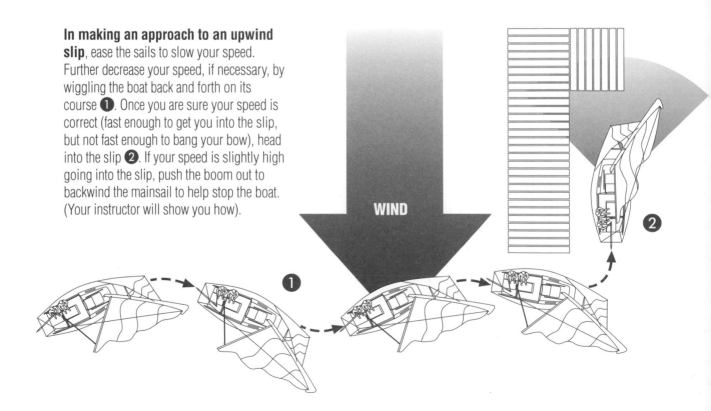

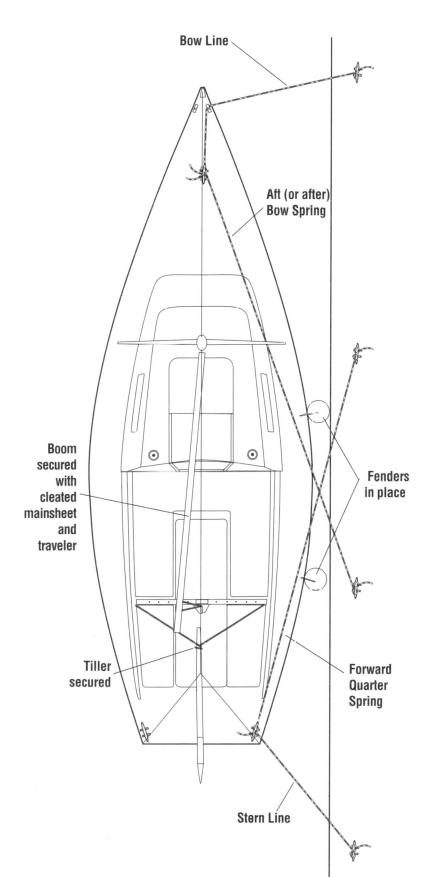

Bow Line

Aft (or after)
Bow Spring

Boom
secured
with
cleated
mainsheet
and
traveler

Fenders
in place

Tiller
secured

Forward
Quarter
Spring

Stern Line

Tying Up at the Dock

Crew members should step off the boat onto the dock. DO NOT JUMP! Falling on the dock or between the dock and the boat is a painful way to end your sail. Nothing other than a fender should be put between the boat and the dock.

Before you leave the boat, double check that the docklines are tied securely with the right amount of tension. All cleated docking lines should be secured with a *cleat hitch* (see photo below).

Docking Lines

▶ **Bow and stern lines** keep the boat close to the dock, but do not prevent it from surging forward or backward in the wind or waves.

▶ **Spring lines** cross each other to keep the boat from moving forward and backward.

Cleated docking lines should always be secured with a cleat hitch

Adjusting Sail Shape

Sails are not flat. They have curvature or shape built into them. The shape of a sail can be adjusted to give it more curvature (*fuller*) or less curvature (*flatter*). In light wind conditions, you want a full sail shape for greater power. As the wind increases, you want to *depower*, or make the sail flatter, to keep the boat under control and sailing well.

The *cunningham*, named after its inventor Briggs Cunningham, is a system used to tension the forward edge (*luff*) of the sail. This changes the shape of the sail and "depowers" it in higher winds. Tightening the outhaul helps to depower the bottom of the sail.

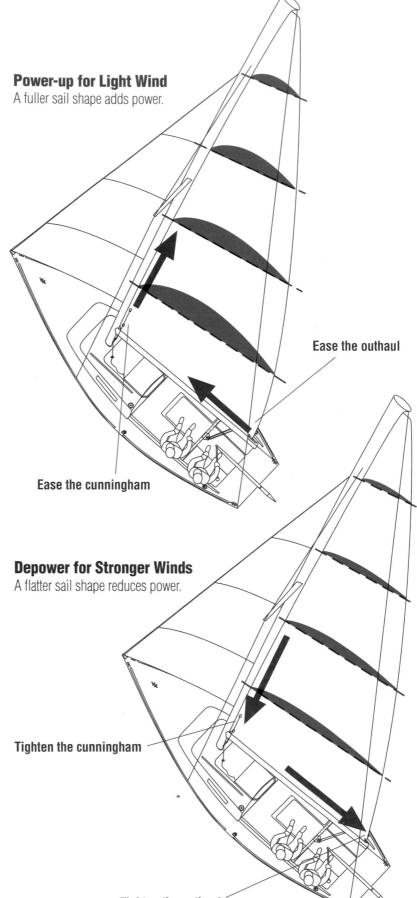

Power-up for Light Wind
A fuller sail shape adds power.

Ease the outhaul

Ease the cunningham

Depower for Stronger Winds
A flatter sail shape reduces power.

Tighten the cunningham

Tighten the outhaul

Depowering Sails

To keep stronger winds from overpowering the boat, you can trim the sails to spill the excess wind (*depower*). Adjusting sail trim this way keeps a boat balanced and sailing at its best. As winds increase, or during gusts, *depower* your sails to help keep the boat in balance, decrease *heel* and make steering easier.

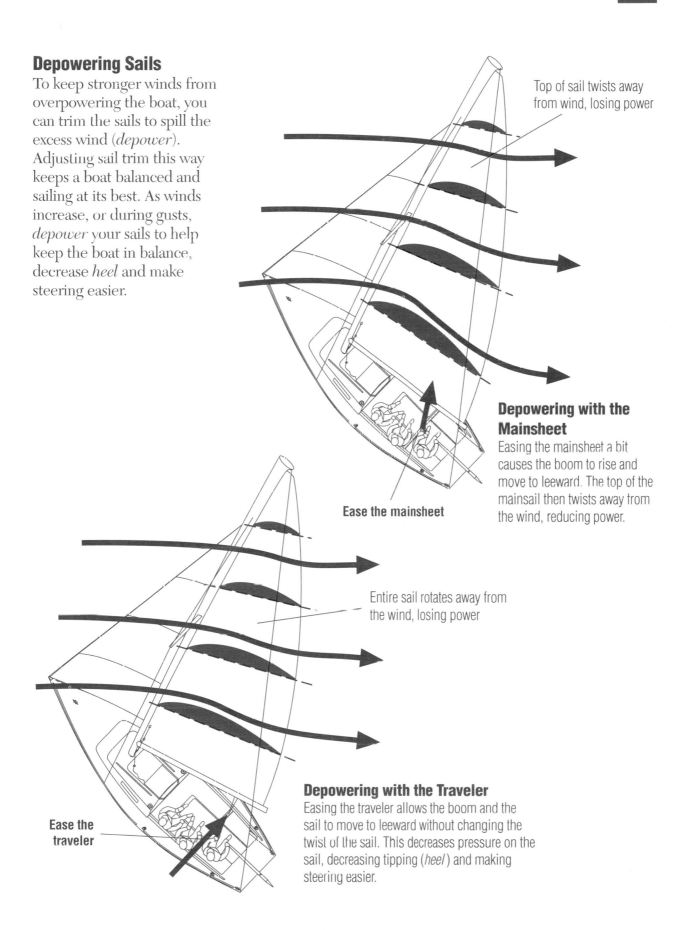

Top of sail twists away from wind, losing power

Ease the mainsheet

Depowering with the Mainsheet

Easing the mainsheet a bit causes the boom to rise and move to leeward. The top of the mainsail then twists away from the wind, reducing power.

Entire sail rotates away from the wind, losing power

Ease the traveler

Depowering with the Traveler

Easing the traveler allows the boom and the sail to move to leeward without changing the twist of the sail. This decreases pressure on the sail, decreasing tipping (*heel*) and making steering easier.

Balance

You can steer a boat with its sails instead of its rudder because of a principle called *balance*. A sailboat is a collection of forces in motion, not all of which are headed in the same direction. There are forces exerted by the mainsail and the jib, both of which pull the boat forward and sideways. There are opposing forces exerted by the water on the keel and rudder.

When all of these forces are *in balance*, the boat will sail forward in a straight line. If they are not, the boat will want to turn. This is why you are able to steer the boat by trimming in or easing either the mainsail or jib. By doing so, you are consciously throwing the boat *out of balance*.

As your sailing skills improve, you will use the principle of balance more and more to get the best performance out of your boat and execute more advanced maneuvers. For now, just understanding balance will help explain why certain things are happening on your boat.

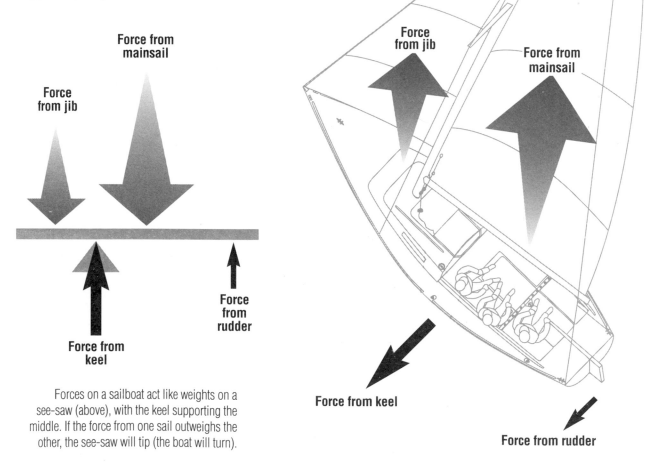

Forces on a sailboat act like weights on a see-saw (above), with the keel supporting the middle. If the force from one sail outweighs the other, the see-saw will tip (the boat will turn).

Tacking Angles

You can reach an upwind destination in several ways. If the course is not obstructed you can take a long zig and a long zag. In a channel or river you may need to use a series of short zig-zags to reach your destination. Sailing upwind requires course changes of about 90° in most boats. A handy way to estimate your course after the next tack is to sight to windward (toward the wind) directly off the side of the boat. If you can pick out a landmark, another sailboat, a cloud or other reference, it helps you get quickly oriented after the new tack.

Jibing Angles

Sailing downwind allows a lot more freedom in your course and point of sail. Sailing with the wind, you can sail more directly toward your destination. Even though the wind is coming from behind, it is desirable to keep the wind coming over one side of the boat or the other, not directly behind.

Jibing angles are a lot more flexible and less structured than tacking angles. With the wind coming from behind, you do not have to contend with the No-Go Zone.

When tacking, your course options are unlimited, but the angle of your tacks is always the same: about 90°.

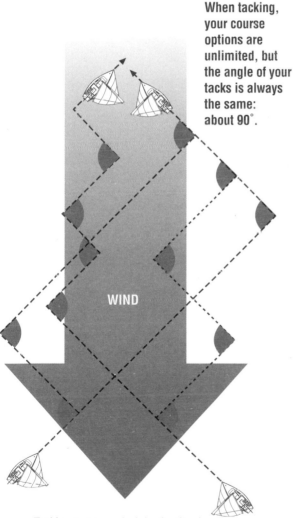

Tacking to an upwind destination is accomplished through a series of steps where you sail as close to the wind as possible.

WIND

WIND

Similar to tacking upwind, you can use either just one or a series of jibes to head downwind

Wind Shifts - Upwind

Even the steadiest wind is constantly changing its direction (*shifting*). These changes range from almost unnoticable to major swings in direction. Wind shifts play a major role in how you sail *upwind*. When the wind shifts, it also swings your No-Go Zone toward one side or the other, affecting the course you are able to sail. You respond to these changes of wind direction by *heading up* or *heading down*. In truly large wind shifts, you might even tack if the new tack will keep you sailing closer to your destination than your current one.

❸ **Shift Forward**
Here the wind has *shifted forward* from the original direction. In order to keep from sailing in the No-Go Zone, the helmsman steers *down* until the boat is in the groove again. A wind shift that forces you to steer *down* is called a *header*.

❶ **Shift Aft**
Here the wind has *shifted aft*, also shifting the No-Go Zone and the groove. The helmsman recognizes the change in wind direction and heads *up*. A wind shift that allows you to head *up* more is called a *lift*.

❶ Here, a boat and its crew are sailing *upwind* "in the groove."

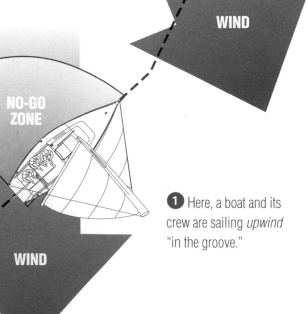

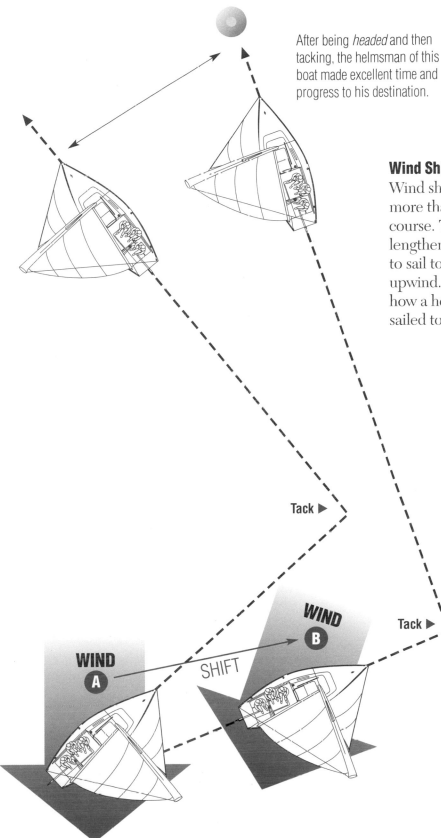

After being *headed* and then tacking, the helmsman of this boat made excellent time and progress to his destination.

Wind Shifts and Distance

Wind shifts (*headers* and *lifts*) do more than force you to change your course. They also shorten or lengthen the distance you will need to sail to reach a destination upwind. The example here shows how a header shortens the distance sailed to an upwind destination.

In this example, a boat is sailing upwind toward a buoy. If wind direction **A** shifts forward to wind direction **B**, the boat can reach the buoy sailing less distance. Because the boat had to head *down* in response to the wind shift, the shift is called a *header*.

Expert Tip:

When sailing upwind in shifty wind, always sail on the tack that has the closest angle to your destination. That way, you will be sailing the shortest distance (and the fastest course) to where you want to go. Try it!

Tack ▶

Tack ▶

WIND A

WIND B

SHIFT

More Leaving and Returning

You don't always leave and return to the dock under the ideal conditions described earlier. Awareness of the wind conditions, forethought, and knowledge of sail handling are necessary for approaching and departing docks, particularly when weather conditions offer a challenge.

Backward Departure

There may be times when you will have to sail the boat backward to leave the dock. Here's how to do it:

❶ Back away: push the boom out all the way in the direction you want the bow to turn (in this case to the left, or port) and hold out (*back*) the jib to the opposite direction. Center the tiller. The boat will sail backward.

❷ Turn out of the No-Go Zone: as soon as the boat has cleared the dock, turn the tiller toward the mainsail (the same direction you want the bow to turn) to turn out of the No-Go Zone.

❸ Sail away: when the boat has turned out of the No-Go Zone and is pointed in the desired direction, release the jib and sheet it in on the correct side, trim the mainsail and center the tiller.

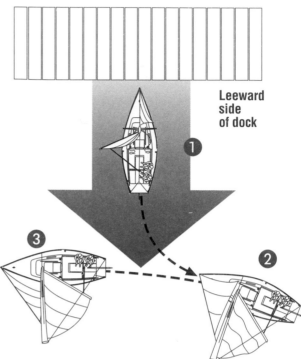

Leeward side of dock

Downwind Approach

The returning methods described on page 48 covered situations where your approach to a dock was made on a reach followed by a turn into the wind and No-Go Zone to stop the boat. In this case the boat is making its approach by sailing downwind. The disadvantage of this method is that you have less control of your boat speed since you cannot luff your sails effectively to slow down when sailing downwind. Here's how to do the downwind approach:

❶ Sail downwind until the boat is three to six boat lengths downwind of the dock.

❷ Turn toward the dock with sails luffing and coast to a stop.

or...

❸ Turn directly into the wind with sails luffing and coast to a stop.

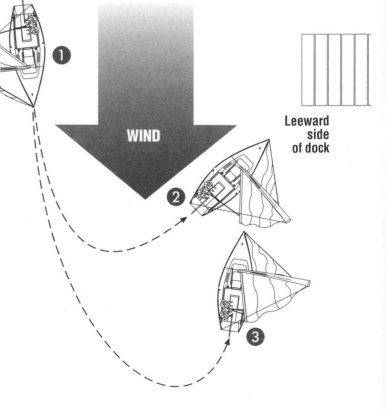

WIND

Leeward side of dock

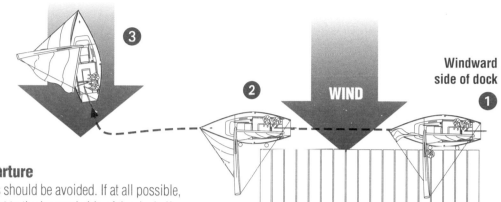

Windward Side Departure

Windward side departures should be avoided. If at all possible, you should move your boat to the leeward side of the dock. If you ever have to make a windward departure, here's how to do it:

❶ With sails lowered, but ready to raise, move your boat to the end of the dock.

❷ At the end of the dock, raise the jib and push the boat away from the dock. Once clear of the dock, sheet in the jib to get the boat moving.

❸ When the boat has picked up enough speed, turn the boat into the wind and hoist the mainsail. Once the mainsail is up, turn to your course.

Windward Side Approach

There may be times when you have no choice but to return to the windward side of the dock. The key point is to lower the mainsail when the boat is to windward of the dock and then drift down to it either with the jib up or lowered. Whether to leave the jib up depends on the conditions and the boat. If it's windy, it is usually a good idea to drop the jib so you won't drift downwind too quickly. It is very important that everyone is thoroughly briefed and understands what they should do and when, because timing is key to the success of a windward side approach. Make sure the fenders are in place before lowering the mainsail.

❶ Turn into the wind and drop your mainsail. Stow it so it won't get in the way.

❷ Turn downwind toward the dock, using the jib to adjust your speed.

❸ As you get near the dock let the jib luff completely or lower it. A crew member should be positioned with bow line in hand to step off on the dock and help slow the boat if necessary by taking a turn around a dock cleat.

Knots and Lines

A good knot is one that is secure with good holding power. It should also come untied easily, so the line can be used. There are many knots used in sailing, but six basic, easy-to-tie knots will handle most, if not all, of your needs. Learn the knots well because an improperly tied knot is useless or worse.

Laid line (top) consists of three large strands twisted around one another. Usually made of nylon, it is very strong but can be rough on the hands. Laid line stretches, which makes it excellent for anchor rode and docklines. Flexible braided line (bottom) made of Dacron™ is excellent for halyards and sheets. Dacron does not stretch as much as nylon, and braided line is relatively gentle on the hands.

The Bowline

The bowline (BOE-lin) puts a non-slipping loop at the end of a line. The knot becomes more secure under pressure, but remains easy to untie. It is the most commonly used knot on sailboats. Among its many applications, the bowline is used to attach the jib sheets to the clew of the jib.

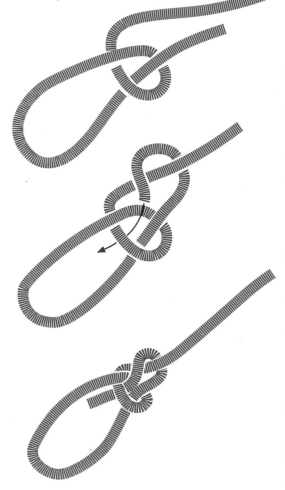

To tie a bowline, put a small loop in the line where you want the knot to be. Make sure the end crosses on top of the standing part of the line. This small loop will end up as part of the knot.

Run the end up through the loop you just made, down behind the standing part, back up over the edge of the loop, and down through the loop again.

Snug the knot together, making sure the knot holds and the remaining loop does not slip.

Figure-8 Knot

The figure-8 knot looks like its name. It is sometimes called a stopper knot, and is tied on the end of a line to keep the line from slipping through a fitting. Easy to untie, it is commonly used on the ends of the jib sheets in the cockpit.

Square Knot

The square knot is used only for sail lashings. It is not recommended for tying two lines together because it can be difficult to untie.

Sheet Bend

A sheet bend is used to tie two different sized lines together. It looks like a bowline, and it is secure and easy to untie.

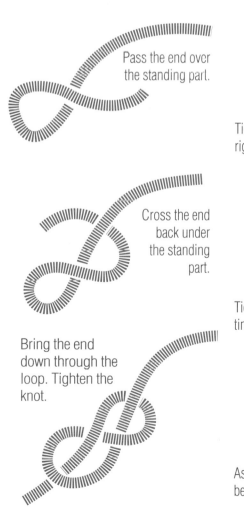

Pass the end over the standing part.

Cross the end back under the standing part.

Bring the end down through the loop. Tighten the knot.

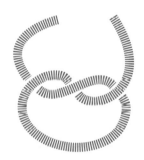

Tie a simple overhand knot with the right end going over the left.

Tie another simple overhand knot, this time crossing left end over right end.

As you tighten the line the knot should be symmetrical.

Make a loop at the end of the smaller line, with the end crossing over on top. Run the larger line up through the loop.

Run the larger line down around the standing part of the smaller line, up over the edge of the loop, and down through the loop again.

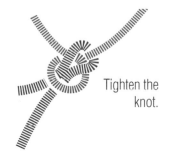

Tighten the knot.

Clove Hitch

A clove hitch is used to tie a line to an object. It is not a very secure knot. It is very easily untied and, with an extra half-hitch, can be used to secure a tiller.

Simply cutting through a line will cause the cut ends to fray. The ends of a cut line should be whipped. Whipping a line by wrapping the end of it with thread will protect it from fraying and unraveling. It's best to whip the line before cutting it. Another alternative with synthetic lines is to use an electric hot knife to cut and fuse the ends.

Wrap a loop of the end around the object.

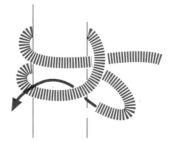

Cross over the standing part and wrap a second loop around the object.

Tuck the end under the crossing you just made and tighten.

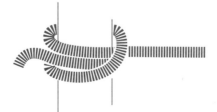

Round Turn and Two Half-hitches

This knot should use a loop to secure a line to an object.

Wrap the end of the line twice around the object.

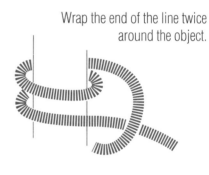

Cross the end over the outside of the standing part.

Use the end to tie two half-hitches onto the standing part.

Line Handling

A line should not be simply left in a tangled pile, but should always be ready to use or release by leaving it coiled.

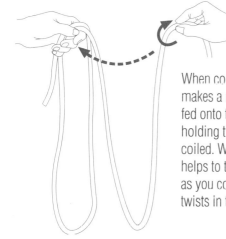

When coiling a line, one hand makes a new loop which is fed onto the other hand holding the loops previously coiled. With some lines, it helps to twist the line slightly as you coil to avoid kinks or twists in the line.

To stow a coiled line, wrap the end of the line around the middle of the coil. Make a loop and pass it through and over the upper end of the coil.

Heaving a Line

When preparing to throw a line, make sure one end is secured. Hold half of the coil in your throwing hand and the other half in your other hand. Swing and throw the coil underhand, allowing the remainder of the line to run free from your other hand.

Weather Basics

Newspapers, radio, television, telephone, and VHF radio forecasts keep sailors informed about predicted wind speed and direction, and storm possibilities.

Weather maps help you predict what kind of weather to expect on the water. High pressure systems (Ⓗ) usually indicate good, mild weather, while low pressure systems (Ⓛ) usually are accompanied by a warm or cold front and inclement weather.

VHF Forecasts. The National Oceanographic and Atmospheric Administration operates 400 VHF transmitters in the US. Each has a range of 40 miles and broadcasts short term weather forecasts. 7 frequencies are used for overlapping coverage. Ask your instructor which frequency is best for your area.

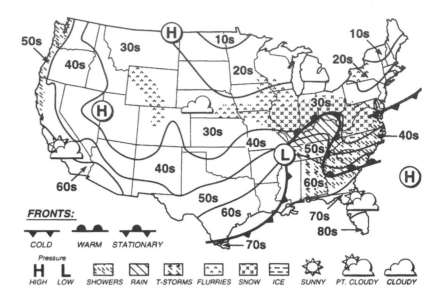

FRONTS:

COLD   WARM   STATIONARY

Pressure

H   L   SHOWERS   RAIN   T-STORMS   FLURRIES   SNOW   ICE   SUNNY   PT. CLOUDY   CLOUDY
HIGH   LOW

Cumulus clouds, which are large, white, and fluffy, are often an indicator of good weather.

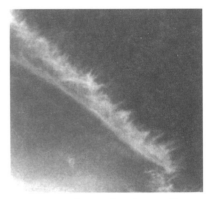

Wispy, thin **cirrus clouds** usually mean good weather for the day, but may be a prediction that a change in weather is on the way.

Towering **cumulonimbus clouds**, or "thunderheads" are usually accompanied by severe conditions, including heavy rain and lightning.

Low layered **stratus clouds** usually bring steady rain.

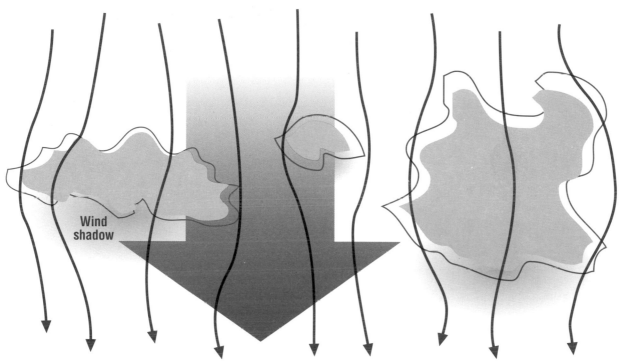

Land Effects

Wind conditions can be affected by nearby land features. Islands, tall buildings, even anchored ships cast *wind shadows* (areas of less wind) on their leeward sides. Sailing from fresh winds into one of these wind shadows greatly depowers a sailboat.

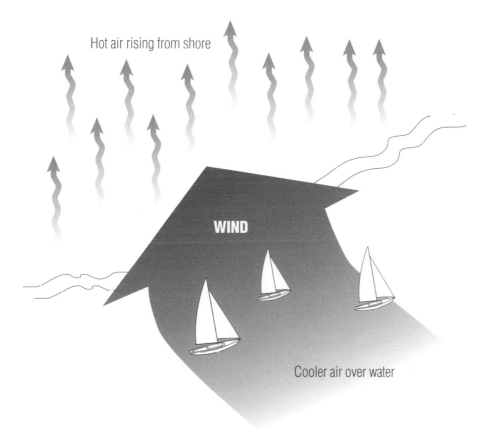

Hot air rising from shore

WIND

Cooler air over water

Thermal Winds

Local winds are often caused by differences in temperature between the shore and neighboring water. As denser cool air is drawn toward rising warm air, wind is created. These winds are commonly referred to as "onshore breezes" and "sea breezes." The technical term is *thermal wind*. The most famous illustration of thermal wind is on San Francisco Bay, where hot air rising out of the Sacramento Valley, about 75 miles inland from San Francisco, creates a vacuum that draws in 25-knot winds through the Golden Gate almost every summer afternoon like clockwork.

Tides and Currents

Tides are the *vertical* change of water level and are caused primarily by the gravitational pull of the moon on the earth. As the moon rotates around the earth, it "pulls" the earth's water toward it. As the moon moves, so does the water level in most bodies of ocean water. Typically there are two high and two low tides each day on the east and west coasts of the U.S. In the Gulf of Mexico there is usually only one high and one low per day. With a watch, a tide table and a chart you can determine the depth of the water in which you are sailing or anchoring at any given time.

Currents are the *horizontal* movement of water and are caused by river flow, wind, or ocean movements. The Gulf Stream off the East Coast of the U.S. is a well known ocean current. In coastal areas, currents are also caused by the tides rising and falling. Depending on their direction, these currents can either assist or hinder your progress while sailing. It is important to know the direction and strength of currents. Charts, tide tables, and a watch are helpful in planning your sail.

These photos, taken at the same location, show the difference between high and low tide. Consulting a tide table and a chart will help you avoid running aground during a low tide.

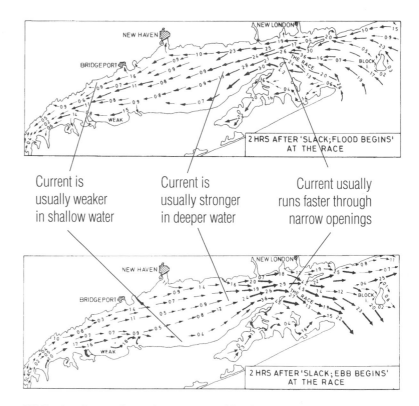

Current is usually weaker in shallow water

Current is usually stronger in deeper water

Current usually runs faster through narrow openings

While the photos above demonstrate *tide*, these charts from a nautical almanac show *current* coming in (*flooding*) and going out (*ebbing*) of Long Island Sound. Charts courtesy Reeds Nautical Almanac

Reading Tides and Current

There are a number of indicators on the water and shoreline that will tell you what the tide and currents are doing.

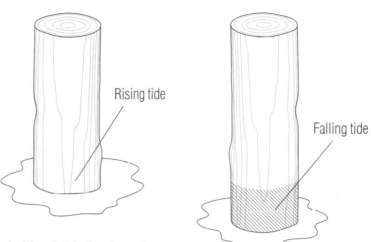

Rising tide

Falling tide

Photo courtesy Anne Martin

Current pulls on this buoy, causing it to lean, and leaves a wake as it flows from left to right.

A piling that is dry above the water level indicates that the tide is rising.
When the piling above the water is wet, the tide is falling. A beach can provide the same information as the piling. A dry beach is indicative of a rising tide; a wet beach is a sign of a falling tide.

Compensating for Current

If you are going to sail across a current you can compensate for the effect it will have on your boat. Instead of steering directly toward your goal, steer for a point upstream, and let the current pull you back to your desired course.

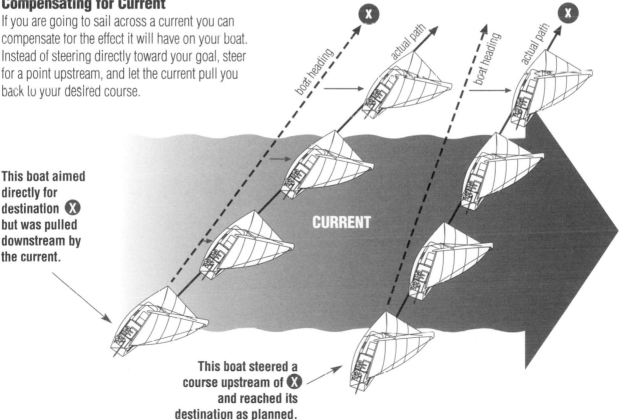

This boat aimed directly for destination X but was pulled downstream by the current.

CURRENT

This boat steered a course upstream of X and reached its destination as planned.

Basic Navigation Rules

The purpose of the Basic Navigation Rules is to avoid collisions. The boat that has right-of-way is the *stand-on vessel* and should maintain course and speed. The *give-way vessel* must keep out of the way and should make its change of course obvious and early. It is always a vessel's obligation to avoid collisions, even if it has the right-of-way.

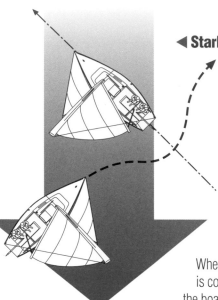

◀ Starboard Tack over Port Tack

A sailboat on a starboard tack has the right-of-way over a sailboat on a port tack. As boats on opposite tacks approach each other, the boat on the port tack is the *give-way vessel*. Its skipper should change course and aim behind the stern of the starboard tack boat. The boat on starboard tack is the *stand-on vessel* and should hold its course.

When sailing on **starboard tack**, the wind is coming over the right (*starboard*) side of the boat. When sailing on **port tack**, the wind is coming over the left (*port*) side of the boat.

◀ Leeward Vessel over Windward Vessel

When approaching another boat on the same tack the windward vessel, the boat upwind, is the *give-way vessel* and should yield to the leeward vessel by steering behind it. The leeward vessel is the *stand-on vessel* and should hold its course.

Overtaken Vessel over Overtaking Vessel ▶

A boat that is passing another should NOT expect the slower boat to clear a path. The boat that is doing the passing is the *give-way vessel*, and its skipper must change course to maneuver around the slower craft. The boat being overtaken is the *stand-on vessel* and should hold its course.

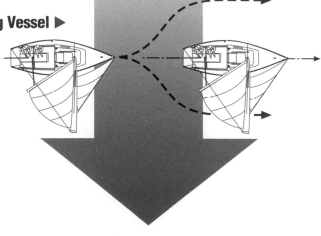

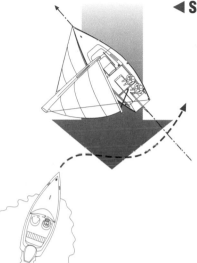

◄ Sailboats over Powerboats

Because a powerboat (or sailboat under power) is more maneuverable, it must yield to a sailboat. The sailboat is the *stand-on vessel* and should hold its course unless the other boat comes uncomfortably close. Then the sailboat should take evasive action.

In general, the priority for stand-on vessels, from top to bottom is:

1. A disabled vessel.
2. A vessel that is difficult to maneuver, such as a dredge.
3. A vessel restricted by draft, such as a tanker in a channel.
4. A vessel engaged in commercial fishing.
5. A sailboat.
6. A powerboat.

If you have any doubts, *yield to the other craft!* Be especially wary of a powerboat. Until you see it turn, don't assume a powerboat will yield to you.

STAY ALERT. BE SAFE!

If you have any doubts about the other vessel's action, do not steer across its bow. If you are the *give-way vessel*, make your course change early and obvious to the other vessel.

Stay Clear of Large Vessels ►

Ships and tugs with tows have difficulty in maneuvering. Always give them a wide berth, and you must give way when they are in a channel. If you see a tugboat crossing ahead, look well behind it to check if a barge is being towed. NEVER try to cross the cable between a tug and its tow.

Basic Navigation Aids

Buoys and channel markers are like road signs and traffic markers on the water. While there are many kinds of buoys and channel markers in use in North America, the most common ones fall into the categories shown here. They have distinct shapes and colors that will help you sail your boat in and out of harbors safely and avoid shallow water. The basic rule to remember in U.S. waters is *"Red, Right, Returning."* This means keep the red markers to your right when you are returning from open water into a harbor. Keep the green buoys on your right when leaving a harbor into open water.

Most buoys, channel markers and other navigation aids are marked on nautical charts. Local charts of your sailing area are available at most marine supply stores. It's a good idea to study a chart of your local area to get familiar with the "traffic signs" you will be encountering as you sail.

Green or red **lighted buoys** are usually spaced relatively far apart and located near the entrances of harbors. Each has a distinct flashing pattern that is indicated on a chart so it can be readily identified. Lighted buoys are especially helpful for navigating at night.

A **can** is an odd-numbered, green buoy that is used to mark the *left* side of a channel when entering (or returning to) a harbor. It has a flat top. When you leave a harbor, cans mark the *right* side of the channel.

A **nun** is an even-numbered, red buoy used to mark the *right* side of a channel when entering (or returning to) a harbor. It has a pointed top. When you leave a harbor, nuns mark the *left* side of the channel.

A **green daymark** is a square, odd-numbered green sign that is mounted to a piling. It marks the side of a channel and should be treated like a can.

A **red daymark** is a triangular, even-numbered, red sign mounted to a piling. It marks the right side of a channel when returning.

Reading a Chart

A chart shows not only the channels and the buoys, but also the shorelines, the water depth, obstructions, shoals, the positions of wrecks, and characteristics of the bottom. In addition, it indicates the positions of landmarks, lighthouses and much more. At the edge of the chart is an important note: "Soundings in Feet," "Soundings in Meters," or "Soundings in Fathoms" which tell you how the water depth is measured on the chart. A meter is a little over three feet, while a fathom is precisely six feet. Always check which measurement is used to indicate water depths (*soundings*) on your chart.

These diamond shapes are **channel buoys**. On a chart they are colored to represent a nun (red) or can (green). In this channel you can see a set of cans (on the left) and nuns (on the right) positioned to guide you safely through the narrow channel opening.

A **contour line** follows a constant water depth. On most charts, areas of shallower waters are indicated by a light blue area.

Charts also indicate **onshore landmarks** that can be used as navigation references. Here a tower is indicated.

The small numbers scattered throughout the water are **soundings** or depths at low tide at those particular points.

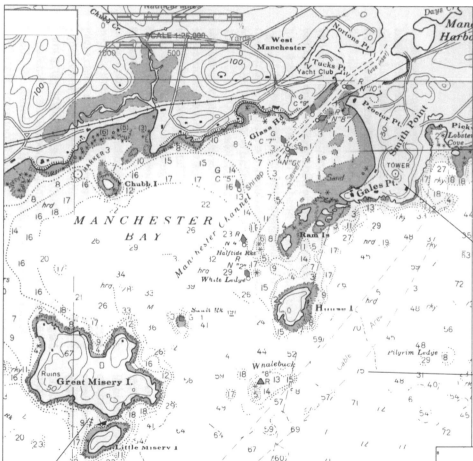

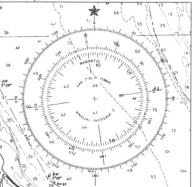

Charts also indicate noteworthy bottom topography, such as hazardous rocks, sunken ships (shown) and other **hidden dangers**.

A **compass rose** (right) is printed on every nautical chart. If your boat has a compass, you use the compass rose to relate your boat's compass *heading* (direction) to a chart and vice versa. The outer circle indicates the degrees of the compass relative to the geographic north pole. The inner circle shows compass degrees relative to the magnetic north pole (yes, they're different). Your boat's compass relates to the inner circle (magnetic north).

Hypothermia and Heat Emergencies

Sailors are often exposed to extreme conditions. Hot, sunny days with no wind, cold rainy days with too much wind, prolonged exposure to wind and spray…all of the things that make sailing challenging and fun can sneak up and bite you if you do not take care of yourself. Your best preparation is to anticipate the extremes. Bring plenty of warm and waterproof clothing if it might get cool and wet. Drink plenty of fluids and wear a hat in hot, sunny weather. Nonetheless, hypothermia and heat emergencies can occur. Here are some signs and solutions.

HYPOTHERMIA

SIGNALS…
- Shivering
- Impaired judgment
- Dizziness
- Numbness
- Change in level of consciousness
- Weakness
- Glassy stare

(Physical symptoms may vary, since age, body size, and clothing will cause individual differences.)

TREATMENT…
Medical assistance should be given to anyone with hypothermia. Until medical assistance arrives, these steps should be taken:
- Check breathing and pulse.
- Gently move the person to a warm place.
- Carefully remove all wet clothing. Gradually warm the person by wrapping in blankets or putting on dry clothes. Do not warm a person too quickly, such as immersing in warm water. Rapid rewarming may cause dangerous heart rhythms. Hot water bottles and chemical heat packs may be used if first wrapped in a towel or blanket before applying.
- Give warm, nonalcoholic and decaffeinated liquids to a conscious person only.

HEAT EXHAUSTION

SIGNALS…
- Cool, moist, pale skin
- Heavy sweating
- Headache
- Dizziness
- Nausea
- Weakness, exhaustion

TREATMENT…
Without prompt care, heat exhaustion can advance to a more serious condition — heat stroke. First aid includes:
- Move person to cool environment.
- Remove clothing soaked with perspiration and loosen any tight clothing.
- Apply cool, wet towels or sheets.
- Fan the person.
- Give person a half glass (4 oz.) of cool water every 15 minutes.

HEAT STROKE

SIGNALS…
- Red, hot, dry or moist skin
- Very high skin temperature
- Changes in level of consciousness
- Vomiting
- Rapid, weak pulse
- Rapid, shallow breathing

TREATMENT…
Heat stroke is life threatening. Anyone suffering from heat stroke needs to be cooled and an EMS technician should be contacted immediately. To care for heat stroke:
- Move person to cool environment.
- Apply cool, wet towels or sheets.
- If available, place ice or cold packs on the person's wrists and ankles, groin, each armpit, and neck.
- If unconscious, check breathing and pulse.

Electrical Hazards

There are some hazards on the water and on your own boat, but there's one very important one you need to look up to see. *Electrical powerlines can be deadly!* Make sure you have the proper clearance before crossing under powerlines, especially when moving boats on trailers onshore. Remember to take into account higher water levels from tides, river runoff, or recent rains.

Another electrical danger in some regions is lightning. Should you be overtaken during a lightning storm, you should head immediately for port and keep your crew away from the mast and any metal or electrical components aboard your boat.

Pre-Sailing Exercises

Before any exercise, including sailing, you should warm up and loosen up by stretching. Keep yourself in reasonably good condition, and before heading out, stretch out. These flexibility exercises should be done for about 30 seconds. Do not stretch to the point of pain, only to increase flexibility.

Bicep stretch
30 seconds on each arm.

Shoulder & upper arm
30 seconds on each arm.

Lower leg stretch
30 seconds on both legs.

Quadricep stretch
30 seconds on each leg.

Sailing requires movements in many unusual positions. Stretching before and after you sail will help minimize the stiffness and discomfort that commonly accompanies using new muscle groups. *NOTE: Do not engage in any of these exercises without consulting with your physician. Some of these exercises could adversely affect students who are not physically fit or have a history of back, shoulder or knee problems.*

Overboard Recovery

All sailors must know how to react quickly to a crew overboard situation. There are three preferred methods of recovering a crew who has fallen overboard. All involve the following seven steps:

1. *Get buoyancy to the victim.*
2. *Keep the victim in sight.*
3. *Head the boat back to the victim.*
4. *Stop the boat alongside the victim.*
5. *Make contact with the victim.*
6. *Attach the victim to the boat.*
7. *Get the victim back on board.*

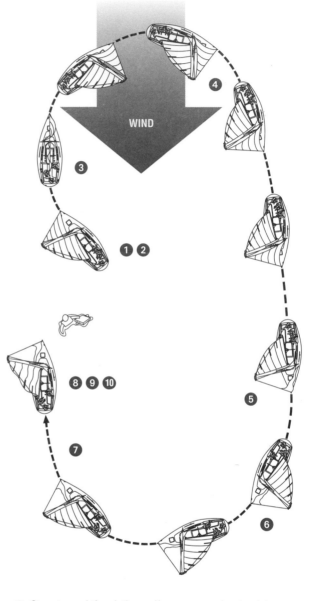

Quick-Stop Recovery

The hallmark of the Quick-Stop recovery method is the immediate reduction of boat speed by turning in a direction to windward and thereafter maneuvering at modest speed, remaining near the victim. This recovery requires these steps:

1. As soon as a crew member falls overboard, throw buoyant objects, such as cushions, PFDs or life rings, to the victim and shout *"Crew Overboard!"* These objects may not only come to the aid of the victim, but will "litter the water" where he or she went overboard and help the spotter to keep him or her in view. It has been determined that the deployment of the standard overboard pole rig requires too much time. The pole rig is saved to "put on top" of the person in case the initial maneuver is unsuccessful.

2. Designate someone to spot and point at the person in the water. The spotter should NEVER take his or her eyes off the victim.

3. Bring the boat into the wind, trimming the mainsail to close-hauled.

4. Continue to turn through the wind, without releasing the headsail, until the wind is almost astern. Do not ease the sails.

5. Hold this course until the victim is aft of the beam, and drop or furl the headsail if possible. If the headsail is lowered, its sheets should not be slacked.

6. Jibe the boat.

7. Steer toward the victim as if you were going to pick up a mooring.

8. Stop the boat alongside the victim by easing or backing sails.

9. Establish contact with the victim with a heaving line or other device. A "throwing sock" containing 75 feet of light floating line and a kapok bag can be thrown into the wind because the line is kept inside the bag and trails out as it sails to the victim. Attach the victim to the boat.

10. Recover the victim on board.
    This method should be executed under sail alone unless there is insufficient wind to maneuver the boat.

Quick-Turn Recovery

The Quick-Turn (or Figure-8) recovery avoids jibing during a recovery. In heavy weather, you may find controlling the boat easier with this recovery technique; *however, it is imperative to keep the victim in sight at all times!* Take the following steps in a Quick-Turn recovery:

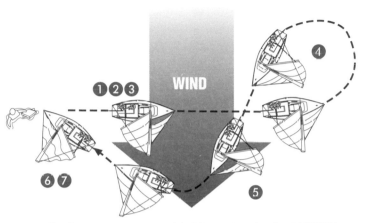

WIND

1. As soon as a crew member falls overboard, call out LOUDLY *"Crew overboard!"*
2. Throw cushions, PFDs or life rings in the direction of the person in the water. Steer the boat on a beam reach.
3. Assign a crew member to watch and point at the person in the water. This crew member should NEVER take his or her eyes off the victim.
4. After sailing a maximum of four boatlengths, tack into the wind and fall off onto a deep broad reach, crossing the boat's original course.
5. The plan is to approach the victim on a close reach. This point of sail gives perfect speed control, using the main sheet as a "gas pedal," together with some space for altering direction. To determine whether you're in position for the close reach approach, steer toward the victim and let off your sheets. If you are on a close reach, both sails will flog. If your approach is too far upwind, your main will fill and slowing down will be impossible. In this case immediately run off almost dead downwind for a length or two. Then steer up for the victim again. In all probability this will position you properly for a close-reach approach. Should you still be too far upwind with a mainsail full of air, bear off hard a second time, etc.
6. Ease sheets to slow the boat and bring it to a stop alongside the victim.
7. Attach the victim to the boat and recover on board.

Attachment. After maneuvering the boat back alongside the victim, it is imperative that the victim be attached to the boat. This should be done so that the boat and victim do not drift apart, necessitating another return. Do not rely on the victim holding onto a line. In descending order of preference, here are some methods:

- Use a Lifesling, if you have one.
- Use the "D" rings of an inflatable harness (if being worn) to tie the victim to the boat.
- Tie a bowline around the victim.
- Once the victim is attached, drop the sails. Do not leave the victim tied to the boat unattended.

Retrieval. This is considerably easier if there are more than two crew members left aboard to assist. On a boat with low freeboard, the crew can often drag the victim aboard. In flat water, and if the boat has a scoop/swim platform, the victim can be dragged up over the stern.

- Especially if shorthanded, you may need to improvise some method to aid in the retrieval:
- A line over the side with a bowline tied in the end to act as a stirrup. Any lines over the side should be tied onto the boat on the opposite side from the victim so they can help themselves get inboard.
- A line over the side with a series of loops tied at intervals so the victim can assist themselves, or even climb back in unassisted.
- A paddle over the side tied in the middle so it becomes a "T" bar for the victim to stand on.
- A block and tackle (preferably four parts) rigged to a pre-hoisted halyard that is then used to lift the victim from the water.
- If you are unable to retrieve the victim, ensure that the victim is securely attached to the boat, and call for help on the VHF radio (MAYDAY), or attract the help of a passing boat.

Aftercare. Be aware that the victim may well be suffering from hypothermia (see page 70). Get the victim back ashore as soon as possible. Unless you are sailing in tropical waters, you should treat this as a serious first aid issue.

Shortening Sail

When the wind is too strong and your boat is heeling too much, you should shorten your sail. Your boat will go just as fast and will be more in control with less sail area exposed to the wind.

Reefing

The area of the mainsail may be reduced by lowering the sail partially and securing the lower portion to the boom.

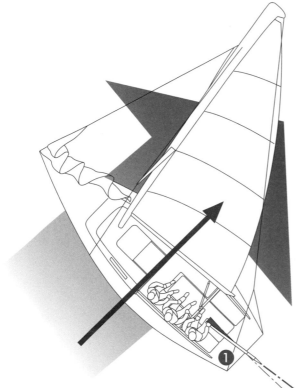

Lowering the Jib

The easiest way to reduce sail is to simply lower the jib. With just the mainsail up, however, the boat is no longer in balance. The wind pressure on the mainsail will tend to rotate the bow of the boat toward the wind. To compensate, you will need to steer with the tiller pulled slightly away from the mainsail ❶ to keep the boat sailing straight.

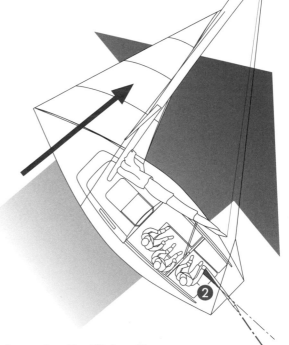

Lowering the Mainsail

The most significant way you can reduce sail is to lower the mainsail. With just the jib up, however, the boat is no longer in balance. The wind pressure on the jib will tend to rotate the bow of the boat away from the wind. To compensate, you will need to steer with the tiller pushed slightly toward the mainsail ❷ to keep the boat sailing straight.

Running Aground

Running aground happens to almost every sailor at some time. If you run aground on a soft, muddy bottom with a rising tide, you'll float off easily with no damage to the boat.

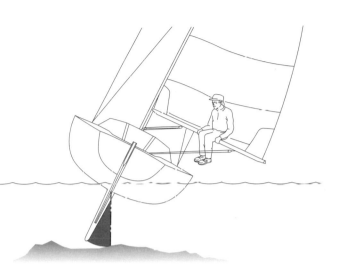

If you get stuck, use the sails and crew weight to heel the boat. You may have to get some crew members to sit on the boom and slowly swing it out over the side to tilt the boat enough to raise the keel off the bottom.

Another method of breaking free is to seek the assistance of a passing powerboater. He can tilt and pull your boat off by *slowly* pulling on a long line attached to your jib halyard. Have the boat pull you from abeam (perpendicular to your boat).

MORE ON SAILING EMERGENCY PROCEDURES

Knockdowns. A knockdown is when a boat heels over so far that one of its spreaders touches the water. This usually happens because it has been carrying too much sail for high wind conditions or because of a mistake by the helmsman or crew. To recover from a knockdown:
▶ Release the sheets and the boom vang.
▶ Get the crew up to the windward rail.
▶ If the rudder responds, head up until the sails luff.

Swamping. A knockdown may cause the boat to fill with water if hatches are left open. If your boat becomes swamped:
▶ Release the sheets.
▶ Lower the sails.
▶ Bail with buckets and bilge pump.

Sinking. If your boat is taking on water and is in danger of sinking:
▶ Make sure everyone is wearing a life jacket.
▶ Bail with buckets and bilge pump.
▶ If the boat has been holed, try to find the source of the leak and plug it.
▶ Try to sail to shore and run it aground before it goes down.
▶ If the boat becomes completely swamped with decks awash, and it looks like it will sink, DO NOT leave the boat...let it leave you by going down.
▶ Make sure you are not tangled in any lines.

Anchoring

As in docking, preparation is the key to successful anchoring. Before anchoring take down and stow the jib. Make sure the foredeck is clear except for the anchor and its line (*rode*), which should be coiled on the deck (laid out in large loops) so it will run freely. If there is a pulpit, make sure the anchor and rode will run under it.

❷ **As the boat comes to a stop**, lower (do not throw or drop) the anchor. After it hits the bottom pay out the anchor line as you drift back.

❶ When everything is prepared, sail **on a reach**, about 3-6 boat lengths downwind of where you want to drop your anchor. When you are directly downwind of where you want to drop it, head up into the wind.

The Danforth anchor is very common. It is strong, lightweight, holds well, and is easy to store.

❸ **When you've reached the spot** where you want the boat to remain, firmly cleat off the rode. Check for adequate scope and that your anchor is holding. Then lower your mainsail.

Scope

The amount of rode that you pay out is not arbitrary. Scope is the ratio of anchor rode to the depth of the water. A scope of 7:1 is considered adequate for most conditions. This means that if the depth of the water where you are anchoring is 10 feet you should pay out 70 feet of rode. Remember charts list the depth of the water at low tide, so check your tide table to find the accurate depth for the time you are anchoring.

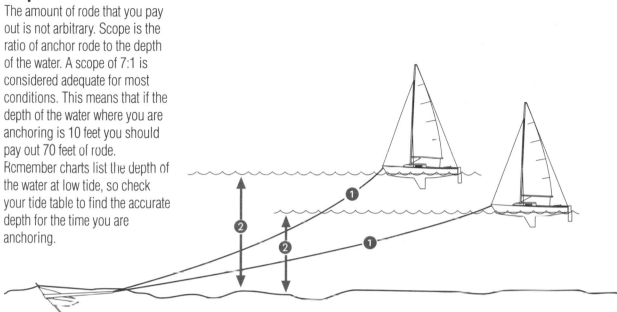

Scope is the ratio of the length of your anchor rode ❶ to the depth of the water ❷

Is your anchor holding?

It's good seamanship to make sure your anchor has a secure hold on the bottom. Here's an easy method: Once you think you've anchored well, sight two objects that are aligned, for instance, a buoy and a house. Both objects can be on shore, such as a fence post and a telephone pole. Do NOT use another boat as one of your objects for sighting.

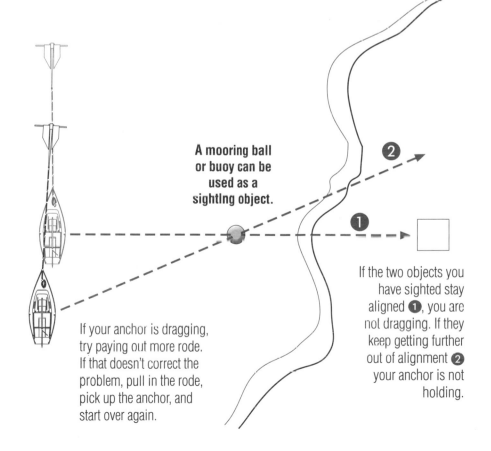

A mooring ball or buoy can be used as a sighting object.

If your anchor is dragging, try paying out more rode. If that doesn't correct the problem, pull in the rode, pick up the anchor, and start over again.

If the two objects you have sighted stay aligned ❶, you are not dragging. If they keep getting further out of alignment ❷ your anchor is not holding.

Safety Equipment

There are a number of safety requirements specified by the US Coast Guard for sailors operating boats on lakes, rivers and the open ocean. Specific information can be gained from a pamphlet titled "Federal Requirements for Recreational Boats." A current copy can be obtained from most chandleries, USCG stations or by writing US Coast Guard, 2100 Second St. SW, Washington, DC 20593. We have provided a summary of current requirements.

The Coast Guard requires pleasure boats to carry safety equipment. This equipment list is a *minimum* and should be augmented by the boat owner.

A well-equipped first aid kit is a necessity on any boat.

Safety Checklist

▶ Recreational boats are bound by both federal and state requirements.
▶ Your boat must be registered in the state of principal use and have a Certificate of Number. This number must be displayed per state requirements. Any change in ownership, address change or boat status must be registered with the state within 15 days.
▶ The US Coast Guard or any law enforcement officials may board your vessel when you are underway and terminate use of your vessel for negligent operation or violation of federal regulations.
▶ USCG approved fire extinguishers must be carried aboard all auxiliary powered vessels. Boats less than 26 feet must have one Type B-1.
▶ USCG approved Personal Flotation Devices (PFDs) of Type I, II, III or V are required for each person aboard the vessel and one Type IV (throwable) for vessels larger than 16 feet in length.
▶ USCG approved Visual Distress Signals must be carried aboard vessels except: boats less than 16 feet in length, boats in organized events such as regattas, open sailboats less than 26 feet in length without auxiliary power, and manually propelled boats.
▶ All vessels must carry a horn.
▶ Vessels operating or anchored between sunset and sunrise are required to display navigation lights.
▶ Vessels with divers in the water must display a rigid replica of the code flag "A". In many states these vessels must display a red flag with a diagonal white stripe.
▶ US law prohibits dumping of refuse in US waters. This includes plastics, oil and hazardous waste.
▶ Vessels equipped with Marine Sanitation Devices must meet USCG requirements.
▶ Boating accidents must be reported to the nearest state authority per the federal requirements.
▶ You are obligated to render assistance, as can be safely provided, to anyone in danger at sea.

Recommended Safety Equipment

▶ Additional means of propulsion such as oars, paddle or auxiliary power.
▶ A manual bailing device such as a bucket or bilge pump.
▶ A basic first aid kit with instructions.
▶ An anchor and anchor line.
▶ A tool kit, spare parts and through-hull plugs.
▶ A VHF radio.
▶ Navigation charts and magnetic compass.

Signaling for Help

Before you decide to ask for outside assistance, determine if you can take care of the problem yourself. You may be able to get back to the harbor under your own power, or accept a tow from a friendly boat. Coast Guard and private search-and-rescue missions are expensive and time-consuming. If you do need to signal for help, use the signals, either separately or together, that are recognized by the Coast Guard and the Navigation Rules.

International Distress Signals

▶ A smoke signal giving off orange-colored smoke.

▶ A rocket parachute flare or a hand flare showing a red light.

USE AND REGULATIONS FOR FLARES: *Flares fired from a pistol or launcher are visible over the horizon day or night. Handheld flares can pinpoint your location for rescuers, but should be used with great caution around a rubber raft. The US Coast Guard requires vessels over 16 feet to have three daylight and three night flares or three combination daylight/night devices readily available, which have not expired.*

▶ Rockets or shells, throwing red stars fired one at a time at short intervals.

▶ Flashlight or other device signaling SOS (*dot-dot-dot, dash-dash-dash, dot-dot-dot*) in the Morse Code.

▶ Continuous sounding of a foghorn.

▶ Flames, such as a fire in a bucket or barrel.

▶ "Mayday" spoken over a radiotelephone.

▶ A signal consisting of a square flag having above or below it a ball or anything resembling a ball.

▶ Flying the international code flags or signals "N" and "C".

▶ Firing a gun or other explosive device at intervals of about a minute.

▶ Slowly and repeatedly waving both outstretched arms.

▶ A high intensity white light flashing at regular intervals from 50 to 70 times per minute.

▶ A radiotelegraph or radiotelephone alarm signal.

▶ Signals transmitted by an emergency position-indicating radio beacon (EPIRB).

Rig Types

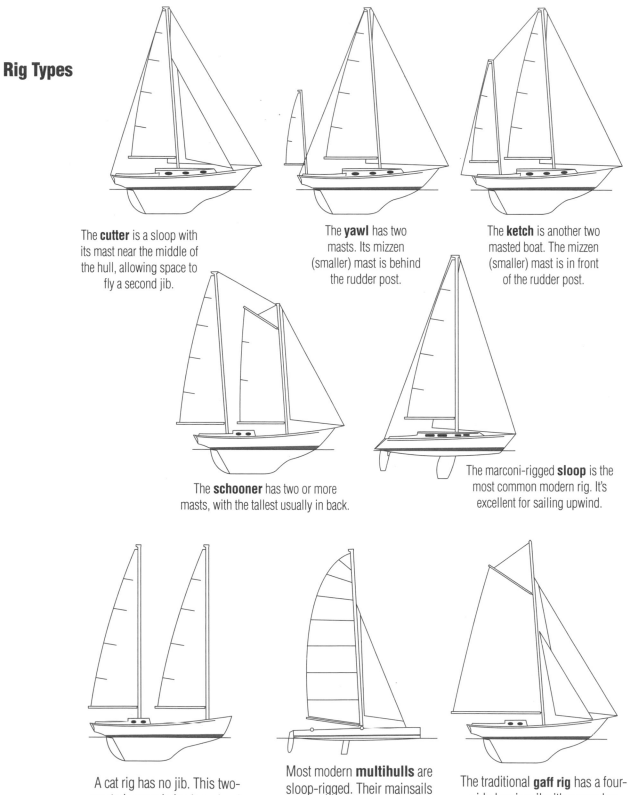

The **cutter** is a sloop with its mast near the middle of the hull, allowing space to fly a second jib.

The **yawl** has two masts. Its mizzen (smaller) mast is behind the rudder post.

The **ketch** is another two masted boat. The mizzen (smaller) mast is in front of the rudder post.

The **schooner** has two or more masts, with the tallest usually in back.

The marconi-rigged **sloop** is the most common modern rig. It's excellent for sailing upwind.

A cat rig has no jib. This two-masted example is also a ketch rig. Hence the name **cat ketch**.

Most modern **multihulls** are sloop-rigged. Their mainsails have full-length battens and a large curved roach (leech).

The traditional **gaff rig** has a four-sided mainsail with a wooden spar (gaff) attached to the top.

Hull Types

A monohull is a boat with a single hull.

The twin-hulled catamaran features speed and acceleration.

The three-hulled trimaran can also carry a lot of sail for speed.

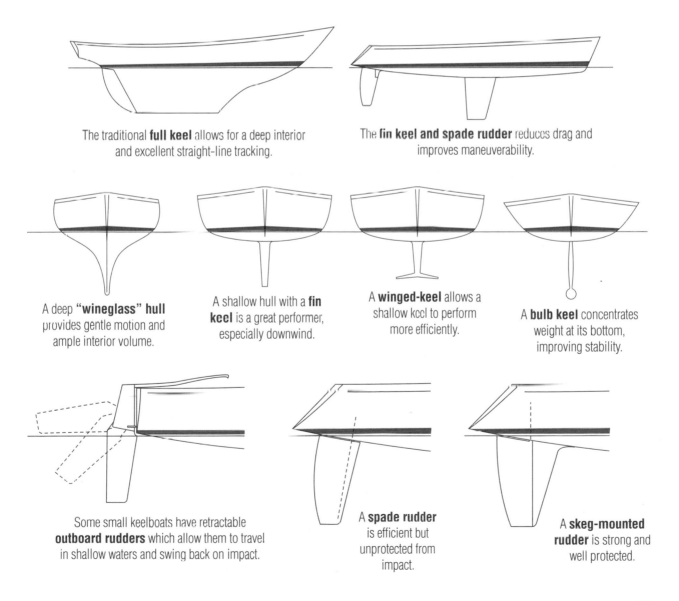

The traditional **full keel** allows for a deep interior and excellent straight-line tracking.

The **fin keel and spade rudder** reduces drag and improves maneuverability.

A deep **"wineglass" hull** provides gentle motion and ample interior volume.

A shallow hull with a **fin keel** is a great performer, especially downwind.

A **winged-keel** allows a shallow keel to perform more efficiently.

A **bulb keel** concentrates weight at its bottom, improving stability.

Some small keelboats have retractable **outboard rudders** which allow them to travel in shallow waters and swing back on impact.

A **spade rudder** is efficient but unprotected from impact.

A **skeg-mounted rudder** is strong and well protected.

A

Abeam - off the side of (at right angle to) the boat.

Aboard - on the boat.

Adrift - a boat drifting without control.

Aft - at or toward the stern or behind the boat.

Aground - a boat whose keel is touching the bottom.

Amidships - toward the center of the boat.

Apparent wind - the wind aboard a moving boat.

Astern - behind the stern of the boat.

Athwartships - across the boat from side to side.

B

Backstay - the standing rigging running from the stern to the top of the mast, keeping the mast from falling forward.

Back - to stop or to propel a boat backward by holding the clew of a sail out to windward.

Bail - to empty a boat of water.

Balance - the capability of a boat to sail straight without changing the tiller position.

Ballast - weight in the keel of a boat that provides stability.

Barometer - a weather forecasting instrument that measures air pressure.

Batten - a thin slat that slides into a pocket in the leech of a sail, helping it hold its shape.

Beam - the width of a boat at its widest point.

Beam reach - (point of sail) sailing in a direction at approximately 90 degrees to the wind.

Bear away - to fall off, head away from the wind.

Bearing - the direction from one object to another expressed in compass degrees.

Beating - a course sailed upwind.

Below - the area of a boat beneath the deck.

Bend - to attach a sail to a spar or a headstay, or to attach a line to a sail.

Bight - a loop in a line.

Bilge - the lowest part of the boat's interior, where water on board will collect.

Bitter end - the end of a line.

Blanket - to use a sail or object to block the wind from filling a sail.

Block - a pulley on a boat.

Boat hook - a pole with a hook on the end used for grabbing hold of a mooring or retrieving something that has fallen overboard.

Boat speed - the speed of a boat through the water.

Bolt rope - the rope sewn into the foot and luff of some mainsails and the luff of some jibs by which the sails are attached to the boat.

Boom - the spar extending directly aft from the mast to which the foot of the mainsail is attached

Boom vang - a block and tackle system which pulls the boom down to assist sail control.

Bottom - 1. - the underside of the boat.
2. - the land under the water.

Bow - the forward part of the boat.

Bow line (BOW - line) - a line running from the bow of the boat to the dock or mooring.

Bowline - (BOE-lin) - a knot designed to make a loop that will not slip and can be easily untied.

Breast line - a short dockline leading off the beam of the boat directly to the dock.

Broach - an uncontrolled rounding up into the wind, usually from a downwind point of sail.

Broad reach - (point of sail) sailing in a direction with the wind at the rear corner of the boat (approximately 135 degrees from the bow).

Bulkhead - a wall that runs athwartships on a boat, usually providing structural support to the hull.

Buoy - a floating marker.

Buoyancy - the ability of an object to float.

By the lee - sailing on a run with the wind coming over the same side of the boat as the boom.

C

Cabin - the interior of a boat.

Can - an odd-numbered, green, flat-topped buoy marking the left side of a channel as you return to port.

Capsize - to tip or turn a boat over.

Cast off - to release a line when leaving a dock or mooring.

Catamaran - a twin-hulled sailing vessel with a deck or trampoline between the hulls.

Catboat - a boat with only a mainsail and the mast located at the bow.

Centerboard - a pivoting board that can be lowered and used like a keel to keep a boat from slipping to leeward.

Centerline - the midline of a boat running from bow to stern.

Chafe - wear on a line caused by rubbing.

Chainplates - strong metal plates which connect the shrouds to the boat.

Channel - a (usually narrow) path in the water, marked by buoys, in which the water is deep enough to sail.

Chart - a nautical map.

Charter - to rent a boat.

Chock - a guide mounted on the deck through which docklines and anchor rode are run.

Chop - rough, short, steep waves.

Cleat - a nautical fitting that is used to secure a line.

Clew - the lower, aft corner of a sail. The clew of the mainsail is held taut by the outhaul. The jib sheets are attached to the clew of the jib.

Close-hauled - the point of sail that is closest to the wind.

Close reach - (point of sail) sailing in a direction with the wind forward of the beam (about 70 degrees from the bow).

Coaming - the short protective wall surrounding the cockpit.

Cockpit - the lower area in which the steering controls and sail controls are located.

Coil - to loop a line neatly so it can be stored.

Come about - see **tack**.

Companionway - the steps leading from the cockpit or deck to the cabin below.

Compass - the magnetic instrument which indicates the direction in which the boat is headed.

Compass rose - the twin circles on a chart which indicate the direction of true north and magnetic north.

Course - the direction in which the boat is steered.

Crew - besides the skipper, anyone on board who helps sail the boat.

Cunningham - a line running through a grommet about eight inches up from the tack of a mainsail that is used to tighten the luff of the sail.

Current - the horizontal movement of water caused by tides, wind and other forces.

Cutter - a single-masted boat with the mast near the middle that is capable of flying both a jib and a staysail.

D

Daysailer - a small sailboat.

Dead downwind - sailing in a direction straight downwind.

Deck - the mostly flat surface area on top of the boat.

Depower - to release the power from the sails by allowing them to luff or making them flatter. This is done to reduce heel.

Dinghy - a small sailboat or rowboat.

Displacement - the weight of a boat; therefore the amount of water it displaces.

Dock - 1. - the wooden structure where a boat may be tied up. 2. - the act of bringing the boat to rest alongside the structure.

Dockline - a line used to secure the boat to the dock.

Dodger - a canvas protection in front of the cockpit of some boats that is designed to keep spray off the skipper and crew.

Downhaul - a line used to pull down on the movable gooseneck on some boats to tighten the luff of the mainsail. The cunningham has the same function on

other boats.

Downwind - away from the direction of the wind.

Draft - the depth of a boat's keel from the water's surface.

E

Ease - to let out a line or sail.

Ebb - an outgoing current.

F

Fairlead - a fitting that guides a jib sheet or other lines back to the cockpit or along the deck.

Fairway - a channel.

Fake - to lay out a line on deck using large loops to keep it from becoming tangled.

Fall off - see **Head down**.

Fast - secured.

Fathom - a measurement of the depth of water. One fathom equals six feet.

Fender - a rubber bumper used to protect a boat by keeping it from hitting a dock.

Fend off - push off.

Fetch - a course on which a boat can make its destination without having to tack.

Fitting - a piece of nautical hardware.

Flood - an incoming current.

Following sea - waves hitting the boat from astern.

Foot - the bottom edge of a sail.

Fore - forward.

Forepeak - a storage area in the bow (below the deck).

Foresail - a jib or a genoa.

Forestay - the standing rigging running from the bow to the mast to which the jib is hanked on.

Forward - toward the bow.

Fouled - tangled.

Foul-weather gear - water-resistant clothing.

Freeboard - the height of the hull above the water's surface.

Full - not luffing.

Furl - to fold or roll up a sail.

G

Gaff - on some boats, a spar along the top edge of a four-sided sail.

Gear - generic term for sailing equipment.

Genoa - a large jib whose clew extends aft of the mast.

Give-way vessel - the vessel required to give way to another boat when they may be on a collision course.

Glide zone - the distance a sailboat takes to coast to a stop.

Gooseneck - the strong fitting that connects the boom to the mast.

Grommet - a reinforcing metal ring set in a sail.

Ground tackle - the anchor and rode (chain and line).

Gudgeon - a fitting attached to the stern of a boat into which the pintles of a rudder are inserted.

Gunwale (GUN-el) - the edge of the deck where it meets the topsides.

Gust - see **puff**.

H

Halyard - a line used to hoist or lower a sail.

Hank - a snap hook that is used to connect the luff of a jib onto the forestay.

"Hard a-lee" - the command given to the crew just prior to tacking.

Hard over - to turn the tiller as far as possible in one direction.

Hatch - a large covered opening in the deck.

Haul in - to tighten a line.

Head - 1. - the top corner of a sail. 2. - the bathroom on a boat. 3. - the toilet on a boat.

Headboard - the reinforcing small board affixed to the head of a sail.

Header - a wind shift which makes your boat head down or sails to be sheeted in.

Heading - the direction of the boat expressed in compass degrees.

Head down - to fall off or bear away, changing course away from the wind.

Head off - see **head down**.

Head up - to come up, changing course toward the wind.

Headsail - a jib, genoa, or staysail.

Headstay - the standing rigging running from the bow to the mast.

Head-to-wind - the course of the boat when the bow is dead into the wind.

Headway - progress made forward.

Heave - to throw.

Heave-to - to hold one's position in the water by using the force of the sails and rudder to counter one another.

Heavy weather - strong winds and large waves.

Heel - the lean of a boat caused by the wind.

Helm - the tiller.

Helmsman - the person responsible for steering the boat.

High side - the windward side of the boat.

Hike - to position crew members out over the windward rail to help balance the boat.

Hiking stick - see **tiller extension**.

Hiking strap - a strap used by people hiking out that holds their feet.

Holding ground - the bottom ground in an anchorage used to hold the anchor.

Hove-to - a boat that has completed the process of heaving-to, with its jib aback, its main loosely trimmed, and its rudder securely positioned to steer it close to the wind.

Hull - the body of the boat, excluding rig and sails.

Hull speed - the theoretical maximum speed of a sailboat determined by the length of its waterline.

I

Inboard - inside of the rail of a boat.

In irons - a boat that is head-to-wind, making no forward headway.

J

Jib - the small forward sail of a boat attached to the forestay.

Jibe - to change direction of a boat by steering the stern through the wind.

"Jibe-ho" - the command given to the crew when starting a jibe.

Jiffy reef - a quick reefing system allowing a section of the mainsail to be tied to the boom.

Jury rig - an improvised, temporary repair.

K

Kedge off - to use an anchor to pull a boat into deeper water after it has run aground.

Keel - the heavy vertical fin beneath a boat that helps keep it upright and prevents it from slipping sideways in the water.

Ketch - a two-masted boat with its mizzen (after) mast shorter than its mainmast and located forward of the rudder post.

Knockdown - a boat heeled so far that one of its spreaders touches the water.

Knot - one nautical mile per hour.

L

Land breeze - a wind that blows over land and out to sea.

Lash - to tie down.

Lay - to sail a course that will clear an obstacle without tacking.

Lazarette - a storage compartment built into the cockpit or deck.

Lazy sheet - the windward side jib sheet that is not under strain.

Lead (LEED) - to pass a line through a fitting or a block.

Lee helm - the boat's tendency to turn away from the wind.

Lee shore - land which is on the leeward side of the boat. Because the wind is blowing in that direction, a lee shore could pose a danger.

Leech - the after edge of a sail.

Leeward (LEW-erd) - the direction away from the wind (where the wind is blowing to).

Leeward side - the side of the boat or sail that is away from the wind.

Leeway - sideways slippage of the boat in a direction away from the wind.

Lifeline - plastic coated wire, supported by stanchions, around the outside of the deck to help prevent crew members from falling overboard.

Lift - 1. - the force that results from air passing by a sail, or water past a keel, that moves the boat forward and sideways. 2. - a change in wind direction which lets the boat head up.

Line - a nautical rope.

Low side - the leeward side of the boat.

Lubber's line - a small post in a compass used to help determine a course or a bearing.

Luff - 1. - the forward edge of a sail. 2. - the fluttering of a sail caused by aiming too close to the wind.

Lull - a decrease in wind speed for a short duration.

M

Magnetic - in reference to magnetic north rather than true north.

Mainmast - the taller of two masts on a boat.

Mainsail (MAIN-sil) - the sail hoisted on the mast of a sloop or cutter or the sail hoisted on the mainmast of a ketch or yawl.

Mainsheet - the controlling line for the mainsail.

Marlinspike - a pointed tool used to loosen knots.

Mast - the large aluminum or wooden pole in the middle of a boat from which the mainsail is set.

Masthead - the top of the mast.

Masthead fly - a wind direction indicator on top of the mast.

Mast step - the structure that the bottom of the mast sits on.

Mizzen - the small aftermost sail on a ketch or yawl hoisted on the mizzen mast.

Mooring - a permanently anchored ball or buoy to which a boat can be tied.

N

Nautical mile - a distance of 6076 feet, equaling one minute of the earth's latitude.

Navigation Rules - laws established to prevent collisions on the water.

No-Go Zone - an area into the wind in which a boat cannot produce power to sail.

Nun - a red, even-numbered, cone-shaped buoy marking the right side of a channel as you return to port. Nuns are usually paired with cans.

O

Offshore wind - wind blowing off (away from) the land.

Offshore - away from or out of sight of land.

Off the wind - sailing downwind.

On the wind - sailing upwind, close-hauled.

Outboard - 1. - outside the rail of a boat. 2. - a portable engine.

Outhaul - the controlling line attached to the clew of a mainsail used to tension the foot of the sail.

Overpowered - a boat that is heeling too far because it has too much sail up for the amount of wind.

Overtaking - a boat that is catching up to another boat and about to pass it.

P

Painter - the line attached to the bow of a dinghy.

Pay out - to ease a line.

PFD - abbreviation for Personal Flotation Device; a lifejacket.

Pinching - sailing too close to the wind.

Pintle - small metal extensions on a rudder that slides into a gudgeon on the transom. The gudgeon/pintle fitting allows the rudder to swing back and forth.

Point - to steer close to the wind.

Points of sail - boat directions in relation to wind direction, i.e., close-hauled, beam reaching, broad reaching, and running.

Port - 1. - the left side of a boat when facing forward. 2. - a harbor. 3. - a window in a cabin on a boat.

Port tack - sailing on any point of sail with the wind coming over the port side of the boat.

Prevailing wind - typical or consistent wind conditions.

Puff - an increase in wind speed for a short duration.

Pulpit - a stainless steel guardrail at the bow and stern of some boats.

Pushpit - a stainless steel guardrail at the stern of some boats.

Push-pull principle - the explanation of how sails generate power.

Q

Quarter - the sides of the boat near the stern.

R

Rail - the outer edges of the deck.

Rake - the angle of the mast.

Range - the alignment of two objects that indicate the middle of a channel.

Reach - one of several points of sail across the wind.

"Ready about" - the command given to the crew to prepare to tack.

"Ready to jibe" - the command given to the crew to prepare to jibe.

Reef - to reduce the size of a sail.

Reeve - to pass a line through a cringle or block.

Rhumb line - a straight course between two points.

Rig - 1. - the design of a boat's mast(s), standing rigging, and sail plan. 2. - to prepare a boat to go sailing.

Rigging - the wires and lines used to support and control sails.

Right-of-way - the right of the stand-on vessel to hold its course.

Roach - the sail area aft of a straight line running from the head to the clew of a sail.

Rode - line and chain attached from the boat to the anchor.

Roller furling - a mechanical system to roll up a headsail (jib) around the headstay.

Rudder - the underwater fin that is controlled by the tiller to deflect water and steer the boat.

Run - (point of sail) sailing with the wind coming directly behind the boat.

Running rigging - lines and hardware used to control the sails.

S

Sail cover - the protective cover used to preserve sails when they are not in use.

Sail ties - pieces of line or webbing used to tie the mainsail to the boom when reefing or storing the sail.

Schooner - a two-masted boat whose foremast is usually shorter than its mainmast.

Scope - the ratio of the amount of anchor rode deployed to the distance from the bow to the bottom.

Scull - to propel a boat by swinging the rudder back and forth.

Scupper - cockpit or deck drain.

Sea breeze - a wind that blows over the sea and onto the land.

Seacock - a valve which opens and closes a hole through the hull for saltwater needed on board or discharge.

Secure - make safe or cleat.

Set - 1. - the direction of a current. 2. - to trim the sails.

Shackle - a metal fitting at the end of a line used to attach the line to a sail or another fitting.

Shake out - to remove a reef and restore the full sail.

Sheave - the rotating wheel inside a block or fitting.

Sheet - 1. - (noun) the line which is used to control the sail by easing it out or trimming it in. 2. - (verb) to trim a sail.

Shoal - shallow water that may be dangerous.

Shroud - standing rigging at the side of the mast.

Singlehanded - sailing alone.

S-Jibe - the controlled method of jibing with the mainsail crossing the boat under control and the boat's path making an "S" shaped course.

Skeg - a vertical fin in front of the rudder.

Skipper - the person in charge of the boat.

Slip - a parking area for a boat between two docks in a marina.

Sloop - a single-masted sailboat with mainsail and headsail.

Snub - to hold a line under tension by wrapping it on a winch or cleat.

Sole - the floor in a cockpit or cabin.

Spar - a pole used to attach a sail on a boat, for example, the mast, the boom, a gaff.

Spinnaker - a large billowing headsail used when sailing downwind.

Splice - the joining of two lines together by interweaving their strands.

Spreader - a support strut extending athwartships from the mast used to support the mast and guide the shrouds from the top of the mast to the chainplates.

Spring line - a dockline running forward or aft from the boat to the dock to keep the boat from moving forward or aft.

Squall - a short intense storm with little warning.

Stability - a boat's ability to resist tipping (heeling).

Stanchions - stainless steel supports at the edge of the deck which hold the lifelines.

Standing rigging - the permanent rigging (usually wire) of a boat, including the forestay, backstay, and shrouds.

Stand-on vessel - the vessel or boat with the right-of-way.

Starboard - when looking from the stern toward the bow, the right side of the boat.

Starboard tack - sailing on any point of sail with the wind coming over the starboard side of the boat.

Stay - a wire support for a mast, part of the standing rigging.

Staysail (STAY-sil) - on a cutter, a second small "inner jib," attached between the bow and the mast.

Stem - the forward tip of the bow.
Step - the area in which the base of the mast fits.
Stern - the aft part of the boat.
Stow - to store properly.
Swamped - filled with water.

T

Tack - 1. - a course on which the wind comes over one side of the boat, i.e., port tack, starboard tack. 2. - to change direction by turning the bow through the wind. 3. the lower forward corner of a sail.
Tackle - a sequence of blocks and line that provides a mechanical advantage.
Tail - to hold and pull a line from behind a winch.
Telltales - 1. - pieces of yarn or sailcloth material attached to sails which indicate when the sail is properly trimmed. 2. - wind direction indicators attached to standing rigging.
Tide - the rise and fall of water level due to the gravitational pull of the sun and moon.
Tiller - a long handle, extending into the cockpit, which directly controls the rudder.
Tiller extension - a handle attached to the tiller which allows the helmsman to sit further out to the side.
Toe rail - a short aluminum or wooden rail around the outer edges of the deck.
Topping lift - a line used to hold the boom up when the mainsail is lowered or stowed.
Topsides - the sides of the boat between the waterline and the deck.
Transom - the vertical surface of the stern.
Traveler - a track or bridle that controls sideways (athwartships) movement of the mainsail.
Trim - 1. - to pull in on a sheet. 2. - how a sail is set relative to the wind.
Trimaran - a three-hulled sailing vessel.
True wind - the actual speed and direction of the wind when standing still.
Tune - to adjust a boat's standing rigging.
Turnbuckle - a mechanical fitting attached to the lower ends of stays, allowing for the standing rigging to be adjusted.

U

Underway - to be under the power of sail or engine.
Unrig - to stow sails and rigging when the boat is not in use.
Upwind - toward the direction of the wind.
USCG - abbreviation for United States Coast Guard.

V

Vang - see **boom vang**.
Vessel - any sailboat, powerboat or ship.

W

Wake - waves caused by a boat moving through the water.
Waterline - the horizontal line on the hull of a boat where the water surface should be.
Weather helm - the boat's tendency to head up toward the wind, which occurs when a sailboat is overpowered.
Weather side - see **windward side**.
Whip - to bind together the strands at the end of a line.
Whisker pole - a pole, temporarily mounted between the mast and the clew of a jib, used to hold the jib out and keep it full when sailing downwind.
Winch - a deck-mounted drum with a handle offering mechanical advantage used to trim sheets. Winches may also be mounted on the mast to assist in raising sails.
Windward - toward the wind.
Windward side - the side of a boat or a sail closest to the wind.
Wing-and-wing - sailing downwind with the jib set on the opposite side of the mainsail.
Working sails - the mainsail and standard jib.
Working sheet - the leeward jib sheet that is being used to trim the jib.

Y

Yawl - a two-masted boat with its mizzen (after) mast shorter than its mainmast and located aft of the rudder post.

US SAILING Basic Keelboat Certification

The Basic Keelboat graduate will have successfully demonstrated the ability to responsibly skipper and crew a simple daysailing keelboat in familiar waters in light to moderate wind and sea conditions.

Recommended Equipment: It is recommended that Basic Keelboat Certification courses and examinations be conducted on 18 to 27 foot daysailing sloop-rigged keelboats with tiller steering and with adequate equipment inventory to complete all required certification outcomes.

Prerequisite: There is no prerequisite for Basic Keelboat Certification.

Certification Requirements: Basic Keelboat Certification requires the successful completion of the following knowledge and skill requirements. These requirements are expected to be able to be performed safely with confident command of the boat in familiar waters with a wind range of 5 to 15 knots. Some regions may have stronger prevailing conditions, which are acceptable if the candidate can safely control the boat and be aware of his or her limitations in these conditions. The certified candidate will be able to skipper a tiller steered keelboat up to 27 feet in length.

Part 1: Minimum Water Skills

Preparation to Sail:
1. Demonstrate ability to recognize and forecast prevailing local weather conditions.
2. Demonstrate how to properly board a boat.
3. Perform a presail check for the boat's flotation integrity, safety and legally required equipment, and crew indoctrination.
4. Demonstrate the proper rigging of the sails, halyards, sheets, blocks, and winches.
5. Check all other equipment specific to your boat not indicated above.

Crew Operations and Skills:
6. Demonstrate how to put on a Personal Flotation Device (PFD).

7. Demonstrate tying and use of knots: stopper knot, bowline, cleat hitch and sail lashing knot.
8. Demonstrate the use of these sail controls: halyards, sheets, cunningham/downhaul and outhaul.

Leaving the Dock or Mooring:
9. Demonstrate appropriate helmsman and crew coordination and skills for departure suitable to the conditions: raising sails, line handling, casting off and boathandling.

Boat Control in Confined Waters:
10. Demonstrate in close quarters under sail: starting, stopping, speed control, tacking, jibing, steering control, sail luffing, the No-Go Zone, getting out of irons, backing the jib, and crew coordination and communication.
11. Demonstrate sailing a predetermined closed course and maneuvering around obstacles.

Navigation (Piloting):
12. Point out Aids to Navigation in the harbor and local waters that you are sailing, and respond accordingly.

Navigation Rules, International-Inland:
13. Demonstrate use of Navigation Rules while sailing.

Boat Control in Open Water:
14. Demonstrate proper sail trim with accurate sheet adjustment of the main and headsails. Make use of the sail telltales and identify points of sail.
15. Perform a heaving-to maneuver per the prescribed method.
16. When appropriate, demonstrate sailing "by the lee" and explain the inherent dangers involved.

Heavy Weather Sailing:
17. Demonstrate how to reef and/or depower sails.

Overboard Recovery Methods:
18. Properly demonstrate one of the overboard recovery methods, which is most appropriate for: your sailing ability, boat type, crew experience, wind and sea conditions, and maintaining constant visual contact with the victim.

Safety and Emergency Procedures:
19. Explain the proper procedure for using an approved distress signal.

Returning to the Dock or Mooring:
20. Demonstrate appropriate helmsman and crew coordination and skills for arrival under sail and/or

power suitable to the conditions: boathandling, deploying fenders, stopping, tying up and lowering sails. Explain at least two different approach plans for other conditions.

Securing the Boat Properly:

21. Demonstrate stowing of sails, rigging and equipment. Thoroughly clean the boat, and install any covers.
22. Check both the electrical and bilge systems for dock operation if required.
23. Check the locks on companionway, lockers and hatches. Make a final check of docklines, spring lines and fender placement.

Part 2: Minimum Knowledge

Preparation to Sail:

1. Describe personal preparation such as clothing and sun protection.

Crew Operations and Skills:

2. Be familiar with the nomenclature for basic parts of the boat, sails, battens and rigging.
3. Describe the proper use of Personal Flotation Devices (PFDs) and throwable flotation devices.
4. Describe the use of sail controls.
5. Explain potential electrical hazards such as overhead electrical wires and lightning.

Sailing Theory:

6. Describe basic sailboat design, sail theory and boat dynamics.
7. Explain how to read the wind and determine all points of sail.
8. Understand what is meant by the term "sailing by the lee" and explain the inherent dangers involved.

Leaving the Dock or Mooring:

9. Understand the effects of wind, tide and currents in relation to the boat and surrounding area while preparing to get underway.
10. Describe the differences and alternatives for leaving under sail and/or power in upwind, crosswind and downwind situations.

Navigation (Piloting):

11. Be familiar with basic chart reading specific to your local waters.
12. Describe Aids to Navigation: buoys, daymarks, regulatory markers, and other markers specific to your local waters.

Navigation Rules, International-Inland:

13. Describe the Navigation Rules, International-Inland, for Stand-On and Give-Way sailboats and powerboats for collision avoidance and understand your state and local boating regulations.

Heavy Weather Sailing:

14. Describe weather warning sources.

Overboard Recovery Methods:

15. Understand the Quick Stop and Quick-Turn overboard recovery methods to include: constant visual contact with the victim, communication, recovery plan, sequence of maneuvers, boathandling, course sailed, pickup approach and coming alongside the victim (or simulated object).
16. Describe methods of getting an overboard recovery victim back on deck after the vessel is stopped alongside.

Safety and Emergency Procedures:

17. Be familiar with treatment of victims of overheating, hypothermia and seasickness.
18. Describe the use and regulations for flares.
19. Be familiar with at least six different distress and emergency signals per Navigation Rule 37.
20. Be familiar with the U.S. Coast Guard requirements for safety equipment.

Anchoring Techniques:

21. Be familiar with anchoring procedures for emergency situations such as loss of boat control, sudden storms, prevention from going aground or injured crew situations.

Returning to the Dock or Mooring:

22. Describe the differences and alternatives for arrival under sail and/or power in upwind, crosswind and downwind situations.

An introduction to US SAILING.

Since 1897 the United States Sailing Association (US SAILING) has provided support for American sailors at all levels of sailing — in all kinds of sailboats. The primary objective of its Training Program is to provide a national standard of quality instruction for all people learning to sail. The US SAILING Keelboat Certification System includes a series of books such as *Basic Keelboat*, a program of student certifications and an extensive educational and training program for instructors. It is one of the most highly developed and effective national training systems for students and sailing instructors and is recognized nationally and internationally.

US SAILING is a non-profit organization and the official National Governing Body of Sailing as designated by the U. S. Congress in the Amateur Sports Act. It has a national Training Program for sailors in dinghies, windsurfers, multihulls and keelboats. It is also the official representative to the International Sailing Federation (IYRU until 1996).

The US SAILING Keelboat Certification System is designed to develop safe, responsible and confident sailors who meet specific performance and knowledge standards. (See US SAILING BASIC KEELBOAT Certification on page 88 for the BASIC KEELBOAT standards.) There are other benefits for you as well. You can start at the BASIC KEELBOAT certification level and progress through BASIC CRUISING, BAREBOAT CRUISING, COASTAL NAVIGATION, and even go on to COASTAL PASSAGE MAKING, CELESTIAL NAVIGATION and OFFSHORE PASSAGE MAKING. With your US SAILING certifications and experience documented in the *Official Logbook of Sailing*, you will have a passport to cruising and chartering boats locally or worldwide.

Basic Keelboat is intended as a supplement to your first sailing lessons, rather than as a substitute for them. It was created to help you accelerate your learning curve and clarify your understanding of the concepts and techniques of sailing.

What Makes Sailing Special?
Within the past 20 years, the advent of fiberglass boatbuilding and other new technologies has opened up the sport of sailing to people of all ages, incomes and abilities. Sailing offers virtually limitless choices of boats, each with its own unique characteristics, and the opportunity to explore an adjacent cove or an exotic tropical location.

Most sailors will acquire entry-level skills quite rapidly. However, mastering them is an experience that will be rewarding, exciting and pleasurable for a lifetime.

As you learn to sail, you will find that sailing is more than simply being pushed and pulled by the wind. For most people, sailing is meeting new friends, enjoying nature's beauty and challenge, and sharing a unique fellowship with all boaters. A tremendous camaraderie exists among sailors, particularly on the water, which makes sailing — and the people who do it — very special.

Please contact us at:
US SAILING
P.O. Box 1260, 15 Maritime Drive
Portsmouth, RI 02871-6015
401-683-0800   Fax: 401-683-0840

What can US SAILING do for you?

US SAILING is committed to helping you discover and enjoy the beauty, relaxation, challenge and friendships of sailing. As part of this commitment we offer:

THE KEELBOAT CERTIFICATION SYSTEM with its various levels of training and certification:

- **Basic Keelboat.** To responsibly skipper and crew a simple daysailing keelboat in familiar waters in light to moderate wind and sea conditions.

- **Basic Cruising.** To responsibly skipper and crew an auxiliary powered cruising sailboat during daylight hours within sight of land in moderate wind and sea conditions.

- **Bareboat Cruising.** To responsibly skipper, crew or bareboat charter an inboard auxiliary powered cruising sailboat within sight of land to a port or an anchorage during daylight hours in moderate to strong wind and sea conditions.

- **Coastal Navigation.** To properly use traditional navigation techniques and electronic navigation for near coastal passage making.

- **Coastal Passage Making.** To responsibly skipper and crew an inboard auxiliary powered cruising sailboat for coastal or offshore passages in strong to heavy conditions, including zero visibility and nighttime, in unfamiliar waters out of sight of land.

- **Celestial Navigation.** To navigate using celestial techniques and integrating celestial with traditional navigation techniques.

- **Offshore Passage Making.** To responsibly skipper and crew an inboard auxiliary powered cruising sailboat to any destination worldwide.

Plus many other useful services:

US SAILING certified instructors help you achieve new skills and knowledge using up to date and safe methods.

Course materials, including this book, presented in a highly visual format to help you gain competency and confidence in your sailing skills and knowledge.

The Official Logbook of Sailing, recognized nationally and internationally, to document your US SAILING certifications and experience and use as a passport to chartering boats locally and worldwide.

A national database so charter companies can confirm your sailing credentials.

A list of sailing schools that use US SAILING certified instructors and US SAILING course materials.

US SAILING Safety-at-Sea seminars.

U.S. Coast Guard recognition of the completion of a safe boating course, often one of the requirements for licensing.

Racing Rules and handicap rating systems.

US SAILING membership making you a part of the National Governing Body for the Sport of Sailing and the recipient of discounts on products and services.

The Keelboat Certification System was developed by volunteers representing sailing schools, charter companies, sailors, and the sailing industry.

—Welcome aboard!

A special acknowledgement to Sail America

US SAILING would like to thank Sail America for their continuing support of quality sailing instruction and the generous grant they provided to help publish this book.

Sail America (originally A.S.A.P.) was formed in 1990 to represent all segments of the sailing industry — from boatbuilders to sailing schools — with the mission of stimulating public interest in sailing and expanding the sailing market in the US.

With this in mind, Sail America creates and manages its own boat shows and then reinvests the money earned from the shows to benefit the sport of sailing. SAIL EXPO Atlantic City is now an established annual show, and in 1995 SAIL EXPO St. Petersburg was successfully launched.

As a result, Sail America has been able to reinvest a substantial percentage of show earnings to benefit sailing through several important programs including:

- Grants to improve the quality of sailing instruction and training (i.e., funding this book)
- A grant for the "Class Afloat" program to stimulate awareness of junior and senior high school students in sailing
- Grants to provide sailing equipment and promotional materials to associations that benefit physically challenged sailors.

Sail America's mission is to promote the growth of sailing as a sport, an industry, and a way of life in harmony with the environment. For more information on Sail America, please call (401) 841-0900.

Sail America

Notes

Notes

Notes

Notes

Transforming Mental Health Services: Implementing the Federal Agenda for Change

Edited by
Howard H. Goldman, M.D., Ph.D.
Jeffrey A. Buck, Ph.D.
Kenneth S. Thompson, M.D.

A Compendium of Articles
From *Psychiatric Services*

Manufactured in the United States of America on acid-free paper
13 12 11 10 09   5 4 3 2 1
First Edition

Originally published in *Psychiatric Services,* Volumes 57–60

American Psychiatric Association
1000 Wilson Boulevard
Arlington, VA 22209-3901
www.psych.org

Library of Congress Cataloging-in-Publication Data

Transforming mental health services : implementing the federal agenda for change / edited by Howard H. Goldman, Jeffrey A. Buck, Kenneth S. Thompson. — 1st ed.
    p. ; cm.
    "A compendium of articles from Psychiatric Services."
    Includes bibliographical references.
    ISBN 978-0-89042-455-1 (alk. paper)
    1. Mental health services—United States. 2. Health care reform—United States. I. Goldman, Howard H.
II. Buck, Jeffrey A. III. Thompson, Kenneth, 1954 Sept. 2– IV. American Psychiatric Association. V. Psychiatric services (Washington, D.C.)
    [DNLM: 1. United States. Substance Abuse and Mental Health Services Administration. 2. United States. President's New Freedom Commission on Mental Health. 3. United States. President's New Freedom Commission on Mental Health. Achieving the promise. 4. Mental Health Services—trends—United States—Collected Works. 5. Health Care Reform—trends—United States—Collected Works. WM 30 T7705 2009]
    RA790.6.T72 2009
    362.196'89—dc22

                                                                            2009018196

British Library Cataloguing in Publication Data
A CIP record is available from the British Library.

Contents

III. STATE EXAMPLES OF TRANSFORMATION

IV. PROGRESS AND NEXT STEPS

Introduction

Howard H. Goldman, M.D, Ph.D.
Jeffrey A. Buck, Ph.D.
Kenneth S. Thompson, M.D.

As one of the first acts of his presidency, George W. Bush announced the New Freedom Initiative on February 1, 2001, followed up by a related Executive Order on June 18, 2001. The New Freedom Initiative was a nationwide effort to remove barriers to community living for persons with disabilities. It supported states' efforts to meet the goals of the *Olmstead* Supreme Court decision of 1999 that required states to administer services, programs, and activities "in the most integrated setting appropriate to the needs of qualified individuals with disabilities."

As part of the New Freedom Initiative, the President established the New Freedom Commission on Mental Health. The Commission's mission was to study the nation's mental health system and to offer recommendations to assist adults with serious mental illnesses and children with serious emotional disturbances to participate fully in their communities.

The Commission disappeared as quickly as it appeared, completing its work in a year between 2002 and 2003. Its report, *Achieving the Promise: Transforming Mental Health Care in America,* highlighted the fragmentation of the existing service system. It recommended a series of reforms, including an emphasis on recovery as an achievable goal and the need for a person-centered orientation in service delivery. Further, it recognized that there was a range of other human services that should be provided if mental health care is to be transformed.

Within the federal government, the Substance Abuse and Mental Health Services Administration (SAMHSA) was given lead responsibility for implementing the recommendations of the Commission. SAMHSA has provided national leadership for the transformation process since 2003. Its initiatives have included a grant program to help states transform their mental health systems and the creation of a "federal partners" workgroup to facilitate interagency collaboration at the federal level.

To help further dissemination of information on transformation-related activities, SAMHSA contracted with *Psychiatric Services* to support the publication of papers on the theme of transformation, which are now collected in this compendium. The understanding was that all papers in the series would be peer reviewed in the usual fashion. Some were solicited, but others were developed independently. Papers accepted by the journal were considered by SAMHSA for inclusion in the series. Jeffrey Buck, Ph.D. and Anita Everett, M.D., initially served as SAMHSA's guest editors for the series. Kenneth Thompson, M.D., replaced Dr. Everett as series coeditor when she left SAMHSA. The result is the 17 papers in this compendium, *Transforming Psychiatric Services,* which were published either as regular articles or columns between January 2006 and May 2009.

Organization of the compendium

The papers are organized into four sections.

The first section presents the work of consultants to several of the Commission's subcommittees. Not all of the background papers prepared for the Commission were published by the government, and some of the background papers required updating. This compendium includes review papers from four subcommittees. The work is that of the authors, all of whom interacted with the commissioners who sat on the various subcommittees. The papers focus on the interface between mental health and general health and on employment, housing, and Medicaid financing.

The second section presents six articles on themes directly related to the work of the Commission. Continuing the focus on financing and Medicaid is an article reporting on a survey of state Medicaid directors and their views on mental health services. Other articles address issues related to school mental health, recovery, data systems, and research.

The third section includes reports from four states—California, New Mexico, Texas, and Missouri—about their transformation activities and a paper describing the structure and function of statewide consumer networks that have been created to ensure that consumers have a strong voice in the development of recovery-oriented services. Four of these papers appeared in the State Mental Health Policy column, edited by Fred C. Osher, M.D., of the Council of State Governments Justice Center.

Two papers make up the final section that concludes this compendium. One is an interview with

Dr. Goldman is editor of Psychiatric Services. *Dr. Buck is chief of the Survey, Analysis, and Financing Branch and Dr. Thompson is associate director of medical affairs at the Center for Mental Health Services of the Substance Abuse and Mental Health Services Administration.*

Michael F. Hogan, Ph.D., director of the New York State Office of Mental Health (NYSOMH), who chaired the President's New Freedom Commission. The other is a paper by A. Kathryn Power, M.Ed., currently the director of the Center for Mental Health Services at SAMHSA and the leader of transformation-related activities in SAMHSA.

Conclusions

The report of the New Freedom Commission represents the first time in more than 20 years that a presidential commission has examined issues in mental health services delivery. The recommendations of the previous commission, which was appointed during the Carter Administration, were shortly superseded by the priorities of the new Reagan Administration. However, the conclusions and recommendations of the Carter Commission continued to shape the thinking of policy makers long after its 1978 report was issued. At the time of this writing, when a new administration has succeeded the one that established the New Freedom Commission on Mental Health, it is not unreasonable to think that the Commission's recommendations will have similar outcomes. Although transformation of mental health care may no longer be an organizing principle for federal mental health policy, it is likely that many of the specific recommendations of the Commission will continue to influence policy development at both state and federal levels.

Transforming Mental Health Care at the Interface With General Medicine: Report for the President's Commission

Jürgen Unützer, M.D., M.P.H.
Michael Schoenbaum, Ph.D.
Benjamin G. Druss, M.D., M.P.H.
Wayne J. Katon, M.D.

This paper is based on a report commissioned by the Subcommittee on Mental Health Interface With General Medicine of the President's New Freedom Commission on Mental Health. Although mental and medical conditions are highly interconnected, medical and mental health care systems are separated in many ways that inhibit effective care. Treatable mental or medical illnesses are often not detected or diagnosed properly, and effective services are often not provided. Improved mental health care at the interface of general medicine and mental health requires educated consumers and providers; effective detection, diagnosis, and monitoring of common mental disorders; valid performance criteria for care at the interface of general medicine and mental health; care management protocols that match treatment intensity to clinical outcomes; effective specialty mental health support for general medical providers; and financing mechanisms for evidence-based models of care. Successful models exist for improving the collaboration between medical and mental health providers. Recommendations are presented for achieving high-quality care for common mental disorders at the interface of general medicine and mental health and for overcoming barriers and facilitating use of evidence-based quality improvement models. (Psychiatric Services 57:37–47, 2006)

The President's New Freedom Commission on Mental Health was charged by President George W. Bush on April 29, 2002. Twenty-two commissioners were asked to conduct a comprehensive study of the U.S. mental health service delivery system, advise the President on methods of improving the system, identify model programs that could be disseminated to diverse settings, and develop policy options that promote the integration of effective treatments into clinical practice, improve service coordination, and improve community integration for individuals with mental illness (1–3).

This paper is based on a background report that was prepared to support the deliberations and recommendations of the Subcommittee on Mental Health Interface With General Medicine, which is one of 15 topical subcommittees of the New Freedom Commission.

The preparation of this report was informed by *Mental Health: A Report of the Surgeon General* and its supplement *Mental Health: Culture, Race, and Ethnicity* (4,5), a selective review of published literature on mental health services at the interface between mental health and general medicine (based on a search of MEDLINE and PsycINFO), and consultation with experts in the field. The paper is not a systematic or evidence-based literature review, such as a Cochrane review. Rather, it is a focused summary of the literature by a group of experts that was intended to help the Subcommittee on Mental Health Interface With General Medicine make recommendations in four specific areas: financing of care, performance standards, technical assistance, and provider training. The original literature review was updated in late 2004 to add relevant citations from 2002 to 2004.

Findings and recommendations from the subcommittee were reported to the full Commission in Arlington, Virginia, on January 8, 2003 (6,7).

Mental illness and the medical care system

Several decades of research have documented the high prevalence of common mental disorders in general medical settings. Evidence suggests that community-dwelling people with common mental disorders frequently present in general medical settings, such as primary care clinics, during the course of an illness episode, al-

Dr. Unützer and Dr. Katon are affiliated with the department of psychiatry and behavioral sciences at the University of Washington Medical Center, Box 356560, Seattle, Washington 98195 (e-mail, unutzer@u.washington.edu). Dr. Schoenbaum is with RAND in Arlington, Virginia. Dr. Druss is with the School of Public Health at Emory University in Atlanta. Originally published in the January 2006 issue of Psychiatric Services.

though relatively few receive specialty mental health care (8,9). Unmet needs for mental health care are particularly prevalent among older adults, children and adolescents, individuals from ethnic minority groups, uninsured patients or patients with low incomes who are seen in the public sector, and individuals with mental health problems who present with primarily physical symptoms (9–18).

Overall, about half of the care for common mental disorders is delivered in general medical settings, leading Regier and colleagues (8) to describe general medical settings as the "de facto mental health care system" in the United States. Thus general medical settings represent an important— perhaps the single most important— point of contact between patients with mental disorders and the health care system. The role of primary care providers is even more important for older adults (19) and patients from racial and ethnic minority groups. For example, among Mexican Americans, almost two-thirds of consultations for treatment of a mood or anxiety disorder are with primary care providers (20). Similarly, African Americans with mental health concerns are more likely to see a primary care physician than a psychiatrist (21).

Efficacious treatments exist for most common mental disorders (4), as do treatment guidelines for primary care providers and mental health specialty care providers for prevalent conditions, such as depression. Nevertheless, a majority of patients with mental illness are not treated effectively in primary care settings or elsewhere (4,8,9)

Co-occurring mental and medical illness

In addition to increasing the personal and societal burdens of mental illness, low rates of effective mental health treatment are also likely to increase the burdens associated with physical illness. Mental disorders frequently co-occur with other medical disorders. For instance, adults with common medical disorders have high rates of depression and anxiety (22). Major depression among patients with chronic medical illnesses in-

creases the burden of somatic symptoms (23), causes additional functional impairment (24,25), and increases medical costs (26,27). Depression also impairs self-care and adherence to treatments for chronic medical illnesses (22) and causes increased mortality, which is perhaps best documented among patients after they experience a heart attack (28). Some of this excess mortality may be explained by direct biological effects of mental disorders on the cardiovascular system (for example, neurohumoral dysregulation and platelet changes) or behavioral factors (for example, poor diet, smoking, alcohol abuse, and obesity). However, poor quality of preventive, acute, and chronic medical care may also contribute to premature cardiovascular deaths (29).

Barriers to effective care

Patient, provider, and system factors all contribute to poor quality of care at the interface of mental health with general medicine. For instance, patients may not recognize or correctly identify their symptoms; be reluctant to seek care, particularly because of stigma; or be reluctant to adhere to treatment recommendations. Primary care providers may lack the necessary training and confidence to provide appropriate treatment for mental health problems, and even well-trained and motivated primary care providers are limited in what they can accomplish in a 12- to 15-minute office visit during which they may also be addressing multiple medical and social problems. Finally, mental health benefits are typically more restricted and heavily managed than other medical benefits, and few insurance plans cover providers' costs for implementing screening, care management, and other proactive services that studies have shown to be effective in increasing the rate of evidence-based treatment, as we discuss below.

Similar factors underlie the poor quality of care for mental disorders other than depression, for the mental health problems of patients with co-occurring medical conditions, and for the medical conditions of people with mental illness. The personal and societal consequences of these quality

gaps at the interface between mental health and general medicine can be substantial—unnecessary suffering, functional impairment, mortality, economic losses, and health care costs.

Quality improvement strategies

Numerous studies have assessed strategies to improve care at the interface of general medicine and mental health. Much of this work has been done in the area of depression, because it is one of the most common disorders seen in general medical settings, and because efficacious treatments have existed for several decades. More recently, parallel research has examined strategies to improve care for anxiety and somatoform disorders and for severe and persistent mental illness among patients with comorbid medical disorders. In this section, we summarize evidence on such strategies.

Case finding and diagnosis

Much of the early research on improving care for mental disorders in general medical settings has focused on case finding and diagnosis. Numerous studies since the 1970s have focused on developing screening instruments for common mental disorders in primary care (4,30), such as the PHQ primary care study (31).

Several studies have coupled screening with systematic feedback of depression diagnoses to primary care providers Although some of these screening studies showed an increase in the rate of diagnosis of mental disorders in primary care, no screening studies have demonstrated a significant effect on clinical outcomes of mental disorders, such as depression (32,33). This evidence suggests that screening and provider feedback are necessary but not sufficient to improve outcomes of adults with common mental disorders.

Correspondingly, the U.S. Preventive Services Task Force recently recommended that primary care providers screen adult patients for depression, as long as they have systems in place to ensure accurate diagnosis, effective treatment, and follow-up (34).

Referral to specialty mental health care

One option for addressing mental health problems in general medical settings is to increase rates of referral to mental health specialty providers, but relatively little research has addressed how to improve these referral processes. Research has shown that primary care providers perceive themselves as having much worse access to suitable mental health providers than to other medical specialists (35,36). Studies have also shown that one-third to one-half of primary care patients who receive a referral to mental health specialty care do not follow through with such a referral (37,38). Finally, successful entry into the specialty mental health care system does not guarantee effective care; many patients treated in specialty mental health clinics do not receive care consistent with existing treatment guidelines (39,40). These findings suggest that although the referral process between general medical settings and mental health specialty care should be improved, reliance on specialty referral alone will fall short of addressing currently unmet needs for mental health care at the interface between mental health and general medicine.

Treatment guidelines and provider education

In the 1990s, several organizations developed and published consensus guidelines for the treatment of common mental disorders, such as depression in primary care (41,42). These guidelines recognized that efficacious treatments, such as antidepressant medications and certain types of psychotherapy, which were originally developed and tested in specialty mental health settings, could also be delivered effectively in primary care settings. Clinical practice guidelines can be an important component of strategies to improve quality of care. However, the consensus in the field is that distributing practice guidelines to primary care providers does not by itself improve quality of care or patient outcomes. It can be difficult for providers to use such guidelines without additional help and changes in the service delivery system. Diagnosing and treating depres-

sion can also be complicated by the fact that as many as 75 percent of depressed primary care patients present predominantly with somatic symptoms. Despite the wide availability of practice guidelines, only about one-third of internal medicine residents in a recent survey of primary care training programs reported that they felt "very prepared" to diagnose and treat depression in the outpatient setting, and residents' level of comfort regarding the management of depression was far lower than for eight other common conditions of outpatients (43).

In this context, researchers have tested strategies that combine practice guidelines with comprehensive training of providers, with mixed results. For instance, one study showed that a comprehensive 20-hour training program improved physicians' knowledge and depression outcomes at three months but not at one year (44). Another study found that intensive guideline-based training of providers on diagnosis and treatment of depression increased the rate of appropriate diagnosis only slightly (from 36 percent to 39 percent) and had no effect on patients' depression status relative to usual care (45).

Overall, these findings suggest that provider education programs, including continuing medical education, academic detailing, and continuous quality improvement, may be an important component of comprehensive quality improvement strategies and that they are likely necessary but not sufficient by themselves to improve care for common mental disorders (46,47)

Collaborative care

Motivated by evidence that strategies such as screening, dissemination of practice guidelines, provider training, and referral to mental health specialists do not appear to be effective on their own, researchers have developed programs that aim to improve care at the interface of mental health and general medicine by training psychiatrists, psychologists, and other mental health specialists to provide depression care in collaboration with patients' primary care providers or by training members of the primary care team, such as nurses, in additional

skills to care for patients with mental health needs. Such professionals are often supported by consultation from a designated mental health professional. We broadly refer to such interdisciplinary care management programs as "collaborative care" (48,49).

Although the programs vary, most effective treatment programs have two key elements. The first is systematic care management by a nurse, social worker, psychologist, or other trained clinical staff to facilitate case identification, coordinate an initial treatment plan and patient education, provide close follow-up, monitor progress, and modify treatment if necessary. Care management can be provided in a primary care clinic or by telephone. The second key element is consultation between a care manager, a primary care provider, and a consulting psychiatrist or other appropriate mental health specialist.

Several recent trials of collaborative care models have attempted to maximize the cost-effectiveness of collaborative care by using a process described as "stepped care" (49,50,51–53). Stepped care usually begins with relatively low-intensity interventions, such as antidepressant medications prescribed by a primary care provider and care management provided by telephone or in the primary care clinic. Under the supervision of a consulting psychiatrist or other appropriate mental health specialist, patients who are not helped by such initial treatments are shifted to progressively more intensive treatment approaches, including referral to specialty mental health care as needed.

Effective treatment programs recognize that usual primary care is better suited to address acute, time-limited medical problems rather than chronic illnesses that require ongoing monitoring and management (54,55). With respect to depression, for instance, half of patients do not improve adequately with the first course of an antidepressant medication, yet the time and resource constraints of usual general medical practice provide little opportunity to monitor patients' progress and adjust treatment.

More than ten studies of collaborative care models for depression in a wide range of health care systems

Suggestions for high-quality mental health care at the interface of general medicine and mental health

1. Educated and prepared consumers, primary care providers, and mental health providers
2. Efficient and effective methods to identify, diagnose, and monitor common mental disorders in general medical settings
3. Information systems that can support proactive tracking of mental health care at the interface between general medicine and mental health
4. Performance criteria for quality of mental health care at the interface between general medicine and mental health
5. Evidence-based treatment protocols that match treatment intensity to clinical outcomes
6. Trained mental health providers who can support primary care providers with education, proactive follow-up, care management, psychotherapy, and consultation for patients who do not respond to first-line treatments in primary care
7. Effective mechanisms to refer patients who do not improve with treatment in primary care to specialty mental health care and to coordinate care between primary care and specialty mental health care
8. Financing mechanisms for evidence-based models of care for common mental disorders in primary care, including payment for care management, consultation, and supervision of mental health care managers by qualified mental health specialists; psychotherapy at copayment rates equal to those for the treatment of physical disorders; and prescription medications for mental disorders

have demonstrated that they are more effective than usual care (56–60). Such models have been shown to improve clinical outcomes, employment rates (61,62), functioning, and quality of life, and they are cost-effective compared with other commonly used medical interventions (61–65).

Collaborative care appears to be particularly beneficial for individuals from ethnic minority groups, who traditionally have low rates of appropriate care, and this approach may reduce ethnic disparities in quality of care (63,66,67). These models have also been successfully extended to adolescents (68) and to older adults, who often have comorbid medical disorders (52,69–71). Analyses from the two largest collaborative care trials for depression suggest that these programs are equally effective for patients with and without comorbid medical disorders (72,73). Similar collaborative care models have been developed for anxiety disorders in primary care (74,75).

Suggestions for high-quality care for common mental disorders at the interface of general medicine and mental health are summarized in the box on this page (17,48,49,54,76–82).

Improving medical care for patients with severe mental illness
Several studies have involved population-based screening for medical problems of patients with mental disorders (83,84). These screening programs did not involve specific efforts to address identified health problems, nor did the researchers assess the impact of the screening per se on clinical outcomes. Nevertheless, there is little reason to expect that screening and case identification alone will be effective in improving treatment of medical conditions among people with severe and persistent mental illness.

To improve medical care for patients with severe mental disorders, some academic leaders have called for systematic efforts to train psychiatrists to recognize and treat their patients' basic medical problems (85,86). As with programs focusing on mental health training for primary care providers, this approach emphasizes knowledge deficits among providers but may not adequately address time and financial constraints, as well as patient factors.

Others have advocated and developed dual training programs in which physicians train and become board eligible in psychiatry and a primary care specialty (87). Currently, about 40 such training programs exist (88). Evidence about the effects of these programs is limited, but the results of one study suggest that only a minority of dually trained physicians actually practice both specialties (87). It is also unlikely that such programs could ever train sufficient numbers of physicians to meet the needs of all in-dividuals with comorbid medical and mental disorders.

A collaborative care framework similar to the models developed in primary care in which mental health providers and primary care practitioners collaborate in the care of patients, may hold promise for improving medical care for patients treated in specialty mental health settings. Although substantially less research has been done in this area than in the treatment of depression in primary care, the results of one randomized trial suggest that on-site, integrated delivery of primary medical care can improve quality and outcomes of medical care for patients with serious mental disorders (89).

Barriers to disseminating quality improvement
With the availability of effective quality improvement models, particularly for depression, efforts are being made to develop strategies to disseminate such models (90–92). Results from this research suggest that successful programs are multifaceted and include various combinations of physician and patient education, "tools" to diagnose and monitor common mental disorders in general medical settings, patient registries or tracking systems, care management, and more effective collaboration between primary care and mental health providers (49,76–79,93–95). More generally, however, a range

of organizational and financial systems affect the scope and quality of health care at the interface of mental health and general medicine.

One major barrier is access to the mental health system. Insurance benefits for mental health care are generally more limited than for general medical care, and some patients, particularly those with severe mental illness, quickly exhaust their benefits. In concept, mental health parity laws are intended to eliminate such differences, and full parity is required in some states and for federal employees. However, although parity laws are an important step, these laws are unlikely in and of themselves to be sufficient to ensure equal access to care (96).

A second barrier is that health insurance reimbursement mechanisms often do not provide incentives for use of evidence-based models of care for mental disorders or for many other chronic conditions (79,97). For instance, neither public nor private health insurance plans provide adequate reimbursement for care management or specialty consultation services, which are key components of collaborative care models for depression and other chronic conditions.

The lack of reimbursement inhibits dissemination, because providers will implement collaborative care interventions only if the benefits of doing so exceed the costs. Although collaborative care and other evidence-based interventions are highly cost-effective from a societal perspective, many of these benefits are experienced as "externalities"—that is, outside the mental health system (for example, via improved medical care) or outside the health system (for example, via improved employment outcomes, reduced need for social services, or reduced suffering of patients' families, friends, and coworkers). Overcoming these potential means of market failure will require purchasers, such as employers and governments, to use targeted financial incentives to promote the use of evidence-based services by providers (97,98).

Other barriers may arise from the separation of mental health care from the mainstream of medicine by managed mental health care (4). Managed behavioral health care organizations and pharmacy benefit managers have become the prevailing form of providing insurance coverage for mental health treatment and prescription drugs, respectively. The separation or carving out of these benefits from the general medical plan can create important organizational barriers to primary care patients who need mental health specialty services or to the effective collaboration of primary care providers and mental health specialists. Several managed behavioral health care organizations have recently made efforts to address this barrier by providing better integrated disease management in collaboration with primary care, and the National Committee for Quality Assurance has released a set of performance indicators for managed behavioral health care organizations that provide incentives for effective collaboration with primary care.

Finally, uninsured patients and individuals covered under Medicaid and other public-sector programs for low-income populations have particularly high rates of common mental disorders, such as depression and anxiety. Although individuals with low incomes who have severe and persistent mental illnesses and who are covered under Medicaid often receive services in specialty mental health care settings, such as community mental health centers, those with common mental disorders, such as depression or anxiety, have limited access to specialty mental health care but substantial unmet medical, emotional, and social needs. For these reasons, it is particularly important to support models of care in which primary care providers caring for patients with low incomes can be supported by specialty mental health professionals. One example of such an effort is an initiative to improve care for depression sponsored by the Bureau of Primary Health Care. More research is needed on the effectiveness of this and similar efforts.

Opportunities to improve quality of care and policy
Recommendations

We have described considerable deficits in the quality of care for people with mental disorders, quality improvement models that have been shown to be effective in addressing some of these deficits, and current barriers to the widespread adoption of such models. We recognize that many of the issues described in this report could benefit from additional research, but we conclude with recommendations that could mitigate some of the existing barriers and facilitate the use of evidence-based quality improvement models. The recommendations are listed in the box on the next page.

Financing for collaborative care services. Our first recommendation is that public and private insurance programs explicitly cover evidence-based collaborative care for common mental disorders. Many of the services in evidence-based collaborative care models, such as in-person consultations and psychotherapy, are reimbursable for providers under current financing mechanisms. Similarly, psychotropic medications are generally covered by health insurance programs, now including Medicare. However, as we have described, key components of the collaborative care model are not currently reimbursable, particularly care management services that provide proactive follow-up and coordination of care for chronic mental disorders and mental health consultations to primary care–based practitioners or care managers that do not have to involve face-to-face contact with patients. Coverage for these services should be coupled with appropriate oversight to ensure that they are provided appropriately, using evidence-based treatment protocols.

One major target for reform must be care management activities, particularly those falling outside the scope of traditional outpatient office visits. Care managers should be reimbursed for time spent consulting with primary care and specialty mental health providers and for coordinating care by these providers, for patient education activities, and for providing proactive monitoring and follow-up (including via telephone). We note that research suggests that people with various types of training, including nurses, clinical social workers, psychologists,

Policy recommendations for overcoming barriers and facilitating use of evidence-based quality improvement models

1. Financing of collaborative care services

♦ Medicare, Medicaid, the Department of Veterans Affairs, other federal- and state-sponsored health insurance programs as well as private insurers should pay for evidence-based collaborative care at the interface of general medicine and mental health, including funding of case management for common mental disorders, supervision of case managers, and consultations to primary care providers by qualified mental health specialists that do not have to involve face-to-face contact with patients.

♦ The government should achieve better coordination of the funding and the clinical care provided to clients of publicly funded community clinics for medical, mental, and substance use disorders.

♦ The federal government should study financial incentives to improve quality of care, particularly in the area of mental health care at the interface of mental health and general medicine.

2. Performance standards

♦ Federal and state government agencies, private insurers, and accrediting organizations, such as the National Committee for Quality Assurance and the Joint Commission on Accreditation of Healthcare Organizations, should develop clear performance standards for the care of individuals with mental disorders at the interface of general medicine and mental health. These standards should include appropriate process and outcome indicators.

♦ Performance standards should also be developed for the recognition and care of common medical disorders among individuals with severe mental illnesses, who are often treated primarily in the specialty mental health care sector.

3. Technical assistance

♦ Government agencies, such as the Agency for Healthcare Research and Quality, the National Institute of Mental Health, the Substance Abuse and Mental Health Services Administration, the Health Resources and Services Administration, the Department of Veterans Affairs, large insurers, and provider organizations, should develop technical assistance programs to help health care providers implement and disseminate evidence-based models to improve care at the interface of general medicine and mental health.

♦ A national technical assistance center should be created to support quality improvement activities at the interface between general medicine and mental health.

4. Provider training

♦ National leadership is needed to help improve the training of medical and mental health practitioners in the care of patients at the interface of general medicine and mental health.

and others, can provide these services effectively if they have adequate training and supervision (49–51,92,99). Some of these providers are not currently reimbursed to provide such care management in some health plans, particularly Medicare. Mental health consultation may involve in-person consultations in which a mental health specialist, such as a psychiatrist or psychologist, evaluates the patient in a medical or mental health setting. Mental health consultation may also involve consultations with a treating primary care provider or a primary care–based care manager that do not involve direct patient contact. Such consultations can occur in person or by telephone and should be documented by the consultant, the care manager (if applicable), and the primary care provider to facilitate coordination of care.

In insurance programs that reimburse providers under a fee-for-service arrangement, such as traditional Medicare, the most direct way to cover these care management and consultation services would be to make them billable in their own right. Mechanically, such an approach may require the creation of new procedure codes, or the adoption of existing codes. It may be as simple as removing existing regulatory barriers to collaborative care, such as current Federally Qualified Health Centers restrictions by Medicare and Medicaid on reimbursing primary care and mental health visits at a single clinic on the same day. In plans with capitation-based or other types of contracts with providers, collaborative care services would become part of the benefit to which patients are entitled, and plans and providers would incorporate these new benefits into rate negotiations.

A second policy recommendation related to the financing of care includes a recommendation that the government achieve better coordination of the funding and the clinical care provided to clients of publicly funded community clinics for medical, mental, and substance use disorders, such as community health centers funded by the Health Resources and Services Administration (HRSA) and community mental health centers supported by the Substance Abuse and Mental Health Services Administration (SAMHSA). Improved coordination of funding streams and clinical care by federal, state, and local government agencies and providers could improve the effectiveness of care at the interface of mental health and general medicine, reduce duplication of services, and prevent clients with mental disorders from "falling through the cracks."

Finally, we endorse a recent recommendation by the Institute of Medicine (100) that the federal government develop research and demonstration programs that study financial incentives to improve the quality of care. These should include incentives for health plans to coordinate medical and mental health services or to meet target outcome criteria for common mental disorders, such as depression. In cases in which behavioral health care is carved out, financial incentives should be shared between managed care organizations, managed behavioral health care organizations, and, when applicable, pharmacy benefit managers. For such financial incentives to be effective, clear performance standards for care at the interface of medicine and mental health need to be developed and applied by federal, state, and private payers.

Performance standards. Our second recommendation concerns performance standards. Successful implementation of evidence-based quality improvement can be strengthened by increasing the accountability of health care providers through performance measurement. Although practice guidelines and performance standards have been developed for a number of common mental disorders by various government agencies and professional organizations, these standards are usually developed for application in either primary care or specialty mental health care settings, and they generally do not address care at the interface of general medicine and mental health and the collaboration of general medical and mental health practitioners.

We recommend that federal and state agencies, private insurers, and accrediting organizations, such as the National Committee for Quality Assurance and the Joint Commission on Accreditation of Healthcare Organizations, develop clear performance standards for the care of individuals with mental disorders. Such standards should extend existing guidelines to include performance standards for care at the interface between mental health and general medicine and mechanisms to audit and track adherence to performance standards. The new standards should

not only include measures of the process of care but also focus on achieving desired health outcomes. Examples of such outcome-oriented criteria include the percentage of depressed patients in a health plan who are documented to experience at least a 50 percent reduction in depression symptoms as measured by a standard instrument, such as the Patient Health Questionnaire (PHQ-9) (101) over a six-month period and the proportion of patients who do not reach 50 percent improvement who receive a change in treatment, such as augmentation of medications, addition of psychotherapy to medications, or referral to specialty mental health care.

We recommend that similar performance standards be developed for the recognition and care of common medical disorders among individuals with severe mental illnesses who are treated in specialty mental health care settings. Medical conditions and treatments should be included along with psychiatric and psychosocial issues in patients' problem lists and treatment plans. If mental health care settings cannot provide basic medical evaluation and treatment on site, they should arrange for appropriate medical care and coordination of care with qualified primary care providers.

Technical assistance. Third, we recommend that public and private stakeholders develop technical assistance programs to help health care providers implement evidence-based models of care at the interface of general medicine and mental health. Relevant organizations include government agencies such as the Agency for Healthcare Quality, the National Institute of Mental Health, SAMHSA, HRSA, the Department of Veterans Affairs (VA), the Centers for Medicare and Medicaid Services (CMS), large insurers, and provider organizations

Successful implementation and dissemination of evidence-based quality improvement programs at the interface of mental health and general medicine will require more than well-educated providers. Organizations that wish to implement and sustain evidence-based models of care at the interface of mental health and gener-

al medicine could greatly benefit from technical assistance programs that could provide the necessary materials and "tools," technical expertise, and consultation to help them implement, disseminate, evaluate, and bill for such programs. Effective technical assistance programs could support provider training, sponsor local and national quality improvement processes, support the development and standardization of necessary information technology, develop business models for sustainability, and develop and disseminate performance standards to monitor care at the interface of mental health and general medicine. Several private and public organizations have developed toolkits to help improve treatment of mental disorders in general medical settings; such efforts, although intended for somewhat different target audiences, can be highly complementary and should be supported to ensure widespread dissemination of evidence-based care models (102–104).

Provider training. Finally, we recommend that public and private stakeholders develop strategies to improve the training of medical and mental health practitioners in the care of patients at the interface of mental health and general medicine and that further research be conducted to evaluate the effectiveness of such programs.

Relevant stakeholders include government agencies that fund or support medical education, such as CMS through Medicare and Medicaid, the VA, and HRSA; professional schools and graduate training programs in medicine, nursing, social work, and clinical psychology; professional organizations, such as the American Medical Association, the American Psychiatric Association, and the American Psychological Association; and licensing, credentialing, and accrediting bodies, such as the American Association of Medical Colleges, the Liaison Committee on Medical Education, and the Accreditation Council for Graduate Medical Education (ACGME). These organizations all have important opportunities to affect the training and certification of primary care and mental health care practitioners in ways that can improve collaboration.

Training programs for medical students and primary care providers should cover the fundamental knowledge and skills required to diagnose and treat common mental disorders, such as depression and anxiety disorders, and to make effective referrals to mental health providers for patients who do not respond to first-line treatments in general medical settings or who prefer treatment from a mental health specialist. Treatment of patients with mental disorders and serious medical disorders often requires a process of interpersonal and emotional growth; several approaches have been developed to teach psychosocial aspects of care to primary care providers (105), and some primary care programs have integrated support groups, such as Balint groups, although there is limited evidence about the effectiveness of such groups.

Training programs for mental health providers should include training in brief, structured psychotherapies that can be delivered in medical settings; effective consultation to and collaboration with primary care providers; recognition of common medical disorders; and effective coordination of the medical care for these disorders with primary care practitioners. Mental health and primary care providers should also receive training in evidence-based behavioral techniques to support effective self-management of chronic medical disorders. A number of reimbursable procedure codes already exist that can be used by psychologists and other qualified mental health providers to bill for counseling individuals with chronic medical disorders. To improve providers' knowledge and skills in these areas, curricula in training programs for nurses, physicians, social workers, and psychologists should be revised.

Such curricular policies have been variably implemented in training requirements for primary care physicians and mental health specialists by the appropriate specialty boards, but additional research is needed to examine their effectiveness. It is also important to point out that although provider knowledge and training may

be necessary to improve mental health care, they may be only a small part of the solution. It is likely that system changes in the way care is delivered will also be needed.

Besides making curricular improvements, it is important to change the location of training in mental health. Too often, mental health providers are still trained in "professional silos," such as psychiatric hospitals or clinics, with little exposure to patients with common mental disorders in general medical settings and with little opportunity to learn effective consultation to and collaboration with primary care practitioners. Coyne and associates (106), among others, have pointed out that psychologists working in primary care can make a number of important contributions to the care of patients with common mental disorders, including diagnosis and treatment of emotional disorders as well as related activities in the areas of health promotion and pain management.

Sample training programs at the interface of mental health and general medicine include the VA program that trains psychiatrists or psychologists to work as part of a multidisciplinary team in primary care (107), a program that trains medical students and psychiatric residents in primary care settings (85), and training programs in "psychosomatic medicine" or "primary care psychiatry" for primary care physicians, psychiatrists, and psychologists. The recent formalization of psychosomatic medicine as an accredited subspecialty of psychiatry with ACGME-accredited fellowship training programs may support the development of mental health practitioners with greater skills in interfacing with medicine. Training programs that emphasize training at the interface between mental health and general medicine should be expanded with support from the federal government, and more research is needed to evaluate their effectiveness.

The role of government
Much of the challenge in improving mental health care is the fact that both the locus of and the responsibility for that care is so diffuse. Persons

with mental disorders may be treated in specialty mental health settings or general medical settings, and care may be financed by the federal government, state government, or private payers. The fragmentation that creates barriers to high-quality care may itself raise challenges to implementing the funding changes, performance standards, technical assistance, and provider training that are needed to overcome those barriers. What, then, is the most appropriate site at which to begin targeting efforts at quality improvement?

As previously discussed, a major barrier to implementation of evidence-based care is the fact that health plans and private payers typically reap only a portion of the benefits that derive from improving quality. Because government represents a broader range of interests, it can play a critical role in spearheading these efforts. A recent report by the Institute of Medicine (100) points out that the federal government is in a unique position to assume a strong leadership role in driving the health care sector to improve the safety and quality of health care services that are provided to the approximately 100 million beneficiaries of the six major government health care programs—Medicare, Medicaid, the State Children's Health Insurance Program, TRICARE, the VA health system, and the Indian Health System—and that the federal government should "vigorously pursue purchasing strategies that encourage the adoption of best practices through the release of public-domain comparative quality data and the provision of financial and other rewards to providers to achieve high levels of quality."

Medicare is currently sponsoring several large-scale demonstration projects that seek to improve care for common chronic conditions. It will be important for these efforts to include mental disorders, both as primary conditions and as comorbid disorders affecting care for other chronic diseases. More broadly, we recommend that the federal government develop a set of sample purchasing specifications for contracts that are based on current best practices at the interface of medicine and mental health services as well as effective methods to measure performance at this interface.

Conclusions

The Subcommittee on Mental Health Interface With General Medicine (6) outlined several policy options in the areas of financing of services, performance standards, technical assistance, and provider training (see box on page 42). In its final report the President's New Freedom Commission on Mental Health (108) prioritized the following recommendations with regard to improving mental health care at the interface with general medicine:

♦ Recommendation 4.4: Screen for mental disorders in primary health care, across the life span, and connect to treatment and supports.

♦ The Commission suggests that collaborative care models should be widely implemented in primary health care settings and reimbursed by public and private insurers.

♦ Medicare, Medicaid, the Department of Veterans Affairs, and other federal- and state-sponsored health insurance programs and private insurers should identify and consider payment for core components of evidence-based collaborative care, including case management, disease management, supervision of case managers, and consultations to primary care providers by qualified mental health specialists that do not involve face-to-face contact with clients. The Commission also recommended that the federal government "could better coordinate the funding and the clinical care provided by publicly funded community health clinics to consumers with multiple conditions, including physical, mental, and co-occurring substance use disorders. This effort would include improved coordination of care between HRSA-funded community health clinics and SAMHSA- or state-supported community mental health centers."

We agree with the emphasis on financing evidence-based treatment programs at the interface of mental health and general medicine, and we believe that financing of such services should be closely tied to outcome-based performance standards for care of common mental disorders at this interface.

Acknowledgments

This article is based on a report prepared for the Subcommittee on Mental Health Interface With General Medicine of the President's New Freedom Commission on Mental Health. The content of this article does not imply endorsement by the U.S. Government or by the Commission. The authors assume full responsibility for the accuracy of the content. This work was funded under task order 280-99-1003 of contract 280-99-1000 with the Substance Abuse and Mental Health Services Administration. The authors acknowledge input from Henry T. Harbin, M.D., the chair of the Subcommittee on Mental Health Interface With General Medicine and other subcommittee members, including Anil G. Godbole, M.D.; Norwood W. Knight-Richardson, M.D., M.B.A.; Nancy C. Speck, Ph.D.; and Deanna F. Yates, Ph.D. The authors are also grateful for comments by Kenneth B. Wells, M.D., M.P.H.; Jeanne Miranda, Ph.D.; Gregory Simon, M.D., M.P.H.; Elizabeth Lin, M.D., M.P.H.; Michael Von Korff, Sc.D.; Christopher Callahan, M.D.; Herbert C. Schulberg, Ph.D.; John Williams, M.D., M.H.S.; and David A. Pollack, M.D.

References

1. Druss BG, Goldman HH: Introduction to the special section on the President's New Freedom Commission report. Psychiatric Services 54:1465–1466, 2003

2. Hogan MF: The President's New Freedom Commission: recommendations to transform mental health care in America. Psychiatric Services 54:1467–1474, 2003

3. New Freedom Commission on Mental Health: Achieving the Promise: Transforming Mental Health Care in America. Rockville, Md, Department of Health and Human Services, 2003

4. Mental Health: A Report of the Surgeon General. Rockville, Md, US Department of Health and Human Services, Substance Abuse and Mental Health Services Administration, Center for Mental Health Services, National Institute of Mental Health, 1999

5. Mental Health: Culture, Race, and Ethnicity: A Supplement to Mental Health: A Report of the Surgeon General. Rockville, Md, US Department of Health and Human Services, Substance Abuse and Mental Health Services Administration, Center for Mental Health Services, National Institute of Mental Health, 2001

6. An Outline for the Draft Report of the Subcommittee on Mental Health Interface With General Medicine. Rockville, Md, Substance Abuse and Mental Health Services Administration, Jan 8, 2003. Available at www.mentalhealthcommission.gov/subcommittee/mhinterface_010803.doc

7. President's New Freedom Commission on Mental Health: Meeting minutes, Arlington, Va, Jan 7–9, 2003. Available at www.mentalhealthcommission.gov/minutes/jan03.htm

8. Regier DA, Narrow WE, Rae DS, et al: The de facto US mental and addictive disorders service system: Epidemiologic Catchment Area prospective 1-year prevalence rates of disorders and services. Archives of General Psychiatry 50:85–94, 1993

9. Young AS, Klap R, Sherbourne CD, et al: The quality of care for depressive and anxiety disorders in the United States. Archives of General Psychiatry 58:55–61, 2001

10. Blazer DG, Hybels CF, Simonsick EM, et al: Marked differences in antidepressant use by race in an elderly community sample: 1986-1996. American Journal of Psychiatry 157:1089–1094, 2000

11. Borowsky SJ, Rubenstein LV, Meredith LS, et al: Who is at risk of nondetection of mental health problems in primary care? Journal of General Internal Medicine 15:381–388, 2000

12. Jackson-Triche ME, Sullivan GJ, Wells KB, et al: Depression and health-related quality of life in ethnic minorities seeking care in general medical settings. Journal of Affective Disorders 58:89–97, 2000

13. Melfi CA, Croghan TW, Hanna MP, et al: Racial variation in antidepressant treatment in a Medicaid population. Journal of Clinical Psychiatry 61:16–21, 2000

14. Mauksch LB, Tucker SM, Katon WJ, et al: Mental illness, functional impairment, and patient preferences for collaborative care in an uninsured, primary care population. Journal of Family Practice 50:41–47, 2001

15. Miranda J, Azocar F, Komaromy M, et al: Unmet mental health needs of women in public-sector gynecologic clinics. American Journal of Obstetrics and Gynecology 178:212–217, 1998

16. Wang PS, Berglund P, Kessler RC: Recent care of common mental disorders in the United States: prevalence and conformance with evidence-based recommendations. Journal of General Internal Medicine 15:284–292, 2000

17. Wells K, Klap R, Koike A, et al: Ethnic disparities in unmet need for alcoholism, drug abuse, and mental health care. American Journal of Psychiatry 158:2027–2032, 2001

18. Unützer J, Katon W, Callahan CM, et al: Depression treatment in a sample of 1,801 depressed older adults in primary care. Journal of the American Geriatrics Society 51:505–514, 2003

19. Klap R, Unroe KT, Unützer J: Caring for mental illness in the United States: a focus on older adults. American Journal of Geriatric Psychiatry 11:517–524, 2003

20. Vega WA, Kolody B, Aguilar-Gaxiola S, et al: Gaps in service utilization by Mexican Americans with mental health problems. American Journal of Psychiatry 156:928–934, 1999

21. Snowden LR, Pingitore D: Frequency and scope of mental health service delivery to African Americans in primary care. Mental Health Services Research 4:123–130, 2002

22. Katon W, Ciechanowski P: Impact of major depression on chronic medical illness. Journal of Psychosomatic Research 53:859–863, 2002

23. Katon W, Sullivan M, Walker E: Medical symptoms without identified pathology: relationship to psychiatric disorders, childhood and adult trauma, and personality traits. Annals of Internal Medicine 134:917–925, 2001

24. Unützer J, Patrick DL, Diehr P, et al: Quality adjusted life years in older adults with depressive symptoms and chronic medical disorders. International Psychogeriatrics 12:15–33, 2000

25. Wells KB, Stewart A, Hays RD, et al: The functioning and well-being of depressed patients: results from the Medical Outcomes Study. JAMA 262:914–919, 1989

26. Simon GE, VonKorff M, Barlow W: Health care costs of primary care patients with recognized depression. Archives of General Psychiatry 52:850–856, 1995

27. Unützer J, Patrick DL, Simon G, et al: Depressive symptoms and the cost of health services in HMO patients aged 65 years and older: a 4-year prospective study. JAMA 277:1618–1623, 1997

28. Frasure-Smith N, Lesperance F, Talajic M: Depression following myocardial infarction: impact on 6-month survival. JAMA 270:1819–1825, 1993

29. Druss BG, Bradford WD, Rosenheck RA, et al: Quality of medical care and excess mortality in older patients with mental disorders. Archives of General Psychiatry 58:565–572, 2001

30. Gilbody SM, House AO, Sheldon TA: Routinely administered questionnaires for depression and anxiety: systematic review. British Medical Journal 322:406–409, 2001

31. Spitzer RL, Kroenke K, Williams JB: Validation and utility of a self-report version of PRIME-MD: the PHQ primary care study. Primary care evaluation of mental disorders: Patient Health Questionnaire. JAMA 282:1737–1744, 1999

32. Katon W, Gonzales J: A review of randomized trials of psychiatric consultation-liaison studies in primary care. Psychosomatics 35:268–278, 1994

33. Klinkman MS, Okkes I: Mental health problems in primary care: a research agenda. Journal of Family Practice 47:379–384, 1998

34. Pignone MP, Gaynes BN, Rushton JL, et al: Screening for depression in adults: a summary of the evidence for the US Preventive Services Task Force. Annals of Internal Medicine 136:765–776, 2002

35. Van Voorhees BW, Wang N-Y, Ford DE: Managed care and primary care physicians' perception of patient access to high quality mental health services. Journal of General Internal Medicine 16(suppl 1):220, 2001

36. Van Voorhees BW, Wang NY, Ford DE: Managed care organizational complexity and access to high-quality mental health services: perspective of US primary care physicians. General Hospital Psychiatry 25:149–157, 2003

37. Callahan CM, Hendrie HC, Dittus RS, et al: Improving treatment of late life depression in primary care: a randomized clinical trial. Journal of the American Geriatrics Society 42:839–846, 1994

38. Grembowski DE, Martin D, Patrick DL, et al: Managed care, access to mental health specialists, and outcomes among primary care patients with depressive symptoms. Journal of General Internal Medicine 17:258–269, 2002

39. Meyers BS, Sirey JA, Bruce M, et al: Predictors of early recovery from major depression among persons admitted to community-based clinics: an observational study. Archives of General Psychiatry 59:729–735, 2002

40. Simon GE, Von Korff M, Rutter CM, et al: Treatment process and outcomes for managed care patients receiving new antidepressant prescriptions from psychiatrists and primary care physicians. Archives of General Psychiatry 58:395–401, 2001

41. Depression in Primary Care: Clinical Practice Guideline 5. Rockville, Md, Agency for Healthcare Policy and Research, 1993

42. Schulberg HC, Katon W, Simon GE, et al: Treating major depression in primary care practice: an update of the Agency for Health Care Policy and Research practice guidelines. Archives of General Psychiatry 55:1121–1127, 1998

43. Wiest FC, Ferris TG, Gokhale M, et al: Preparedness of internal medicine and family practice residents for treating common conditions. JAMA 288:2609–2614, 2002

44. Tiemens BG, Ormel J, Jenner JA, et al: Training primary-care physicians to recognize, diagnose, and manage depression: does it improve patient outcomes? Psychological Medicine 29:833–845, 1999

45. Thompson C, Kinmonth AL, Stevens L, et al: Effects of a clinical-practice guideline and practice-based education on detection and outcome of depression in primary care: Hampshire Depression Project randomised controlled trial. Lancet 355:185–191, 2000

46. Simon GE: Evidence review: efficacy and effectiveness of antidepressant treatment in primary care. General Hospital Psychiatry 24:213–224, 2002

47. Hodges B, Inch C, Silver I: Improving the psychiatric knowledge, skills, and attitudes of primary care physicians, 1950–2000: a review. American Journal of Psychiatry 158:1579–1586, 2001

48. Katon W, Von Korff M, Lin E, et al: Population-based care of depression: effective disease management strategies to decrease prevalence. General Hospital Psychiatry 19:169–178, 1997

49. Katon W, Von Korff M, Lin E, et al: Re-

thinking practitioner roles in chronic illness: the specialist, primary care physician, and the practice nurse. General Hospital Psychiatry 23:138–144, 2001

50. Katon W, Von Korff M, Lin E, et al: Collaborative management to achieve treatment guidelines: impact on depression in primary care. JAMA 273:1026–1031, 1995

51. Katon W, Robinson P, Von Korff M, et al: A multifaceted intervention to improve treatment of depression in primary care. Archives of General Psychiatry 53:924–932, 1996

52. Unützer J, Katon W, Williams JW Jr, et al: Improving primary care for depression in late life: the design of a multicenter randomized trial. Medical Care 39:785–799, 2001

53. Von Korff M, Tiemens B: Individualized stepped care of chronic illness. Western Journal of Medicine 172:133–137, 2000

54. Von Korff M, Unützer J, Katon W, et al: Improving care for depression in organized health care systems. Journal of Family Practice 50:530–531, 2001

55. Wagner EH, Austin BT, Von Korff M: Organizing care for patients with chronic illness. Milbank Quarterly 74:511–544, 1996

56. Badamgarav E, Weingarten SR, Henning JM, et al: Effectiveness of disease management programs in depression: a systematic review. American Journal of Psychiatry 160:2080–2090, 2003

57. Bijl D, van Marwijk HW, de Haan M, et al: Effectiveness of disease management programmes for recognition, diagnosis and treatment of depression in primary care. European Journal of General Practice 10:6–12, 2004

58. Gilbody S, Whitty P, Grimshaw J, et al: Educational and organizational interventions to improve the management of depression in primary care: a systematic review. JAMA 289:3145–3151, 2003

59. Weingarten SR, Henning JM, Badamgarav E, et al: Interventions used in disease management programmes for patients with chronic illness: which ones work? Meta-analysis of published reports. British Medical Journal 325:925–932, 2002

60. Gilbody DS: Review: disease management programmes improve detection and care of people with depression. Evidence-Based Mental Health 7(3):80, 2004

61. Schoenbaum M, Unützer J, Sherbourne C, et al: Cost-effectiveness of practice-initiated quality improvement for depression: results of a randomized controlled trial. JAMA 286:1325–1330, 2001

62. Schoenbaum M, Unützer J, McCaffrey D, et al: The effects of primary care depression treatment on patients' clinical status and employment. Health Services Research 37:1145–1158, 2002

63. Schoenbaum M, Miranda J, Sherbourne C, et al: Cost-effectiveness of interventions for depressed Latinos. Journal of Mental Health Policy and Economics 7:69–76, 2004

64. Simon GE, Katon WJ, VonKorff M, et al: Cost-effectiveness of a collaborative care program for primary care patients with persistent depression. American Journal of Psychiatry 158:1638–1644, 2001

65. Simon GE, Von Korff M, Ludman EJ, et al: Cost-effectiveness of a program to prevent depression relapse in primary care. Medical Care 40:941–950, 2002

66. Miranda J, Duan N, Sherbourne C, et al: Improving care for minorities: can quality improvement interventions improve care and outcomes for depressed minorities? Results of a randomized, controlled trial. Health Services Research 38:613–630, 2003

67. Wells K, Sherbourne C, Schoenbaum M, et al: Five-year impact of quality improvement for depression: results of a group-level randomized controlled trial. Archives of General Psychiatry 61:378–386, 2004

68. Asarnow JR, Jaycox LH, Anderson M: Depression among youth in primary care models for delivering mental health services. Child and Adolescent Psychiatric Clinics of North America 11:477–497, 2002

69. Bruce ML, Ten Have TR, Reynolds CF 3rd, et al: Reducing suicidal ideation and depressive symptoms in depressed older primary care patients: a randomized controlled trial. JAMA 291:1081–1091, 2004

70. Lin EH, Katon W, Von Korff M, et al: Effect of improving depression care on pain and functional outcomes among older adults with arthritis: a randomized controlled trial. JAMA 290:2428–2434, 2003

71. Williams JW, Jr, Katon W, Lin EH, et al: The effectiveness of depression care management on diabetes-related outcomes in older patients. Annals of Internal Medicine 140:1015–1024, 2004

72. Koike A, Unützer J, Wells KB: Comorbid medical disorders and the effectiveness of quality improvement interventions for depression in primary care. American Journal of Psychiatry 159:1738–1745, 2002

73. Harpole LH, Williams JW Jr, Olsen MK, et al: Improving depression outcomes in older adults with comorbid medical illness. General Hospital Psychiatry 27:4–12, 2005

74. Katon WJ, Roy-Byrne P, Russo J, et al: Cost-effectiveness and cost offset of a collaborative care intervention for primary care patients with panic disorder. Archives of General Psychiatry 59:1098–1104, 2002

75. Roy-Byrne PP, Katon W, Cowley DS, et al: A randomized effectiveness trial of collaborative care for patients with panic disorder in primary care. Archives of General Psychiatry 58:869–876, 2001

76. Ford DE, Pincus HA, Unützer J, et al: Practice-based interventions. Mental Health Services Research 4:199–204, 2002

77. Pincus HA, Hough L, Houtsinger JK, et al: Emerging models of depression care: multi-level ('6 P') strategies. International Journal of Methods in Psychiatric Research 12:54–63, 2003

78. Pincus HA: The future of behavioral health and primary care: drowning in the mainstream or left on the bank? Psychosomatics 44:1–11, 2003

79. Pincus HA, Pechura CM, Elinson L, et al: Depression in primary care: linking clinical and systems strategies. General Hospital Psychiatry 23:311–318, 2001

80. Schulberg HC: Treating depression in primary care practice: applications of research findings. Journal of Family Practice 50:535–537, 2001

81. Von Korff M, Katon W, Unützer J, et al: Improving depression care: barriers, solutions, and research needs. Journal of Family Practice 50:E1, 2001

82. Wells KB, Miranda J, Bauer MS, et al: Overcoming barriers to reducing the burden of affective disorders. Biological Psychiatry 52:655–675, 2002

83. Koran LM, Sox HC Jr, Marton KI, et al: Medical evaluation of psychiatric patients: I. results in a state mental health system. Archives of General Psychiatry 46:733–740, 1989

84. Koryani EK: Morbidity and rate of undiagnosed physical illness in a psychiatric clinic population. Archives of General Psychiatry 36:414–419, 1979

85. Dobscha SK, Ganzini L: A program for teaching psychiatric residents to provide integrated psychiatric and primary medical care. Psychiatric Services 52:1651–1653, 2001

86. Shore JH: Psychiatry at a crossroad: our role in primary care. American Journal of Psychiatry 153:1398–1403, 1996

87. Stiebel V, Schwartz CE: Physicians at the medicine/psychiatric interface: what do internist/psychiatrists do? Psychosomatics 42:377–381, 2001

88. Doebbeling CC, Pitkin AK, Malis R, et al: Combined internal medicine-psychiatry and family medicine-psychiatry training programs, 1999–2000: program directors' perspectives. Academic Medicine 76:1247–1252, 2001

89. Druss BG, Rohrbaugh RM, Levinson CM, et al: Integrated medical care for patients with serious psychiatric illness: a randomized trial. Archives of General Psychiatry 58:861–868, 2001

90. Belfiglio G: Approaches to depression care. Healthplan 42:12–17, 2001

91. Wells KB: The design of Partners in Care: evaluating the cost-effectiveness of improving care for depression in primary care. Social Psychiatry and Psychiatric Epidemiology 34:20–29, 1999

92. Wells KB, Sherbourne C, Schoenbaum M, et al: Impact of disseminating quality improvement programs for depression in managed primary care: a randomized controlled trial. JAMA 283:212–220, 2000

93. Oxman TE, Dietrich AJ, Williams JW Jr, et al: A three-component model for reengineering systems for the treatment of depression in primary care. Psychosomatics 43:441–450, 2002

94. Oxman TE, Dietrich AJ, Schulberg HC: The depression care manager and mental health specialist as collaborators within primary care. American Journal of Geriatric Psychiatry 11:507–516, 2003

95. Von Korff M, Goldberg D: Improving outcomes in depression. British Medical Journal 323:948–949, 2001

96. Frank RG, Goldman HH, McGuire TG: Will parity in coverage result in better mental health care? New England Journal of Medicine 345:1701–1704, 2001

97. Frank RG, Huskamp HA, Pincus HA: Aligning incentives in the treatment of depression in primary care with evidence-based practice. Psychiatric Services 54:682–687, 2003

98. Schoenbaum M, Kelleher K, Lave JR, et al: Exploratory evidence on the market for effective depression care in Pittsburgh. Psychiatric Services 55:392–395, 2004

99. Unützer J, Katon W, Callahan CM, et al: Collaborative care management of late-life depression in the primary care setting: a randomized controlled trial. JAMA 288:2836–2845, 2002

100. Institute of Medicine: Leadership by Example: Coordinating Government Roles in Improving Health Care Quality. Washington, DC, National Academy Press, 2002

101. Kroenke K, Spitzer RL, Williams JB: The PHQ-9: validity of a brief depression severity measure. Journal of General Internal Medicine 16:606–613, 2001

102. Depression Management Tool Kit. Chicago, MacArthur Foundation, 2004. Available at www.depression-primarycare.org

103. Changing Practice, Changing Lives: Depression Training Manual. Health Disparities Collaboratives, Feb 2004. Available at www.healthdisparities.net

104. Project IMPACT: Improving Primary Care for Depression in Late Life. Available at www.impact.ucla.edu

105. Kern DE, Branch WT, Jr, Jackson JL, et al: Teaching the psychosocial aspects of care in the clinical setting: practical recommendations. Academic Medicine 80:8–20, 2005

106. Coyne JC, Thompson R, Klinkman MS, et al: Emotional disorders in primary care. Journal of Consulting and Clinical Psychology 70:798–809, 2002

107. Department of Veterans Affairs: VHA Program Guide 1103.2: Provision of Primary Care Services for Mental Health Clinicians. Washington, DC, VHA Mental Health Strategic Health Group, 1997

108. New Freedom Commission on Mental Health: Achieving the Promise: Transforming Mental Health Care in America. Final Report. DHHS pub no SMA-03-3832. Rockville, Md, Department of Health and Human Resources, 2003

Employment Barriers for Persons With Psychiatric Disabilities: Update of a Report for the President's Commission

Judith A. Cook, Ph.D.

A major public policy problem is the extremely low labor force participation of people with severe mental illness coupled with their over-representation on the public disability rolls. This situation is especially troubling given the existence of evidence-based practices designed to return them to the labor force. This article reviews research from the fields of disability, economics, health care, and labor studies to describe the nature of barriers to paid work and economic security for people with disabling mental disorders. These barriers include low educational attainment, unfavorable labor market dynamics, low productivity, lack of appropriate vocational and clinical services, labor force discrimination, failure of protective legislation, work disincentives caused by state and federal policies, poverty-level income, linkage of health care access to disability beneficiary status, and ineffective work incentive programs. The article concludes with a discussion of current policy initiatives in health care, mental health, and disability. Recommendations for a comprehensive system of services and supports to address multiple barriers are presented. These include access to affordable health care, including mental health treatment and prescription drug coverage; integrated clinical and vocational services; safe and stable housing that is not threatened by changes in earned income; remedial and postsecondary education and vocational training; benefits counseling and financial literacy education; economic security through asset development; legal aid for dealing with employment discrimination; peer support and self-help to enhance vocational self-image and encourage labor force attachment; and active involvement of U.S. business and employer communities. (*Psychiatric Services* 57:1391–1405, 2006)

Two major policy issues in the United States today are the persistently low employment rate of individuals with disabilities, coupled with dramatic growth in the public disability rolls. Research confirms that both of these trends are magnified among people with psychiatric disabilities. Evidence further suggests that this situation is perpetu-ated by a series of intended and unintended consequences that arise from current U.S. health care, disability, labor, and economic policies.

In 2002, the Subcommittee on Employment and Income Supports of the President's New Freedom Commission on Mental Health commissioned a report to examine these issues. I prepared this report, which was reviewed and approved by the Subcommittee (1), and some parts of it were incorporated into the Commission's final report, *Achieving the Promise: Transforming Mental Health Care in America*, issued in 2003 (2). This article is an updated version of the subcommittee report, including more recently published research, a section on new federal policy initiatives in the fields of health care, mental health, and disability, and a series of recommendations, some of which were contained in the original report and others that are my own.

Prevalence of disabling mental disorders

Of the adult U.S. civilian noninstitutionalized population aged 18 or older, it is estimated that 3.5 percent, or 6.7 million people, have a mental health disability, defined as a mental disorder that interferes with performance of one or more major life activities, such as the ability to live independently, work, attend school, or manage activities of daily living (3). According to the World Health Organization, mental disorders are the leading cause of disability in the United States for individuals between the ages of 15 and 44 years (4). In a nationally representative cohort of non-institutionalized, working-age adults, mental health conditions were identified as the third leading cause of work disability (5).

Labor force participation and psychiatric disability

Individuals with disabling mental disorders are less likely to be working and more likely to be unemployed, out of the labor force, or un-

Dr. Cook is professor and director of the Center on Mental Health Services Research and Policy, Department of Psychiatry, University of Illinois at Chicago, 1601 West Taylor Street, 4th Floor M/C 913, Chicago, IL 60612 (e-mail: cook@ripco.com). Originally published in the October 2006 issue of Psychiatric Services.

deremployed than those without such disorders. Four nationally representative surveys conducted between 1989 and 1998 found that people who had any mental illness (but who were not necessarily disabled by these disorders) had lower employment rates (48 to 73 percent) than people who did not report mental illness (76 to 87 percent) (6). Employment rates for people who met criteria for disabling mental illness were even lower, ranging from 32 to 61 percent, and lower still—22 to 40 percent—among those with diagnoses associated with high levels of disability such as schizophrenia and related disorders.

To be classified as unemployed, individuals must be actively seeking paid work. Individuals who are not seeking employment because of a disability, ill health, or other reasons are referred to as "out of the labor force," or OLF. In an analysis of data from the Healthcare for Communities study (7), one of the four surveys cited above, the proportion of unemployed among men with disabling mental illness was 27.2 percent and the proportion OLF was 20.8 percent, compared with 4.1 percent and 5.0 percent, respectively, among those with no mental disorder. Almost a quarter (24.7 percent) of women with disabling mental illness were unemployed and 25.8 percent were OLF, compared with 6.7 percent and 14.4 percent, respectively, among women with no mental disorder. Even a college education does not ameliorate this disadvantageous position in the labor market. In the National Health Interview Survey–Disability Supplement (NHIS-D), another of the studies cited above, 43 percent of individuals with mental health disabilities who had college degrees were not working, compared with only 13 percent of college graduates without mental health disabilities (8).

Underemployment or the inadequate utilization of labor (9) is also a serious problem. Underemployment is measured in a number of ways, including being substantially overqualified for the occupation one holds, working less than full-time for eco-

nomic reasons, and earning very low income (10,11). In the NHIS-D, nearly two-fifths (38 percent) of workers with mental health disabilities had jobs that paid near minimum wage, compared with only one-fifth (20 percent) of people without disabilities (8). In 1994–1995 people with mental health disabilities earned a median hourly wage of only $6.33, compared with $9.23 for those without disabilities, and more than one-third (36 percent) of all workers with mental health disabilities were employed in part-time jobs, compared with only 16 percent of their nondisabled counterparts (8). Among a large group of individuals with psychiatric disabilities participating in a multisite, randomized controlled trial of supported employment services called the Employment Intervention Demonstration Program (EIDP) (12), the majority of those with college degrees (70 percent) earned less than $10 an hour (equivalent to an annual salary of $21,000) at their highest-level job, and the majority (54 percent) were employed only part-time.

Disabling mental disorders and public disability income

Two primary federal programs of benefits and entitlements administered by the Social Security Administration (SSA) currently assist disabled individuals who are unable to work. As argued below, there is evidence that these programs unintentionally discourage those who are capable of returning to work from doing so, thus presenting barriers to employment. Supplemental Security Income (SSI) is a means-tested income assistance program for individuals with disabilities who have little or no income and are unable to engage in substantial gainful activity because of a physical or mental impairment that is expected to last for at least 12 months or result in death (13). According to SSA's Monthly Statistical Snapshot for June 2006 (14), there were approximately 4.1 million SSI recipients between the ages of 18 and 64 years who were classified as disabled, and these individuals received an average of $470.30 per month (many states

supplement this amount to varying degrees).

Social Security Disability Insurance (SSDI) is a social insurance program for disabled individuals that provides monthly benefits to covered individuals who qualify for cash payments based on their prior contribution to the system through a compulsory tax on earnings (13). In June 2006, approximately 6.6 million recipients of SSDI were classified as disabled workers, and they received an average of $943.40 per month (14). Also in June 2006 an additional 1.4 million individuals were "dual beneficiaries" (14), meaning that they qualified for SSDI on the basis of their tax contributions but received monthly payments low enough to qualify them for SSI under the means test. These programs were originally designed for individuals over 50 years of age with work-related disabilities, but policy analysts have noted that SSDI has evolved to meet a growing number of social welfare needs and new congressional mandates, while SSI has become a large cash-benefit program for a population that is younger and less attached to the labor force than the program was originally intended to support (15).

People with psychiatric disabilities constitute the largest working-age disability group receiving public income supports. In December 2002 they constituted over a third (33.7 percent) of all working-age SSI beneficiaries and over a quarter (28.1 percent) of all disabled workers receiving SSDI benefits (38.2 percent of those younger than age 50 were receiving SSDI benefits) (16). In addition, for more than a decade the number of SSI beneficiaries with psychiatric disabilities has been increasing at a rate higher than total program growth (15). From 1988 to 2001 the number of SSI recipients with psychiatric disabilities more than tripled, from 411,800 to 1.5 million (the total number of all SSI recipients also rose more than two and a half times during that period) (3). The percentage of SSDI recipients with disabling mental disorders also increased over time but not as rapidly. Less than .5 percent of all beneficiaries at any point in time leave the rolls because of employment (17,18), and people with disabling mental illness are no exception. In fact, SSI beneficiaries with psychiatric disabilities are significantly less likely to work than those with other disabilities (19), and SSDI beneficiaries with disabling mental disorders remain on the rolls significantly longer than those with other diagnoses (20).

Preference for employment

Numerous research studies indicate that individuals with disabling mental disorders want to work, consider themselves able to work, and express the need for job training, services, and supports. Opinion surveys repeatedly find that a majority of people with psychiatric disabilities desire paid employment, with many expressing the need for vocational rehabilitation (21–24). In a national household probability survey (NHIS-D), half of all working age adults with mental health disabilities who were not working considered themselves able to work if supported adequately (25).

Questions of the President's Commission Subcommittee

Given these issues, the President's Commission Subcommittee on Employment and Income Supports, which was charged with making recommendations on employment and income supports, raised a series of questions. Why do so many individuals with disabling mental illness find themselves out of work when so many express the desire to work? Why do they constitute such a disproportionate share of the public disability rolls? Are evidence-based practice services available to help them return to and remain in the labor force? Do most people who want such services receive them? Do public disability policies support or discourage beneficiaries' attempts to work? Do laws protect them from unfair hiring practices and discrimination in the workplace?

The research reviewed here used different definitions of disabling mental disorders, depending on the data sources and research questions. However, unless otherwise noted, all focused on individuals whose mental disorders and related symptoms were disabling—that is, accompanied by impairment that substantially interfered with their ability to manage daily activities (3).

Barriers to employment
Low educational attainment

Many individuals with disabling mental disorders lack the necessary high school and postsecondary education and training required to build careers. This education and training gap stems from multiple causes. The onset of disabling mental illness occurs early; half of all lifetime cases begin by age 14 and three-quarters by age 24 (26), often interrupting secondary and postsecondary education. This is reflected in the graduation and dropout rates of youths classified as having severe emotional disturbance, a designation equivalent to that of mental health disability among adults. Severe emotional disturbance is defined by emotional, behavioral, or interpersonal difficulties that are experienced over a long period and to a marked degree and that adversely affect a child's educational performance or ability to relate to teachers, peers, and others (27).

According to the U.S. Department of Education, in school year 1998–1999 the dropout rate for students with severe emotional disturbance was 50.6, the highest of all disability categories (3). The NHIS-D found that only 38 percent of special education students with severe emotional disturbance had graduated from high school, while another 6 percent received a certificate such as a General Equivalency Diploma, and the remaining 56 percent did not complete their schooling (25). The National Longitudinal Transition Study, a survey of young people exiting special education programs in 303 nationally representative school districts, found that youths with severe emotional disturbance had the highest percentage of high school noncompletion and failing grades (28). One to two years after exiting high school, only 18 percent were employed full-time, another 21 percent worked part-time, and their post–high school work experiences were characterized by greater instability than all other disability groups (29).

These gaps in education are important because advanced education is increasingly essential to securing a high-paying, career-advancing job. A multivariate analysis of employment among individuals with disabling mental disorders who participated in the NHIS-D found that education was a significant predictor of employment in executive, administrative, and professional specialty occupations (30). In 2004 all but one of the 50 highest-paying occupations in the United States required a college degree or graduate education (31). Labor market projections for 2004 to 2014 by the federal Bureau of Labor Statistics indicate that among the 20 fastest-growing occupations an associate's or bachelor's degree is the most significant source of training and education for ten of them (31). It is especially important to prepare people with psychiatric disabilities to enter high-growth industries because of research that has found higher employment and retention rates for people with disabilities in these industries; workers with disabilities are now almost as likely as nondisabled workers to be employed in high-growth industries but not in non-growth industries (32).

Lowered productivity

Another reason for the low labor force participation rates in this population is lower productivity and higher absenteeism that accompany disabling mental disorders, creating an economic burden for workers, their employers, and society at large. In a study of individuals with diagnoses of mood disorders, anxiety disorders, and substance use disorders—but not restricted to those disabled by these disorders—Kessler and Frank (33) found an average of 31 work-cutback days (reduced work activity) per month per 100 workers and an average of 100 work-loss days (days unable to work) per month per 100 workers that were attributable to mental health–related difficulties. In another study, workers with depression—again, not necessarily disabling depression—reported significantly higher health-related "lost productivity time" (hours per week absent plus hour-equivalents per week of reduced performance) than workers without depression, an average of 5.6 hours per week compared with an expected average of 1.5 hours per week, respectively (34).

Analyses of "moment-in-time" work performance found that compared with six other medical conditions, such as arthritis and back pain, major depression was the only condition associated with reductions in both task focus and productivity—approximately 2.3 lost days per month per worker (35). In the recent National Comorbidity Study Replication, bipolar disorder was associated with an annual average of 65.5 lost work days per ill worker and major depressive disorder with 27.2 lost work days (36). On average, those with bipolar disorder experienced $9,619 annual human capital loss per ill worker, while those with major depression had an annual loss of $4,426 per worker; projections to the U.S. labor force were $14.1 billion per year resulting from bipolar disorder and $36.6 billion resulting from major depression (36).

Unfavorable labor market dynamics

Studies show that labor force participation of people with disabilities is closely tied to overall U.S. labor market dynamics (37). Yelin and colleagues (38) showed that long-term labor market trends from 1970 to 1992, including changes in the gender, age, and ethnic makeup of the U.S. workforce, were mirrored in the labor market participation of individuals with disabilities. However, although people with disabilities experienced proportionally larger gains than nondisabled people during periods of market expansion, they also evidenced greater losses during times of market contraction (38). The combination of mental disorders and disability is particularly severe because the effect of such disorders tends to magnify the ef-

fects of disability. According to labor force participation trends from 1982 to 1991, those with disabling mental disorders were 36 percent as likely as all nondisabled persons to be in the labor force, and those with nondisabling mental disorders were 62 percent as likely as nondisabled persons (39). In this study mental disorders were also found to intensify the effects of age and race, in addition to disability status, on labor force participation.

The fact that individuals with disabling mental illness are affected by general labor market trends is evident in the employment patterns in the EIDP study, where those residing in areas with high unemployment had poorer outcomes than those in areas with lower unemployment (40). However, participants receiving evidence-based supported employment services (a model described below) in areas with high unemployment rates had outcomes superior to those in control groups in areas with low unemployment rates. This suggests that use of evidence-based supported employment can help to ameliorate the effects of a poor labor market.

Lack of effective vocational services

Given their desire to work, coupled with low labor force participation, it is disconcerting that many people with mental illness receive few or no employment services. Among a stratified random sample of persons in two states diagnosed as having schizophrenia, only 23 percent of outpatients were receiving vocational rehabilitation services (41). In a study of 2,749 adults with disabling mental disorders who received services in Vermont, only 24 percent received any employment services and more than half received fewer than six service contacts (42). State mental health authorities have not traditionally viewed vocational rehabilitation as part of their mandate for this population. In a survey conducted by the National Alliance on Mental Illness in the late 1990s, only 16 state mental health authorities required that treatment address vocational rehabilitation goals

(43). A survey conducted by the National Association of State Mental Health Program Directors Research Institute in 2004 found that only 36 of 50 state authorities used state general revenue or federal Mental Health Block Grant monies to fund supported employment services (44).

The authority charged with vocational rehabilitation of individuals with disabilities in the United States is the state-federal vocational rehabilitation system. By federal legislative mandate, the Rehabilitation Services Administration (RSA), an agency of the U.S. Department of Education, uses federal and state dollars to fund vocational rehabilitation programs in each state to provide job placement and training services to people with disabilities. In fiscal year 1995, the latest year for which statistics are available, 1.3 million adults were clients of state-run vocational rehabilitation programs, accounting for 12 percent of all Americans estimated to have health conditions or impairments that limited their ability to work (45).

People with disabilities who apply for state vocational rehabilitation services work with a rehabilitation counselor to determine their eligibility for services, select a vocational goal, and develop and implement an individualized plan of services to achieve that goal. According to section 102(a) of the Rehabilitation Act of 1973, as amended, eligibility is defined by, first, having a physical or mental impairment that constitutes a substantial impediment to employment, and second, by being capable of benefiting from vocational rehabilitation services to prepare for, secure, retain, or regain employment (46). Those receiving SSI or SSDI or both are presumed to be eligible for state vocational rehabilitation services unless they are deemed too significantly impaired to benefit. Eligibility does not guarantee receipt of services, however, because state programs are now required to serve individuals with the most severe disabilities when there are not enough resources to serve everyone who is eligible (46).

Researchers have studied the effectiveness of state-federal vocational rehabilitation programs over time by examining longitudinal trends in client outcomes. One such trend is toward selectively serving individuals with severe disabilities, the policy shift described above that was instituted in the 1980s. In the early 1990s Andrews and colleagues (47) examined outcomes of all state vocational rehabilitation clients whose cases were closed from 1977 to 1984. They found that the percentage change in number competitively employed at closure had improved significantly among individuals with severe physical disabilities but not among those with severe psychiatric disabilities.

Beginning in 1995 RSA funded a national follow-up study of a random sample of 8,500 applicants, current users, and former users of state vocational rehabilitation services who were tracked for three years (48). Results indicated that, even after the analyses controlled for age, receipt of SSI or SSDI, gross motor function, and cognitive function, individuals with psychiatric disabilities were significantly less likely than those with other disabilities to achieve employment at closure or to achieve competitive employment (48). Further multivariate analyses indicated that services positively associated with achieving employment were job placement, on-the-job training, supported employment, and business and vocational training. Services associated with competitive employment included job development, job placement, on-the-job training, business and vocational training, and postsecondary education. Individuals with psychiatric disabilities were more likely to earn low wages (defined as no more than $5 per hour) than high wages (more than $9 per hour) (49). Moreover, receipt of postsecondary education through a state vocational rehabilitation agency and achievement of a postsecondary degree were both significantly related to higher earnings, even after the analyses controlled for other educational characteristics.

Lack of effective clinical services
In addition to research showing that individuals with disabling mental disorders receive low levels of vocational services or none at all, a body of research beginning in the 1980s (50) has found that large proportions of this population receive no clinical services and that those who do fail to receive adequate care (51,52). In a national probability survey of U.S. households, 60 percent of individuals diagnosed as having disabling mental illness reported receiving no treatment, 24.7 percent received treatment deemed "not minimally adequate," and only 15.3 percent received minimally adequate treatment, defined as either appropriate psychotropic medication and four or more visits with a doctor or mental health specialist or, when appropriate, eight or more visits with a mental health specialist (53). Failure to receive any psychiatric treatment or appropriate types of services is a critical problem given that integration of clinical and vocational services has been associated with superior employment outcomes in a number of studies (54–56)

Labor force discrimination
Given the high level of social stigma attached to mental illness in American society, it is not surprising that people with disabling mental disorders experience labor force discrimination (57). In surveys over the past five decades, employers have expressed more negative attitudes about hiring workers with psychiatric disabilities than about almost any other group (58–60). In 2004 individuals with disabling mental disorders lodged a fifth of all U.S. court cases alleging employment discrimination (61). In a national survey of more than 1,300 individuals with disabling mental disorders, almost a third (32 percent) reported that after disclosure of mental illness they were turned down for a job for which they felt qualified (62). In-depth follow-up interviews with a subsample of 100 respondents from this survey revealed the negative impact of such disclosure by self or others on work outcomes, including instances in which job offers were rescinded or individuals were fired or asked to leave and demotions, reductions in hours

or responsibilities, social isolation, and harassment by coworkers (63).

In a national probability sample drawn from the NHIS-D, one-third (32 percent) of individuals with mental health disabilities reported having been fired, laid off or told to resign, refused employment, refused a transfer, refused a promotion, or refused a training opportunity because of their mental disorder (25). Although factors other than discriminatory treatment undoubtedly influenced some of these reports (for example, lower productivity during periods of illness or negative business trends, such as corporate downsizing), it is also likely that many of these accounts reflect illegal and actionable instances of employment discrimination.

Baldwin and Johnson (64) studied disability-related employment discrimination by examining earnings differentials and applying econometric techniques previously used to study race and sex discrimination. After they accounted for productivity differentials related to functional limitations and other productivity-related individual characteristics, such as education, occupation, and part-time employment, large unexplained variance in wage differentials between people with and without disabilities remained. The authors attributed these differentials to discrimination in the labor market and, in subsequent analyses, showed that wage differentials were even larger for individuals with disabilities that were thought to evoke "greater prejudice" (defined as including mental illness) compared with those with impairments evoking "milder prejudice."

Failure of protective legislation
One piece of legislation that showed much initial promise for preventing job discrimination is the Americans With Disabilities Act (ADA) (65). Enacted in 1990, this landmark legislation extended civil rights protection to people with disabilities by prohibiting discrimination in employment, state and local government services, public transportation, public accommodations, commer-

cial facilities, and telecommunications. Under the ADA, discrimination in job application procedures, hiring, firing, advancement, compensation, fringe benefits, and job training is prohibited. The law allows individuals with disabilities to request "reasonable accommodations"—changes to the work process or environment that enable workers to perform their jobs. However, these accommodations must not create "undue hardship" for employers, meaning that they must not be unduly expensive, extensive, or disruptive or change the nature or operation of a business. Additionally, individuals seeking accommodations must disclose their disability to employers in order to request and be granted an accommodation (65).

The ADA defines an individual with a disability as someone with a physical or mental impairment that substantially limits one or more major life activities or someone who has a record of such impairment or who is regarded as having such impairment. To be protected from employment discrimination under the ADA, individuals must also be "qualified." This means that they must meet the skill, experience, education, and other requirements of a position and can perform the essential functions of the position either with or without reasonable accommodations.

Since the law was enacted, ADA protections have become increasingly circumscribed for individuals with psychiatric disabilities and other types of conditions. For example, recent Supreme Court rulings have declared that ADA protections do not extend to workers with illnesses "controlled by medications" (66–68) and those whose limitations are not considered "central to most people's daily lives" (69,70).

Additional evidence of the failure of the ADA to protect workers with psychiatric disabilities has been found in studies of the ADA claims adjudication process (71). Claims filed by individuals with psychiatric disabilities are more likely to be classified by the Equal Employment Opportunity Commission as "low-priority," and this priority assignment is

associated with a decreased likelihood that a claimant will receive some benefit in the form of an actual monetary payment (compensatory damages or back pay) or projected monetary gain (assumed to co-occur with hiring, promotion, or reinstatement) (72). As a result, claimants with psychiatric disabilities are significantly less likely than those with other disabilities to receive monetary benefits. Despite these outcomes, ADA claims by persons with psychiatric disability constitute 21 percent of all cases brought to trial in federal court in 2004, in which 76 percent of the decisions favored the employer, 24 percent were unresolved, and none favored the claimant (61). The necessity of disclosure in order to request reasonable accommodations or pursue ADA claims is another disadvantage of this law, given anecdotal evidence that disclosure is related to subsequent discrimination, harassment, and isolation (62,63,73).

Poverty-level income

People with disabilities are among the poorest in the nation, especially those with psychiatric disabilities (74,75). However, the proportion of individuals with disabling mental illness who live in poverty or in near-poverty is difficult to estimate from nationally representative surveys because of the ways in which questions are asked and populations defined as well as the choices researchers make in constructing the variables that they analyze. In one recent analysis of data from the NHIS-D (76), almost a third (31.8 percent) of individuals with mental disabilities fell below the federal poverty line in 1994–1995; however, the definition of mental disability used in this analysis included a wide range of factors, such as diagnoses (for example, schizophrenia, major depression, and antisocial personality) as well as symptoms and impairments (for example, trouble concentrating, confusion and disorientation, and trouble making or keeping friends).

Data from the Survey of Income and Program Participation, a nationally representative household survey conducted by the Bureau of the Cen-

sus (77), indicate that individuals with activity limitations resulting from mental or emotional problems had a median annual income of $9,492 in 1997, when the poverty level was $8,350 for one-person households for persons younger than 65 and $10,805 for two-person households (78). This suggests that between one-third and one-half of individuals with disabling mental disorders are at or near the poverty level.

Even if persons with disabling mental disorders qualify for SSI or SSDI disability cash payments, the level of benefits in these programs coupled with the tenuous economic and career trajectories of this group constitutes what some policy analysts have referred to as a "poverty trap" (79). The maximum federal SSI benefit is now only about 75 percent of the federal poverty standard for an individual (79). In 2004 the monthly income of a person with a disability receiving SSI benefits was $564, while the national average monthly rent for a one-bedroom apartment was $676 (80). Thus, at 105 percent of 2004 SSI benefits, the average national rent for a one-bedroom housing unit exceeded total yearly SSI income. The average annual income of a disabled SSI beneficiary in 2004 was less than a fifth (18.4 percent) of the national one-person median household income (80).

Taken together, this evidence suggests that whether they work, qualify for SSI or SSDI, or receive money from friends and relatives or other sources, income levels of people with psychiatric disabilities are inadequate to help them meet basic needs for food and shelter, let alone the requisites of education, job training, and job seeking. Poverty-level income prevents individuals with adequate work skills from successful job-seeking when they reside in neighborhoods where jobs are scarce and they cannot afford transportation outside their communities to find work. Poverty disqualifies individuals from holding jobs for which they must provide their own tools, uniforms, or other equipment. Poverty inhibits those with low levels of education and work skills from obtaining postsecondary education or training to enhance their skill levels. Research confirms these barriers, suggesting that poverty is an important mediator of the relationship between mental illness and unemployment, in some cases with a larger influence on labor force participation than the psychiatric disorder itself (81).

Linkage of health care to disability beneficiary status
Many individuals with severe mental illness rely on disability income support programs for the health care and medication coverage they provide. Individuals on SSI qualify for Medicaid, and those on SSDI qualify for Medicare after a mandatory waiting period of up to two years. In a study of individuals with schizophrenia who were followed for an average of five years after their first hospitalization, 72 percent relied on SSI, SSDI, or Aid to Families With Dependent Children throughout most of the follow-up period (82). Individuals with high-cost major mental disorders and those requiring expensive medications are especially dependent on Medicare and Medicaid because of the lack of parity in most private health and mental health care systems (83,84). This is important because uncontrolled symptoms, impaired functioning, and comorbid medical conditions and illnesses are associated with inability to achieve vocational success in this population (85,86).

Disadvantages upon labor force reentry
The vulnerability of those who return to work while on the federal disability income support rolls is evident in studies showing that most reenter the labor force because of financial need rather than medical improvement (87). Those who do return to work tend to be younger and better educated than those who do not. Their initial post-SSDI jobs are lower paying, and they work for fewer hours than at the job held before they received SSDI. Moreover, the first job attempt after SSDI benefits are terminated has the greatest chance of leading to successful labor force reentry; the likelihood of positive

outcomes decreases significantly with subsequent job attempts (88). Finally, although workplace accommodations may extend the average duration of employment for those with disabilities (89), there is evidence that some injured workers who receive job accommodations also receive lower wages, in essence "paying the price" of their own accommodations (90). Evidence that SSI and SSDI recipients with psychiatric disabilities return to jobs that do not provide benefits comes from the EIDP, in which only 24 percent of full-time jobs provided medical coverage, 16 percent dental coverage, 8 percent mental health coverage, and 20 percent sick leave (12).

Employment disincentives
SSA disability income support policies create a number of unintended employment disincentives that help contribute to under- and unemployment (91). First, federal regulations mandate an administrative review of an individual's disability status upon return to work—called the continuing disability review—which discourages many beneficiaries from seeking employment (18). Second, once they become employed, beneficiaries find that their cash payments are sharply reduced as their earnings increase. SSDI beneficiaries can earn up to SSA's substantial gainful activity (SGA) level each month ($830 in 2006) with no loss of benefits; however, once earnings exceed that amount for nine nonconsecutive months plus a three-month grace period, all SSDI cash benefits cease—a phenomenon called the "earnings cliff" (92). SSI beneficiaries face a different penalty; once their earnings reach $65 per month, their cash payment is reduced by $1 for $2 of additional earnings, a tax rate of 50 percent, which far exceeds that paid by the wealthiest individuals (79).
A third disincentive is an "implicit tax" on disabled workers, whose labor force participation and resulting loss of beneficiary status causes them to lose additional benefits, such as health insurance, housing subsidies, utility supplements, transportation

stipends, and food stamps (93). Finally, SSDI beneficiaries who return to work in the first 24 months of eligibility become ineligible for health coverage under Medicare, regardless of whether their jobs provide medical benefits (92). Research has indicated that people with psychiatric disabilities are aware of these disincentives and report that they plan their labor force participation accordingly (93,94).
The effects of work disincentives are also evident in studies comparing the employment outcomes of individuals who do and do not receive public disability income support. In the EIDP cohort, those receiving SSI or SSDI cash benefits were significantly less likely to work competitively, to work 40 for more hours per month, and to have high earnings, regardless of study condition, demographic and clinical characteristics, work history, or study site (95). Research on both national and statewide cohorts of state vocational rehabilitation service recipients with psychiatric disabilities has found that employment rates are significantly lower among SSI and SSDI beneficiaries than among nonbeneficiaries, even after the analyses controlled for demographic features, level of family support, and functional impairment (48,96). Veterans with psychiatric (and other) disabilities are less likely to work, earn less money, and work fewer hours if they receive full veterans disability benefits, as opposed to partial benefits, or if they receive more generous benefit amounts; these analyses controlled for a series of confounding demographic and clinical factors (97,98).
Given evidence suggesting that people respond to work disincentives by altering their labor force participation, it follows that policies designed to discourage reliance on disability income may paradoxically discourage substantial work attempts that could lead to exit from the rolls. Instead, many individuals receiving SSI and SSDI find themselves out of the labor force or trapped in low-paying, entry-level jobs where they remain, prevented from realizing their full career potential (79,99).

Ineffective work incentive legislation

Recognizing this problem, various work incentive provisions have been legislated by Congress. The Employment Opportunities of Disabled Americans Act of 1986 (PL 99-643), Section 1619(b), provided for continued SSI eligibility and access to Medicaid as long as earnings remain below a threshold established by each state (100). Another mechanism permitting individuals to work above SGA while retaining Medicaid benefits was the Medicaid Buy-In state plan option under the Balanced Budget Act of 1997 (101).

The newest piece of disability legislation designed to address work disincentives is the Ticket to Work and Work Incentives Improvement Act of 1999 (102). This legislation was intended to give people with disabilities increased vocational service options and reduce employment disincentives while simultaneously reducing government spending on people with disabilities (103). To accomplish the first objective, vouchers, or "tickets," were mailed to all work-disabled SSI and SSDI beneficiaries to be redeemed for five years of vocational services from providers of their own choosing (104). In addition, Ticket to Work participants were offered free counseling about their benefits and entitlements to help them gauge the effects of employment on their cash benefits and other unearned income. SSA also placed a moratorium on continuing disability reviews for Ticket to Work participants and encouraged state Medicaid buy-ins enabling people to keep their health insurance after cash benefits ceased. Savings for SSA would result from a payment structure based on an "outcome payment" design in which providers would be paid only for months individuals earned above SGA or only at the time that the beneficiaries left the rolls as a result of employment.

Although anyone can apply to become a Ticket to Work service provider, the vast majority of providers are state vocational rehabilitation authorities, with a much smaller percentage comprised of not-for-profit and for-profit employment and disability programs, businesses, and corporations (105). In the early stages of the program, economists forecasted that the outcome-focused payment system would offer providers too little financial incentive to serve clients with substantial vocational barriers, such as those with psychiatric disabilities (106). They argued that by "backloading" the payment structure to reward providers whose customers rapidly reached earnings levels exceeding SGA, the program lacked incentives for serving populations that would take longer to move into higher-paying, competitive jobs, such as those with psychiatric or intellectual disabilities (107). These predictions were supported by the findings of a study simulating Ticket to Work provider payments that used 24-month earnings of SSDI beneficiaries with psychiatric disabilities who were receiving vocational rehabilitation (104). The study found that earnings of a large majority (74 percent) remained below SGA for two years.

The national evaluation of the Ticket to Work program has identified several problems with its implementation (108). First, the rate of participation in the program is very low. Even in states where it has operated the longest, just 1.1 percent of beneficiaries have assigned their ticket to a provider. Second, the rate of provider participation is similarly low. As of June 2004 only 40 percent of all providers had accepted tickets. Moreover, consistent with the simulation study (104), the evaluators' analysis of providers' costs and revenues suggests that those relying solely on Ticket to Work payments would have lost money after two years of operation. Despite this pessimistic picture, Ticket to Work participation is relatively vigorous among individuals with disabling mental disorders, who have the fifth-highest rate of participation among the 21 primary disabling conditions examined (106). At the same time, there is also evidence of reluctance to serve this population because one-third of providers interviewed for the evaluation mentioned psychiatric or other disabilities as a challenge to finding jobs for Ticket to Work beneficiaries.

Availability of evidence-based vocational rehabilitation models

Despite the bleak economic and employment situations of people with severe mental illnesses, accumulated research evidence indicates that they can successfully participate in the open labor market (54,109). That is, they can secure and retain jobs that are socially integrated (that is, where not all coworkers have disabilities), for which anyone can compete (that is, not set aside for individuals with disabilities), that pay minimum wage or above, and that belong to the worker rather than belonging to a mental health or rehabilitation agency.

The service delivery approach with demonstrated efficacy in establishing competitive employment is called supported employment (109). Although a number of evidence-based supported employment models have been developed specifically for this population, they share common features (110). All deliver integrated and coordinated clinical and vocational services that are provided by multidisciplinary teams, including both mental health and rehabilitation professionals, with rapid job search and placement into competitive positions in the client's preferred fields and settings, with the availability of services and supports that are not time limited (111). A multisite randomized, controlled trial of supported employment found that 55 percent of those receiving evidence-based supported employment achieved competitive employment compared with 34 percent of a control group that received services as usual or comparison interventions (95). In addition, 51 percent worked 40 or more hours in a given month, compared with 39 percent of the control group, and the average salary earned was $122 per month, compared with $99 per month for workers in the control group. These results have been confirmed by reviews and meta-analyses of single-site randomized controlled trials of supported employment programs for this population (112–114), showing that this approach is more effective than prevocational training or nonvocational community care.

Although most individuals with psychiatric disabilities do not receive any vocational rehabilitation services, others receive services that are not delivered according to best-practice standards (115). Often they receive employment services from a program that is separate from their clinical provider, with poor or nonexistent coordination between the various parties (116). In other instances their career preferences and individual financial circumstances are not taken into account, and they are offered generic job placements in entry-level positions (84). They may be served by employment staff who have little or no knowledge of mental disorders, psychotropic medications and side effects, work-based stigma and discrimination unique to mental illness, or appropriate vocational assessment techniques for this population. Often, so-called "ongoing" supports have an implicit time limit, after which the consumer is encouraged to "graduate" and services are terminated. This limited service duration is due, in part, to the fact that state vocational rehabilitation services are typically provided for relatively brief time periods, with limited opportunities for ongoing job support (115). Similarly, most vocational rehabilitation services are not reimbursable under Medicaid, even in states that have Medicaid's Rehabilitation Option, which creates a funding vacuum that helps to account for fact that this population is vastly underserved (110,116).

Taken together, the foregoing body of evidence suggests that people with psychiatric disabilities face a number of formidable, sometimes interrelated, and often unintended barriers to occupational success and economic security. The next section is a brief discussion of how U.S. policy reform efforts in health care, disability, and mental health have addressed these obstacles in the past several decades. This discussion is followed by recommendations for an integrated system of services and supports, legislative reforms, and business initiatives to address these problems, as called for by the President's Commission.

National policy reform efforts

Incrementalism in U.S. health care policy reform

Scholars of the development of recent health care policy in the United States have characterized its approach to change as incrementalist (117). In incrementalism, targeted policy changes and reforms are applied piecemeal to limited populations, as opposed to inclusive, large-scale reforms, such as universal health care or universal mental health parity. Aaron (118) described a "voluntary incrementalism" in which employer-based and market-driven health insurance serves as the primary source of health care coverage for U.S. citizens, while publicly funded programs are broadened to include, as necessary, certain groups outside the labor force depending upon need and political clout.

Since the establishment of the Medicare and Medicaid programs in the 1960s, expansion of publicly funded health care coverage has followed this policy of incremental reform. For example, Congress has extended coverage to selected groups according to age (Medicare for those 65 years of age or older), disability (Medicaid and Medicare provided through SSI and SSDI), income level (Medicaid for impoverished single-parent families and pregnant women), and even organ system (Medicare for end-stage renal disease patients) (119). The disadvantages of this approach include high levels of complexity in eligibility determination and associated difficulties in outreach to and enrollment of targeted groups. The question of higher costs associated with this approach to policy change also remains unresolved.

U.S. disability policy reform

Employment policy initiatives, such as the ADA and Ticket to Work program, reflect a paradigm shift to a social model of disability (120) as exemplified by the "new paradigm of disability" (121). The new paradigm views disability as an interaction between characteristics of individuals and features of their cultural, social, natural, and built environments; it was adopted in 1999 to guide federally funded disability research (121). In this framework, disability does not lie within the person but in the interface between individuals' characteristics (such as their functional status or personal or social qualities) and the features of the environments in which they operate. The old paradigm views a person with a disability as someone who cannot function because of an impairment, whereas the new paradigm views this person as someone who needs an accommodation in order to function (122). The new paradigm acknowledges the civil rights of qualified individuals with disabilities to work and to receive accommodations, in contrast to the deficit model of disability that dominated American federal policy for most of the 20th century (123).

Current reforms therefore focus on restructuring public disability policy to remove work disincentives, enhance economic security, improve access to effective services, and protect the rights of workers to freedom from discrimination in hiring and employment. However, debate rages regarding the success of these policy reforms given their uncoordinated, piecemeal nature (124,125). Some analysts argue that a policy approach aimed at correcting specific problems with specific disability programs fails to address a multitude of related problems, adding complexity to the programs that makes the programs more difficult to administer and threatens their long-term fiscal health (79). An additional complication lies in the fact that policies are assembled across multiple federal agencies such as SSA, RSA, and the U.S. Department of Labor. As a result, much U.S. disability policy lacks a coordinated, cohesive focus and policy making occurs far outside the realm of mental health and health care (84).

Sequential incrementalism in mental health policy

In the mental health policy arena, recent decades have also witnessed a deemphasis on broad, comprehensive reforms, such as those championed in the federal Mental Health Systems Act of 1980 (PL96-398) that grew out of the first presidential mental health commission established in 1977 during the Carter administration (126). With the repeal of this act at the beginning of the Reagan administration in 1981, ensuing decades witnessed a period of "quiet success" (127) in policy change, during which advocates, policy makers, and legislators worked to implement many of the specific recommendations that had been made in the 1980 National Plan for the Chronically Mentally Ill (128). These included changes in SSI and SSDI eligibility determination and coverage; expansion of the Medicare mental health benefit; use of Medicaid funding for "new" community mental health services, such as case management and psychosocial rehabilitation; and implementation of a "community support" paradigm that viewed housing, employment, education, vocational rehabilitation, and support services as necessary for community integration, in addition to traditional mental health and substance abuse treatment.

This de facto mental health policy has been described as "sequential incrementalism" (129), referring to its gradual, piecemeal approach to change. Grob and Goldman's account (129) of policy formation during this period concluded that, by the year 2000, a new federalism had emerged that, paradoxically, increased the role of states in mental health policy formation while also dramatically increasing the federal government's share of the costs. Another outcome of this series of incremental changes, however, was increased complexity and fragmentation of the service system, a key challenge identified by the second presidential mental health commission.

The New Freedom Commission on Mental Health

Twenty-five years after the Carter presidential commission, George W. Bush established the President's New Freedom Commission on Mental Health in 2002. The Commission was charged with identifying policies that would maximize use of existing resources, improve coordination of treatments and services, and promote successful community integration for children and adults with serious mental illness. Early on, Commission members identified unmet needs for employment and income support as major policy issues requiring resolution, which was reflected as a major goal—goal 2—in the Commission's final report (2). Several of the report's more specific recommendations are germane to this area. The first is that "return-to-work should be consumer-driven" and the second calls for a dramatic increase in the quality and availability of evidence-based supported employment services.

The report also noted that "return to work should involve a multi-systemic approach" and that states should have "the flexibility to combine federal, state, and local resources in creative, innovative, and more efficient ways, overcoming the bureaucratic boundaries between health care, employment supports, housing and the criminal justice system." Finally, the report recommended that SSA evaluate the possibility of removing disincentives to employment in the SSI and SSDI programs.

What would a multisystemic approach to employment and income supports look like? It would encompass federal, state, and local systems responsible for employment, income support, supported employment, mental health, health care, housing, education, legal aid, criminal justice, asset accumulation, and other social services, as well as the business community and mental health advocacy communities. Elements of such a system might include

♦ Ongoing health care coverage for medical, mental health, and prescription drugs, regardless of the individual's labor force status

♦ Integrated and coordinated clinical services and vocational services shown to promote employment in this population

♦ Greater availability of secondary and postsecondary education to help individuals complete interrupted educational careers and obtain college degrees necessary for success in today's labor market

♦ Benefits planning and financial literacy education regarding the effects of earned income on SSI and SSDI cash payments, as well as development of life-long financial plans

♦ Asset development through matched savings accounts called Individual Development Accounts, authorized by the federal Assets for Independence Act (130), allowing low-income workers to accumulate savings for postsecondary education or capitalization of small businesses, thereby building financial security and enabling career development without reduction of SSI or SSDI cash benefits (131)

♦ Housing that is safe and affordable for individuals living on SSI or SSDI and that is not threatened by income increases resulting from labor force participation

♦ Legal aid to deal with labor force discrimination, ensure access to state and local vocational rehabilitation services, and pursue enforcement of the Americans With Disabilities Act

♦ Peer support and self-help to combat mental illness stigma and provide role models for maintaining hope and optimism in the face of daunting barriers

♦ Involvement of employers and the business community in education, advocacy, and workforce development efforts that meet the needs of job seekers and organizations employing them.

The New Freedom Commission report also noted that the extreme fragmentation of our country's mental health system requires that it be transformed. This policy of transformation "calls for profound change; an upheaval and reorganization of what we know, what we do, and how we go about doing it" (132). An extensive review of the literature on transformation noted that it is a complex, multidimensional process operating on many levels that requires visionary leadership, mobilization of scarce resources, persuasive communication, careful coordination of activities, and incorporation of ongoing feedback and readjustment of activities to reach particular goals (133). To accomplish such a challenging agenda, the translation of research into practice is essential. Knowledge translation addresses the vexing problem, in the fields of both physical and behavioral health, of underutilization of evidence-based practice in designing and operating service systems (134–136). Although similar to dissemination or diffusion, translation is distinguished by its emphasis on application of knowledge to systems rather than groups or organizations and by an interactive and engaged process between research and systems of care (137–139).

The aforementioned trends offer the possibility that evidence-based return-to-work services can be coupled with public policy reforms and increased mental health and disability activism to promote employment and economic security for people with psychiatric disabilities. Policy reforms might include changes in Medicaid funding that make supported employment a reimbursable service integral to mental health recovery, removal of work disincentives, labor market restructuring through tax breaks and incentives for workers and employers, and enhanced access to postsecondary education and vocational training, in addition to addressing the causes and consequences of labor force discrimination. Reform also requires the stimulation and nurturance of transformational leadership at all levels of public policy formation and implementation, aimed at the translation of research into practice across entire systems.

Given the inertia and resistance to change of large state and federal bureaucracies, we might ask who will take the lead in either large-scale transformation efforts or gradual reforms? July 2005 saw the release of an action agenda created by seven cabinet-level departments of the federal government—Health and Human Services, Education, Housing and Urban Development, Justice, Labor, Veterans Affairs, and SSA. The agenda is entitled *Transforming Mental Health Care in America* (140). The report endorses the concept of transformation and presents 70 specific steps that will

be taken by federal agencies. Many of the steps focus on enhancing employment opportunities and access to employment services. Around the same time, the Campaign for Mental Health Reform, a collaboration of 16 national mental health advocacy organizations, released its own report, *Emergency Response: A Roadmap for Federal Action on America's Mental Health Crisis*, also endorsing the need for transformation and calling for the improvement of employment outcomes and elimination of disincentives for economic self-sufficiency (141).

Many of the changes being discussed and debated have trade-offs that need to be considered in policy decision making. For example, instituting a $1 for $2 income disregard for SSDI beneficiaries, so that they could retain half of their employment earnings as well as disability cash benefits and entitlements, may not encourage individuals to earn more and leave the rolls but instead may make it more comfortable to remain on the rolls indefinitely (142). Increasing the generosity of SSI and SSDI benefits may also result in "induced entry," which occurs when individuals enter the rolls who would not otherwise have done so (143). Scholars attempting to estimate the effects of induced entry resulting from implementing a $1 for $2 disregard in the SSDI program have predicted increases in the rolls, ranging from a low of 75,000 to a high of 400,000 new beneficiaries over a ten-year period, which would cost between $410 million and $5.1 billion (143–145). Others argue that such a policy change might reasonably be expected to result in budget neutrality or even savings to SSA in returned cash benefits or "induced exit" resulting from larger numbers of individuals leaving the rolls (146). Still others caution against the use of work incentive programs for individuals with disabilities, noting that there is little convincing evidence of their effectiveness in studies of other populations, such as welfare recipients (147).

As these issues are discussed and debated, advocacy organizations in-

cluding those for people in recovery from mental illness, their families, disability advocates, and others can contribute a "value critical" policy analysis to this change process, which is based on social justice and economic fairness through the use of taxpayer dollars (148,149).

As is evident from the foregoing and also noted in the New Freedom Commission's report, researchers must assume responsibility for creating policy-relevant knowledge by carefully matching policy questions with appropriate research designs (81,115,150). First and foremost, a better understanding of labor force participation by people with psychiatric disabilities is needed on both regional and national levels, using standard labor force indicators collected from representative samples (111,150). Second, meaningful data must be gathered and analyzed regarding access to, use of, and results of employment services across multiple state agencies by developing integrated reporting and management information systems along with classification of services and outcomes that is applicable across delivery systems (42). Third, analysis of administrative data and follow-up research designs should be used to locate and interview individuals who seek but do not receive state and local employment services as well as those who are accepted as clients but who leave service systems before their rehabilitation plans are implemented (115).

Fourth, qualitative, ethnographic studies of experiences with discrimination in the job-seeking process and at the workplace are needed to gain a better understanding of how inequality persists in the face of legislation designed to combat it (123). Fifth, interviews with key informants within and outside large delivery systems can help us identify areas of inefficiency, inadequate resource allocation, and bureaucratic "irrationality" in organizational operation (115). Sixth, we must insist on the use and linkage of electronic records in state and federal systems, in a way that maintains client privacy and confidentiality, to address questions regarding cost-effectiveness and cost-benefit ratios of clinical and vocational rehabilitation services, disability income support, and Medicaid and Medicare coverage (99).

Conclusions

Regardless of whether the coming decades witness wide-scale policy transformation or piecemeal reform, change will depend on the political will of federal, state, and local governments as well as the actions of people with psychiatric disabilities and other advocates, given their already ongoing role in active transformation of the mental health system (151). Observers have noted that the public's interest in the welfare of this population waxes and wanes in cycles (84). Nevertheless, in difficult economic times such as these, efforts to enhance employment and economic self-sufficiency should be perceived as risks worth taking, given the potential for a more productive, more diverse, better prepared, and more highly motivated workforce. Great promise lies in the enhancement of our country's economy and its human capital by implementing responsive and responsible policies that address work and income support. These policies have the potential to benefit all U.S. citizens, not just those with psychiatric disabilities.

Acknowledgments

This article is based on a report prepared for the Subcommittee on Employment and Income Supports of the President's New Freedom Commission on Mental Health. The author is grateful to subcommittee members and Commission staff for their active engagement in discussing both research and policy issues described herein. Also acknowledged are the intellectual contributions of Jane K. Burke-Miller, M.S., Dennis D. Grey, B.A., Jessica A. Jonikas, M.A., David E. Marcotte, Ph.D., and Carol A. Petersen, M.Ed. Preparation of this article was funded, in part, by the National Institute on Disability and Rehabilitation Research of the U.S. Department of Education and the Center for Mental Health Services of the Substance Abuse and Mental Health Services Administration (cooperative agreement H133-B05-0003). The contents of this article do not represent the policy or position of any federal agency and no endorsement by the federal government should be inferred.

References

1. Cook JA: Employment and Income Supports: Issue Paper Prepared for the President's New Freedom Commission on Mental Health. Chicago, University of Illinois at Chicago, 2005. Available at www.cmhsrp.uic.edu/download/newfreedomcommreport.pdf

2. Achieving the Promise: Transforming Mental Health Care in America. Final Report. Pub no SMA-03-3832. Rockville, Md, Department of Health and Human Services, President's New Freedom Commission on Mental Health, 2003

3. Jans L, Stoddard S, Kraus L: Chartbook on Mental Health and Disability in the United States: An InfoUse Report. Washington, DC, US Department of Education, National Institute on Disability and Rehabilitation Research, 2004

4. The World Health Report 2004: Changing History. Geneva, World Health Organization, 2004

5. Kapteyn A, Smith JP, Van Soest A: Self-reported work disability in the US and the Netherlands. RAND Working Paper WR-206, Nov 2004. Available at www.rand.org/pubs/working_papers/2004/RAND_WR206.pdf

6. McAlpine DD, Warner L: Barriers to employment among persons with mental illness: a review of the literature. Working Paper, Institute for Health, Health Care Policy, and Aging Research, Rutgers University, 2001. Available at www.dri.uiuc.edu/research/p01-04c/final_technical_report_p01-04c

7. Gresenz CR, Sturm R: Mental health and employment transitions. Economics of Gender and Mental Illness 15:95–108, 2004

8. Kaye HS: Employment and Social Participation Among People With Mental Health Disabilities. Presented at the National Disability Statistics and Policy Forum, Washington, DC, Oct 28, 2002

9. Hauser PM: The measurement of labor utilization. Malayan Economic Review 19:1–17, 1974

10. Clogg CC: Measuring Underemployment: Demographic Indicators for the United States. New York, Academic Press, 1979

11. Jensen L, Slack T: Underemployment in America: measurement and evidence. American Journal of Community Psychology 13:21–31, 2003

12. Cook JA: The promise of vocational rehabilitation: results of the SAMHSA Employment Intervention Demonstration Program: 2002. Available at www.psych.uic.edu/eidp

13. Disability Planner: What We Mean by Disability. Washington DC, Social Security Administration. Available at www.ssa.gov/dibplan/dqualify4.htm

14. Monthly Statistical Snapshot, June 2006. Washington, DC, Social Security Administration, 2006. Available at www.ssa.gov/policy/docs/quickfacts/stat_snapshot/index.html

15. Mashaw JL, Reno VP: Balancing Security and Opportunity: The Challenge of Disability Income Policy: Final Report of the Disability Policy Panel. Washington, DC, National Academy of Social Insurance, 1996

16. Annual Statistical Supplement, 2003. Washington, DC, Social Security Administration, 2003

17. Berkowitz M: The Ticket to Work program: the complicated evolution of a simple idea, in Vocational Rehabilitation: Will Provider Incentives Work for Ticket to Work. Edited by Rupp K, Bell SH. Washington, DC, Urban Institute, 2003

18. Newcomb C, Payne S, Waid MD: What do we know about disability beneficiaries' work and use of work incentives prior to Ticket? in Vocational Rehabilitation: Will Provider Incentives Work for Ticket to Work. Edited by Rupp K, Bell SH. Washington, DC, Urban Institute, 2003

19. Muller LS, Scott CG, Bye BV: Labor-force participation and earnings of SSI disability recipients: a pooled cross-sectional time series approach to the behavior of individuals. Social Security Bulletin 59(1):22–42, 1996

20. Hennessey JC, Dykacz JM: Projected outcomes and length of time in disability insurance program. Social Security Bulletin 52(9):2–41, 1989

21. Campbell J, Schreiber R, Temkin T: The Well-Being Project: Mental Health Clients Speak for Themselves. Sacramento, California Department of Mental Health, Office of Prevention, 1989

22. Rogers A, Walsh ES, Masotta D, et al: Massachusetts Survey of Client Preferences for Community Support Services. Final Report. Boston, Boston University, Center for Psychiatric Rehabilitation, 1991

23. Uttaro T, Mechanic D: The NAMI consumer survey analysis of unmet needs. Hospital and Community Psychiatry 45:372–374, 1994

24. Van Dongen CJ: Quality of life and self-esteem in working and nonworking persons with mental illness. Community Mental Health Journal 32:535–548, 1996

25. Kaye HS: Disability Watch: Vol 2. Oakland, Calif, Disability Rights Advocates, 2001

26. Kessler RC, Berglund P, Demler O, et al: Lifetime prevalence and age-of-onset distributions of DSM-IV disorders in the National Comorbidity Survey Replication. Archives of General Psychiatry 62:593–768, 2005

27. Hoges K, Xue Y, Wotring J: Use of the CAFAS to evaluate outcome for youths with severe emotional disturbance served by public mental health. Journal of Child and Family Studies 13:325–339, 2004

28. Wagner MM, Blackorby J: Transition from high school to work or college: how special education students fare. Future of Children 6(1):103–120, 1996

29. Wagner M: Outcomes for youths with serious emotional disturbance in secondary

school and early adulthood. Future of Children 5(2):90–112, 1995

30. Mechanic D, Bilder S, McAlpine DD: Employing persons with serious mental illness. Health Affairs 21(5):242–253, 2002

31. Occupational Outlook Handbook, 2004–05 Edition. Washington DC, US Department of Labor, Bureau of Labor Statistics, 2004

32. Kaye HS: Improved Employment Opportunities for People With Disabilities. Disability Statistics Report no 17. Washington DC, US Department of Education, National Institute on Disability and Rehabilitation Research, 2002

33. Kessler RC, Frank RG: The impact of psychiatric disorders on work loss days. Psychological Medicine 27:861–873, 1997

34. Stewart WF, Ricci JA, Chee E, et al: Cost of lost productive time among US workers with depression. JAMA 289:3135–3144, 2003

35. Wang PS, Beck AL, Berglund P, et al: Effects of major depression on moment-in-time work performance. American Journal of Psychiatry 161(10):1885–1891, 2004

36. Kessler RC, Akiskal HS, Ames M, et al: The prevalence and effects of mood disorders on work performance in a nationally representative sample of US workers. American Journal of Psychiatry 163:1561–1568, 2006

37. Yelin E: The impact of labor market trends on the employment of persons with disabilities. American Rehabilitation 26:21–33, 2001

38. Yelin EH, Katz PP: Labor force trends of persons with and without disabilities. Monthly Labor Review 117:36–42, 1994

39. Yelin EH, Cisternas MG: Employment patterns among persons with and without mental conditions, in Mental Disorder, Work Disability, and the Law. Edited by Bonnie RJ, Monahan J. Chicago, University of Chicago Press, 1997

40. Cook JA, Grey DD, Burke-Miller JK, et al: Effects of unemployment rate on vocational outcomes in a randomized trial of supported employment for individuals with severe mental illness. Journal of Vocational Rehabilitation 25(2):1–10, 2006

41. Lehman AF, Steinwachs DM, Dixon LB, et al: Translating research into practice: the Schizophrenia Patient Outcomes Research Team (PORT) treatment recommendations. Schizophrenia Bulletin 24:1–10, 1998

42. Pandiani JA, Banks SM, Simon MM: Employment services and employment outcomes for adults with serious mental illness. Research in Community and Mental Health 13:83–105, 2004

43. Noble JH: Policy reform dilemmas in promoting employment of persons with severe mental illness. Psychiatric Services 49:778–781, 1998

44. State Mental Health Agency Profiling System, 2004. Alexandria, Va, National Association of State Mental Health Program Directors Research Institute, 2004. Available at www.nri-inc.org/profiles

45. Kaye HS: Vocational rehabilitation in the United States. Disability Statistics Abstract 20:1–4, 1998

46. Frequently Asked Questions (FAQs) About RSA. Washington, DC, US Department of Education, Office of Special Education and Rehabilitative Services. Available at www.ed.gov/about/offices/list/osers/rsa/faq.html#vrp

47. Andrews H, Barker J, Pittman J, et al: National trends in vocational rehabilitation: a comparison of individuals with physical disabilities and individuals with psychiatric disabilities. Journal of Rehabilitation 51:7–16, 1992

48. Hayward B, Schmidt-Davis H: The Context of VR Services: Third Final Report, Office of Special Education and Rehabilitative Services. Research Triangle Park, NC, Research Triangle Institute, 2005

49. Schmidt-Davis H, Kay H, Hayward BJ: Basic skills and labor market success: findings from the VR Longitudinal Study. American Rehabilitation 25(3):11–18, 1999

50. Robins LN, Regier DA (eds): Psychiatric Disorders in America: the Epidemiologic Catchment Area Study. New York, Free Press, 1990

51. Lehman AF, Steinwachs DM: Patterns of usual care for schizophrenia: initial results from the Schizophrenia Patient Outcomes Research Team client survey. Schizophrenia Bulletin 24:11–19, 1998

52. Wang PS, Berglund PA, Kessler RC: Recent care of common mental disorders in the US: prevalence and conformance with evidence-based recommendation. Journal of General Internal Medicine 15:284–292, 2000

53. Wang PS, Demler O, Kessler RC: Adequacy of treatment for serious mental illness in the United States. American Journal of Public Health 92:92–98, 2002

54. Bond GR: Supported employment: evidence for an evidence-based practice. Psychiatric Rehabilitation Journal 27:377–383, 2003

55. Drake RE, Becker DR, Bond GR, et al: A process analysis of integrated and non-integrated approaches to supported employment. Journal of Vocational Rehabilitation 18:51–58, 2003

56. Cook JC, Lehman AF, Drake R, et al: Integration of psychiatric and vocational services: a multisite randomized, controlled trial of supported employment. American Journal of Psychiatry 162:1948–1956, 2005

57. Stefan S: Unequal Rights: Discrimination Against People With Mental Disabilities and the Americans With Disabilities Act. Washington, DC, American Psychological Association, 2001

58. Cook JA, Razzano L, Straiton DM, et al: Cultivation and maintenance of relationships with employers of persons with severe mental illness. Psychosocial Rehabilitation Journal 17:103–116, 1994

59. Diksa E, Rogers ES: Employer concerns about hiring persons with psychiatric dis-

ability: results of the Employer Attitude Questionnaire. Rehabilitation Counseling Bulletin 40:31–44, 1996

60. Manning C, White PD: Attitudes of employers to the mentally ill. Psychiatric Bulletin 19:541–543 1995

61. Allbright AL: 2004 employment decisions under the ADA Title I: survey update. Mental and Physical Disability Law Reporter 29:513–516, 2005

62. Wahl O: Mental health consumers' experience of stigma. Schizophrenia Bulletin 25:467–478, 1999

63. Wahl O: Telling Is Risky Business: Mental Health Consumers Confront Stigma. New Brunswick, Rutgers University Press 1999

64. Baldwin ML, Johnson WG: Dispelling the myths about work disability, in New Approaches to Disability in the Workplace. Edited by Thomason T, Burton JF, Hyatt DE. Madison, Wis, Industrial Relations Research Association, 1998

65. Americans with Disabilities Act of 1990, Public Law No 101-36

66. Sutton v United Air Lines, 000 US 97-1943 (1999)

67. Murphy v United Parcel Service, 000 US 97-1992 (1999)

68. Toyota Motor Manufacturing, Kentucky, Inc v Williams, 000 US 00-1089 (2002)

69. Paetzold RL: Mental illness and reasonable accommodations at work: definition of a mental disability under the ADA. Psychiatric Services 56:1188–1190, 2005

70. Mathis JM, Giliberti M: Limitation on Major Life Activities Caused by Psychiatric Disabilities: Memorandum. Washington, DC, Bazelon Center for Mental Health Law, August, 1999

71. Moss K, Ullman M, Starrett BE, et al: Outcomes of employment discrimination charges filed under the Americans With Disabilities Act. Psychiatric Services 50:1028–1035, 1999

72. Ullman MD, Johnsen MC, Moss K, et al: The EEOC charge priority policy and claimants with psychiatric disabilities. Psychiatric Services 52:644–649, 2001

73. Schulze B, Angermeyer MC: Subjective experiences of stigma: a focus group of schizophrenia patients, their relatives and mental health professionals. Social Science and Medicine 56:299–312, 2003

74. Cohen CI: Poverty and the course of schizophrenia: implications for research and policy. Hospital and Community Psychiatry 44:951–959, 1993

75. Ware NC, Goldfinger SM: Poverty and rehabilitation in severe psychiatric disorders. Psychiatric Rehabilitation Journal 21:3–9, 1997

76. Magg E: A Guide to Disability Statistics From the National Health Interview Survey: Disability Supplement. Washington DC, Urban Institute, 2006

77. McNeil J: Employment, Earnings, and Disability (1991/92, 1993/4, 1994/5 and 1997 Data From the Survey of Income and Program Participation). Presented at the annual conference of the Western Economic Association International, Vancouver, Canada, 2000. Available at www.vocecon.com/technical/ftp/bibliography/mcnempl.pdf

78. Poverty Thresholds in 1997, by Size of

Family and Number of Related Children Under 18 Year. Washington DC, US Census Bureau. Available at www.census. gov/hhes/www/poverty/threshld/thresh97.html

79. Stapleton DC, O'Day B, Livermore GA, et al: Dismantling the poverty trap: disability policy for the 21st century. Milbank Quarterly, in press

80. O'Hara A, Cooper E, Buttrick J: Priced out in 2004: the escalating housing crisis affecting people with disabilities. Boston, Technical Assistance Collaborative, 2005. Available at www.c-c-d.org/od-oct05.htm

81. Draine J, Salzer MS, Culhane DP, et al: Role of social disadvantage in crime, joblessness, and homelessness among persons with serious mental illness. Psychiatric Services 53:565–573, 2002

82. Ho B, Andreasen N, Flaum M: Dependence on public financial support early in the course of schizophrenia. Psychiatric Services 48:948–950, 1997

83. Sing M, Hill SC: The costs of parity mandates for mental health and substance abuse insurance benefits. Psychiatric Services 52:437–440, 2001

84. Mechanic D: Policy challenges in improving mental health services: some lessons from the past. Psychiatric Services 54:1227–1232, 2003

85. Razzano L, Cook JA, Burke-Miller J, et al: Clinical factors associated with employment among people with severe mental illness: findings from the Employment Intervention Demonstration Program. Journal of Nervous and Mental Disease 193:705–713, 2005

86. Cook JA, Pickett-Schenk SA, Grey DD, et al: Vocational outcomes among formerly homeless persons with severe mental illness in the ACCESS program. Psychiatric Services 52:1075–1087, 2001

87. Schecter ES: Work while receiving disability insurance benefits: additional findings from the New Beneficiary Follow-up Survey. Social Security Bulletin 60(1):3–17, 1997

88. Hennessey JC: Job patterns of disabled beneficiaries. Social Security Bulletin 59 (4):3–11, 1996

89. Burkhauser RV, Butler JS, Kim YW: The importance of employer accommodations for the job duration of workers with disabilities: a hazard model approach. Labour Economics 3:109–130, 1995

90. Gunderson M, Hyatt D: Do injured workers pay for reasonable accommodation? Industrial and Labor Relations Review 50:92–104, 1996

91. Burkhauser RV, Wittenburg D: How current disability transfer policies discourage work: analysis from the 1990 SIPP. Journal of Vocational Rehabilitation 7:9–27, 1996

92. White JS, Black WE, Ireys HT: Explaining Enrollment Trends and Participant Characteristics of the Medicaid Buy-In Program, 2002–2003. Princeton, NJ, Mathematica Policy Research Inc, 2005

93. Polak P, Warner R: The economic life of se-

riously mentally ill people in the community. Psychiatric Services 47:270–274, 1996

94. MacDonald-Wilson KL, Rogers ES, et al: A study of the Social Security work incentives and their relation to perceived barriers to work among persons with psychiatric disability. Rehabilitation Psychology 48:301– 309, 2003

95. Cook JA, Leff S, Blyler C, et al: Results of a multi-site randomized clinical trial of supported employment interventions for individuals with severe mental illness. Archives of General Psychiatry 62:505–512, 2005

96. Cook JA: One-year follow-up of Illinois state vocational rehabilitation clients with psychiatric disabilities following successful closure into community employment. Journal of Vocational Rehabilitation 18:25–32, 2003

97. Rosenheck R, Frisman L, Sindelar J: Disability compensation and work among veterans with psychiatric and nonpsychiatric impairments. Psychiatric Services 46:359–365, 1995

98. Drew D, Drebing CE, Van Omer A: Effects of disability compensation on participation in and outcomes of vocational rehabilitation. Psychiatric Services 52:1479–1484, 2001

99. Cook JA, Burke J: Public policy and employment of people with disabilities: exploring new paradigms. Behavioral Science and the Law 20:541–557, 2002

100. Employment Opportunities for Disabled Americans Act: Public Law no 99-643, 1986

101. Balanced Budget Act of 1997: Public Law 105-33, 1997

102. Ticket to Work and Work Incentives Improvement Act (TWWIIA): Public Law 106-170, 1999

103. Stapleton DC, Livermore GA: A conceptual model and evaluation strategy for the empirical study of the adequacy of incentives in the Ticket to Work program, in Paying for Results in Vocational Rehabilitation: Will Provider Incentives Work for Ticket to Work? Edited by Rupp K, Bell SH. Washington, DC, Urban Institute, 2003

104. Cook JA, Leff HS, Blyler CR, et al: Estimated payments to service providers for persons with mental illness in the Ticket to Work program. Psychiatric Services 57:465–471, 2006

105. Huynh M, O'Leary P: Issues affecting alternatives to the Ticket to Work incentive structure, in Paying for Results in Vocational Rehabilitation: Will Provider Incentives Work for Ticket to Work? Edited by Rupp K, Bell SH. Washington, DC, Urban Institute, 2003

106. Salkever DL: Tickets without takers? Potential economic barriers to the supply of rehabilitation services to beneficiaries with mental disorders, in Paying for Results in Vocational Rehabilitation: Will Provider Incentives Work for Ticket to

Work? Edited by Rupp K, Bell S. Washington, DC, Urban Institute, 2003

107. Wehman P, Revell G: Lessons learned from the provision and funding of employment for the MR/DD population: implications for assessing the adequacy of the SSA Ticket to Work, in Paying for Results in Vocational Rehabilitation: Will Provider Incentives Work for Ticket to Work? Edited by Rupp K, Bell S. Washington, DC, Urban Institute, 2003

108. Thornton C, Fraker T, Livermore G, et al: Evaluation of the Ticket to Work Program: Implementation Experience During the Second Two Years of Operations (2003–2004). Washington, DC, Mathematica Policy Research Inc. and Cornell Institute for Policy Research, 2006. Available at www.human.cornell.edu/che/CUIPR/upload/ThorntonEvalTTW.pdf

109. Lehman AF: Vocational rehabilitation in schizophrenia. Schizophrenia Bulletin 21:645–656, 1995

110. Bond GR, Becker DR, Drake RE: Implementing supported employment as an evidenced-based practice. Psychiatric Services 52:313–322, 2001

111. Cook JA, Razzano L. Vocational rehabilitation for persons with schizophrenia: recent research and implications for practice. Schizophrenia Bulletin 26:87–103, 2000

112. Crowther RE, Marshall M, Bond GR, et al: Helping people with severe mental illness to obtain work: a systematic review. British Medical Journal 322:204–208, 2001

113. Twamley EW, Jeste DV, Lehman AF: Vocational rehabilitation in schizophrenia and other psychotic disorders: a literature review and meta-analysis of randomized controlled trials. Journal of Nervous Mental Disease 191:515–523, 2003

114. Wewiorski NJ, Fabian ES: Association between demographic and diagnostic factors and employment outcomes for people with psychiatric disabilities: a synthesis of recent research. Mental Health Services Research 6(1):9–21, 2004

115. Cook JA: Understanding the failure of vocational rehabilitation: what do we need to know and how can we learn it? Journal of Disability Policy Studies 10(1):127–132, 1999

116. Burt MR, Aron LY: Promoting Work Among SSI/DI Beneficiaries With Serious Mental Illness. Washington, DC, Urban Institute, 2003

117. Altman DE: Two views of a changing health care system, in Applications of Social Science to Clinical Medicine and Health Policy. Edited by Mechanic D, Aiken LH. New Brunswick, NJ, Rutgers University Press, 1987

118. Aaron HJ: Serious and Unstable Condition: Financing America's Health Care. Washington, DC, Brookings Institution, 1991

119. Budetti PP: Health insurance for children: a model for incremental health reform.

New England Journal of Medicine 338: 541–542, 1998

120. Gross BH, Hahn H: Developing issues in the classification of mental and physical disability. Journal of Disability Policy Studies 15(3):130–134, 2004

121. Seelman KD: Long Range Plan, 1999–2003. Washington, DC, US Department of Education, Office of Special Education and Rehabilitative Services, National Institute on Disability and Rehabilitation Research, 1999

122. DeJong G, O'Day B: Materials prepared for the NIDRR Long Range Plan, 1999–2003. Washington, DC, US Department of Education, Office of Special Education and Rehabilitative Services, National Institute on Disability and Rehabilitation Research, 1991

123. Blanck PD, Schartz HA: Towards Researching a National Employment Policy for Persons With Disabilities. 2001 Switzer Monograph. Mary E Switzer Memorial Seminar: Emerging Workforce Issues: WIA, Ticket to Work, and Partnerships. Washington DC, US Department of Education, 2000

124. Switzer JV: Disabled Rights: American Disability Policy and the Fight for Equality. Washington, DC, Georgetown University Press, 2002

125. Metts RL: Disability Issues, Trends and Recommendations for the World Bank. SP Discussion Paper no 0007. Washington, DC, World Bank, Feb 2000 Available at www-wds.worldbank.org

126. Goldman HH: Making progress in mental health policy in conservative times: one step at a time. Schizophrenia Bulletin 32: 424–427, 2006

127. Koyanagi C, Goldman HH: The quiet success of the National Plan for the Chronically Mentally Ill. Hospital and Community Psychiatry 42:899–905, 1991

128. Toward a National Plan for the Chronically Mentally Ill. Washington, DC, Department of Health and Human Services, US Public Health Service, Steering Committee on the Chronically Mentally Ill, 1980

129. Grob GN, Goldman HH: The Dilemma of Federal Mental Health Policy: Radical Reform or Incremental Change? New Brunswick, NJ, Rutgers University Press, 2006

130. Assets for Independence Act. Public Law 105-285, Title IV, Oct 27, 1998, 112 Statute 2759 (42 USC 604 note)

131. Cook JA: Promoting Self-Determination for Individuals With Psychiatric Disabilities Through Self-Directed Services: A Look at Federal, State and Public Systems as Sources of Cash-Outs and Other Fiscal Expansion Opportunities. Chicago, University of Illinois at Chicago, 2004. Available at www.psych.uic.edu/uicnrtc/sd-samhsaconfsentver3.pdf

132. Power AK: Achieving the promise through workforce transformation: a view from the Center for Mental Health Services. Administration and Policy in Mental Health 32:489–495, 2005

133. Mazade NA: Concepts of Transformation. Alexandria, Va, National Association of State Mental Health Program Directors Research Institute, Jan 2005

134. Glasgow RE, Lichtenstein E, Marcus AC: Why don't we see more translation of health promotion research to practice? Rethinking the efficacy-to-effectiveness transition. American Journal of Public Health 93:1261–1267, 2003

135. Drake RE, Goldman HH, Leff HS, et al: Implementing evidence-based practices in routine mental health service settings. Psychiatric Services 52:179–182, 2001

136. Davis D, Evans M, Jadad A, et al: The case for knowledge translation: shortening the journey from evidence to effect. British Medical Journal 327:33–35, 2003

137. Jacobson N, Butterill D, Goering P: Development of a framework for knowledge translation: understanding user context. Journal of Health Services Research and Policy 8:94–99 2003

138. Lavis JN, Robertson D, Woodside JM, et al: How can research organizations more effectively transfer research knowledge to decision makers? Milbank Quarterly 81:221–248, 2003

139. What Is Knowledge Translation? Focus: Technical Brief No 10. Austin, Tex, National Center for the Dissemination of Disability Research. Available at www.ncddr.org/kt/ktplan.html

140. Transforming Mental Health Care in America: The Federal Action Agenda: First Steps. Rockville, Md, Substance Abuse and Mental Health Services Administration, Jul 2005. Available at www.samhsa.gov/federalactionagenda/nfc_toc.aspx

141. Emergency Response: A Roadmap for Federal Action on America's Mental Health Crisis. Alexandria, Va, Campaign for Mental Health Care Reform, 2005 Available at www.mhreform.org/emergency/index.htm

142. Fagnoni CM: Social Security Disability: Multiple Factors Affect Return to Work. Testimony before the Subcommittee on Social Security, Committee on Ways and Means, House of Representatives, March 11, 1999

143. Time-Limiting Federal Disability Benefits. Memorandum. Washington, DC, Congressional Budget Office, 1997

144. Tuma N: Approaches to evaluating induced entry into a new SSDI program with a $1 reduction in benefits for each $2 in earnings. Palo Alto, Stanford University, Department of Sociology, 2001

145. Benéitez-Silva H, Buchinsky M, Rust J: Induced entry effects of a $1 for $2 offset in SSDI benefits. Stony Brook, NY, State University of New York, Stony Brook, Apr 2006. Available at http://econ.ucsd.edu/seminars/0506seminars/Buchinsky_SP06.pdf

146. Ruth D, Hill M, Carlson B, et al: Costs and Savings to Taxpayers for a $1/$2 Disability Insurance Offset and a Sliding-Scale Medicare Buy-In. Richmond, Virginia Commonwealth University, 1997

147. Hynes HW, Moffitt R: The effectiveness of financial work incentives in Social Security Disability Insurance and Supplemental Security Income: lessons from other transfer programs, in Disability, Work and Cash Benefits. Edited by Mashaw J. Kalamazoo, Mich, Upjohn Institute for Employment Research, 1996

148. Rein M: Value-critical policy analysis, in Ethics, the Social Sciences and Policy Analysis. Edited by Callahan D, Jennings B. New York, Plenum, 1983

149. Lynn LE: A place at the table: policy analysis, its postpositive critics, and the future of practice. Journal of Policy Analysis and Management 18:411–425, 1999

150. Silverstein R, Julnes G, Nolan R: What policymakers need and must demand from research regarding the employment rate of persons with disabilities. Behavioral Sciences and the Law 23:399–448 2005

151. Cook JA, Jonikas JA: Self-determination among mental health consumers/survivors: using lessons from the past to guide the future. Journal of Disability Policy Studies 13:87–95, 2002

Housing for People With Mental Illness: Update of a Report to the President's New Freedom Commission

Ann O'Hara

A significant barrier to participation in community life for people with serious mental illness is the lack of decent, safe, affordable, and integrated housing of their choice linked with supportive services. The nation's affordable housing and mental health systems have historically failed to address consumers' housing needs and choices. The lack of housing has resulted in disproportionately high rates of homelessness and chronic homelessness. The author summarizes these issues, which were examined by the Subcommittee on Housing and Homelessness of the President's New Freedom Commission, and discusses the subcommittee's recommendations to end chronic homelessness among people with mental illness, expand access to affordable housing resources for consumers, and promote evidence-based practices. There has been uneven progress nationwide in ameliorating the widespread and multidimensional housing and homelessness problems that were exposed in the subcommittee's paper. The permanent supportive housing model, including "housing first" approaches, has proven effective in preventing and ending homelessness among consumers, but efforts to expand the supply are hampered by significant reductions in federal funds for housing. State and local mental health systems are also struggling to reconfigure service system resources to better address housing and homelessness issues. Apparent reductions in chronic homelessness will be short-lived unless affordable housing policies and mental health services are reoriented to both prevent and end homelessness for people with mental illness. *Psychiatric Services* 58:907–913, 2007

In 2004 a seminal background paper was published by a team of national experts in the housing and mental health field who served together on the Subcommittee on Housing and Homelessness of the President's New Freedom Commission on Mental Health (1). The Commission's intent was to enable persons with serious mental illness to live, work, learn, and participate fully in the community. The subcommittee's paper was an analysis of the interplay of unmet housing needs with these goals and an agenda for how to initiate change in this arena.

The Commission's final report, *Achieving the Promise: Transforming Mental Health Care in America* (2), identified adequate and affordable housing in the community as essential for consumers to participate fully in their communities. Recognizing that traditional reform measures were not enough, the Commission recommended fundamentally transforming how mental health care is delivered in America, including access to integrated community-based permanent housing. Since the report's publication, there has been uneven progress nationwide in ameliorating the widespread and multidimensional housing and homeless problems that were exposed in the subcommittee's paper.

This article serves as an update to the subcommittee's paper three years after it was issued. It recasts, in an abbreviated format, the paper's problem issues and policy options and reports on progress related to its key recommendations. This article begins with a summary of the affordable housing and homelessness issues presented in the first paper, all of which continue to interfere with the stability and integration of persons with mental illness into our wider society. It restates policy options and program innovations that were recommended to federal, state, and local governments by the subcommittee and provides an update on the status of key federal housing programs. The achievements of several state and local mental health systems that are focused on affordable housing as a core component of mental health transformation activities are also described.

Defining the problem

Housing is more than a basic need. The lack of decent, safe, affordable, and integrated housing is a significant barrier to participation in community life for people with serious mental illnesses (3). Today, many such individuals do not have decent, safe, and affordable permanent housing that meets their preferences and needs. Historically, housing for people with mental illnesses has been in segregated, congregate residential

Ms. O'Hara is associate director, Technical Assistance Collaborative, Inc., 535 Boylston St., Suite 1301, Boston, MA 02116 (e-mail: aohara@tacinc.org). Originally published in the July 2007 issue of Psychiatric Services.

treatment settings, such as group homes (4). Yet studies have shown that people with mental illnesses prefer to live in less restrictive, independent housing that is integrated in the community (5–7). Consumer preference or choice has also been found to be an important predictor of housing success (8,9). Success in housing also requires access to services and supports that reinforce consumers' dignity, independence, and ability to live in the community.

The lack of affordable housing and accompanying support services often causes people with serious mental illnesses to cycle between jails, institutions, shelters, and the streets; to remain unnecessarily in institutions; or to live in large, segregated facilities or substandard housing (10). Research demonstrates that people with serious mental illnesses also make up a large percentage of those who are repeatedly homeless or who are homeless for long periods of time (11–13). Many more face the constant stress of losing their housing or living in dangerous and unsafe housing conditions. People with co-occurring mental illnesses and substance use disorders are in particular need. They make up a significant percentage of people who are homeless and chronically homeless (11). Such individuals are also likely to have acute and chronic physical health problems; exacerbated, ongoing psychiatric symptoms; excessive alcohol and drug use; and a higher likelihood of victimization and incarceration (14).

Analysis of problem issues
Understanding and addressing the housing and homelessness issues that confront people with serious mental illnesses requires analyzing the following key issues.

Housing affordability gap
People with serious mental illnesses often have pronounced difficulties in affording housing (2). They share the same housing affordability problems experienced by all very-low-income Americans who, according to federal guidelines, should pay no more than 30% of income for housing. Households that include per-

sons with disabilities are more likely to have housing problems because they are twice as likely to have incomes below federal poverty guidelines (15). In 2004 five million households in the bottom income quartile were headed by a nonelderly disabled person, and in 2.6 million of these households housing cost burdens were severe or residents lived in crowded conditions (16).

The widening gap between rents and Supplemental Security Income (SSI) payments means that the lowest-income people with serious mental illness are completely priced out of the rental housing market. In 2006, on the basis of data from the U.S. Department of Housing and Urban Development (HUD) regarding the national average for rental units, a person with a mental illness relying on SSI would have needed to pay 113% of his or her monthly income to rent a modest one-bedroom apartment (17). The federal government deems that a very-low-income household paying more than 50% of monthly income for housing is "seriously rent burdened" and has "worst case" housing needs (10). In recent years, the relative value of SSI payments has continued to decline and in 2006 was equivalent to only 18.2% of the median national income (17). An overall decline in the number of affordable housing units being produced has further exacerbated these severe housing affordability problems (18).

Mental illness and homelessness
In addition to poverty and the lack of affordable housing options for people with extremely low incomes, individual risk factors, such as disabling health and behavioral health issues increase a person's vulnerability to homelessness. People with serious mental illnesses are particularly vulnerable and are overrepresented among the homeless population (19). According to a study by the Urban Institute, as many as 46% of people who are homeless have a mental illness (11). Furthermore, this same research indicates that 31% of individuals using homeless services report a combination of mental health and substance use problems within the previous year (11). The symptoms of

serious mental illness and co-occurring substance use may contribute to an individual's risk of becoming homeless, just as they may be caused or worsened by homelessness. The fragmentation of mental health systems, a lack of resources, and the continuation of traditional models of service delivery have also contributed to the vulnerability of this population and the volume of acute cases that lead to homelessness (4).

As a result, people with serious mental illnesses often have greater difficulty exiting homelessness on their own and are more vulnerable to experiencing chronic homelessness, defined as being continuously homeless for a year or more or having had at least four episodes of homelessness in the past three years (20). Experts believe that between 150,000 and 200,000 people with disabling conditions such as mental illness are chronically homeless (21).

Inadequate response from the affordable housing system
The State of the Nation's Housing 2006, published by the Joint Center for Housing Studies of Harvard University (16), noted the housing challenges faced by people with extremely low incomes who have disabilities and the lack of response from the federal government. Federal "elderly only" housing policies enacted in the 1990s prevent people with mental illness and people with other disabilities under age 62 from accessing many federally subsidized rental properties (22). Programs that can help people with mental illness obtain affordable housing, including the Section 8 Housing Choice Voucher program and the Section 811 Supportive Housing for Persons With Disabilities program, have experienced a decline in federal support in recent years (16,23,24). With the notable exception of funding targeted specifically to people who are chronically homeless, recent federal housing policy has focused on homeownership opportunities for households above 30% of median income rather than on increasing the availability of affordable rental housing for the lowest-income Americans (25).

Where housing opportunities exist, major barriers prevent people with serious mental illnesses from obtaining more access to housing intended to benefit people with the lowest incomes. For one, affordable housing programs are extremely complex, highly competitive, and difficult to access. In addition, during the 1990s the federal government devolved decision making for most housing programs to state and local housing officials, state housing finance agencies, and public housing agencies, which often do not understand or prioritize the needs of people with mental illnesses (26).

Inadequate response from the mental health system

Affordable housing and the community support services that consumers need to access and retain housing are often overlooked priorities for state and local mental health systems. This is evidenced by most systems' conventional categorical funding streams, bureaucratic program requirements, administrative approaches to resource allocation and management, and staff skills that are not geared toward rigorously supporting consumers in normal housing (27). Underlying this problem is the perception shared by many mental health systems that housing and housing stability are not their responsibility. Also at work is a preference of mainstream payers, who cover mental health services, for traditional office-based care rather than "in vivo" models of service. Such traditional approaches do not provide the flexibility and mobility necessary to support and sustain consumers in community-based permanent housing.

In addition, traditional case managers must deal with large caseloads, leaving them insufficient time to provide the more intensive support typically needed by persons with serious mental illnesses, such as found in the assertive community treatment approach (28). In general, mental health systems have been unresponsive to the needs of their constituents who are homeless (29). Categorical or "silo" funding streams, which are widespread in mental health systems, also make it difficult to serve the multiple needs of people who are homeless and have serious mental illnesses. These difficulties are amplified for persons with mental illness who are chronically homeless and must navigate a fragmented service system with gaps in the social services safety net (20).

Consumer choice and housing approaches

In addition to affordability, effective housing solutions for persons with mental illness should also reflect the housing choices of consumers themselves. Consistently, research demonstrates that this preference is for an innovative and independent form of housing known as supported housing, or more recently as permanent supportive housing (5,22). The term supported housing (30) was initially used to describe an alternative to residential treatment models that required consumers to progress from more to less restrictive living situations as they were deemed housing "ready." Permanent supportive housing, the term now more commonly used, offers affordable rental housing chosen by the consumer linked with voluntary community-based supports and specifically does not make housing conditional on participation in a supportive services program (22,31). Extensive consumer preference studies show a desire to live in one's own house or apartment, a disregard for segregated settings, and greater housing and neighborhood satisfaction with the permanent supportive housing model (5,32).

Permanent supportive housing is more effective at engaging and housing hard-to-serve people with mental illness than are residential treatment programs that use housing as leverage for treatment compliance (33). Permanent supportive housing has also been shown to be a cost-effective solution to homelessness (12). Research on a specific type of permanent supportive housing called "housing first" provides strong evidence for the impact of consumer choice on positive outcomes for people with mental illnesses. Clients of Pathways to Housing, a choice-based housing first program in New York City for homeless people with co-occurring serious mental illness and substance use disorders, demonstrated an 88% retention rate in housing over five years compared with 40% for those housed in residential treatment settings (14). Further, individuals in the Pathways program, which does not require mental health treatment or sobriety, reported greater perceived choice and achieved stable housing without compromising mental health or substance abuse symptoms (9,34). Research by Pathways staff has also demonstrated the effectiveness of engaging consumers in substance abuse treatment by using a harm-reduction approach that tailors intervention to an individual's stage of recovery (9). Converting traditional congregate residential facilities and office-based service approaches to the permanent supportive housing model preferred by consumers and making low-demand programs available for those who need them is central to the challenge of transforming the mental health system nationwide.

Progress in housing and system transformation strategies

The Housing and Homelessness Subcommittee made a number of recommendations on housing and homelessness issues that are key to effective mental health system transformation. Their recommendations sought to end chronic homelessness among people with mental illness, expand access to affordable housing resources for consumers, and promote evidence-based practices, including the use of Medicaid financing mechanisms, for people with mental illness who are homeless or at risk of homelessness.

Strategies to prevent and end chronic homelessness

In 2002 the Bush Administration announced its policy objective to end chronic homelessness in ten years. In the midst of the subcommittee's work in 2003, HUD, the U.S. Department of Health and Human Services (HHS), and the U.S. Department of Veterans Affairs (VA) in partnership with the U.S. Interagency Council on Homelessness initiated the first of

To support and advance the goal of ending chronic homelessness among people with serious mental illness, the subcommittee recommended that HUD—in partnership with HHS and VA—develop and implement a comprehensive plan designed to facilitate access to 150,000 units of permanent supportive housing for chronically homeless individuals over the next ten years. They called for the plan to include specific cost-effective approaches, strategies, and action steps to be implemented at the federal, state, and local levels.

Five years into the federal commitment to end chronic homelessness, progress to expand permanent supportive housing for chronically homeless people is evident. In addition to the federal interagency initiatives, HUD appropriations legislation since 2002 has included new McKinney-Vento Homeless Assistance funds to develop between 5,000 and 10,000 new units of permanent supportive housing for chronically homeless people (36). Policy incentives have also been adopted to redirect existing permanent supportive housing units to people with disabilities who have been homeless for long periods of time (37). At the state and local levels, communities are creating plans to end chronic homelessness that focus on improving outreach activities, discharge planning, and housing and community supports for people with mental illness and others who experience chronic homelessness (38). Private philanthropic organizations and national homeless advocacy groups are actively promoting this agenda and providing financial support for these initiatives (39).

Strategies to expand access to affordable housing

The Housing and Homelessness Subcommittee recognized that to end homelessness among people with mental illness, federal housing policy must also respond to the needs of consumers at risk of homelessness. Toward that end, the subcommittee's report included several recommendations designed to improve mental health consumers' access to government-funded affordable housing opportunities. These recommendations

recognized the importance of federal housing policies in facilitating access to a complex array of federal housing programs administered through a myriad of state and local public and private housing agencies and providers. In particular, the subcommittee noted the important role that HUD could play through structured partnerships with HHS and other federal agencies and by providing guidance and technical assistance to state and local housing officials and public housing agencies. Unlike the sustained federal effort to create new housing opportunities for chronically homeless people, there has been very little response from the federal government to address the housing problems of the lowest-income consumers before they become homeless.

Housing experts agree that federal housing funds—including so-called "mainstream" housing programs as well as housing programs targeted to people with disabilities—are essential to close the housing affordability gap that affects people with mental illness with the lowest incomes. Flexible capital funding through programs such as the Low Income Housing Tax Credit and the HOME Investment Partnerships programs are core components of affordable rental housing strategies in local communities. However, for units in these types of properties to be affordable for consumers with extremely low incomes, permanent rent subsidies provided through programs such as the Housing Choice Voucher program and the Section 811 Supportive Housing for Persons With Disabilities program are also essential.

During the past five years federal support for the rent subsidy programs needed by people with serious mental illness has declined significantly. In 2002 a successful policy initiated in 1997, which provided approximately 50,000 new Housing Choice Vouchers for people with disabilities, was eliminated (24). From 2003 to 2006 Congress and HUD created fiscal policies that contributed to the loss of more than 150,000 existing Housing Choice Vouchers and also weakened efforts to rejuvenate and preserve the nation's supply of housing for the lowest-income households (23). During

this same period, HUD also repeatedly proposed legislation that would have redirected existing voucher funds to households above 30% of median income (25).

The Section 811 Supportive Housing for Persons With Disabilities program has also been adversely affected by recent federal housing policy (16). Section 811 is the only federal housing program dedicated to expanding the supply of affordable and accessible supportive housing for people with serious and long-term disabilities. Recognizing the value and symbolism of this program, the subcommittee report called for reforms and improvements in Section 811, but none have been enacted. During the past four years the number of new rental units for people with disabilities produced through the Section 811 program has declined by more than 25% (40).

As new federal housing resources for the lowest-income households have steadily declined, more state and local mental health authorities have elected to create policies and housing approaches that rely on mental health system resources to expand affordable and permanent supportive housing opportunities for consumers. During recent years the State of California has reduced hospitalizations, incarceration, and homelessness and achieved substantial cost savings through the development of permanent supportive housing. These outcomes prompted the passage of Proposition 63 and an unprecedented state commitment to finance the creation of 13,000 new units of permanent supportive housing over the next ten years (41). Over the past decade state mental health–funded "bridge" subsidy programs have helped link thousands of consumers to Housing Choice Vouchers in Ohio, Connecticut, Oregon, and Hawaii. Given the recent cutbacks in the voucher program, the effectiveness of these bridge subsidies to link consumers to Housing Choice Vouchers may now be in question.

At the local level, counties and municipalities are also increasingly tapping discretionary mental health funds, such as savings from managed care, to leverage scarce government housing dollars. In 2004 and 2005 Arlington County, Virginia, and Allegheny County, Pennsylvania, both successfully implemented housing strategies for people with serious mental illness on the basis of this leveraging principle. Although these noteworthy state and local efforts have certainly helped some consumers obtain affordable housing, they are not sufficient to fill the gap created by declining federal support for housing programs that assist the lowest-income households.

The subcommittee's report emphasized that housing funding alone could not solve consumers' housing problems. Their recommendations reinforced the complexity of the housing issue for people with mental illness by calling for the creation of public-private partnerships between developers, landlords, housing agencies, and the mental health system. These types of partnerships were first modeled through the Robert Wood Johnson Foundation's Program on Chronic Mental Illness, which demonstrated the importance of housing planning and the important role of nonprofit housing corporations in mental health housing policy (42). Today, mental health nonprofit housing development corporations in numerous states own and manage thousands of units of permanent housing permanently set aside for consumers. However, the scarcity of new housing funding from programs such as Section 811 may reduce the number of new units that these development corporations could otherwise produce each year.

Mental health systems that have made significant progress on affordable housing issues do so by strengthening linkages with the affordable housing system (22). Strategies to implement this approach typically include dedicating one or more full-time staff members to work exclusively on housing and homeless issues. These mental health system staff must have the expertise to facilitate partnerships with housing agencies, track housing program and policy changes, obtain the scarce housing resources that are available, and provide training and technical assistance

on housing issues. Today, Tennessee stands out as a strong example of this practice in action. The state has hired seven regional housing facilitators who have been instrumental in creating well over 2,000 units of affordable housing for persons with mental illness since 2002. Other state mental health authorities that have successfully used this model include Connecticut, Kentucky, Massachusetts, Ohio, and Oregon.

Strategies to promote evidence-based practices

Mental health care programs and practitioners often rely on clinical and service delivery practices that, although widely accepted in the field, are not evidence based (43). The subcommittee recommended that HHS establish funding policies to ensure that initiatives related to evidence-based practices and the integration of federal and state funding resources are tailored to people with mental illnesses who are homeless or at risk of homelessness. Evidence-based practices that are known to be effective in assisting people with mental illnesses who are homeless (or at risk of homelessness) to gain and sustain independent living in the community include assertive community treatment, integrated services for people with co-occurring substance use disorders and mental illnesses, supported employment, and illness self-management.

Financing and implementation of evidence-based practices have been adopted as a core principle and objective of the Substance Abuse and Mental Health Services Administration (SAMHSA) mental health system transformation effort. Implementation of these practices poses a significant challenge for state and local systems electing to reconfigure mainstream resources. At the service delivery level, a lack of knowledge of evidenced-based practices, readiness issues, fiscal disincentives, and inadequate support for the change process can often derail potentially successful systems change activities (43).

The subcommittee also recommended that HHS and its Centers for Medicare and Medicaid Services

(CMS) improve and expand the ways in which Medicaid funding is used to maximum effect in serving people who are homeless, at risk of homelessness, or moving from homelessness to permanent supportive housing. Existing Medicaid statutes and regulations support some flexibility and ability to implement community-based services of importance to people with mental illnesses who are homeless or at risk of homelessness. However, best-practice services are optional as opposed to mandatory in state Medicaid plans, and thus states vary widely in how these service approaches are implemented. The subcommittee recommended that CMS exercise strong national leadership to engender the inclusion of best-practice services into state Medicaid plans and service requirements.

CMS has acted on these recommendations through its policy guidance to state Medicaid directors, through a set of system change grants to states designed to reduce institutional care and increase integrated community service provision, and through active participation in HHS's mental health transformation agenda. However, it should be noted that Medicaid resources are being restricted and curtailed at both the state and federal levels at the same time that efforts are being made to expand Medicaid coverage for best-practice services targeted to people with serious mental illness. Stringent eligibility requirements for Medicaid and difficulties navigating the SSI application process can restrict access to services, particularly for homeless people with serious mental illnesses (4).

Housing as a key factor in transformation planning

To ensure that housing and other essential resources are available to consumers and families in a transformed mental health system, the commission called on states to develop comprehensive mental health plans to outline responsibility for coordinating and integrating programs. Through the accountability envisioned in the planning process, the commission postulated that states would have the flexibility to combine federal, state, and local resources in creative, innovative, and more efficient ways, overcoming the bureaucratic boundaries between the health care, housing, employment support, and criminal justice systems (2). The background paper of the Subcommittee on Housing and Homelessness made note of a similar vision articulated in policies that apply to federally mandated housing planning activities (that is, the Consolidated Plan, the Public Housing Agency Plan, the Continuum of Care Plan, and the Qualified Allocation Plan) required of state and local government housing agencies as a condition of receiving federal affordable housing funding.

In 2005 SAMHSA awarded Mental Health Transformation State Incentive Grants (MHT-SIGs) to seven states to advance the vision and goals of the Commission's final report. These grants are intended to support an array of infrastructure and service delivery improvement activities to help grantees build a solid foundation for delivering and sustaining effective mental health and related services. It is too early in the MHT-SIG planning process to determine whether state mental health systems will build the housing capacity necessary to successfully leverage interagency partnerships and the limited resources that are available from state and local housing systems and this planning process. It is clear, however, that these collaborations are essential for a transformed system.

Conclusions

Preliminary results achieved in several major cities suggest that federal policies targeted to end chronic homelessness are working. Denver, Philadelphia, and Portland, Oregon, all report significant reductions in street homelessness achieved through aggressive permanent supportive housing strategies and outreach strategies (21). Although progress toward this goal is encouraging, it may be short lived if the housing resources—and community-based supportive services—are not in place to prevent consumers from becoming homeless.

As *The State of the Nation's Housing 2006* makes clear, housing affordability problems are intensifying across the nation, particularly for households with the lowest incomes. For people with mental illness those acute problems are further exacerbated by stigma and housing discrimination. The report realistically concludes that "prospects for a turnaround are bleak" and notes that after nearly 20 years of increases in federal housing assistance, growth ground to a halt in the second half of the 1990s. Successful efforts to transform mental health system service approaches—including increased support for the implementation of evidence-based practices—will be compromised if these policies remain in place and consumers are unable to obtain decent and affordable places to live that are well integrated in neighborhoods and communities.

It is important for mental health systems, including consumers and family members, to join with other groups working to reorient affordable housing policy to focus on the needs of households with extremely low incomes. Collectively, these efforts must create the political will to support increased funding for the Housing Choice Voucher program as well as programs such as Section 811 and McKinney-Vento Homeless Assistance resources that focus exclusively on the needs of people with disabilities who are homeless or most at risk of homelessness. A new National Housing Trust Fund could also provide incentives for the creation of new rental housing affordable to people with disabilities whose income is below 30% of the median. The National Low Income Housing Coalition is leading the effort to create this new resource, including policies that would prioritize the needs of extremely low-income households (44).

In addition to the federal government, state and local governments can also play an important role in housing policy for people with mental illness. The success achieved by mental health advocates in California demonstrates that elected officials and voters can be convinced to support housing and supportive services

policies that directly benefit people with mental illness. The key to success at all levels is to ensure that government housing officials are educated about the housing and supportive services barriers that exist today for people with mental illness and about the eventual—and higher—cost to the taxpayer if nothing is done to address this critical need.

Acknowledgments and disclosures

The author reports no competing interests.

References

1. Subcommittee on Housing and Homelessness: Background Paper. Rockville, Md, US Department of Health and Human Services, New Freedom Commission on Mental Health, 2004

2. Achieving the Promise: Transforming Mental Health Care in America. Pub no SMA-03-3832. Rockville, Md, US Department of Health and Human Services, New Freedom Commission on Mental Health, 2003

3. US Department of Health and Human Services: Cooperative Agreements to Evaluate Housing Approaches for Persons With Serious Mental Illness: Guidance for Applicants. Rockville, Md, Substance Abuse and Mental Health Services Administration, Center for Mental Health Services, 1997

4. Blueprint for Change: Ending Chronic Homelessness for Persons With Serious Mental Illnesses and Co-occurring Substance Use Disorders. Rockville, Md, Substance Abuse and Mental Health Services Administration, Center for Mental Health Services, 2003

5. Tanzman B: An overview of surveys of mental health consumers' preferences for housing and support services. Hospital and Community Psychiatry 44:450–455, 1993

6. Yeich S, Mowbray C, Bybee D, et al: The case for a "supported housing" approach: a study of consumer housing and support preferences. Psychosocial Rehabilitation Journal 18(2):75-86, 1994

7. Fakhoury W, Murray A, Shepherd G, et al: Research in supported housing. Social Psychology and Psychology Epidemiology 37:301–315, 2002

8. Srebnik D, Livingston J, Gordon L, et al: Housing choice and community success for individuals with serious and persistent mental illness. Community Mental Health Journal 31:139–152, 1995

9. Tsemberis S, Gulcur L, Nakae M: Housing First, consumer choice, and harm reduction for homeless individuals with a dual diagnosis. American Journal of Public Health 94:651–656, 2004

10. A Report on Worst Case Housing Needs in 1999: New Opportunity Amid Continuing Challenges. Executive Summary. Washington, DC, US Department of Housing and

Urban Development, Office of Policy Development and Research, 2001

11. Burt M: What Will It Take to End Homelessness? Washington, DC, Urban Institute Press, 2001

12. Culhane, DP, Metraux, S, Hadley, T: Public service reductions associated with placement of homeless persons with severe mental illness in supportive housing. Housing Policy Debate 13:107–163, 2002

13. Levy C: State panel seeks changes in homes for mentally ill. New York Times, Sept 24, 2002, p A1

14. Tsemberis S, Eisenberg R: Pathways to housing: supported housing for street-dwelling homeless individuals with psychiatric disabilities. Psychiatric Services 51:487–493, 2000

15. American Community Survey. Washington, DC, US Census Bureau, 2005. Available at http://factfinder.census.gov

16. The State of the Nation's Housing 2006. Cambridge, Mass, Joint Center for Housing Studies of Harvard University, 2006

17. Priced Out in 2006. Boston, Technical Assistance Collaborative, Inc, 2007

18. Meeting Our Nation's Housing Challenges: Report of the Bipartisan Millennial Housing Commission. Washington, DC, US Government Printing Office, 2002

19. Rosenheck R, Bassuk E, Salomon A: Special populations of homeless Americans, in Practical Lessons: The 1998 National Symposium on Homelessness Research. Edited by Fosburg L, Dennis D. Washington, DC, US Department of Housing and Urban Development and US Department of Health and Human Services, 1999

20. Ending Chronic Homelessness: Strategies for Action. Report From the Secretary's Work Group on Ending Chronic Homelessness. Washington, DC, US Department of Health and Human Services, 2003

21. Chronic Homelessness Issue Brief. Washington, DC, National Alliance to End Homelessness, 2006

22. Technical Assistance Collaborative, Inc: Permanent Supportive Housing: A Proven Solution to Homelessness. Opening Doors, issue 20, Jan 2003. Available at www.tacinc.org/pubs/odpubs.htm#20

23. Center on Budget and Policy Priorities: The Effects of the Federal Budget Squeeze on Low-Income Housing Assistance. Washington, DC, Center on Budget and Policy Priorities, 2007

24. Priced Out in 2004. Boston, Technical Assistance Collaborative, Inc, 2005

25. Newly Proposed Housing Legislation Would Leave Public Housing Agencies Vulnerable to Substantial Funding Cuts and Shifting HUD Mandates. Washington, DC, Center on Budget and Policy Priorities, 2005

26. Technical Assistance Collaborative and the Consortium for Citizens With Disabilities Housing Task Force: Affordable Housing in Your Community: What You Need to Know! What You Need to Do! Opening Doors, issue 8, Sept 1999. Available at www.tacinc.org/pubs/odpubs.htm#20

27. Carling P: Housing, community support, and homelessness: emerging policy in mental health systems. New England Journal of Public Policy 8:281–295, 1992

28. Morse G: A review of case management for people who are homeless: implications for practice, policy, and research, in Practical Lessons. The 1998 National Symposium on Homelessness Research. Edited by Fosburg L, Dennis D. Washington, DC, US Department of Housing and Urban Development and US Department of Health and Human Services, 1999

29. Holes in the Safety Net: Mainstream Systems and Homelessness. San Mateo, Calif, Charles and Helen Schwab Foundation, 2003

30. Carling P: Housing and supports for persons with mental illness: emerging approaches to research and practice. Hospital and Community Psychiatry 44:439–449, 1993

31. Strategic Framework for Ending Long-Term Homelessness. New York, Corporation for Supportive Housing, 2002

32. Newman S: Housing attributes and serious mental illness: implications for research and practice. Psychiatric Services 52:1309–1317, 2001

33. Allen M: Waking Rip van Winkle: Why developments in the last 20 years should teach the mental health system not to use housing as a tool of coercion. Behavioral Sciences and the Law 21:503–521, 2003

34. Greenwood R, Schaefer-McDaniel N, Winkel G, et al: Decreasing psychiatric symptoms by increasing choice in services for adults with histories of homelessness. American Journal of Community Psychology 36:223–238, 2005

35. US Departments of Housing and Urban Development, Health and Human Services, and Veterans Affairs: Notice of Funding Availability (NOFA) for the Collaborative Initiative to Help End Chronic Homelessness. Federal Register 68:4018–4046, 2003

36. HUD's Homeless Assistance Programs. Washington, DC, National Alliance to End Homelessness, 2006

37. FY 2006 Super NOFA: Continuum of Care Homeless Assistance Programs. Washington, DC, US Department of Housing and Urban Development, 2006

38. The Ten Year Plan to End Homelessness. Washington, DC, National Alliance to End Homelessness, 2005

39. Partnership to End Long Term Homelessness: Nine Partners Join Together to Galvanize a National Effort to End Long-Term Homelessness, Millions of Dollars Dedicated to Promote Awareness and Build Supportive Housing, New Data From Nine Cities Shows Supportive Housing is Cost-Effective Alternative to Chronic Homelessness, 2006. Available at www.endlongtermhomelessness.org

40. FY 2006 Notice of Funding Availability: Section 811 Supportive Housing Program for Persons With Disabilities. Washington, DC, US Department of Housing and Urban Development, 2006

41. The Importance of State Investment in Permanent Supportive Housing. New York, Corporation for Supportive Housing, 2004

42. Cohen M, Somers S: Supported housing: insights from the Robert Wood Johnson Foundation Program on Chronic Mental Illness. Psychosocial Rehabilitation Journal 13(4):43–50, 1990

43. Hyde P, Falls K, Morris J, et al: Turning Knowledge Into Practice: A Manual for Behavioral Health Administrators and Practitioners About Understanding and Implementing Evidence-Based Practices. Boston, Technical Assistance Collaborative and the American College of Mental Health Administration, 2003

44. Housing Trust Funds Grow Nationwide. Washington, DC, National Low Income Housing Coalition, 2007 Available at www.nlihc.org

Issues in Medicaid Policy and System Transformation: Recommendations From the President's Commission

Stephen L. Day, M.S.W.

Efforts to ensure that people with disabilities participate fully in their communities have raised awareness of current Medicaid policies that impede provision of best-practice mental health services. The author summarizes issues that were examined by the Medicaid Subcommittee of the President's New Freedom Commission and its recommendations in four areas: access, service delivery, service coordination, and quality. Because of Medicaid's substantial role as a payer for mental health services, more creative and flexible program policies can promote system transformation. Current eligibility rules and time-consuming procedures can inhibit timely access to Medicaid coverage for people with mental illness. Medicaid benefit plans may create financial incentives for maintaining more traditional but less effective models of care. Some policies impede states' ability to coordinate Medicaid funding with other sources of funding to create systems of community-based care. Medicaid does not provide specific requirements to ensure that individuals with depression are identified and offered informed choices about treatment through primary or specialty care providers. Action steps to address these and other issues include use of presumptive eligibility and parity, retention of coverage as enrollees enter the workplace, guidance to states on evidence-based practices and service coordination with other agencies, more flexible financing mechanisms, improved data collection and reporting, and enhanced integration of primary and mental health care. (*Psychiatric Services* 57:1713–1718, 2006)

In 2002 President Bush charged the New Freedom Commission on Mental Health with recommending strategies to enable people with mental illnesses to live, work, learn, and participate fully in their communities. The Commission established several working subcommittees to identify issues and make recommendations related to this overarching goal. The Medicaid Subcommittee examined a range of Medicaid requirements and practices that influence the financing and delivery of mental health services. The sub-committee also received information from a variety of stakeholders, including consumers, family members, providers, state mental authority leaders, and other interested parties. The subcommittee reviewed the work of other subcommittees of the President's Commission to see how the recommendations of those groups might interact with the Medicaid recommendations. I assisted the committee to analyze the Medicaid issues presented and drafted the report and recommendations that were adopted by the Commission.

This article summarizes policy implications of the Medicaid program for mental health services as adopted by the Medicaid Subcommittee. The subcommittee accepted the recommendations summarized here and sent them forward to the Commission for final action. Many of the subcommittee's recommendations were incorporated in the final report of the Commission. The article provides background information on the role of Medicaid in funding public mental health services, and issues and barriers related to the use of Medicaid for best-practice mental health services are identified. The recommendations that were made to and adopted by the New Freedom Commission on Mental Health are listed.

Several events have taken place at the federal and state levels since the Medicaid working paper was developed and the Commission's final report was published (1). The most significant federal actions have been implementation of the new Medicare Part D pharmacy benefit and enactment of the 2006 Deficit Reduction Act. Implications of the act for mental health are discussed in a column on page 1711 of this issue (2). In addition, since 2002, many states have implemented changes in their Medicaid plans, in part to reduce future costs and in part to expand Medicaid funding for best-practice community service models. Despite these changes, the key findings of the Medicaid Subcommittee and the recommendations it made in 2002 to the President's New Freedom Commission remain as relevant today as they were then.

The author is executive director of the Technical Assistance Collaborative, 535 Boylston Street, Suite 1301, Boston, MA 02116 (e-mail: info@tacinc.org). Originally published in the December 2006 issue of Psychiatric Services.

The policy context for Medicaid

Medicaid is a significant force in the development, implementation, and funding of mental health services for adults and children in the United States. In each state a designated Medicaid state agency develops a state Medicaid plan that determines which individuals are covered and for what services, which optional services are included in the plan, what types of providers qualify for Medicaid reimbursement, and how providers are paid for services rendered. The federal Medicaid statute identifies mandatory services that all states must include in their Medicaid state plans. For mental health the only mandatory services are inpatient hospitalization in general hospitals, medical care provided by a psychiatrist, and Early Periodic Screening Diagnosis and Treatment (EPSDT). All other common adult mental health services, such as outpatient therapy, case management, inpatient care in freestanding psychiatric hospitals, psychiatric medications, and rehabilitation services, are optional components that states may or may not include in their Medicaid state plans.

Because most community mental health services are not mandatory, there is considerable variation among the states in covered services and related Medicaid requirements. Almost all states now have some form of Medicaid waivers and managed care arrangements that have an impact on the delivery and administration of public mental health services. These waivers and managed care approaches have helped states overcome some of the policy issues discussed in this article and at the same time have added complexity to state Medicaid programs and have led to variation among programs. It is not possible within the scope of this article to discuss the various local approaches to implementation of mental health services under Medicaid.

Medicaid as a primary payer for mental health services

Medicaid plays a substantial role as a payer for mental health specialty services, such as inpatient and outpatient services provided by entities and independent practitioners that are specifically organized to provide behavioral health services for Medicaid-enrolled children and adults who have mental health needs and for whom mental health services are a medical necessity. Studies that combined information from Medicaid, mental health, and substance abuse agencies in three states have indicated that between 20 and 25 percent of all nonelderly adult mental health service users receive publicly funded mental health services only through Medicaid and that between 7 and 13 percent of Medicaid enrollees are mental health service users (3,4). Ninety-eight percent of children and adolescents receiving public mental health services receive at least some of their services through Medicaid (5).

In 2001 Medicaid spent almost $27 billion, accounting for 26 percent of all behavioral health spending in the United States and 35 percent of all public expenditures for mental health services (6). Medicaid's role in funding mental health services has grown in recent years and will continue to grow (7). In 2003 Medicaid accounted for more than 50 percent of all public funding for mental health services in the United States and could account for as much as two-thirds of such spending by 2013 (8). As a result, public mental health systems have evolved, or "tilted," in the direction of accommodating Medicaid-covered individuals and services (9). Because state general appropriation funds traditionally used for a variety of generic community mental health services have been converted to Medicaid matching funds and states have typically not increased non-Medicaid funding for mental health in recent years, resources have become proportionately less available for uninsured individuals with low incomes who are not able to qualify for Medicaid (9). Thus, although increased Medicaid funding has substantially expanded access to mental health services, it has also increased the importance of state-level efforts to coordinate Medicaid financing policy within each state's overall public mental health policy framework and service system design.

In addition, the "refinancing" of public mental health services with Medicaid has contributed to the conversion of public mental health systems from a grant-funded provider-driven model to a fee-for-service insurance model (8). This has increased the responsiveness of mental health services to the needs and choices of individual consumers, but it has also resulted in fundamental changes in the nature of relationships between consumers, service providers, and payers for services. To remain financially viable, service providers once considered to be part of the social and mental health safety net now must seek out consumers who are eligible for Medicaid and then must deliver services that qualify for Medicaid reimbursement. At the same time, state mental health authorities must find new ways to ensure that fee-for-service revenues sustain essential safety net services, such as crisis stabilization and flexible community support services, throughout public mental health systems of care.

Medicaid has now surpassed Medicare spending at the federal level and is the single largest component of state spending after education (10). Health care economists project that Medicaid expenditures will rise between 10 and 15 percent each year over the next several years (11). As a consequence, both state and federal policy makers are looking for new ways to decrease or at least contain increasing Medicaid costs (12,13). The growth in expenditures leaves Medicaid a likely target for additional funding cuts to balance both federal and state budgets, especially in the area of optional services. The 2006 Deficit Reduction Act contains provisions that could result in coverage and access limitations for services and reimbursement requirements for targeted case management and rehabilitative services that have become important components of public mental health systems (14).

Medicaid as a force for system transformation

At the same time that Medicaid has become the primary source of financing for mental health services, it has also become an important source of resources to reform traditional long-term care and behavioral health services within the states. Early in his administration, on June 19, 2001, President Bush issued an Executive Order requiring swift and effective implementation of the U.S. Supreme Court's 1999 opinion in *Olmstead v. L.C.* The *Olmstead* decision affirmed that people with disabilities have a right under the Americans With Disabilities Act to live in integrated community settings as opposed to institutions. That 2001 Executive Order is the logical precursor of the Executive Order on April 29, 2002, that established the President's New Freedom Commission on Mental Heath.

These efforts have resulted in progress at the federal and state levels to ensure that people with psychiatric disabilities have maximum opportunities to "live, work, learn, and participate fully in their communities" (1). At the same time, these efforts have resulted in increased understanding at the federal and state levels of limitations in current Medicaid policies and practices that impede use of Medicaid for a range of best-practice services focused on community living. Some of these limitations also affect the ability of states to coordinate Medicaid funding with other sources of funding to create comprehensive systems of community-based mental health services and supports for children, adolescents, and adults.

For example, Medicaid medical-necessity criteria and unit-of-service documentation requirements sometimes make it difficult to deliver flexible and mobile community supports as opposed to facility-based services for people with serious mental illness. Medicaid service definitions or provider requirements often differ from child welfare service policies, which can impede the integration of mental health and child welfare social services for children and their families. In addition, given the extensive statutory and regulatory basis of Medicaid at both the federal and state levels, it often takes a considerable amount of time for the rules and

regulations to catch up with the science of best-practice mental health services.

Medicaid issues and barriers

The Medicaid Subcommittee identified several critical operational issues and barriers associated with Medicaid requirements. For example, complex eligibility rules and time-consuming procedures can inhibit timely access to Medicaid coverage for people with mental illness, particularly when disability must be established as a condition for Medicaid eligibility (for example, for single adults between the ages of 22 and 64 in states where Medicaid eligibility is linked to eligibility for Supplemental Security Income). Some states also have different eligibility requirements for children than for adults, which can impede smooth transition from the child mental health system to the adult mental health system. In addition, eligibility rules in some states result in parents' having to relinquish custody to gain Medicaid eligibility for children in need of residential treatment or other Medicaid-reimbursed interventions. Some states have used Medicaid waivers to overcome barriers to eligibility, particularly with regard to disability criteria applied to single adults between the ages of 22 and 64.

In regard to covered services, traditional Medicaid benefit plan definitions and provider qualifications frequently do not reflect best practices and may have the unintended effect of maintaining financial incentives for more traditional but less effective models of care for both children and adults. For example, established evidence-based best practices such as assertive community treatment and multisystemic therapy are not yet included in all state Medicaid plans.

Furthermore, the Medicaid exclusion of service coverage for adults in an Institution for Mental Disease (IMD) makes many state-funded psychiatric hospital services and residential services ineligible for Medicaid reimbursement. This increases state costs and reduces opportunities for coordination of services across service modalities. Also, because the costs of

IMD services are not reimbursed by Medicaid, states found it difficult before 2006 to meet the requirement for "revenue neutrality" in the Medicaid Home and Community Based Waiver Program as it applies to people with mental illness. Since the DRA was enacted in 2006, the specific revenue neutrality provision has been removed. The Home and Community Based Waiver Program has allowed states to develop flexible community-based services as opposed to institutional care for people with developmental disabilities or physical disabilities or elderly persons with needs for assistance with activities of daily living.

Another key issue is employment, which is viewed by consumers and professionals as a key element of recovery. The supported employment service model is one of the recognized evidence-based practices. Nonetheless, there remain eligibility and service definition limitations within the Medicaid program that provide disincentives to supported employment and moving toward self-sufficiency. Few states have implemented the Medicaid buy-in option associated with the federal Ticket to Work program, which means that most Medicaid recipients face the loss of needed medications, clinical treatment, and community supports as they increase their wages through employment. Also, because the Medicaid regulations specifically prohibit reimbursement for employment, states have had to be cautious in the degree to which Medicaid is used to fund services associated with the supported employment best-practice model.

Two final issues identified by the Medicaid Subcommittee are related to depression and the use of Medicaid data for planning. As emphasized in *Mental Health: Report of the Surgeon General* (15), depression is eminently treatable, and good outcomes can be expected with a combination of medication and related clinical approaches, including psychotherapy. In Medicaid as well as in most other third-party insurance programs, screening and care for depression are typically conducted by primary care physicians

Table 1

Medicaid policies and action steps recommended by the President's New Freedom Commission on Mental Health

Policy area and recommendation	Action steps
Access: improve Medicaid recipients' access to needed and desired best-practice mental health services	Use presumptive eligibility to facilitate access to needed benefits for people with mental illness or serious emotional disturbance
	Establish a principle of parity of mental health coverage with general medical care benefits within Medicaid plans and waivers and between Medicaid and Medicare
	Assure retention and flexibility of Medicaid coverage for people who are moving toward work and self-sufficiency and for people who are overcoming functional limitations through recovery
Service delivery: foster the development and implementation of evidence-based practices and models at the state level and increase integrated community services while reducing institutional or out-of-home care. Out of home care includes residential treatment facilities and foster care.	Provide federal policy guidance to states to incorporate evidence-based service definitions in Medicaid plans for adults and youths
	Support Medicaid waivers and related demonstration programs that stimulate integration of funding streams and provide financial incentives for the implementation of best practices
	Expand federal financial incentives for community-based care as opposed to institutional care
	Explore additional flexible financing mechanisms, including payments for recovery-based outcomes, which could further stimulate adoption of best practices at the state level
Service planning and coordination: enhance coordination, collaboration, and data-driven planning activities between Medicaid and other federal and state funding streams and service program requirements	Provide federal guidance to improve state-level planning and coordination among state agencies that administer Medicaid and other related public mental health service programs for adults and youths
	Encourage state governors to exercise leadership in planning state mental health system improvement strategies across all aspects of state government (for example, housing, employment, criminal justice, juvenile justice, child welfare, and public health)
	Ensure improved data collection and reporting among Medicaid and other federal and state funding streams for mental health services
Quality and consumer responsiveness: increase the degree to which Medicaid-funded services respond to consumers' needs and choices and continuously improve methods for service delivery to high-priority Medicaid mental health consumers	Promote consumer choice and control through recovery-oriented service models, including peer supports
	Foster early identification and intervention for youths with potential serious emotional disturbance
	Enhance the integration of primary health and mental health under the Medicaid program (with an initial emphasis on primary health interventions for depression)

or in primary care clinics, and treatment of depression consists primarily of medication prescription and management, with few requirements for, or tracking of, referrals to therapists or psychiatric specialists. Medicaid does not provide specific requirements or incentives to ensure that individuals with depression are identified and offered informed choices about treatment and have opportunities to receive care through health care providers or specialty behavioral health care providers.

Federal data-reporting requirements for Medicaid are extensive, and in most states the Medicaid data files are the best available source of information on mental health service access, utilization, and costs. New service definitions and reporting codes implemented under the Health Insurance Portability and Accountability Act have resulted in consistent and comparable Medicaid data reporting among all Medicaid jurisdictions. However, in most states Medicaid data are not comparable to data collected on non-Medicaid state and local mental health service delivery and expenditures. Also, most state mental health authorities do not have access to the Medicaid data files for planning and for assessing service access and use of best practices. Thus this rich source of Medicaid claims data for planning and accountability has not been tapped in most states.

Summary of Medicaid policy issues

On the basis of the analysis of Medicaid policy and operational issues presented here, the President's New Freedom Commission on Mental Health concluded that Medicaid is a critical funding source with opportunities for state-level creativity and flexibility. However, the Commission also recognized that Medicaid is very complex and is often administered outside of the mental health arena at the state level. Thus specialized expertise and strong federal encouragement are frequently needed to ensure best use of Medicaid to meet states' objectives for their mental health system. For example, there are well-known evidence-based practices in the mental health field, but few states have taken full advantage of Medicaid financing opportunities to implement these practices.

Nonetheless, the Commission also recognized that Medicaid by itself cannot meet all the financial and program guidance needs of state and local mental health systems. Not all people in need of services will be eligible for Medicaid, and not all services will qualify for Medicaid reimbursement. In addition, Medicaid lacks specific mechanisms or incentives that foster joint planning, collaboration or coordination of funding, and service approaches. For the reasons described above, federal action is needed to ensure that Medicaid is a key component of efforts to transform state mental health systems.

The Medicaid Subcommittee recommended four key policy initiatives that were subsequently accepted by the New Freedom Commission and incorporated into its final report. These are briefly summarized in Table 1.

Discussion

Many of the recommendations of the Medicaid Subcommittee were incorporated into the final report of the President's New Freedom Commission, *Achieving the Promise: Transforming Mental Health Care in America*. After the report was published, the federal Substance Abuse and Mental Health Services Administration (SAMHSA) adopted the report's major recommendations and has led in the development of Transforming Mental Health Care in America: The Federal Action Agenda, a federal multiagency action plan to implement many of the Commission's recommendations (16). SAMHSA has also provided funds to seven states— Connecticut, Maryland, Ohio, Oklahoma, New Mexico, Texas, and Washington—to begin multiagency planning for mental health system transformation, with Medicaid as a key participant in and focus of the planning efforts.

The purchasing collaborative model being implemented in New Mexico is a prime example of mental health system transformation that incorpo-

rates Medicaid and many other key payers for mental health and substance abuse services and the administering agencies into a unified system with standard service definitions and access criteria, seamless payment mechanisms, and uniform strategies for implementing evidence-based services (17). Experience gained in this initiative could be beneficial in the design and implementation of systems in other federal and state transformation efforts in which Medicaid plays a substantial part.

In addition to SAMHSA's system transformation efforts, several states —Georgia, Hawaii, North Carolina, and New York—as well as the District of Columbia have recently amended their Medicaid plans to incorporate evidence-based or promising practices in their covered benefits for people with mental illness or serious emotional disturbance. These evidence-based services are consistent with the Medicaid policy recommendations contained in the New Freedom Commission's report and provide models that could be implemented in other states with no changes in Medicaid requirements or practices at the federal level.

At the same time, federal and state budget challenges have overshadowed efforts to expand Medicaid coverage and foster delivery of evidence-based services for adults with mental illness and children with serious emotional disturbance. The 2006 Deficit Reduction Act calls for more than $40 billion in cuts in federal Medicaid expenditures over the next five years. The act does provide states with some additional flexibility in both eligibility and covered benefits, but the assumption is that this flexibility will be used to reduce costs rather than to expand services and eligibility categories. Thus improvements in federal and state Medicaid financing strategies as part of a larger mental health system transformation must be accomplished with fewer dollars rather than with expanded resources.

Conclusions

The President's New Freedom Commission on Mental Health followed in the footsteps of the Surgeon Gener-

al's report on mental health by recommending feasible strategies and evidence-based service approaches for making the best use of Medicaid in concert with Medicare and state general fund resources to attain positive outcomes and successful community living for people with mental illness or serious emotional disturbance. It is now up to consumers, families, providers, practitioners, and other stakeholders to create demand and support for implementation of these strategies at the state level. Federal leadership is essential, but at this point Medicaid changes to implement best practices and other related recommendations of the Commission can be designed and implemented only at the state level.

For the longer term an opportunity exists to review the current patchwork of Medicaid optional services and state-level variations and to consider a more consistent national Medicaid (and possibly Medicare) benefit plan for adults with serious mental illness and children with serious emotional disturbance. The evidence about what services are most effective and beneficial for individuals and their parents and families is clear. The financing models and interagency planning and implementation mechanisms are in development. The adoption of a standard national benefit plan with local variability has proven effective for more than 30 years for elders, persons with physical disabilities, and persons with developmental disabilities. The 2006 Deficit Reduction Act will allow states to define specialty benefit plans for certain narrowly defined population groups. These provisions could create the incentives necessary to move toward national standards for a benefit plan for adults with serious mental illness and youths with serious emotional disturbance, similar to the plan that now exists for people with intellectual and developmental disabilities.

References

1. Achieving the Promise: Transforming Mental Health in America. Pub no SMA-03-3832. Rockville, Md, Department of Health and Human Services, President's New Freedom Commission on Mental Health, 2003

2. Koyanagi C: The Deficit Reduction Act: should we love it or hate it? Psychiatric Services 57:1711–1712, 2006

3. Buck JA: Spending for state mental health care. Psychiatric Services 52:1294, 2001

4. Larson MJ, Farrelly MC, Hodgkin DL, et al: Payments and use of services for mental health, alcohol, and other drug abuse disorders: estimates from Medicare, Medicaid and private health plans, in Mental Health United States, 1998. Edited by Manderscheid RW, Henderson M. DHHS pub no SMA 99-3285. Washington, DC, US Government Printing Office, 1999

5. Teich JL, Buck JA, Graver L, et al: Utilization of public mental health services by children with serious emotional disturbances. Administration and Policy in Mental Health 30:523–534, 2003

6. Mark T, Coffey RM, McKusick D, et al: National Estimates of Expenditures for Mental Health and Substance Abuse Treatment, 1991–2001. SAMHSA pub no SMA-05-3999, Rockville, Md, Substance Abuse and Mental Health Services Administration, 2005

7. Mark TL, Buck JA, Dilonardo JD, et al: Medicaid expenditures on behavioral health care. Psychiatric Services 54:188–194, 2003

8. Buck JA: Medicaid, health care financing trends, and the future of state-based public mental health services. Psychiatric Services 54:969–975, 2003

9. Frank RG, Goldman HH, Hogan M: Medicaid and mental health: be careful what you ask for. Health Affairs 22(1):101–113, 2003

10. Desonia R: Running on Empty: The State Budget Crises Worsen. Issue brief no 783. Washington, DC, George Washington University, National Health Policy Forum, Sept 2002

11. Boyd DJ, Scheppach RC: The Disappearing State Surpluses: How Come, How Long, and How Will They Affect Social Service Programs? Issue brief no 769. Washington, DC, George Washington University, National Health Policy Forum, Oct 2001

12. Guyer J: The Role of Medicaid in State Budgets. Washington, DC, Kaiser Commission on Medicaid and the Uninsured, 2001. Available at www.kff.org/medicaid/4024index.cfm

13. Medicaid Spending Growth: Results From a 2002 Survey. Washington, DC, Kaiser Commission on Medicaid and the Uninsured, 2002. Available at www.kff.org/medicaid/4064-index.cfm

14. Perkins J: Advocacy Tips for Responding to the Deficit Reduction Act of 2005. Washington, DC, National Disability Rights Network, Training and Advocacy Support Center, Apr 27, 2006

15. Mental Health: A Report of the Surgeon General. Washington, DC, US Department of Health and Human Services, US Public Health Service, 1999

16. Transforming Mental Health Care in America: Highlights of the Federal Action Agenda. Rockville, Md, Substance Abuse and Mental Health Services Administration, 2005. Available at www.samhsa.gov/pubs/mhc/mhcagenda.htm

17. Hyde P: A unique approach to designing a comprehensive behavioral health system in New Mexico Psychiatric Services 55:983–985, 2004

Insights and Opportunities: Medicaid Directors Identify Mental Health Issues

Barbara Coulter Edwards, M.P.P.
Vernon K. Smith, Ph.D.

Medicaid has become central to financing public mental health services, and state Medicaid directors are now in a position to wield considerable influence over the direction that mental health policy takes in a state. As state mental health authorities seek to shape state and local mental health systems, they should find it useful, perhaps critical, to understand the perspectives and opinions of Medicaid directors. (*Psychiatric Services* 58:1032–1034, 2007)

In preparing a 2006 Medicaid issues briefing for the Substance Abuse and Mental Health Services Administration (SAMHSA), Health Management Associates informally asked Medicaid directors what they viewed as their most important mental health challenges and what they saw as effective strategies for improving collaboration between Medicaid and the mental health system. Medicaid officials in 35 states responded to our inquiries. Strong common themes emerged across states.

Our research uncovered a keen interest in mental health issues among Medicaid officials. They were aware of the federal call for transformation of the mental health system to promote recovery through consumer-centered and evidence-based care. A significant number of state Medicaid officials reported the need for new or redesigned mental health services, including options for community-based services, improved continuity of service options, and care management and coordination. Others identified concern about inadequate access to mental health professionals for children and in rural areas.

Medicaid directors and their key mental health staff also expressed strong frustration relating to two issues. First, there was a fairly widespread belief that state and local behavioral health systems fail to fully understand the fundamental parameters—and therefore the limitations—of Medicaid as a funding mechanism for public mental health systems. Second, the most frequently raised concern was what Medicaid officials described as conflicting priorities and policy directions between the Centers for Medicare and Medicaid Services (CMS) and SAMHSA.

Local tension and opportunities

CMS describes Medicaid's primary purpose as helping to fund medically necessary services and has issued guidance that state plan services in support of evidence-based practices in mental health treatment must be medical services (1). Several Medicaid directors noted that Medicaid's "medical model" causes much mental health system discontent. The need to build service delivery with licensed providers, the requirement for medical justification and documentation of a patient's progress to support a claim, restrictions on treating family members not covered by Medicaid, and the inability to cover nonmedical support services that may be part of effective treatment were cited as points of frustration for mental health systems. Other basic federal Medic-

aid tenets that can be in conflict within state and local mental health systems include the requirements that the same benefit package be available statewide (2), that comparable services be available to all Medicaid consumers (3), and that consumers have free choice of providers (4).

Medicaid directors across the country expressed concern over the cost of mental health services (especially pharmacy) as well as over the impact that inadequate treatment of mental health conditions has on other costs borne by Medicaid. Many called for improved accountability for outcomes and predicted that a focus on outcomes would find significant common ground for collaboration between Medicaid and mental health authorities. As one director put it, "accountability and outcomes" was "a language Medicaid could understand." In addition, improved management of pharmacy services and effective integration of behavioral health services with primary care are high on many lists of state Medicaid issues.

Medicaid officials expressed optimism that Medicaid's support for mental health consumers at the state level could be improved by joint planning and collaboration between the state mental health authorities and the Medicaid agency. Directors cited successful collaborations that were accomplished both through the combined administrative direction of an umbrella agency and through cross-department initiatives. Directors stressed that common goals and a shared understanding of Medicaid program opportunities and limitations were key to more successful mental health strategies.

Shared goals may become even more important, because state Medic-

The authors are affiliated with Health Management Associates, Inc., 37 W. Broad St., Suite 1150, Columbus, OH 43215 (e-mail: bedwards@healthmanage ment.com). Fred C. Osher, M.D., is editor of this column. Originally published in the August 2007 issue of Psychiatric Services.

aid programs have been given additional flexibility in defining benefit packages for some populations under the Deficit Reduction Act of 2005, including the flexibility to limit mental health care or other coverage for target populations. The Deficit Reduction Act also provides states with opportunities to create community-based service options for mental health populations through Money Follows the Person grants, a demonstration opportunity to create home-based alternatives for children in residential care, and new state plan options to offer home and community care.

Federal constraints

Despite optimism about the potential for local collaboration, Medicaid directors overwhelmingly expressed concern about a growing disconnect between what the mental health system views as "best practice" and what the Medicaid program is able to cover. The U.S. Department of Health and Human Services, through SAMHSA, is encouraging innovation and adoption of evidence-based mental health services, whereas the same federal department, through CMS, is pursing an agenda of tighter compliance with a medical model that in the mental health community might be considered an outdated model of benefit design. Some Medicaid officials described recent experiences where CMS resisted or disallowed implementation of evidenced-based practices endorsed by SAMHSA, observations that are consistent with past research that has examined Medicaid policy challenges to achieving the goals of the President's New Freedom Commission (5).

Another major concern in several states is related to new federal regulations and guidance regarding what costs can be considered in the calculation of managed care capitation rates (6). This issue may influence the ability of Medicaid to support innovative mental health services within capitated arrangements. Directors also remain concerned that, for those with mental health medication needs, coverage for individuals dually eligible for Medicare and Medic-

aid under Medicare Part D may disrupt continuity of care and effective care management.

Furthermore, many state Medicaid officials are concerned about the direction that federal policy is taking regarding the coverage options most often used by states to support community mental health services. The Deficit Reduction Act tightened the definition of targeted case management (7), and the federal government has announced an intention to issue regulations in 2007 to similarly "clarify" the use of the rehabilitation option. These actions raise questions as to whether federal policy will support continued Medicaid financing of key state and local mental health services.

Recent audit activities by the Office of the Inspector General and increased CMS scrutiny in the review of community mental health–related state plan amendments have spurred further concern about federal intentions.

Medicaid officials generally believe that the increased federal focus on program integrity underscores longstanding compliance expectations regarding documentation and the assurance that Medicaid services are billed only for Medicaid-eligible consumers. However, officials also see new questions being raised about the role of local authorities, the use of certified public expenditures, and definitions of allowable services.

These federal policy challenges, as well as ongoing financial pressures around the larger Medicaid program, led several directors to question the mental health system's dependence on Medicaid as the primary source of new revenue to meet growing demands. Some officials recommended that the mental health systems in their states should broaden their financing strategies for the future to include other public-sector and even private resources. This was an intriguing comment, because mental health system experts predict that Medicaid will grow to pay for two-thirds of state mental health services in the next ten to 20 years (8).

When asked to recommend strategies to improve Medicaid and mental health system collaboration, many state Medicaid officials recommend-

ed that SAMHSA and CMS should engage in joint planning to clarify federal direction and to identify effective Medicaid benefit parameters. This federal collaboration was seen as key to achieving the goals of the President's New Freedom Commission on Mental Health.

Conclusions

There is sometimes a concern that state Medicaid officials do not pay sufficient attention to mental health issues. Mental health expenditures tend not to dominate state-level concern the way nursing home or hospital expenditures can.

On the other hand, some in the mental health system are concerned that Medicaid policies are overly influential and create pressures and constraints that skew the system away from critical priorities or more effective treatments. Because the Single State Medicaid Agency is prohibited by federal law from delegating policy making for Medicaid mental health expenditures to the mental health authority, states are presented with a fundamental and potentially difficult dilemma. Although the mental health authority may be best prepared to set effective policy direction for the mental health system, its preferred direction may compromise the availability of much needed federal Medicaid funding. With Medicaid now the largest source of funding for the public mental health system, who, indeed, is to set policy for state mental health systems?

State leaders in the mental health system would be well served to take the initiative to engage and foster partnerships with Medicaid at both the state and national levels. Our review of key issues with Medicaid directors suggests there is real opportunity to forge effective state-level relationships by focusing on goals that are shared by both Medicaid and the mental health system. Overall, Medicaid officials described a relatively high level of engagement on their part in mental health issues in their states. Many expressed a sense of frustration at feeling trapped between evolving mental health system expectations on the one hand and federal Medicaid constraints on the other, but in no case did Medicaid directors indicate the slightest desire to be in charge of their states' mental health systems. Rather, many Medicaid directors indicated a strong willingness to engage with the mental health system to find effective Medicaid program and funding options, especially if accountability for outcomes and cost would be a part of the equation.

In addition, it is clear that long-standing inconsistent and ambiguous federal policy is creating tension at the state and local levels regarding the role of Medicaid in the public mental health system. It can be argued that SAMHSA and CMS, as branches of a single federal department, have the opportunity and even obligation to develop consistent federal policy regarding financing effective mental health services. Recent national association efforts to bring state Medicaid directors and state mental health directors into joint activity could become a springboard toward mutual efforts to achieve consistency in federal mental health policy.

Acknowledgments and disclosures

The authors report no competing interests.

References

1. Centers for Medicare and Medicaid Services: Medicaid Support of Evidence-Based Practices in Mental Health Programs. Available at www.cms.hhs.gov/promisingpractices/downloads/ebpbasics.pdf

2. Social Security Act, section 1902(a)(1)

3. Social Security Act, section 1902(a)(10)(C)

4. Social Security Act, section 1902(a)(23)

5. Day SL: Issues in Medicaid policy and system transformation: recommendations from the President's Commission. Psychiatric Services 57:1713–1718, 2006

6. 42 CFR 438.6

7. Deficit Reform Act of 2005, section 6052 (PL 109-171)

8. Mark TL, Coffey RM, Vandivort-Warren R, et al: US spending for mental health and substance abuse treatment, 1991–2001. Health Affairs, Mar 29, 2005, pp W5-133– W5-142. Available at content.healthaffairs.org/cgi/content/abstract/hlth aff.w5.133

Transformation of Children's Mental Health Services: The Role of School Mental Health

Sharon Hoover Stephan, Ph.D.
Mark Weist, Ph.D.
Sheryl Kataoka, M.D., M.S.H.S.
Steven Adelsheim, M.D.
Carrie Mills, B.S.

The New Freedom Commission has called for a transformation in the delivery of mental health services in this country. The commission's report and recommendations have highlighted the role of school mental health services in transforming mental health care for children and adolescents. This article examines the intersection of school mental health programs and the commission's recommendations in order to highlight the role of school mental health in the transformation of the child and adolescent mental health system. Schools are uniquely positioned to play a central role in improving access to child mental health services and in supporting mental health and wellness as well as academic functioning of youths. The New Freedom Commission report articulated several goals related to school mental health: reducing stigma, preventing suicide, improving screening and treating co-occurring disorders, and expanding school mental health programs. The authors suggest strategies for change, including demonstrating relevance to schools, developing consensus among stakeholders, enhancing community mental health–school connections, building quality assessment and improvement, and considering the organizational context of schools. (*Psychiatric Services* 58:1330–1338, 2007)

The failure of the nation's child mental health system to fully address the mental health needs of children and adolescents has been well documented and points to the need to reconsider current policy and practice (1–4). The lack of clear direction or a unified vision to guide efforts within the system arguably contributes to the inadequacy of care received by our nation's youths.

In 2002, President George W. Bush established the President's New Freedom Commission on Mental Health to analyze the state of the country's mental health system. After a year of study and input from more than 2,000 stakeholders, the commission concluded that "the mental health delivery system is fragmented and in disarray . . . leading to unnecessary and costly disability, homelessness, school failure and incarceration" (5). The final report of the commission, *Achieving the Promise: Transforming Mental Health Care in America* (5), highlighted unmet needs and barriers to care, including fragmenta-tion and gaps in care for children and lack of a national priority for mental health care. The report articulates six goals and 19 recommendations that target dramatic transformation and improvement of child, adolescent, and adult mental health systems (see box on page 49).

The commission unequivocally recognized that mental health services in schools are a critical component in rebuilding our mental health system for children. Given that the recommendations of the New Freedom Commission report are consistent with the goals of most school mental health programs, efforts have been made to identify the implications of the New Freedom Commission report for advancing a school mental health policy agenda (6,7). The New Freedom Commission report includes very specific and direct linkage to school mental health services and programs as described in goal 4, "Early mental health screening, assessment, and referral to services are common practice." To reach this goal, the commission recommended that we "improve and expand school mental health programs" (recommendation 4.2).

This article examines the intersection of school mental health and the New Freedom Commission recommendations in order to highlight the role of school mental health in the transformation of the child and adolescent mental health system. We conclude with specific recommendations for utilizing the New Freedom Commission report as a meaningful and useful framework for system transformation.

Dr. Stephan and Dr. Weist are affiliated with the Department of Psychiatry, University of Maryland School of Medicine, 737 W. Lombard St., Rm. 426, Baltimore, MD 21201 (e-mail: sstephan@psych.umaryland.edu). Dr. Kataoka is with the Department of Psychiatry, University of California, Los Angeles. Dr. Adelsheim is with the Department of Psychiatry, University of New Mexico, Albuquerque. Ms. Mills is with the Department of Population, Family, and Reproductive Health, Johns Hopkins Bloomberg School of Public Health, Baltimore. Originally published in the October 2007 issue of Psychiatric Services.

School mental health

Throughout the United States schools offer youths unparalleled access to resources to address interrelated academic, emotional, behavioral, and developmental needs. With more than 52 million youths attending over 110,000 schools and more than six million adults working in schools, one-fifth of the U.S. population can be reached in schools (5). In fact, reports have documented that of the small percentage of children and adolescents who receive needed mental health services, schools are the most common setting in which children access this care (1,8,9). Further, data indicate that these services are indeed reaching youths, including youths from ethnic minority groups and students with less obvious problems, such as depression and anxiety, who are unlikely to access services in specialty mental health settings (10–13).

School mental health programs offer increased accessibility to students by reducing many of the barriers to seeking care in traditional settings, such as transportation, child care, and stigma, and by reducing the inefficiency of "no shows"; that is, when a student does not keep an appointment, a school-based provider has the ability to serve other students in the time slot (14). Further, evidence suggests that school mental health programs reduce stigma associated with seeking mental health support (15), increase opportunities to promote generalization and maintenance of treatment gains (16), and enhance capacity for mental health promotion activities as well as universal and targeted prevention effort (17,18). Compared with traditional outpatient mental health services, school mental health services can offer more ecologically grounded roles for mental health clinicians (that is, roles based in the natural environment of the student) (19). School mental health services have been shown to enhance clinical productivity, because students are more accessible to mental health staff (20).

In addition to these inherent advantages of school mental health services, there is growing evidence that school mental health programs can have a positive impact on a number of student, family, and school outcomes. These services have resulted in reduced emotional and behavioral problems, decreased disciplinary referrals, increased prosocial behavior, increased family engagement, and improvement in school outcomes, such as fewer disciplinary referrals, improved school climate, and fewer special education referrals (21–28).

Further, there is growing recognition by policy makers and consumers of the value of school mental health programs and services. A recent policy statement on school mental health released by the American Academy of Pediatrics (29) underscores many of these advantages, including improved access to a range of services and enhanced opportunities for service coordination. The policy statement advocates for effective collaboration between educators, primary health care providers, and mental health professionals in implementing high-quality school-based mental health services.

School mental health and the commission report

The University of Maryland Center for School Mental Health has convened meetings and conducted policy analyses to identify the most important connections between the New Freedom Commission report and the Achieving the Promise Initiative and school mental health. Four specific recommendations of the New Freedom Commission report were determined to have the most proximal connections to school mental health: reduce stigma, prevent suicide, screen and treat comorbid mental and substance use disorders, and the obvious, improve and expand school mental health programs. Ideas explored by the Center for School Mental Health in relation to each of these themes are discussed below, with an emphasis on the role of school mental health in creating system transformation.

Reduce stigma

Recommendation 1.1 of the New Freedom Commission report advocates for the implementation of a national campaign to reduce the stigma of seeking mental health care and a national strategy for suicide prevention. Less than 30% of individuals with psychiatric disorders seek treatment (30,31), and stigma is a significant barrier to help seeking and accessing services (32). Schools are a key venue for supporting a campaign to reduce stigma, and school mental health services naturally reduce obstacles to care related to stigma (32).

Focusing on mental health in schools provides both natural and formal opportunities for promoting antistigma messages related to mental health. With appropriate training and community support, school staff can normalize mental illness, convey positive messages about mental health, and encourage students to engage in activities that promote mental wellness. Formal avenues for reducing mental health stigma in schools include integration of mental health awareness into special and regular education curricula, including universal programs on social and emotional learning, prevention programs, and specialized interventions for problems. Simple messages, such as "mental health refers to thoughts, feelings and actions that contribute to success in life," can help to generalize the concept of mental health as applicable to everyone and to dispel negative connotations that mental health refers only to those with chronic mental illness.

Schools also reduce stigma by offering a naturalistic environment for youths and families to seek assistance for mental health needs. In contrast to traditional community mental health settings, which may be seen as disconnected from a family's daily environment, schools offer an ecologically sound alternative, providing services directly in the living and learning environment of children. The availability and accessibility of school mental health providers, access to key informants such as teachers, and the typical proximity of schools to children's neighborhoods all further increase the likelihood of care seeking. Because of their historic ties to children, families, and communities, schools can also serve as a natural place for families to be exposed to information about mental health and available services.

Prevent suicide

Schools are also a critical venue for developing and executing the second proposal of recommendation 1.1—to implement a national strategy to prevent suicide. As noted, schools offer a desirable site for both suicide prevention campaigns and programs for youths because of schools' ability to reach most youths, their inherent ties to families and communities, and the multiple opportunities for both formal and informal education about and prevention of mental health problems and psychosocial problems, including suicide.

Data from the 2003 Youth Risk Behavior Survey of a nationally representative sample of more than 15,000 high school students throughout the United States indicate that in the 12-month period preceding the survey 16.9% had seriously considered attempting suicide, 16.5% had made a plan for attempting suicide, 8.5% had attempted suicide one or more times, and 2.9% had made an attempt requiring medical attention (33). More than 60% of adolescents who commit suicide have mental health problems, which often have existed for a year or more before the suicide (34). There is increasing national focus on preventing teen suicide, as reflected in the Call to Action to Prevent Suicide by the U.S. Surgeon General (35) and the more recent strategy document (36) developed by the U.S. Department of Health and Human Services, the National Strategy for Suicide Prevention, (www.mentalhealth.samhsa.gov/suicideprevention). The latter effort represents the first national blueprint to address suicide and calls on schools to play a significant role in efforts to prevent suicide nationwide. Specifically, schools are encouraged to collaborate with other agencies, increase the implementation of research-supported prevention programs, train key school personnel to identify youths at risk of suicide, and develop effective suicide screening programs that are directly

---

President's New Freedom Commission Goals and Recommendations

1.1. Advance and implement a national campaign to reduce the stigma of seeking care and a national strategy for suicide prevention
1.2. Address mental health with the same urgency as physical health
2.1. Develop an individualized plan of care for every child with a serious emotional disturbance
2.2. Involve consumers and families fully in orienting the mental health system toward recovery
2.3. Align relevant federal programs to improve access and accountability for mental health services
2.4. Create a comprehensive state mental health plan
2.5. Protect and enhance the rights of people with mental illness
3.1. Improve access to high-quality care that is culturally competent
3.2. Improve access to high-quality care in rural and geographically remote areas
4.1. Promote the mental health of young children
4.2. Improve and expand school mental health programs
4.3. Screen for co-occurring mental and substance use disorders and link with integrated treatment strategies
4.4. Screen for mental disorders in primary health care across the life span and connect individuals to treatment and supports
5.1. Accelerate research to promote recovery and resilience and ultimately to cure and prevent mental illnesses
5.2. Advance evidence-based practices by using dissemination and demonstration projects and create a public-private partnership to guide their implementation
5.3. Improve and expand the workforce providing evidence-based mental health services and supports
5.4. Develop the knowledge base in four understudied areas: mental health disparities, long-term effects of medication, trauma, and acute care
6.1. Use health technology and telehealth to improve access and coordination of mental health care, especially for Americans in remote areas or in under served populations
6.2. Develop and implement integrated electronic health record and personal health information systems

---

linked to needed services. It is also noteworthy that the Substance Abuse and Mental Health Services Administration (SAMHSA) is providing key federal leadership in suicide prevention, including a grant program that specifically emphasizes school-based activities.

School-based efforts to address suicide have been evaluated with mixed results (37). One suicide prevention strategy that is being implemented in a number of districts across the country is the school gatekeeper training model, which has several key components: training school personnel (gatekeepers) to improve their knowledge, attitudes, and skills to appropriately intervene with students at risk of suicide; providing crisis intervention to engage suicidal students' support networks; and facilitating suicidal students' referrals for treatment and counseling

(38). A recent study found that among students who had been previously identified as at risk of suicide, use of this gatekeeper model can increase the proportion of students who access specialty mental health services in the community (39).

Some screening and prevention efforts, including Columbia University's TeenScreen Program (www.teenscreen.org) and the SOS Suicide Prevention Program (40), have demonstrated positive findings with respect to identifying at-risk youths, increasing knowledge about suicide and depression, and reducing suicide attempts. However, their success has also been paired with controversy related to concerns about the large number of false-positive screens and the limited capacity of schools to respond to serious mental health issues that may be unveiled when screening programs are implemented (41). Some of the concerns regarding school-based universal suicide screening are likely rooted in the stigma associated with mental health problems compared with other medical issues, such as vision and hearing, for which there is already schoolwide screening.

Federal support for universal mental health screening, as evidenced in the New Freedom Commission recommendations, reflects the recognition that for most individuals with mental illness symptoms begin in childhood, which suggests that early screening can play a critical role in providing prevention and early intervention to delay or eliminate the onset of symptoms (30). Weist and colleagues (42) have outlined a process for addressing concerns about school-based mental health screening that includes intensive planning, collaboration, training, supervision, and support to ensure the selection of age-appropriate screening methods; parental consent and student assent; trained and available staff and mental health providers to conduct screenings and follow-up treatment; and resolution of logistical and liability issues.

Screen and treat co-occurring disorders

The New Freedom Commission argues for the screening and integrated treatment of comorbid mental and substance use disorders in recommendation 4.3. The reality is that co-occurring disorders are more common than not among people with mental illness or substance use disorders (43). Even though the rate of youth substance use has been declining overall in the past decade, half of adolescents have tried an illicit drug by the time they graduate from high school (44). Of youths identified as having substance use disorders, it is estimated that up to 75% may have a co-occurring mental health disorder (45).

Despite this reality most communities do not have the capacity to respond to any level of substance abuse concerns among youths because of stigma, resource limitations, limited evidence-based approaches, and the

failure of child-serving systems to take responsibility for the problem (46). Lack of ownership by a single community system is also reflected in schools, where substance abuse services are often not well integrated into the full continuum of mental health service delivery for youths (47). Although school-based mental health providers are often the "default" providers of substance abuse services, limitations in preservice training and lack of supervision and support in evidence-based substance abuse treatment for mental health providers leave many providers unprepared to address co-occurring mental health and substance use problems (48).

Despite the existing challenges to providing high-quality services to youths with comorbid mental and substance use problems, schools offer inherent advantages in this arena. Specifically, the federal focus on funding prevention programs, such as Safe and Drug Free Schools and initiatives of the Center for Substance Abuse Prevention, have advanced the integration of substance abuse programming into schools across all grade levels. Further, when evidence-based substance abuse prevention activities are implemented appropriately in schools, outcomes are positive and strong, including delayed initiation of use, decreased frequency of use, and slowed or arrested progression to the use of more hazardous substances (49). As discussed above, schools are also uniquely staged to offer screening of co-occurring mental health and substance use problems, given their ability to reach many students, the growing infrastructure to implement screening, and the evolution of guidelines to promote responsible, effective screening protocols (42). In addition, a number of prevention and intervention programs have been successfully implemented in school settings.

Improve and expand school mental health programs

Recommendation 4.2 of the New Freedom Commission report is to "improve and expand school mental health programs." When detection, prevention, and early intervention

services for youths are provided in the context of schools, negative consequences such as school failure and comorbid substance abuse can be prevented. Coordinated school service approaches have been described that integrate assessments with on-campus prevention services, early intervention programs, and more intensive systems-of-care services for the few students who require multimodal treatments across child-serving agencies. However, as the *Blueprint for Change: Research on Child and Adolescent Mental Health* from the National Institute of Mental Health has noted, research advances in the development of efficacious mental health treatments for children and adolescents have had minimal translation into community practice settings such as schools (50).

Contributing to the slow progress of bringing improved services into schools is the reality that schools are underresourced to address nonacademic barriers to learning. Most districts offer mental health supports to only a small percentage of students, often those in or being referred to special education. Further, the quality of services for emotional or behavioral disabilities that are provided to youths in special education is questionable (51), with many youths receiving "no or poor" services to address their individual needs (52).

SAMHSA recently released the report of the first national survey of school mental health in the United States for the 2002–2003 school year (53). According to the report, over 80% of U.S. schools provided assessment for mental health issues, consultation for behavioral problems, and some level of crisis intervention services. Children with more serious issues are commonly referred to community agencies. Around two-thirds of schools reported providing individual and group counseling and some case management services. However, because of the way the survey was structured, respondents could indicate that a service was provided even it was for only one student or a few students, which likely resulted in exaggeration of services actually provided. Also notable was that education leaders at local and state levels expressed the perception that mental health needs of students were increasing while funding was not adequate to meet these needs and was predicted to decrease, not increase. These school leaders also expressed concern about the many barriers to successfully referring students for services in other community agencies. Thus these findings suggest that the majority of schools offer some level of mental health services but that these services are not sufficient to meet youths' needs and that connections with other community systems remain a significant challenge.

It has been challenging to advocate for school mental health services as a transformative force in children's mental health when schools are in essence undergoing their own transformation related to the No Child Left Behind Act. Despite evidence linking empirically supported mental health promotion to academic achievement and school success (28, 54–58), education system reform has directed relatively little attention to nonacademic barriers to learning. Instead, these educational reforms have for the most part focused on grades and test scores for reading and math to the exclusion of other subjects, with no attention to the mental health and well-being of students. Further research is needed to bridge this divide between educational reform efforts and the transformation of school mental health and to encourage greater collaboration between educators and school mental health providers in the development of programs that support academic success.

School mental health and transformation

An analysis of school mental health services and the New Freedom Commission report reveals their mutual goal of maximizing healthy development and success for all children through the provision of high-quality mental health services in a public health framework that ensures access to all youths and families. Although the New Freedom Commission report reviews critical dimensions for

needed change, it does not detail how such change will occur or be funded. Systemic change is extremely challenging partly because of limited resources and resistance to movement away from the status quo. Without purposeful action from a diversity of stakeholders aimed at implementation of the New Freedom Commission recommendations, it is likely that the document will remain relatively unused. From a historical perspective, Friedman (59) noted, "the mere articulation of policy through legislation or regulation is rarely adequate to accomplish the goals of the policy." Below are suggestions for facilitating transformation of child and adolescent mental health services through the school system.

Demonstrate relevance to schools
In an era of paramount attention to the academic achievement of our children, school mental health has the advantage of articulating a powerful message linking mental health to school success. The argument for integrated approaches to reduce both academic and nonacademic barriers to learning is supported by mounting evidence demonstrating a strong positive association between psychological wellness and academic success (28,54–58). Research suggests that 46% of the failure to complete secondary school is attributable to psychiatric disorders (60). Thus it is not difficult to conceive of advocacy and public awareness efforts that highlight the need for attention to school mental health in overall mental health system change. For the transformation of children's mental health services to expand school mental health, it is necessary to generate understanding and buy-in from educators through the dissemination of clear and strong messages about the importance of mental health and the negative impact of mental illness on school success. To that end, the school mental health field must clearly define specific academic factors—for example, grades, discipline referrals, promotion, dropout, and school connectedness—that are influenced by mental health promotion and intervention.

Develop consensus among stakeholders
One way to develop messages about school mental health and programs that speak to the school community more clearly is to develop consensus across diverse school stakeholders in a true participatory partnership. From mental health antistigma campaigns on campus to early mental health intervention programs targeting at-risk students, all school mental health activities would benefit from being informed, created, implemented, and disseminated through a partnership of school stakeholders, including youths, families, educators, administrators, providers, and community members and leaders. This would help to ensure that the multiple missions and goals of school and community stakeholders are addressed and that school mental health programs are both feasible and culturally relevant and acceptable.

There is a significant need to promote true involvement of the public in discussions about mental health and transformation of the education system and ideas to advance school mental health. A number of strategies could be used to promote such public involvement. First, the New Freedom Commission report can be used as a tool for discussions about school mental health among diverse stakeholder groups. This is currently being done by the IDEA Partnership (www. ideapartnership.org and www.shared work.org). Second, the interdisciplinary nature of school mental health (with families and youths included as one of the disciplines) can be acknowledged, and interdisciplinary networking and training can be increased, such as the networking and training that occurs at the Center for School Mental Health annual conference on advancing school mental health (csmh.umaryland.edu). Third, social marketing efforts can be developed that speak to the promise and challenges of school mental health in plain language written for diverse stakeholder audiences.

Enhance community mental health–school connections
A major focus for the authors of this article has been advancing a shared

family-school-community agenda, evidenced by strong family and youth leadership and strong collaboration between the education system and the child and adolescent mental health system in building school mental health. This has also been a major theme in the expanded school mental health framework and at the University of Maryland Center for School Mental Health.

A number of strategies to strengthen these partnerships are promising. A first strategy is reaching out to and encouraging leadership in relevant professional organizations to support this agenda. Such organizations include the National Association of State Directors of Special Education, the National Association of State Mental Health Program Directors, the Council of Chief State School Officers, the National Council of State Legislatures, and the American College of Mental Health Administrators, which already espouse and demonstrate support for such an integrated agenda. A second strategy is tracking strong examples of family-school-community collaboration to advance school mental health, which is done at annual conferences and in books (61,62), and moving toward Internet-based evolving directories of programs to promote networking and collaboration across communities, states, and organizations (www.sharedwork.org). A third strategy to strengthen partnerships is to capitalize on federal grant opportunities that promote such partnerships, such as System of Care (SAMHSA), Safe Schools/ Healthy Students (SAMHSA and Department of Education), and Mental Health Integration Into the Schools (Department of Education).

Build quality assessment and improvement

An overarching construct in school mental health is advancing quality assessment and improvement, which can be viewed as inclusive of all relevant processes—needs assessment and resource mapping; stakeholder involvement; coordination of services in schools; connecting school mental health services in schools to related community programs and efforts; selecting, training, supporting, and coaching staff; emphasizing high-quality and evidence-based services; evaluating services provided to individual students and at the program level; and connecting evaluation findings to continuous quality improvement cycles and advocacy efforts. There is a great need for approaches to measure and improve the quality of school mental health services, and some measures are now available, including the School Mental Health Quality Assessment Questionnaire (63) and the Mental Health Planning and Evaluation Template (www.nasbhc.org).

Central in the quality agenda, and receiving increased attention, is the goal of making evidence-based services feasible in schools (64,65). Several successful models of development and implementation of mental health services in schools exist along the continuum of care and should be considered examples for future work in the area. Two representative examples are LifeSkills Training (www.lifeskillstraining.com) and Cognitive Behavioral Intervention for Trauma in Schools (66), both of which were developed for implementation in schools. These two programs have demonstrated positive outcomes among participants according to both psychosocial and academic indicators and have been endorsed by SAMHSA as model programs.

It is important to note that promoting quality assessment and improvement in school mental health will help to increase the likelihood of effective services that achieve outcomes valued by families and schools. This in turn will help to propel school mental health agendas in communities and states, contributing to real systems transformation as called for by the Achieving the Promise initiative.

Consider the organizational context of schools

In addition to improving the quality of school mental health at the provider and program levels, transformation of mental health services for youths must also attend to the system and organizational issues that are relevant for schools. Leadership support within an organization has been found to be an important factor in the adoption of new programs, and commitment from school administrators has been shown to strongly influence the implementation of prevention programs (67,68). Successful adoption of mental health programs has also been shown to be related to the climate and structure of the organization (69,70) and may be related to the readiness of a school to adopt a new school mental health program. Similarly, school mental health programs may be more successfully implemented if there is minimal burden on instructional staff in schools, especially given heightened pressures to perform under No Child Left Behind.

As evidence-based mental health programs are implemented in the school system, factors such as federal and state policies that influence the financing of school mental health programs can also greatly influence dissemination of evidence-based programs in schools. For example, SAMHSA's National Child Traumatic Stress Initiative has supported the dissemination of trauma-informed best practices in community settings such as schools (www.nctsn.org), which has resulted not only in improved quality of services in schools for traumatized youths but also in sustained services through community-school partnerships (25,71). Similarly the Mental Health Services Act in California provides for additional funds through state taxes to support the dissemination of mental health care, including prevention and early intervention services for children and adolescents in school settings. By having access to funding that does not compete with education dollars, schools may have more incentive to support mental health services on campus.

Conclusions

The President's New Freedom Commission report provides a launching point from which school mental health programs can expand the scope and depth of child mental health services. By delivering these services in a naturalistic community setting that minimizes some of the barriers to accessing care for youths and their families, school mental health programs can play a critical role in operationalizing the recommendations of the New Freedom Commission report, both in terms of supporting the resiliency of youths and providing effective services for those who need mental health care. The New Freedom Commission has built upon previous federal initiatives, such as the U.S. Surgeon General's reports on mental health (8,9) and the Children's Mental Health Conference (72), by emphasizing the need to improve the dissemination of evidence-based treatments in community settings and increasing the awareness of mental health issues across child-serving agencies.

This article has outlined some of the ways in which national school mental health efforts are aligned with the goals and recommendations of the New Freedom Commission. From this national agenda for transforming mental health care in the United States, several key strategies have also been discussed in terms of addressing these goals in schools, including demonstrating relevance to schools, developing consensus among stakeholders, enhancing community mental health–school connections, building quality assessment and improvement, and transforming school mental health services in the organizational context of schools.

Implications for a research agenda to support this transformation would also involve greater collaboration across academic disciplines and true partnerships with community stakeholders that inform the direction of the research questions and the design, implementation, and dissemination of services in schools. If school mental health programs are to improve and expand effectively, joint efforts by education and mental health researchers toward the achievement of both academic success and emotional well-being for students are necessary. Greater participatory research with school-community partners can enlighten the research agenda in such a way that barriers to providing services on campuses are reduced. Ap-

proaching mental health services in schools through the lens of an educator, a student, or an administrator will enhance the development of novel approaches to address stigma, treat co-occurring disorders, and prevent suicide—all of which are relevant to the school culture as well as culturally appropriate for the community being served.

Recent federal legislation to support mental health in schools reflects progress in advancing the school mental health agenda. Namely, the Mental Health in Schools Act of 2007, introduced by Senators Dodd, Domenici, and Kennedy, proposed significant funding to local education agencies to expand existing school mental health efforts through community-family-school partnerships. The bipartisan legislation emphasizes a public health approach to mental health that includes prevention and promotion, positive behavioral supports, and targeted intervention and stresses cultural and linguistic competence. Further, the proposed legislation underscores the importance of program accountability by requiring the use of evidence-based practices and outcome measurement.

Two other recent Senate bills reflect critical federal support for school-based services, including mental health: Senate Bill 600, the School-Based Health Clinic Establishment Act (introduced February 15, 2007) and Senate Bill 1669, the Healthy Schools Act of 2007 (introduced June 20, 2007). If passed, Senate Bill 600 would authorize the first-ever federal program for school-based health centers, the large majority of which would include mental health providers and all of which would provide at least some level of mental health care to students. The Healthy Schools Act of 2007 similarly supports the inclusion of mental health services in school-based health centers by ensuring procedures for payment under Medicaid and the State Children's Health Insurance Program to school centers certified by the Department of Health and Human Services. In addition, the legislation recognizes that mental health must be considered a part of compre-

hensive care by establishing a minimum criterion for "primary health services" as the core group of services offered by school-based health centers, including comprehensive health and mental health assessments, intervention, and treatment. Together with enhanced advocacy, effective policy, and development of established models of mental health care in schools, federal legislation of this nature is necessary to ensure that transformation of the children's mental health system is inclusive of schools.

Acknowledgments and disclosures

This work was supported by cooperative agreement U45-MC-00174-10-0 from the Office of Adolescent Health, Maternal and Child Health Bureau (Title V, Social Security Act), Health Resources and Services Administration, with cofunding from the Center for Mental Health Services, Substance Abuse and Mental Health Services Administration. It was also supported by grant 1-R01-MH-71015-01-A1 from the National Institute of Mental Health.

The authors report no competing interests.

References

1. Burns BJ, Costello EJ, Angold A, et al: Children's mental health services use across sectors. Health Affairs 14(3):147–159, 1995

2. Youngsters' Mental Health and Psychosocial Problems: What Are the Data? Los Angeles, Center for Mental Health in Schools, 2003

3. Kataoka S, Zhang L, Wells KB: Unmet need for mental health care among US children: variation by ethnicity and insurance status. American Journal of Psychiatry 159:1548–1555, 2003

4. Leaf PJ, Alegria M, Cohen P: Mental health service use in the community and schools: results from the four-community MECA study. Journal of the American Academy of Child and Adolescent Psychiatry 35:889–897, 1996

5. Achieving the Promise: Transforming Mental Health Care in America: Executive Summary. Pub no SMA-03-3831. Rockville, Md, Department of Health and Human Services, President's New Freedom Commission on Mental Health, 2003

6. Integrating Agenda for Mental Health in Schools Into the Recommendations of the President's New Freedom Commission on Mental Health. Los Angeles, Center for Mental Health in Schools, 2004

7. Mills C, Stephan SH, Moore E, et al: The President's New Freedom Commission: capitalizing on opportunities to advance school-based mental health services. Clinical Child and Family Psychology Review 9:149–161, 2006

8. Mental Health: A Report of the Surgeon

General: Executive Summary. Rockville, Md, Department of Health and Human Services, US Public Health Service, 1999

9. Mental Health: Culture, Race and Ethnicity: A Report of the Surgeon General. Rockville, Md, Department of Health and Human Services, US Public Health Service, 2001

10. Foster EM, Conner T: Public costs of better mental health services for children and adolescents. Psychiatric Services 56:50–55, 2005

11. Weist MD: Expanded school mental health services: a national movement in progress, in Advances in Clinical Child Psychology. Edited by Ollendick T, Prinz RJ. New York, Plenum, 1997

12. Kataoka SH, Stein BD, Jaycox LH, et al: A school-based mental health program for traumatized Latino immigrant children. Journal of the American Academy of Child and Adolescent Psychiatry 42:311–318, 2003

13. Kutash K, Rivera VR: What Works in Children's Mental Health Services: Uncovering Answers to Critical Questions. Baltimore, Brookes Publishing, 1996

14. Weist MD: Challenges and opportunities in expanded school mental health. Clinical Psychology Review 19:131–135, 1999

15. Nabors LA, Reynolds MW: Overcoming challenges in outcome evaluations of school mental health programs. Journal of School Health 70:206–209, 2000

16. Evans S: Mental health services in schools: utilization, effectiveness and consent. Clinical Psychology Review 19:165–178, 1999

17. Elias MJ, Gager P, Leon S: Spreading a warm blanket of prevention over all children: guidelines for selecting substance abuse and related prevention curricula for use in the schools. Journal of Primary Prevention 18:41–69, 1997

18. Weare K: Promoting Mental, Emotional and Social Health: A Whole School Approach. London, Routledge, 2000

19. Atkins MS, Adil JA, Jackson M, et al: An ecological model for school-based mental health services, in 13th Annual Research Conference Proceedings: A System of Care of Children's Mental Health: Expanding the Research Base. Edited by Newman C, Liberton C, Kutash K, et al. Tampa, University of South Florida, Louis de la Parte Florida Mental Health Institute, Research and Training Center for Children's Mental Health, 2001

20. Flaherty LT, Weist MW: School-based mental health services: the Baltimore models. Psychology in the Schools 36:379–389, 1999

21. Armbruster P, Lichtman J: Are school-based mental health services effective? Evidence from 36 inner city schools. Community Mental Health Journal 35:493–504, 1999

22. Burns EJ, Walrath C, Glass-Siegel M, et al: School-based mental health service in Baltimore. Behavior Modification 28:491–512, 2004

23. Horner RH, Sugai G, Todd AW, et al: School-wide positive behavior support: an alternative approach to discipline in schools, in Individualized Support for Students With Problem Behaviors: Designing Positive Behavior Plans. Edited by Bambara L, Kern L. New York, Guilford, 2005

24. Scott TM: A school-wide example of positive behavioral support. Journal of Positive Behavior Interventions 3:88–94, 2001

25. Stein BD, Jaycox LH, Kataoka SH, et al: A mental health intervention for schoolchildren exposed to violence. JAMA 290:603–611, 2003

26. Stormshak B, Dishion T, Light J: Implementing family-centered interventions within the public middle school: linking service delivery to change in student problem behavior. Journal of Abnormal Child Psychology 33:723–733, 2005

27. Sugai G, Sprague J, Horner RH, et al: Preventing school violence: the use of the office discipline referrals to assess and monitor school-wide discipline interventions. Journal of Emotional and Behavioral Disorders 8:94–101, 2000

28. Zins JE, Weissberg RP, Wan MC, et al: Building School Success Through Social and Emotional Learning. New York, Teachers College Press, 2004

29. Committee on School Health: School-based mental health services. Pediatrics 113:1839–1845, 2004

30. Kessler RC, Berglund PA, Bruce ML, et al: The prevalence and correlates of untreated serious mental illness. Health Services Research 36:987–1007, 2001

31. Regier DA, Narrow WE, Rae DS, et al: The de facto US mental and addictive disorders service system: Epidemiologic Catchment Area prospective 1-year prevalence rates of disorders and services. Archives of General Psychiatry 50:85–94, 1993

32. Owens PL, Hoagwood K, Horowitz L, et al: Barriers to children's mental health services. Journal of the American Academy of Child and Adolescent Psychiatry 41:731–738, 2002

33. Grunbaum JA, Kann L, Kinchen S, et al: Youth risk behavior surveillance: United States, 2003. Morbidity and Mortality Weekly Report 53:1–95, 2004

34. Shaffer D, Gould MS, Fisher P, et al: Psychiatric diagnosis in child and adolescent suicide. Archives of General Psychiatry 53:339–348, 1996

35. The Surgeon General's Call to Action to Prevention of Suicide. Washington, DC, US Public Health Service, 1999

36. National Strategy for Suicide Prevention: Goals and Objectives for Action. Rockville, Md, Department of Health and Human Services, US Public Health Service, 2001

37. Gould MS, Greenberg T, Velting DM, et al: Youth suicide risk and preventive interventions: a review of the past 10 years. Journal of the American Academy of Child and Adolescent Psychiatry 42:386–405, 2003

38. Enhanced Pediatric Nutrition Surveillance System (PedNSS) Manual. Atlanta, Centers for Disease Control and Prevention, 1994

39. Kataoka S, Stein BD, Nadeem E, et al: Who gets care? Mental health service use following a school-based suicide prevention program. Journal of the American Academy of Child and Adolescent Psychiatry, in press

40. Aseltine R, DeMartino R: An outcome evaluation of SOS suicide prevention program. American Journal of Public Health 94:446–451, 2004

41. Coyne JC, Gaba CG, Benazon NR, et al: Distress and psychiatric morbidity among women from high risk breast and ovarian cancer families. Journal of Consulting and Clinical Psychology 68:864–874, 2000

42. Weist MD, Rubin M, Moore E, et al: Mental health screening in schools. Journal of School Health 77:53–58, 2007

43. Power K, DeMartino R: Co-occurring disorders and achieving recovery: the Substance Abuse and Mental Health Services Administration perspective. Biological Psychiatry 56:721–722, 2004

44. Johnston L, O'Malley P, Bachman J, et al: Monitoring the Future National Results on Adolescent Drug Use: Overview of Key Findings, 2004. Bethesda, Md, National Institute on Drug Abuse, 2004

45. Greenbaum P, Foster-Johnson L, Petrila A: Co-occurring addictive and mental disorders among adolescents: prevalence research and future directions. American Journal of Orthopsychiatry 66:52–60, 1996

46. Lamb S, Greenlich MR, McCarty D: Bridging the Gap Between Research and Practice: Forging Partnerships With Community-Based Drug and Alcohol Treatment. Washington, DC, National Academy Press, 1998

47. Connecting Substance Abuse Prevention and Intervention to School-Based Mental Health. Baltimore, University of Maryland School of Medicine, Center for School Mental Health Assistance, 2000. Available at csmh.umaryland.edu

48. Jaffe SL, Mogul RJ: Alcohol and substance abuse in children and adolescents, in Handbook of Child and Adolescent Outpatient, Day Treatment and Community Psychiatry. Edited by Ghuman H, Sarles R. Philadelphia, Brunner/Mazel, 1998

49. Botvin G, Baker E, Dusenbury L, et al: Long-term follow-up results of a randomized drug abuse prevention trial in a white middle-class population. JAMA 273:1106–1112, 1995

50. Blueprint for Change: Research on Child and Adolescent Mental Health. Washington, DC, National Advisory Mental Health Council, Workgroup on Child and Adolescent Mental Health Intervention and Development and Deployment, 2001

51. Kutash K, Duchnowski A: The mental health needs of youth with emotional and behavioral disabilities placed in special education programs in urban schools. Journal of Child and Family Studies 13:235–248, 2004

52. Nelson M: Through a glass darkly: reflections on our field and its future. Behavioral Disorders 28:212–216, 2003

53. Foster S, Rollefson M, Doksum T et al: School Mental Health Services in the United States, 2002–2003. DHHS pub no SMA-05-4068. Rockville, Md, Substance Abuse and Mental Health Services Administration, Center for Mental Health Services, 2005

54. Bishop JH, Bishop M, Gelbwasser L, et al: Why we harass nerds and freaks: a formal theory of student culture and norms. Journal of School Health 74:235–251, 2004

55. Catalano RF, Haggerty K, Oesterle S, et al: The importance of bonding to school for health development: findings from the Social Development Research Group. Journal of School Health 74:252–261, 2004

56. Klern AM, Connell JP: Relationships matter: linking teacher support to student engagement and achievement. Journal of School Health 74:262–273, 2004

57. McNeely C, Falci C: School connectedness and the transition into and out of health-risk behavior among adolescents: a comparison of social belonging and teacher support. Journal of School Health 74:284–292, 2004

58. Wilson D: The interface of school climate and school connectedness and relationships with aggression and victimization. Journal of School Health 74:293–299, 2004

59. Friedman RM: A conceptual framework for developing and implementing effective policy in children's mental health. Journal of Emotional and Behavioral Disorders 11:11–18, 2003

60. Stoep AV, Weiss NS, Kuo ES, et al: What proportion of failure to complete secondary school in the US population is attributable to adolescent psychiatric disorder? Journal of Behavioral Health Services and Research 30:119–124, 2003

61. Robinson KE: Advances in School-Based Mental Health Interventions: Best Practices and Program Models. New York, Civic Research Institute, 2004

62. Weist MD, Evans SW, Lever NA: Handbook of School Mental Health: Advancing Practice and Research. New York, Kluwer, 2003

63. Weist MD, Sander MA, Walrath C, et al: Developing principles for best practice in expanded school mental health. Journal of Youth and Adolescence 34:7–13, 2005

64. Martin JL, Weisz JR, Chorpita BF, et al: Moving evidence-based practices into everyday clinical care settings: addressing challenges associated with pathways to treatment, child characteristics, and structure of treatment. Emotional and Behavioral Disorders in Youth 7:5–21, 2006

65. Ringeisen H, Henderson K, Hoagwood K: Context matters: schools and the "research to practice gap" in children's mental health. School Psychology Review 32:153–168, 2003

66. Jaycox L: Cognitive Behavioral Intervention for Trauma in Schools. Longmont, Colo, Sopris West, 2004

67. Kallestad JH, Olweus D: Predicting teachers' and schools implementation of the Olweus Bullying Prevention Program: a multilevel study, in Prevention and Treatment, vol 6. Washington, DC, American Psychological Association, 2003

68. Rohrbach LA, Backer TE, Montgomery SB: Diffusion of school-based substance abuse prevention programs. American Behavioral Scientist 39:919–934, 1996

69. Gotham HJ: Diffusion of mental health and substance abuse treatments: development, dissemination, and implementation. Clinical Psychology: Science and Practice 11:160–172, 2004

70. Glisson C: The organizational context of children's mental health services. Clinical Child and Family Psychology Review 5:233–253, 2002

71. Wong M: Commentary: building partnerships between schools and academic partners to achieve a health-related research agenda. Ethnic Disparities 16(1 suppl):S149–S153, 2006

72. Report on the Surgeon General's Conference on Children's Mental Health: A National Action Agenda. Washington, DC, US Government Printing Office, 2000

The Top Ten Concerns About Recovery Encountered in Mental Health System Transformation

Larry Davidson, Ph.D.
Maria O'Connell, Ph.D.
Janis Tondora, Psy.D.
Thomas Styron, Ph.D.
Karen Kangas, Ed.D.

The notion of "recovery" has recently taken center stage in guiding mental health policy and practice. However, it is not yet clear what the term means and what is to be entailed in transforming the nation's mental health system to promote it. The authors discuss the various meanings of recovery as applied to mental illness and list the top ten concerns encountered in efforts to articulate and implement recovery-oriented care. These concerns include the following: recovery is old news, recovery-oriented care adds to the burden of already stretched providers, recovery involves cure, recovery happens to very few people, recovery represents an irresponsible fad, recovery happens only after and as a result of active treatment, recovery-oriented care is implemented only through the addition of new resources, recovery-oriented care is neither reimbursable nor evidence based, recovery-oriented care devalues the role of professional intervention, and recovery-oriented care increases providers' exposure to risk and liability. These concerns are addressed through discussion of the two overarching challenges that they pose, namely the issues of resources and risk. (*Psychiatric Services* 57: 640–645, 2006)

"Don't tell me that recovery is not evidence based. I'm the evidence."— Woman with serious mental illness

With the publication of the President's New Freedom Commission report, *Achieving the Promise: Transforming Mental Health Care in America* (1), the notion of "recovery" has taken center stage in guiding mental health policy and practice. With the combination of the commission's recommendations and those of the Surgeon General's unprecedented *Report on Mental Health* (2)—which emphasized that all mental health care should be consumer- and family-driven and have as its overarching aim the promotion of recovery—policy makers, program managers, and practitioners are finding themselves under increasing pressure to make services more "recovery oriented."

However, it is not entirely clear what the term "recovery" means in this context or what precisely is to be entailed in transforming America's mental health system to promote it (3–6). This lack of clarity is likely related to a deeper ambiguity about what the term recovery means as applied to mental illness. Recovery, which has been used with various connotations for the past two decades, has been the object of debate among advocates, providers, family members, and other stakeholders. The only thing about which these diverse groups appear to agree at present is that the term can be confusing and, at times, even contradictory (3).

To begin to clarify the range of issues involved in use of the term recovery in relation to mental illness, we offer a brief discussion of this term and a list of the top ten concerns we have encountered in attempting to articulate and implement care based on such a vision. Although we consider all ten concerns worthy of examination (7), within the context of this article we limit our discussion to the two overarching challenges that appear common to these concerns—namely, issues of resources and risk—and suggest possible ways to address them in the work of systems change.

A brief introduction to recovery

Given the broad heterogeneity that has been found in the outcome of serious mental illness (8–10), several different meanings of the term recovery are relevant for people with this condition. For the fortunate persons

The authors are affiliated with the Yale University program for recovery and community health and the Connecticut Department of Mental Health and Addiction Services. Send correspondence to Dr. Davidson at the Department of Psychiatry, Yale University School of Medicine, Erector Square 6 West, Suite 1C, 319 Peck Street, New Haven, Connecticut 06513 (e-mail, larry.davidson@yale.edu). Originally published in the May 2006 issue of Psychiatric Services.

who have only one episode of mental illness and then return to their previous functioning with little, if any, residual impairment, the usual sense of recovery used in primary care is the most relevant. Such people recover from an acute episode of psychosis or major depression in ways that are more similar to, than different from, recovery from acute medical conditions. Persons who recover from an episode of major affective disorder but who continue to view themselves as vulnerable to future episodes may instead consider themselves to be re-covering in ways that are not unlike recovering from a heart attack.

Many others will recover from mental illness over a longer period, after perhaps 15 or more years of disability, constituting an additional sense of recovery found in relation to some other medical conditions, such as asthma. Individuals who are concerned as much with the effects of having been diagnosed with a mental illness as with the effects of the illness itself might also consider themselves to be recovering from the trauma of having been treated as a mental patient, whereas those who view taking control of their illness and minimizing its disruptive impact as the major focus of their efforts might find the sense of recovery used in the addiction self-help community to be most compatible with their own experience. Such a sense of recovery has been embraced, for example, among persons with co-occurring psychiatric and substance use disorders who consider themselves to be in "dual recovery."

To further complicate the picture, there is at least one additional meaning of the term, which is derived by some individuals with a history of serious mental illness from the Independent Living Movement led by people with physical disabilities (11). This vision is focused more on the fundamental rights of people with disabilities—primarily rights to self-determination and community inclusion—than on their clinical or functional status per se.

It is useful in considering this final sense of recovery to recall that individuals with other forms of disability were not always accorded a life in the community to the same degree that they are today. Before passage of the Rehabilitation Act of 1973, in fact, there were no legal assurances for people with mobility impairments that they would find curbs cut into sidewalks or other means of access, such as wheelchair ramps and bathrooms equipped with handrails, when they attempted to participate in community life alongside their nondisabled peers. The Independent Living Movement played a key role in passage of the Americans With Disabilities Act of 1990, which established that a person with paraplegia need not regain use of his or her legs and a person with a visual or auditory impairment need not regain use of his or her eyes or ears for that person to have access to a safe, dignified, and full life in the community (12). It is this vision of social inclusion and self-determination that lies at the heart of this most recent sense of recovery for an increasing number of individuals living with what have come to be considered "psychiatric disabilities."

In the context of this vision, serious mental illness is viewed more in terms of the prolonged disability, impairment, or secondary consequences that result from the illness rather than in terms of the illness per se. This concept of recovery—a concept we suggest be considered "recovery in" serious mental illness as opposed to "recovery from" serious mental illness (7)—is not to be confused with cure but rather calls for the provision of accommodations and supports that enable people with psychiatric disabilities to lead safe, dignified, and full lives in the community. Once the rights and responsibilities of citizenship have in this way been restored to people with mental illness, the major challenge becomes identifying and providing the accommodations and supports the person needs in order to participate fully in the community in ways that he or she chooses. To capture the shift in practice required by this form of recovery, we have defined care oriented to these goals as that which "identifies and builds upon each individual's assets, strengths, and areas of health and competence to support the person in managing his or her condition while regaining a meaningful, constructive, sense of membership in the broader community" (3).

Even if we achieve conceptual clarity in these distinctions between various forms of recovery, confusion is reintroduced by virtue of the fact that a person may experience more than one form of recovery at any given time, as well as move in and out of different forms of recovery over time. So robust is the heterogeneity found in mental illness, and so little is known about what determines individual outcomes, that there is considerable fluidity between these various forms of recovery. As one way of reducing this complexity for the purpose of formulating policy and guiding practice, we propose accepting this final definition of recovery as having the most profound and far-reaching implications for the work of transformation.

We believe that there are two fundamental reasons that this definition is the most inclusive. First, this form of recovery speaks most directly and forcefully to the issues of civil rights and membership in society—issues that people with serious mental illnesses have identified as even more entrenched and difficult to address than those posed by the illnesses themselves (13,14). These issues are discrimination, second-class citizenship, inclusion, self-determination, and, most fundamentally, power. As suggested by its parallel in the Independent Living Movement, this form of recovery requires that persons with serious mental illnesses remain in control of their own lives, including their own mental health care, until, unless, and only for as long as there are clear and convincing reasons, grounded in law, for their sovereignty to be handed over temporarily to others. This requirement does not mean merely that they can no longer be confined to hospitals against their will for protracted periods of time. It also means that they can make their own decisions; pursue their own hopes, dreams, and aspirations; and select and participate in the activities they enjoy or find meaningful in the settings of their choice, even while disabled.

Just as it is unreasonable and unethical to insist that a person with paraplegia regain his or her mobility to live independently or that a person with visual impairments regain his or her vision to be gainfully employed or attend school, it is both unreasonable and unethical to insist that a person with a serious mental illness no longer experience symptoms or no longer have functional impairments to have sex or attend church. The fact that this principle applies to anyone with a serious mental illness, regardless of the severity of the illness or the various types of recovery accessible to the person, suggests the second reason that we propose the civil-rights sense of recovery in mental illness as the most inclusive. Focusing solely on promoting recovery from mental illness runs the risk of abandoning people with severe disabilities—people who in this sense are not recovering—to repeated failure and despair. On the other hand, restoring to people their civil rights and focusing on their hopes and participation in the enjoyable and meaningful activities of their choice would not seem to run the risk of leaving anyone behind. In fact, research suggests that identification and pursuit of activities consistent with a person's interests and learning ways to manage and minimize the destructive effects of the illness contribute to the process of recovering from serious mental illness—over a period of weeks, months, or years (15,16). For example, a focus on learning how to live with auditory hallucinations appears to result in a decrease in their severity and frequency (17), while simply waiting for the symptoms to disappear leaves a person inactive, isolated, and alone.

With this brief introduction in mind, we can now turn to our list of top ten concerns. They are listed in brief form in the box above.

The top ten concerns about recovery

The concerns listed in the accompanying box have been culled from a series of presentations, discussions, and training sessions conducted over the

---

Top ten concerns about recovery in serious mental illness

10. Recovery is old news. "What's all the hype? We've been doing recovery for decades."
9. Recovery-oriented care adds to the burden of mental health professionals who already are stretched thin by demands that exceed their resources. "You mean I not only have to care for and treat people, but now I have to do recovery too?"
8. Recovery means that the person is cured. "What do you mean your clients are in recovery? Don't you see how disabled they still are? Isn't that a contradiction?"
7. Recovery happens for very few people with serious mental illness. "You're not talking about the people I see. They're too disabled. Recovery is not possible for them."
6. Recovery in mental health is an irresponsible fad. "This is just the latest flavor of the month, and one that also sets people up for failure."
5. Recovery only happens after, and as a result of, active treatment and the cultivation of insight. "My patients won't even acknowledge that they're sick. How can I talk to them about recovery when they have no insight about being ill?"
4. Recovery can be implemented only through the introduction of new services. "Sure, we'll be happy to do recovery, just give us the money it will take to start a (new) recovery program."
3. Recovery-oriented services are neither reimbursable nor evidence based. "First it was managed care, then it was evidence-based practice, and now it's recovery. But recovery is neither cost-effective nor evidence based."
2. Recovery approaches devalue the role of professional intervention. "Why did I just spend ten years in training if someone else, with no training, is going to make all the decisions?"
1. Recovery increases providers' exposure to risk and liability. "If recovery is the person's responsibility, then how come I get the blame when things go wrong?"

---

last several years as the state of Connecticut has moved toward a recovery-oriented system of care (18). As the work of transformation can at times elicit tensions and conflict, the rubric of "top ten concerns"—derived from *Late Night With David Letterman*—was chosen to introduce some levity into the situation. Because of space limitations, we cannot take each concern separately but will address, and offer alternatives to, the two most significant challenges that appear common across the specific concerns—namely, those of resources and risk.

Recovery and resources

Many of the concerns about recovery derive from a misunderstanding of the nature of the processes involved and who is responsible for which aspects of the recovery process. In our training, we have found it useful to discuss the various meanings of recovery as they relate to mental illness (as we did above) but also, and perhaps even more important, to distinguish between recovery, which pertains to the role and responsibility of the person with a serious mental illness, and recovery-oriented care, which pertains to the role and responsibility of mental health providers.

Recovery is a process in which the person engages to figure out how to manage and live with his or her disorder. It is not a fad, an added burden, or a new and as yet unproven practice imposed on already stretched providers. As such, it is neither something providers can do to or for people with mental illness, nor is it something that can be promoted after or separate from treatment and other clinical services. Rather, the New Freedom Commission has argued for recovery to be adopted as the overarching aim of all mental health services (with the exception of forensic services for offenders with mental illness, the primary aim of which may be containment or community safety). It is thus insufficient for mental health providers to agree that they could do more to enhance quality-of-life domains among people with mental illness if they had new or additional resources. Many providers, for example, are happy to open new "recovery programs" or to decrease caseload size if offered the requisite resources. But recovery-oriented care cannot be conceptualized as an add-on to existing services.

Providers who argue that they must provide treatment first and can then perhaps focus on offering rehabilitation (if there is the time or resources), should be asked: If what you are offering is not oriented to promoting recovery, then what is it for? And if there are ways in which what you offer could be more recovery-oriented, and thereby more effective at achieving its aims, would you not want to learn about it and try it?

We are not suggesting that offering recovery-oriented care does not require the expenditure of resources. However, we cannot afford to have a recovery-oriented system grow up parallel to, and distinct from, existing systems of care, conceptualized as an adjunctive or ancillary service. Resources will be needed to fund services and supports and to carry out the staff training and consultation needed to retool the mental health workforce, but these resources will have to be derived, in large part, from the resources currently allocated to fund existing services, supports, and training.

Rather than being contradictory to recovery, this approach is one way in which the current emphasis on evidence-based practices can be used to promote recovery-oriented care. If there is no evidence supporting the effectiveness of a given practice in promoting an individual's ability to manage, overcome, or live with his or her mental illness, then why should scarce resources be used to fund it? Why should those resources not be reallocated to support practices that are more effective in achieving the overarching aim of the system of care? In this respect, it makes no sense to ask whether recovery or recovery-oriented care is "evidence based." There is ample evidence, documented extensively over 30 years, that people can and do learn how to

live with and recover from serious mental illness in the various senses described above (19). The question about evidence-based practices is which interventions, provided by whom, are most effective at promoting which of these various forms of recovery under what circumstances. It is true that new or existing resources will need to be devoted to answering this question in the future if transformation is to be optimally effective in achieving its aims.

Recovery and risk

The second commonly expressed concern about recovery involves issues of ethics and risk. How can the idea of recovery be relevant to someone experiencing an acute episode of psychosis or mania? It would seem that such a person would need to get better first before recovery can be discussed or even considered. Similarly, some staff question the ethics of focusing on strengths, hopes, and dreams when a person may be faced with such urgent needs as safety, shelter, and stabilization. Self-determination and client choice are touted as cornerstones of the recovery process. But what sense does it make to afford choices to a population of individuals whose judgment is impaired by the very conditions we are charged with treating? Doesn't honoring the choices of someone with an acute or severe mental illness involve abandoning him or her to the ravages of the illness, often to the streets? Doesn't this amount to leaving a vulnerable population of people "to rot with their rights on" (20)? Finally, providers ask, How can you tell us to promote client choice and self-determination on one hand while holding us responsible for adverse events on the other? Doesn't increasing client choice increase provider risk?

Most people who may be described as in recovery from mental illness neither think nor talk about the term "recovery" at all. They talk about getting a job, making friends, having faith, living on their own, and generally getting their lives back. Their engagement in this process is equally relevant to all phases and forms of treatment, although the goals of each

phase or form may differ. For example, in terms of acute episodes, recovery doesn't start after the episode resolves, nor can it be put on hold while the person is receiving treatment. From the person's perspective, it is rather that the acute episode has temporarily disrupted his or her ongoing process of recovery (or it may be an anticipated part of the process), and care received during this period can more or less promote or undermine that process.

Recovery requires reframing the treatment enterprise from the professional's perspective to the person's perspective. In this regard, the issue is not what role recovery plays in treatment but what role treatment plays in recovery. This shift has important implications for how we conceptualize and deliver care and the degree to which this care is acceptable to, and effective for, the people we serve. For example, if we accept the premise that mental illness is a condition that many people can learn to live with, our emphases on choice and self-determination become inevitable rather than optional. How else can people learn how to manage their condition in particular, and their life more generally, if they are not allowed to make their own decisions?

But mental illness is different from other illnesses, providers suggest, because of the issue of risk. To this concern we have several responses. First, a majority of people with mental illness pose no risks to the community (21–23). In fact, surveys have shown consistently that this population is much more likely to be victimized than to victimize others (24,25). These findings suggest that people with mental illness—like all other American citizens—should be presumed innocent until proven otherwise. In the realm of choice, this presumption means being allowed to make one's own decisions unless and until there are clear and persuasive grounds for imposing restrictions on this most fundamental of our civil rights (26). A core principle of the recovery paradigm is the appropriate application of established constructs of informed consent and permission to treat to a majority of individuals with serious mental illness a majority of the time. Application of this principle means that—as in other forms of medicine—no matter how expert or experienced the provider, it is ideally left up to the person and his or her loved ones to make informed decisions about care. It is not the practitioner's role to make such health care decisions for the person.

But doesn't such an approach result in devaluing or disregarding the knowledge and expertise of the professional? We suggest, to the contrary, that a recovery-oriented approach brings psychiatry closer to other medical specialties in which it is the specialist's role to assess the person's functioning, diagnose his or her condition, educate the person about the costs and benefits of the effective interventions available to treat the condition, and then, with provision of informed consent and permission to treat, competently provide the appropriate interventions. If mental illness is an illness like any other, it should be treated as such, by medical staff as well as by the general public. If this basic tenet is accepted, it is difficult to understand how providers could view their roles as any less important, or as requiring any less skill, than those of other specialists, such as cardiologists or oncologists.

However, given that one of the obligations of public mental health systems is to protect the community, we understand, and insist, that—just as in other forms of medicine—there are exceptions to this rule. These exceptions, as clearly delineated in federal and state statutes, invariably involve a person who poses some degree of risk, either to him- or herself or to others. In these cases, just as in emergency medicine, the issue of informed consent and permission to treat is suspended temporarily to perform life-saving measures. These cases do not contradict recovery but pose important challenges to it—challenges that may in the future be addressed through such mechanisms as psychiatric advance directives or other creative means to enable people to retain control over their lives, even in such extenuating circum-

stances. In the interim, rather than arguing about whether or not recovery-oriented care increases risk (an issue about which we do not yet have data), we suggest that it is more useful to highlight the ways in which a recovery-oriented approach clarifies and reinforces the need that already exists for appropriate risk assessment and management. Within the context of a recovery-oriented system of care, the competent conduct of risk assessments will be needed precisely in order to identify the rare circumstances in which people cannot be allowed to act in ways that put others or themselves at risk.

By defining the cases or periods of time in which people pose sufficient risk to have others step in and make decisions for them (to protect them and the public), competent risk assessment leads to the additional byproduct of delimiting a domain of behavior and a population of people for whom there is no such need. This byproduct is important, because the recovery vision emphasizes not only the rights of people with mental illness but also the responsibilities they carry associated with community membership. In a majority of circumstances in which people do not pose immediate risks to self or others, it is not only their right to make their own decisions but also their responsibility. As Deegan (27) has suggested, people need to have "the dignity of risk" and "the right to fail" in order to learn from their own mistakes. Given the social climate in which mental health care is currently offered, it will be primarily through the appropriate use of risk assessment and management strategies that this latitude will become possible. For this reason, advocates are neither afraid of nor do they dismiss the scrutiny of risk assessment. They welcome it. But they welcome it on the condition that, in a majority of cases, when people are found not to pose serious or imminent risks to themselves or others, they are allowed to make their own choices and, by necessity, their own mistakes. Thus, although a recovery orientation might in fact increase risk, it is primarily the person's access to opportunities for taking risks that needs to be

increased, not necessarily the provider's or the community's exposure to risk.

Conclusions

Recovery-oriented systems of care will not stop offering active treatment to reduce the signs and symptoms of mental illness, nor will they stop offering rehabilitative interventions to address functional impairments. What primarily will be different about recovery-oriented systems of care, as we envision them, is that these interventions and supports will be provided in ways much more similar to than different from other health care services for other health conditions. The people receiving these services will likewise continue on with their ordinary lives, either recovering from the illness when possible or, when not yet possible, gaining access to the technologies, tools, and environmental accommodations they need to incorporate the illness or disability into their lives as only one component of a multidimensional existence and multifaceted sense of personal identity. In doing so, they will have to face no more discrimination or externally imposed threats to their personal sovereignty (as opposed to threats posed by the nature of the illness itself) than people with diabetes, asthma, or arthritis.

Some well-meaning providers believe that this form of recovery-oriented care is something that is already being provided, and perhaps in some exemplary communities it is. Systemic transformation, however, will take time, and we expect that the paradigm shift involved will require at least a generation to materialize in any substantive way. In the interim, it is ironic, perhaps, that taking the risk of offering recovery-oriented care promises to be one of the few ways possible to increase available resources. The more that programs implement elements of choice and self-determination and a focus on life goals and aspirations, and the more data are collected to demonstrate effectiveness, the better are our chances of advocating successfully for more adequate funding of care. The more responsive our care, the more likely it is that people in recovery and their loved ones will join us in these advocacy efforts and support—rather than challenge—the legitimacy of the work we do.

Finally, the more effective our efforts at promoting community inclusion, the less people will need from mental health care, allowing us to reduce caseload sizes and spend more of our time in pursuit of the aims that brought us into the field to begin with. Once it is firmly established, the recovery vision will allow us to see, albeit in retrospect, that the costs incurred by not taking such risks—the costs of chronicity, institutionalization, and homelessness—far outweigh the costs of doing so.

References

1. Achieving the Promise: Transforming Mental Health Care in America. Pub no SMA-03-3832. Rockville, Md, Department of Health and Human Services, President's New Freedom Commission on Mental Health, 2003

2. Mental Health: A Report of the Surgeon General. Rockville, Md, Department of Health and Human Services, 1999

3. Davidson L, O'Connell M, Tondora J, et al: Recovery in serious mental illness: a new wine or just a new bottle? Professional Psychology Research and Practice 36:480–487, 2005

4. Jacobson N, Greenley D: What is recovery? A conceptual model and explication. Psychiatric Services 52:482–485, 2001

5. Jacobson N: In Recovery: The Making of Mental Health Policy. Nashville, Tenn, Vanderbilt University Press, 2004

6. Liberman RP, Kopelowicz A: Recovery from schizophrenia: a concept in search of research. Psychiatric Services 56:735–742, 2005

7. Davidson L, Tondora J, O'Connell MJ, et al: A Practical Guide to Recovery-Oriented Practice: Tools for Transforming Mental Health Care. New York, Oxford University Press, in press

8. Carpenter WT, Kirkpatrick B: The heterogeneity of the long-term course of schizophrenia. Schizophrenia Bulletin 14:645–652, 1988

9. Davidson L, McGlashan TH: The varied outcomes of schizophrenia. Canadian Journal of Psychiatry 42:34–43, 1997

10. McGlashan TH: A selective review of recent North American long-term follow-up studies of schizophrenia. Schizophrenia Bulletin 14: 515–542, 1988

11. Deegan PE: The Independent Living Movement and people with psychiatric disabilities: taking back control over our own lives. Psychosocial Rehabilitation Journal 15:3–19, 1992

12. Davidson L, Stayner DA, Nickou C, et al: "Simply to be let in": inclusion as a basis for recovery from mental illness. Psychiatric Rehabilitation Journal 24:375–388, 2001

13. Onken S, Dumont JM, Ridgway P, et al: Mental Health Recovery: What Helps and What Hinders? A National Research Project for Development of Recovery Facilitating System Performance Indicators. Alexandria, Va, National Association of State Mental Health Program Directors, National Technical Assistance Center for State Mental Health Planning, 2001

14. Chamberlin J: Rehabilitating ourselves: the psychiatric survivor movement. International Journal of Mental Health 23:39–46, 1995

15. Davidson L, Stayner DA, Lambert S, et al: Phenomenological and participatory research on schizophrenia: recovering the person in theory and practice. Journal of Social Issues 53:767–784, 1997

16. Becker DR, Drake RE: Individual placement and support: a community mental health center approach to vocational rehabilitation. Community Mental Health Journal 30:193–206, 1994

17. Chadwick P, Birchwood M, Trower P: Cognitive Therapy for Hallucinations, Delusions, and Paranoia. Chichester, England, Wiley, 1996.

18. Davidson L, Kirk T, Rockholz P, et al: Creating a recovery-oriented system of behavioral health care: moving from concept to reality. Psychiatric Rehabilitation Journal, in press

19. Davidson L, Harding CM, Spaniol L: Recovery From Severe Mental Illnesses: Research Evidence and Implications for Practice, vol 1. Boston, Boston University, Center for Psychiatric Rehabilitation, 2005

20. Appelbaum PS, Gutheil TG: "Rotting with their rights on": constitutional theory and clinical reality in drug refusal by psychiatric patients. Bulletin of the American Academy of Psychiatry and the Law 7:306–315, 1979

21. Monahan J: "A terror to their neighbors": beliefs about mental disorder and violence in historical and cultural perspective. Bulletin of the American Academy of Psychiatry and the Law 20:191–195, 1992

22. Monahan J, Arnold J: Violence by people with mental illness: a consensus statement by advocates and researchers. Psychiatric Rehabilitation Journal 19:67–70, 1996

23. Mulvey EP: Assessing the evidence of a link between mental illness and violence. Hospital and Community Psychiatry 45:663–668, 1994

24. Dailey WF, Chinman MJ, Davidson L, et al: How are we doing? A statewide survey of community adjustment among people with serious mental illness receiving intensive outpatient services. Community Mental Health Journal 36:363–382, 2000

25. Sells D, Rowe M, Fisk D, et al: Violent victimization of persons with co-occurring psychiatric and substance use disorders. Psychiatric Services 54:1253–1257, 2003

26. From Privileges to Rights: People Labeled With Psychiatric Disabilities Speak for Themselves. Washington, DC, National Council on Disability, 2000. Available at www.ncd.gov/newsroom/publications/2000/privileges.htm

27. Deegan PE: Recovering our sense of value after being labeled mentally ill. Journal of Psychosocial Nursing 31:7–11, 1993

THEMES FROM THE COMMISSION

Barriers to Recovery and Recommendations for Change: The Pennsylvania Consensus Conference on Psychiatry's Role

Joseph A. Rogers, A.A.
Michael J. Vergare, M.D.
Richard C. Baron, M.A.
Mark S. Salzer, Ph.D.

Objective: **Recovery has emerged over the past decade as a dominant theme in public mental health care. _Methods:_ The 2006 Pennsylvania Consensus Conference brought together 24 community psychiatrists to explore the barriers they experienced in promoting recovery and their recommendations for change. _Results:_ Twelve barriers were identified and classified into one of three categories: psychiatry knowledge, roles, and training; the need to transform public mental health systems and services; and environmental barriers to opportunity. Participants made 22 recommendations to address these barriers through changes in policies, programs, and psychiatric knowledge and practice. _Conclusions:_ The recommendations identify areas for change that can be accomplished through**

individual psychiatrist action and organized group efforts. (**_Psychiatric Services_ 58:1119–1123, 2007**)

Recovery has emerged as the dominant theme in the transformation of public mental health policy, practice, and research (1–5) and is at the heart of the report from the President's New Freedom Commission on Mental Health, _Achieving the Promise: Transforming Mental Health Care in America_ (6). The expansion of recovery's influence, however, has proceeded without an exploration of how community psychiatry and its practitioners view recovery and its challenges (7,8). Specifically, what do psychiatrists think about recovery, their own role in promoting hope, empowerment, and opportunity, and the barriers they may face in moving the recovery agenda forward? What recommendations do they have for overcoming those barriers and enhancing their ability to promote recovery?

Methods

This brief report presents findings from a one-day meeting in Philadelphia in January 2006 of 24 psychiatrists from institutional and community settings who were clinicians, administrators, and educators. After a series of plenary presentations that reviewed the fundamentals of recovery, participants chose to attend one of three work groups that focused on policy, program, or practice issues. Each group was asked to address two questions: What do you perceive as barriers to ex-

panding psychiatry's role in supporting recovery? and What recommendations would you make to address these barriers at that level and strengthen psychiatry's efforts in promoting recovery? The facilitator of each group documented the points that were raised. A final large group session was held to discuss the identified barriers and recommendations. Participants were informed that the issues and recommendations they raised would be captured in a report, presented here. The project was determined to be exempt from institutional review board approval by the Office of Regulatory Affairs at the University of Pennsylvania.

Results

The barriers to promoting recovery fell into three clusters based on a thematic analysis conducted by the authors: psychiatry knowledge, roles, and training; transforming public mental health systems; and environmental barriers to opportunity. Each set of barriers is discussed separately, with recommendations for addressing each barrier provided in Table 1.

The most prominent consensus points were the need to enhance community psychiatrists' knowledge of recovery, the need to redefine their roles in ways that support their efforts to promote recovery, and the need to invest in recovery-oriented training for psychiatrists throughout their careers.

Barrier 1

Many psychiatrists in the public mental health system lack sufficient knowl-

Mr. Rogers is affiliated with the Mental Health Association of Southeastern Pennsylvania, Philadelphia. Dr. Vergare is with the Department of Psychiatry, Thomas Jefferson University, Philadelphia. Mr. Baron and Dr. Salzer are with the Department of Psychiatry, University of Pennsylvania, Philadelphia. Send correspondence to Dr. Salzer at the Department of Psychiatry, University of Pennsylvania, 3535 Market St., 3rd Floor, Center for Mental Health Policy and Services Research, Philadelphia, PA 19104 (e-mail: mark. salzer@uphs.upenn.edu). Originally published in the August 2007 issue of Psychiatric Services.

edge and appreciation of recovery and have limited opportunities to learn more. Although participants in the program felt that most psychiatrists accepted recovery's values and beliefs—articulated by the comment "A great many of us went into the field of psychiatry precisely because we believe that people can get better and lead full lives"—the term recovery and the best ways for psychiatrists to act on those values and beliefs remained too vague in their minds. Participants felt that psychiatrists in administrative positions tended to be better informed and more enthusiastic about applying recovery principles, but those providing clinical supervision or working day to day with patients had little training and too few opportunities to learn about recovery and its implications for their work.

Barrier 2

Experienced psychiatrists are sometimes discouraged by the frequent perceived "failure" of their patients to move forward with their lives. Participants believed that they and their colleagues felt a keen sense of responsibility for their patients' welfare, and although they were aware of the external barriers to success (including the failures of many public mental health systems and the impact of prejudice and discrimination), many were uncomfortable with encouraging patients to take substantial risks in pursuit of self-determined goals. Participants recognized that this aversion to risk sometimes conflicted with recovery's emphasis on hope and empowerment.

Barrier 3

Community psychiatrists have limited time to work with patients and few incentives to pursue recovery goals with them. Participants were especially concerned about their evolving roles and the lack of opportunity to work more effectively with individuals. These complaints were especially heartfelt: "Is it really asking too much for me to spend more than ten minutes a month with a patient?" Psychiatrists often feel that they have only a fleeting relationship with patients and are marginalized as persons who only prescribe medications (9) and as barriers to clients' pursuit of nonclinical goals.

Barrier 4

Psychiatrists have not exercised sufficient leadership in promoting recovery throughout the public mental health system. Participants felt that psychiatry's leaders have neither done enough to promote the importance of recovery within the field nor encouraged other fields within the public mental health arena to consider recovery as the basis for system transformation. They expressed concern that although there are prominent psychiatrists promoting recovery within the public mental health system, at the local level there is not enough outspoken advocacy—in partnership with consumers and other practitioners—to emphasize recovery.

Barrier 5

There are too few community psychiatrists in the field today, and there is too little interest among future psychiatrists in working in public mental health. The participants were concerned that the field of community psychiatry appears to have little allure: practicing psychiatrists are leaving the field, and the numbers of psychiatric residents choosing community psychiatry are dwindling. The problems—low pay, the attenuated professional role of psychiatrists in community programs, and the severity of the problems experienced by clients of public mental health systems—have diminished the ranks of existing and emerging community psychiatrists (10). There was a sense that an emphasis on recovery might reignite interest in the field.

Participants felt that public mental health systems continue to face substantial administrative, financial, and clinical problems that frustrate efforts to work within a more recovery-oriented framework.

Barrier 6

Current mental health reimbursement systems do not support recovery. Participants pointed out that federal, state, and local public mental health systems have not framed financial reimbursement systems to reflect recovery-oriented care. Despite the emphasis on recovery in public state-

ments and formal planning documents, public mental health providers are still primarily focused on symptom remission and client stabilization, with limited opportunities to expand the number of reimbursable programs that emphasize community integration and recovery. Participants believed that both the existing framework of community support services and the emerging network of consumer-run programs are starved for funding.

Barrier 7

There are too few public mental health programs emphasizing recovery issues—such as empowerment, employment, and education—to which psychiatrists can refer patients. Participants were concerned that many core programs, including consumer-run services, employment-oriented programs, and housing opportunities, are not readily available. Without supports to address patient needs, including both spiritual connections and comprehensive health care, the public mental health system often fails to respond to the most basic recovery principles. Participants argued for a transformed mental health system that redirected funds to critical needs without limiting much-needed clinical services.

Barrier 8

Public mental health systems are uncoordinated, underfunded, and overly focused on symptom reduction, stabilization, and maintenance. Participants often commented on the lack of coordination among systems of services and supports, which made service planning and progress more difficult; the increasing demands for greater funding for acute care, which limited the availability of funding for community integration activities; and the continuing emphasis on symptoms as opposed to recovery.

Barrier 9

There is no systematic or standardized way in which most mental health systems can assess their effectiveness in achieving recovery-oriented goals at the individual or system levels. Despite efforts to clarify the definition of recovery and establish measure-

Table 1

Recommendations for community psychiatry efforts to promote recovery

Barrier	Recommendation
1. Psychiatrists in the public mental health system lack sufficient knowledge and appreciation of recovery and have limited opportunities to learn more.	1. Medical education for psychiatrists and other mental health professionals needs to place more emphasis on recovery and its implications for practice. Greater exposure to the basic principles of recovery, to consumer advocates, and to psychiatrists who apply recovery approaches can better prepare medical students for the evolving roles of psychiatrists in the public mental health system. State financial support for "recovery education modules" within the medical school curriculum would broden young psychiatrists' awareness. 2. Psychiatric residents and psychiatrists at the start of their careers need greater exposure to recovery and community integration principles. The role of more seasoned community psychiatrists as mentors should be supported and should include a focus on recovery approaches. 3. A rapid expansion of recovery-based in-service training opportunities and continuing medical education courses on recovery and community integration would broaden knowledge about and support for recovery and help both to redefine the role of community psychiatrists and to transform the psychiatrist-patient relationship.
2. Experienced psychiatrists are sometimes discouraged by the frequent perceived "failure" of their clients' attempts to move forward with their lives.	4. Psychiatrists in the public mental health arena need more consistent exposure to recovery's success, both to patients in recovery and to the psychiatrists who have worked with them. Success stories can serve as models for others and help lift the pervasive pessimism among psychiatrists that sometimes overshadows their day-to-day clinical work. 5. Improved systems to document risk and promote innovative risk-management approaches are vitally needed if psychiatrists are to feel comfortable working with patients in recovery. For example, participants spoke of how difficult it was for both patients and psychiatrists to risk destabilization and rehospitalization if they choose to manage their own medications or to risk the loss of Social Security support if they return to work. The risks implicit in a recovery approach require greater discussion and guidelines for responsible practice.
3. Community psychiatrists have limited time to work with clients and few incentives to pursue recovery goals with them.	6. Redefine the role of community psychiatrists to emphasize their importance in supporting recovery. Reimbursement mechanisms and program guidelines need to ensure that psychiatrists have more time with each patient in order to permit a greater focus on recovery and community integration issues, to continue to manage medications, and to permit effective consultation with other team members. 7. Community psychiatrists should contribute to the development of best-practice guidelines that document a range of approaches to support recovery goals and planning in their clinical work with examples that emphasize hope, empowerment, and opportunity. 8. Federal, state, and local systems of care should specify recovery-oriented outcomes for clinical psychiatric work and provide training in implementation and documentation to ensure that psychiatrists are encouraged to focus their engagement with individual patients around both clinical and more practical recovery-oriented outcomes.
4. Psychiatrists have not exercised sufficient leadership in promoting recovery throughout the public mental health system.	9. Leaders in the field of community psychiatry should be encouraged to focus on recovery issues within their contributions to professional journals, conference presentations, and their research and program responsibilities, both individually and in partnership with consumers and other mental health professionals. 10. A series of partnerships between psychiatrists and consumer and other mental health professional groups should explore how they can take effective action at policy, program, and practice levels to support recovery-oriented systems of care and highlight the success of recovery-based services and supports.
5. There are too few psychiatrists in community settings, and there is too little interest among future psychiatrists in working in public mental health.	11. Revised working conditions for community psychiatrists—a substantial redefinition of their roles and responsibilities, a reexamination of pay and benefit structures, and a revision of their clinical responsibilities—would improve the attractiveness of community psychiatry for both existing practitioners and those in training and would likely improve overall job satisfaction. 12. Transforming the public mental health system to emphasize recovery and community integration principles and the central role of community psychiatry in promoting recovery could help to increase the number and diversity of community psychiatrists and their commitment to the field.
6. Current mental health reimbursement systems often do not support recovery practices.	13. A greater funding balance must be found between psychiatric services and community integration and recovery outcomes. While continuing to support clinical care and stabilization of clients in need of acute care, public mental health dollars must cover a wide range of alternative programs that emphasize community integration and recovery. 14. A greater emphasis is needed both on defining more specific recovery-oriented outcomes and documenting client progress in this regard, as a way to ensure that fund-

Continues on next page

Table 1

Continued from previous page

Barrier	Recommendation
	ing continues to respond to real client needs and genuine program achievements. Reimbursement for recovery-based results is an important system goal.
7. There are too few public mental health programs that emphasize recovery issues, such as empowerment, employment, and education, to which psychiatrists can refer.	15. Public mental health systems need to provide—and psychiatrists need to advocate increased funding for—a wide range of supports and services in community settings for people with serious mental illnesses, including a wider array of housing, employment, socialization, health care, spiritual, civic, and related community integration opportunities.
	16. Public mental health systems need to provide—and psychiatrists need to advocate increased funding for—the continued expansion of consumer-run supports and services as well as the hiring of consumers of mental health services within the network of traditional mental health support agencies in the public sector.
	17. Public mental health systems need to ensure that consumers are fully empowered, with new initiatives to broaden clinical understanding of the role of consumers in setting their own goals and framing their own treatment and rehabilitation plans, as well as their participation on boards and committees at agency and system levels.
8. Public mental health systems are uncoordinated, underfunded, and overly focused on symptom reduction, stabilization, and maintenance.	18. The public mental health system must better meet clients' needs, providing greater coordination among clinical and rehabilitative programs, as well as stronger linkages to non–mental health services and supports in community settings, to ensure that clients have the widest possible range of opportunities to participate in community life.
9. There are no standardized approaches to assess effectiveness in achieving recovery-oriented goals at either the individual or system levels.	19. A committee of consumers, policy makers, and psychiatrists should review current recovery outcome measures and work together to develop a consensus document providing guidelines for measuring both recovery initiatives and recovery outcomes, as part of a multisite study project.
10. Prejudice toward people with psychiatric disabilities remains a powerful factor and blunts opportunities through discriminatory public policies and exclusionary social practices.	20. Psychiatrists should play a leading role in a community education campaign to focus on the realities of mental illness, mental health treatment, and the importance of recovery. Antidiscrimination and antistigma campaigns linked to the core concepts of recovery and community integration—hope, empowerment, and opportunity—should be cooperative ventures at national, state, and local levels.
11. Community support, expressed through the political process, still provides too limited financial support and public policy advocacy to ensure that those with psychiatric disabilities receive services and can claim the rights they deserve.	21. Psychiatrists at all levels need to play a more direct role in the political process on behalf of and in partnership with those with psychiatric disabilities in order to eliminate discriminatory public policies (such as zoning exclusions and custody awards) and increase public funding for supports and services.
12. Many people with psychiatric disabilities are poor and are thus victimized by the same sets of social conditions (poor housing, low wages, and limited social participation) as other people who live in poverty.	22. Psychiatrists should play leadership roles—in partnership with consumers, other mental health professionals, and advocates for other people who are disadvantaged or disabled—in addressing the social policies that limit opportunities for people to live in hope, with empowerment, and with abundant opportunities.

ment standards, there is still considerable confusion about what mental health systems and psychiatrists should be achieving in a recovery-oriented system.

Much of the discussion about the need for improvements in the delivery of mental health services hinged on the broader issues of environmental barriers that limited opportunities for people to successfully participate in the community. Several commented on the public's continuing misperceptions about the presence of people with psychiatric disabilities in community settings and current polit-

ical philosophy that government should play limited roles in people's lives.

Barrier 10
Community prejudices toward people with psychiatric disabilities remain a powerful factor in the lives of those with mental illnesses, blunting many opportunities through discriminatory public policies and exclusionary social practices. The participants felt that people with psychiatric disabilities often make only limited progress toward recovery-oriented goals within the context of a wary and sometimes hos-

tile community in which such basic resources as housing, jobs, and social interactions are limited.

Barrier 11
Community support, expressed through the political process, still provides too-limited financial support and public policy advocacy to ensure that those with psychiatric disabilities in public mental health programs receive the services and can claim the rights they deserve. Participants were clear that the lack of community understanding about psychiatric disabilities translated into a series of public

policy decisions that limited the funding for supports as well as the rights of people with psychiatric disabilities.

Barrier 12

Many people with psychiatric disabilities in public mental health systems are poor and are thus victimized by the same sets of social conditions—poor housing, low wages, and limited social participation, for example—as other people who live in poverty. Participants also saw people with psychiatric disabilities, particularly those who were poor and from minority, immigrant, or otherwise disenfranchised communities, as struggling against the same sets of social factors that limit the lives of their peers without disabilities.

Discussion

The goal of the symposium was to identify key barriers and recommend solutions for facilitating psychiatry's efforts in promoting recovery. The participants clearly indicated that psychiatrists must be far more active in aligning psychiatric policies, programs, and practices with recovery and community integration efforts. The recommendations that emerged from the one-day symposium lay out an ambitious agenda for community psychiatry. They suggest that there is much work to be done, not only within psychiatry but also within the sprawling public mental health system and, indeed, within the broader community. Although this was a first attempt to assess the views of psychiatrists about their ability to integrate recovery into their public policy and clinical roles, the barriers they have identified and the recommendations they have developed are reasonable and present a realistic challenge to the field.

The formidable and complex nature of that challenge is underlined by the way this identification of barriers and recommendations raises more subtle issues: two particular concerns are raised here, but there are likely many others. First, it may be that underlying psychiatrists' concerns about their roles are the dramatic changes under way in the roles of psychiatrists. Changes in the relationships between psychiatrists and patients (for whom self-determination is a fundamental issue), between psychiatrists and other mental health professionals (who now want a broader role for themselves), and between psychiatrists and public or private insurers (with their demands for an emphasis on pharmacologic treatment) raise wide-ranging issues about the future roles and responsibilities of psychiatrists in facilitating recovery.

Second, participants in this conference were more readily able to identify and support aspects of recovery that suggested the need for a greater focus and more substantial funding for a wide range of rehabilitation programs that respond to recovery-oriented goals than to identify and promote ways in which recovery principles could be integrated into their clinical practice. They were aware of few models, guidelines, or practice recommendations that could help individual psychiatrists move toward transforming the treatment environment—ways in which hope, empowerment, and opportunity would play out in the psychiatric milieu.

Conclusions

Our ambition is for this initial dialogue to help shape local, regional, and national discussion among psychiatrists and other mental health professionals within the mental health system, which would then lead to determined action in partnership with patients. This first look at psychiatric perspectives on these critical issues may serve as an impetus for enhancing psychiatry's role in promoting recovery.

Acknowledgments and disclosures

This study was partially supported by grant H133-B031109 to the University of Pennsylvania Collaborative on Community Integration from the National Institute on Disability and Rehabilitation Research (Dr. Salzer, principal investigator). The authors thank Christine Simiriglia, Betsy Gorski, L.S.W., Ken Thompson, M.D., and Estelle Richman, M.A., for their support and involvement in this effort.

The authors report no competing interests.

References

1. Anthony WA: Recovery from mental illness: the guiding vision of the mental health services system in the 1990s. Psychiatric Rehabilitation Journal 16:11–23, 1993

2. Spaniol L, Gagne C, Koehler M: Recovery from serious mental illness: what is it and how to support people in their recovery, in The Psychological and Social Impact of Disability, 4th ed. Edited by Marinelli RP, Dell Orto AE. New York, Springer, 1999

3. Lieberman RP, Kopelowicz A: Recovery from schizophrenia: a concept in search of research. Psychiatric Services 56:735–742, 2005

4. Jacobson N, Greenley D: What is recovery? A conceptual model and explication. Psychiatric Services 52:482–485, 2001

5. Bellack AS: Scientific and consumer models of recovery in schizophrenia: concordance, contrasts, and implications. Schizophrenia Bulletin 32:432–442, 2006

6. Achieving the Promise: Transforming Mental Health Care in America. Executive summary, pub no SMA-03-3832. Rockville, Md, Department of Health and Human Services, President's New Freedom Commission on Mental Health, 2003

7. Blanch AK, Fishs D, Tucker W, et al: Consumer-practitioners and psychiatrists share insights about recovery and coping. Disabilities Studies Quarterly 13:17–20, 1993

8. Davidson L, O'Connell M, Tondora J, et al: The top ten concerns about recovery encountered in mental health system transformation. Psychiatric Services 57:640–645, 2006

9. Gabbe GO: The psychiatrist as psychotherapist, in Psychiatry in the New Millennium. Edited by Weissman S, Sabshin M, Eist H. Washington, DC, American Psychiatric Press, 1998

10. Arce AA, Vergare MJ: Psychiatrists and interprofessional role conflicts in Community Mental Health Centers, in Community Mental Health Centers and Psychiatrists. Washington, DC, and Rockville, Md, Edited and published by the Joint Steering Committee of the American Psychiatric Association and the National Council of Community Mental Health Centers, 1985

Transforming Mental Health and Substance Abuse Data Systems in the United States

Rosanna M. Coffey, Ph.D.
Jeffrey A. Buck, Ph.D.
Cheryl A. Kassed, Ph.D.
Joan Dilonardo, Ph.D.
Carol Forhan, M.B.A.
William D. Marder, Ph.D.
Rita Vandivort-Warren, M.S.W.

State efforts to improve mental health and substance abuse service systems cannot overlook the fragmented data systems that reinforce the historical separateness of systems of care. These separate systems have discrete approaches to treatment, and there are distinct funding streams for state mental health, substance abuse, and Medicaid agencies. Transforming mental health and substance abuse services in the United States depends on resolving issues that underlie separate treatment systems— access barriers, uneven quality, disjointed coordination, and information silos across agencies and providers. This article discusses one aspect of transformation—the need for interoperable information systems. It describes current federal and state initiatives for improving data interoperability and the special issue of confidentiality associated with mental health and substance abuse treatment data. Some achievable steps for states to consider in reforming their behavioral health data systems are outlined. The steps include collecting encounter-level data; using coding that is compliant with the Health Insurance Portability and Accountability Act, including national provider identifiers; forging linkages with other state data systems and developing unique client identifiers among systems; investing in flexible and adaptable data systems and business processes; and finding innovative solutions to the difficult confidentiality restrictions on use of behavioral health data. Changing data systems will not in itself transform the delivery of care; however, it will enable agencies to exchange information about shared clients, to understand coordination problems better, and to track successes and failures of policy decisions. (*Psychiatric Services* 59:1257–1263, 2008)

About 30% of U.S. adults experience a mental or substance use disorder during the course of a year (1). Co-occurring disorders are common: about 9% of those with a mental disorder and about 60% of those with a substance use disorder struggle with both (2). Many people with behavioral health problems also have serious physical health problems. These individuals are often the most in need of coordinated care in many aspects of their lives.

How data systems can enhance care quality

Optimal service delivery to individuals with co-occurring mental and substance use disorders requires an integrated approach—providers of various client services who communicate with each other about what the client needs, support clients to obtain referral appointments without delay, follow up with clients to be sure they obtained care, and monitor patients' medication use for compliance and outcome. In addition, for this population, services that wrap around clinical care are essential— social support services (jobs, housing, social networks, and peer support groups), community reentry programs for people who have been incarcerated, ongoing monitoring and maintenance of client progress and compliance with treatment regimens, and so on. Effective data systems can enhance the delivery of such services without making success dependent on a single service coordinator and without losing clients through handoffs and disconnections between services and programs. Data systems that link information from different program and care settings can facilitate coordination and, at the same time, support evaluations of programs to deter-

Dr. Coffey, Dr. Kassed, Ms. Forhan, and Dr. Marder are affiliated with the health care business of Thomson Reuters, 4301 Connecticut Ave., Washington, D.C. 20008 (e-mail: rosanna.coffey@thomsonreuters.com). Dr. Buck and Ms. Vandivort-Warren are with the Substance Abuse and Mental Health Services Administration, Rockville, Maryland. Dr. Dilonardo is a consultant for Thomson Reuters. Originally published in the November 2008 issue of Psychiatric Services.

mine what works to improve patient outcomes. Better data systems have the potential to help researchers and clinicians understand clinical interventions on a large scale.

Typically, public treatment systems for mental disorders in the United States are separate from those for substance use disorders, and both are distinct from states' Medicaid programs (3,4). Silos of information do not communicate with one another (5), which inhibits effective and efficient coordination of services, continuity of care, and assessment of treatment outcomes and costs, resulting in suboptimal patient care (6). The President's New Freedom Commission on Mental Health recognized this fragmentation and further noted that reducing service fragmentation in behavioral health care required transformation of data systems (7). The commission recommended steps to harness the power of health information technology and to leverage human and economic resources through better federal, state, and local collaborations (7). The importance of these recommendations was emphasized by an Institute of Medicine (IOM) report that highlighted how mental health and substance abuse services lag behind general health care in using information technology to promote improved, evidence-based patient care (8). The IOM recommended the development of policies and infrastructures to link patient records and other mental health and substance abuse service data, as well as to standardize data requirements at the national, state, and local levels.

Both the New Freedom Commission and the IOM endorsed electronic health records, better coding and reporting of mental health and substance abuse interventions, and collection of client-level information by use of payment transactions standardized under the Health Insurance Portability and Accountability Act (HIPAA) (7,8). The application of information technology has improved care for chronic illnesses, including mental illness (9). Within the context of a "comprehensive quality improvement model," information technology

has been critical in improving chronic disease management (10).

This article focuses on one aspect of mental health and substance abuse treatment transformation in the United States—the need for interoperable information systems. Our aim is to reach high-level state policy makers who have the authority and ability to make information more accessible across their health and social service programs. The article describes current federal and state initiatives for improving health data interoperability and the special issue of confidentiality associated with mental health and substance abuse treatment data. Some achievable first steps for states to consider in reforming their behavioral health data systems are outlined. Even though the article focuses on data systems in the United States, the general principles of data integration may be applicable in any country that has separate data systems for administering separate public programs of health care.

Current federal and state initiatives

Data interoperability is the ability of dispersed, separately owned, and separately managed information systems to communicate with one another electronically to share specific bytes of data. Agreements between owners of information systems define the purpose, parameters, and safeguards for the exchange. Although businesses across the U.S. economy have rapidly driven data interoperability and exchange, the adoption has been painfully slow in health care and even more so in behavioral health care. As a result, a number of government initiatives over the past decade have attempted to make the case for why and how health data systems should interoperate.

The value of interoperability for mental health, substance abuse, and Medicaid data was demonstrated in a project sponsored by the Substance Abuse and Mental Health Services Administration (SAMHSA) (2,11, 12). The Integrated Database Project assembled data from state agencies for program evaluation purposes and revealed challenges to interoperabili-

ty among existing data systems. Data collected at the client level and analyzed within three states and across three public programs—mental health, substance abuse, and Medicaid—revealed duplication of services and costs among the three systems in each state, especially for clients with complex co-occurring disorders. Of note, the project highlighted many challenges to implementing interoperability among existing systems—different concepts and data elements, incompatible definitions for the same data elements (clinical, demographic, or resource related), local coding schemes for concepts (substance use problems, procedures, and provider identifiers), varying record-keeping practices (service records bundled together versus service-specific records), and missing clinical elements (physical and behavioral health history, diagnostic specificity and completeness, medications records, response to medications, and outcomes and disposition of the patient). State and local data systems need a better foundation to support interoperable mental health, substance abuse, and Medicaid data systems. Standards that have evolved over decades for physical health services have barely infiltrated data collection for mental health and substance abuse services.

Various federal and state initiatives have aimed to improve the data environment to allow exchange of health information to benefit patient care. Establishment of electronic payment transactions with related standards for data content, confidentiality, and security and promotion of the adoption of comprehensive electronic patient records are setting the foundation for interoperability of electronic health data for integrated behavioral health care.

HIPAA, which was enacted in 1996, outlined a vision for administrative simplification and set national health data standards for health care business transactions (13). HIPAA data content standards have been set for eligibility determination, enrollment, and health care claims used in fee-for-service systems. In addition, HIPAA required the eventual adoption of a standard unique identifier for health care providers, and in 2007 the National Provider Identifier (NPI) became effective for all HIPAA standard transactions.

The Health Information Technology initiative of 2004 of the U.S. Department of Health and Human Services set a ten-year goal of implementing electronic health records for most Americans in order to prevent medical errors, decrease paperwork, improve quality of care, and expand access to affordable care (14). SAMHSA identified data interoperability and electronic health records as major goals of its data strategy (15) and has addressed—and continues to consider—the special issue of patient privacy and behavioral health data confidentiality (16).

The Medicaid information technology architecture (MITA), created by the Centers for Medicare and Medicaid Services (CMS), aims to support improved care quality through integrated and patient-centered information systems and program administration (17). The MITA framework was developed to enable state Medicaid enterprises to meet common objectives while still supporting unique local needs (18). It incorporates existing and evolving standards developed by national organizations, fosters shared leadership and partnerships, and encourages use of nonproprietary systems and open-source code for data interoperability. SAMHSA and CMS are collaborating to promote integration among Medicaid data systems, state mental health data systems, and state substance abuse data systems by using the MITA framework.

States have been trying to overcome the problems of fragmented, nonlinkable health data that were highlighted by the SAMHSA Integrated Database Project. One approach has been for states to develop "data warehouses" that combine siloed data to increase their utility. For example, Washington State linked client data across community mental health centers and state Medicaid claims (but not with substance abuse system data). Integrated data allowed administrators in that state to

analyze and understand that providing outpatient mental health treatment to the most needy and disabled clients was likely to reduce medical care costs in the state (19). South Carolina linked data from a large number of its health and social service programs. The state's integrated database has allowed it to identify and serve children with special health care needs and those without health insurance (20). Another approach taken by states has been linking and then deidentifying data for specific research projects. Connecticut successfully linked data between the Department of Mental Health and Addiction Services and the Department of Corrections and showed the value of treating substance abuse among prison inmates—much lower reincarceration rates among those treated, with cost savings to society of 1.8 to 5.7 times the costs of the treatment programs (21).

Aligning state data systems with each other and with national standards can have an enormous positive impact on transforming mental health and substance abuse treatment systems and showing the social value of better treatment systems. Informed by the lessons of the SAMHSA Integrated Database Project, a few state efforts are focusing on front-end harmonization to create interoperability for existing administrative behavioral health data systems. Oklahoma, Maryland, and Indiana are exploring ideas for mental health and substance abuse data system integration projects with Medicaid (22–24), using MITA strategies. The states are developing consistent client identifiers within the state, aligning data element definitions, and considering secure Web-based technologies for data sharing. These projects exemplify steps toward achieving the goals outlined by the New Freedom Commission.

Ideally, investing in new point-of-care information systems would help states reach these goals, but such systems are expensive and in their infancy. Restructuring existing mental health and substance abuse administrative data systems presents a more practical, affordable, and manage-

able approach to client-centered information exchange in the immediate future.

The special issue of data confidentiality

Strict laws and regulations about the confidentiality of client information, which have existed for decades, complicate data exchange for behavioral health care providers and programs. Such rules are a consequence of the stigma and discrimination that has been associated with mental and substance use disorders. Social and legal risks continue to be associated with disclosure of protected behavioral health information, including removal of a child from a parent, lost employment, and criminal prosecution (25–29).

Because of such rules and risks, mental health and substance abuse treatment providers and program administrators are reluctant to share patient data for any purpose, even including treatment (30). The state-administered programs, to which providers must report individual patient data for eligibility and coverage determinations, also must abide by federal and state confidentiality restrictions on the use of behavioral health data. Specifically, these include the HIPAA Privacy Rule, which applies to all health data used for payment transactions, including for mental health and substance abuse services; 42 CFR Part 2, the more stringent federal confidentiality regulation associated with substance abuse treatment; and any applicable state laws or regulations.

Each of the federal rules permits disclosure of deidentified health data and of identified data under restricted circumstances. Some state laws also regulate how information about treatment for mental health or substance abuse conditions can be shared and may restrict disclosure to deidentified data (31,32). Here we discuss the federal laws to clarify how state program administrators in states that do not impose more stringent rules can link and share data to improve programs while adhering to federal confidentiality laws.

HIPAA defined individually identifiable health information and criteria for its protection (33). Personally identifiable health information comprises any past, present, or future physical or mental health data that also includes direct or indirect person identifiers. These identifiers include direct identifiers such as name and address, as well as identifiers that are not unique, such as birth date and zip code, that might inadvertently identify a person. Such data must be protected through administrative policies and procedures specified by HIPAA. When protections are in place, HIPAA encourages use of personally identifiable health data for routine health care operations, public health activities, and research without the administrative burden of patient consent for each discrete disclosure (34). HIPAA permits the use of protected health information for research if an institutional review board approves the use and the researcher certifies that the request is for the minimum data necessary, that the identifiable data will be used only for the research, and that the data will not be removed from the organization (33).

However, 42 CFR Part 2 (often referred to as Part 2) has tighter requirements that organizations with personally identifiable substance abuse treatment data must follow in addition to HIPAA. Part 2 permits disclosure and use of person-level substance abuse treatment data without patient consent for limited program purposes—audits, program evaluation, and research (35). Without patient consent, personally identifiable substance abuse treatment records cannot be redisclosed for routine health care operations outside the organization from which the data were obtained; thus, independent treatment professionals may not share data about individual clients without client consent. Because the most restrictive disclosure rule applies, overlapping federal and state rules add to the complexity of interpreting and applying appropriate data-sharing procedures.

Nevertheless, a number of states have successfully shared personally identifiable information across agencies for research purposes. This is permissible under both HIPAA and Part 2 without patient consent, although specific requirements noted above must be met. Some state mental health, substance abuse, and Medicaid agencies may already be able to share information because of their organizational structure; Part 2 and HIPAA permit sharing of personally identifiable information between components of the same organization with authority to collect the data. Thus, for mental health, substance abuse, and Medicaid agencies in some states, it may be possible to house data sharing and analyses within the government office with authority over these agencies.

Some data system developers are designing patient consent into interoperable data systems (36). Rates of patient consent in one research study of nearly 16,000 patients showed that 90% of patients gave authorization for use of their data in medical research, regardless of their diagnosis; for patients with mental health conditions, the rate was 88% (37). For a patient in substance abuse treatment, a consent form for release of personally identifiable information must specify the authorized users of an information system, the period of time that the consent will be in effect, the specified uses of the data, plus all of the consent requirements of Part 2, HIPAA, and any relevant local restrictions (Wattenberg S, Substance Abuse and Mental Health Services Administration, personal communication, 2007). Although consent may be difficult to design and obtain for clients with substance use disorders, it is possible (35).

The future of electronic patient records for clients with substance use disorders hinges on innovative solutions to maximize patient consent. Such a solution should address the benefits of sharing personal data and confidentiality protections afforded it. Existing Internet technology can address HIPAA-compliant security for personally identifiable information with authorized access on a "need- to- know" basis. Systems can be configured for access by various types of users with different preassigned authorizations. Secured access can be controlled with user identifiers, multilayered password protection, and electronic signature authentication. Privacy advocates argue for designing into these systems patient ownership of their own data, encompassing all associated issues in regard to access, tracking, and control of the data.

Achievable steps for reforming behavioral health data systems

The general principles for creating and sustaining interoperable data systems do not differ greatly from those that guide other operational or organizational restructuring efforts (38). For example, engaging a top-level champion, perhaps even the governor, can provide visionary leadership, remove political and financial barriers, and motivate separate agencies toward collaboration and data sharing (39). Benchmarks established by a multistakeholder planning group can facilitate consensus-building and transformation efforts. Identifying financial resources to sustain progress toward system change can enhance motivation and efforts to ensure the permanency of improvements once they are made. Small steps toward new standards for mental health and substance abuse data integration and transparency are a sensible way to begin, are achievable, and can provide an early and tangible return on investment. A return on investment is essential to ensure support for continuation and expansion of data integration efforts.

Within this general approach, there are concrete actions that states may find useful to consider as incremental steps toward increasing the interoperability of mental health and substance abuse data systems. Although systemwide change may seem overwhelming, undertaking even some of the following activities can result in positive strides toward improvements in data linking and patient care.

Collect encounter-level transactions

Encounter data (that is, one record for each interaction between a provider and a patient) can be used to monitor access to, costs of, and quality of health care treatments provided, which is what administrators and consumers want to know. The advantage of collecting data at the level of the encounter is that it can be aggregated and viewed from many perspectives—services, conditions, providers, payers, and programs. Certainly, data content of encounter records can be improved; for example, codes for procedures can be developed that are more specific to mental health, substance abuse, and integrated treatments; and coding of all relevant diagnoses can be required. The improved coding that resulted from basing hospital prospective payments on diagnosis-related groups showed that reimbursement rewards are an effective way to stimulate improved coding and that using and reporting such data at the provider level results in improved data collection by providers (40).

Redesigning data collection to capture encounter-level transactions may seem daunting for mental health and substance abuse agencies that require only a record at intake or discharge from their provider networks, but many behavioral health providers already submit claims or encounter data to other payers. National standards for submitting encounter or claims data exist as a ready-made system that state mental health and substance abuse agencies can embrace with modest investment. Medicaid already adheres to these standards.

Use HIPAA-compliant coding
Collection of encounter-level transactions by using HIPAA-compliant national data standards will require states to harmonize mental health and substance abuse data elements with those standards. It is essential to review a state's mental health and substance abuse data element definitions and coding and compare them with the appropriate implementation guides (inpatient, outpatient, and so forth) for HIPAA transactions (41). The National Association of State Mental Health Program Directors and the National Association of State Alcohol and Drug Abuse Directors are collaborating with part-

ners in the behavioral health industry to ensure that the national codes represent the range of mental health and substance abuse treatment services (42). When aligned with national health data standards, behavioral health data could be analyzed with other data, such as that from Medicaid, private insurance, and statewide all-payer claims systems. Such linkages would provide comparative treatment data and information on clients' comorbid physical and mental conditions. Realignment of data systems at the front end (where concepts, definitions, and coding are established) to be compliant with HIPAA would not only yield savings in dollars and time for special projects but would also ease transition to electronic health records. HIPAA-compliant data will be a necessary condition for electronic health records that are fully interoperable. Once undertaken, these preparations will support behavioral health care systems at many levels in improving patient care.

Forge linkages with other information systems
There are many linkage possibilities with other state data systems. An obvious choice for most states and a helpful starting point would be linkages to Medicaid because of that program's substantial role in financing mental health and substance abuse treatment. Other linkages to emergency department records, inpatient data, and even criminal justice records, for example, would allow a deeper understanding of treatment effectiveness and offer opportunities for remedying disparities and service gaps. Because an increasing proportion of inmates in correctional facilities have a history of drug use that eventually leads to unmet health care needs (43), the corrections system offers a unique opportunity to link vulnerable populations with needed behavioral and physical health services, particularly after incarceration.

Align identifiers with those of other agencies
Provider-specific and client-specific identifiers that are compatible with

other data systems are keys to interoperability. States could require each mental health and substance abuse treatment provider to obtain a NPI (44) and to report data using the NPI. Also, client identifiers should align among agencies whose data are to be integrated or linked with mental health and substance abuse agency data. Synthetic client identifiers can be created between data systems to enable alignment across agencies' client-level records while helping to protect patient privacy.

Invest in flexible and adaptable systems and processes
Agencies commonly purchase or create software and hardware systems that are unique to one agency. Alternatively, using nonproprietary software and open-source code fosters system interoperability and enables easy communication and rapid adaptation in response to changing agency and community needs (45). The CMS MITA framework can lead states through the possibilities for incorporating these capabilities (18,46). MITA also encourages interoperability between the Medicaid management information system and other health information systems to measure and improve client outcomes and manage health care costs. In addition, Medicaid MITA projects may be eligible for varying percentages of federal matching funds.

Analyze and generate information
To be viable and sustainable, information systems must demonstrate a return on investment. Patients, providers, policy makers, and analysts should decide together how the data will be used. They should make these decisions ahead of investments in the data system. Dedicated, trained staff should be available to address important policy questions with the client-linked, enhanced data systems. Unless the effort to integrate data systems shows projected and continuing worth in how it is used, governors, state budget officers, program administrators, legislators, and federal supporting agencies will be unwilling to invest in it.

Conclusions

Service fragmentation undermines effective mental health and substance abuse treatment, creating an often-insurmountable barrier when patients try to obtain, and providers try to give, effective treatment. Incomplete information about a patient's physical and mental health stymies treatment providers' abilities to apply best practices to help the patient achieve optimal wellness.

The IOM and the President's New Freedom Commission recognized the need to redesign behavioral health care, emphasizing the need for shared knowledge and cooperation among stakeholders. Strategies to achieve this aim have noted that the technology for information sharing exists but needs to be applied expeditiously to improve the lives of individuals who struggle with mental or substance use disorders.

In this article we have presented an approach to improving existing state systems of health data so that they are able to communicate and to describe health care comprehensively rather than piecemeal. The approach includes aligning behavioral health data systems with general health data systems; collecting encounter-level data; using HIPAA-compliant coding, including NPIs; forging linkages with other state data systems and developing unique synthetic client identifiers among state systems; investing in flexible and adaptable data systems and business processes; and finding innovative solutions to the difficult confidentiality restrictions on use of behavioral health data. Although we have focused on integration of mental health, substance abuse, and Medicaid data systems, these ideas also apply to other public data systems, such as criminal justice, child welfare, and school health systems. State agencies may want to focus on integrating one or two systems to demonstrate the feasibility of the concept in their state, while keeping others in mind for future enhancements.

Data interoperability for behavioral health care is an important step toward sharing and use of data for significant improvements in patient care and public policy. Although linking data systems will not in itself transform the delivery of care, it will enable agencies to exchange information about shared clients, to better understand problems of coordination, and to track successes and failures of policy decisions. Several federal initiatives have provided an impetus for improving health care data interoperability and increasing the adoption of electronic health records. With public funding, dedicated support, and engagement from consumers, providers, administrators, and policy makers, behavioral health information systems may be poised for meaningful change and better quality of care for individuals with mental and substance use disorders.

Acknowledgments and disclosures

Development of this article was funded by SAMHSA under the Integrated Database Project (contract 270-01-7087) between Thomson Medstat (now Thomson Reuters) and two SAMHSA centers—the Center for Substance Abuse Treatment and the Center for Mental Health Services.

The authors report no competing interests.

References

1. Kessler RC, Chiu WT, Demler O, et al: Prevalence, severity, and comorbidity of 12-month DSM-IV disorders in the National Comorbidity Survey Replication. Archives of General Psychiatry 62:617–627, 2005

2. Coffey R, Dilonardo J, Vandivort-Warren R, et al: Expenditures on Clients Receiving Treatment for Both Mental Illness and Substance-Use Disorders: Results From an Integrated Data Base of Mental Health, Substance Abuse, and Medicaid Agencies for Three States in 1997. SAMHSA pub no SMA-07-4263. Rockville, Md, Substance Abuse and Mental Health Services Administration, 2007

3. Burnam MA, Watkins KE: Substance abuse with mental disorders: specialized public systems and integrated care. Health Affairs 25:648–658, 2006

4. Mark T, Levit K, Coffey R, et al: National Expenditures for Mental Health Services and Substance Abuse Treatment, 1993–2003. SAMHSA pub no SMA 07-4227. Rockville, Md, Substance Abuse and Mental Health Services Administration, 2007

5. Coffey RM, Chalk M, Dilonardo JD: Increasing interoperability in health information systems: what is the value to stakeholders—consumers, providers, state and federal governments, and taxpayers? in Increasing Interoperability in Health Information Systems for Medicaid, Mental Health, and Substance Abuse Treatment: A Compilation of Papers Presented at the Conference, January 24–25, 2007, Washington, DC. Baltimore, Centers for Medicare and Medicaid Services, and Rockville, Md, Substance Abuse and Mental Health Services Administration, 2007

6. Whalen D, Pepitone A, Graver L, et al: Linking client records from substance abuse, mental health and Medicaid State agencies. SAMHSA pub no SMA-01-3500. Rockville, Md, Substance Abuse and Mental Health Services Administration, Center for Substance Abuse Treatment and Center for Mental Health Services, July 2001

7. Achieving the Promise: Transforming Mental Health Care in America. Pub no SMA-03-3832. Rockville, Md, Department of Health and Human Services, President's New Freedom Commission on Mental Health, 2003

8. Institute of Medicine: Improving the Quality of Health Care for Mental and Substance-Use Conditions. Washington, DC, National Academies Press, 2006

9. Dorr D, Bonner LM, Cohen AN, et al: Informatics systems to promote improved care for chronic illness: a literature review. Journal of the American Medical Informatics Association 14:156–163, 2007

10. Green CJ, Fortin P, Maclure M, et al: Information system support as a critical success factor for chronic disease management: necessary but not sufficient. International Journal of Medical Informatics 75:818–828, 2006

11. Forhan C: Lessons learned through building and using integrated Medicaid, mental health, and substance abuse data, in Increasing Interoperability in Health Information Systems for Medicaid, Mental Health, and Substance Abuse Treatment: A Compilation of Papers Presented at the Conference, January 24–25, 2007, Washington, DC. Baltimore, Centers for Medicare and Medicaid Services, and Rockville, Md, Substance Abuse and Mental Health Services Administration, 2007

12. Coffey R, Graver L, Schroeder D, et al: Mental Health and Substance Abuse Treatment: Results From a Study Integrating Data From State Mental Health, Substance Abuse, and Medicaid Agencies. SAMHSA pub no SMA-01-3528. Rockville, Md, Substance Abuse and Mental Health Services Administration, 2001

13. Public Law 104-191: Health Insurance Portability and Accountability Act of 1996, Aug 21, 1996. Available at aspe.hhs.gov/admnsimp/pl104191.htm

14. Health Information Technology: President's Vision for Health IT. Washington, DC, US Department of Health and Human Services, 2004. Available at dhhs.gov/healthit/vision.html

15. SAMHSA Data Strategy FY 2007 to FY 2011. Rockville, Md, Substance Abuse and Mental Health Services Administration, 2007

16. The Confidentiality of Alcohol and Drug Abuse Patient Records Regulation and the HIPAA Privacy Rule: Implications for Alcohol and Substance Abuse Programs. Rockville, Md, Substance Abuse and Mental Health Services Administration, Center for Substance Abuse Treatment, 2004. Available at www.hipaa.samhsa.gov

17. Medicaid Information Technology Architecture (MITA): Overview. Baltimore, Md, Centers for Medicare and Medicaid Services, 2005. Available at www.cms.hhs.gov/medicaidinfotecharch

18. Bazemore D, Shugart A: What is the Medicaid information technology architecture (MITA)? in Increasing Interoperability in Health Information Systems for Medicaid, Mental Health, and Substance Abuse Treatment: A Compilation of Papers Presented at the Conference, January 24–25, 2007, Washington, DC. Baltimore, Centers for Medicare and Medicaid Services, Rockville, Md, Substance Abuse and Mental Health Services Administration, 2007

19. Mancuso D, Estee S: Washington State Mental Health Services Cost Offsets and Client Outcomes. Technical report 3.29. Olympia, Washington State Department of Social and Health Services, Management Services Administration, Research and Data Analysis Division, 2003

20. Bailey WP: Integrated State Data Systems, Part 2, Book 3: Tools for Monitoring the Health Care Safety Net. AHRQ pub no 03-0027. Rockville, Md, Agency for Healthcare Research and Quality, 2003. Available at ahrq.gov/data/safetynet/bailey.htm

21. Daley M, Love CT, Shepard DS, et al: Cost-effectiveness of Connecticut's in-prison substance abuse treatment. Journal of Offender Rehabilitation 39:69–92, 2004

22. Stoner H: The recovery collaborative of Oklahoma, in Increasing Interoperability in Health Information Systems for Medicaid, Mental Health, and Substance Abuse Treatment: A Compilation of Papers Presented at the Conference, January 24–25, 2007, Washington, DC. Baltimore, Centers for Medicare and Medicaid Services, Rockville, Md, Substance Abuse and Mental Health Services Administration, 2007

23. Lehman C: Multi-agency IT projects: building bridges and sharing data, in Increasing Interoperability in Health Information Systems for Medicaid, Mental Health, and Substance Abuse Treatment: A Compilation of Papers Presented at the Conference, January 24–25, 2007, Washington, DC. Baltimore, Centers for Medicare and Medicaid Services, Rockville, Md, Substance Abuse and Mental Health Services Administration, 2007

24. Liljestrand I: CMS-SAMHSA health information collaboration: developing consumer-centric driven services for Medicaid, in Increasing Interoperability in Health Information Systems for Medicaid, Mental Health, and Substance Abuse Treatment: A Compilation of Papers Presented at the Conference, January 24–25, 2007, Washington, DC. Baltimore, Centers for Medicare and Medicaid Services, Rockville, Md, Substance Abuse and Mental Health Services Administration, 2007

25. Unjust denial of parental rights overturned. News release. Washington, DC, Bazelon Center for Mental Health Law, Jan 10, 2007. Available at bazelon.org/newsroom/2007/UNJUST011107.html

26. Anti-stigma: do you know the facts? Fact sheet. Rockville, Md, Substance Abuse and Mental Health Services Administration, Center for Mental Health Services, 2003. Available at mentalhealth.samhsa.gov/publications/allpubs/oel99-0004/default.asp

27. Schroedel JR, Fiber P: Punitive versus public health oriented responses to drug use by pregnant women. Yale Journal of Health Policy Law Ethics 1:217–235, 2001

28. Lindenthal JJ, Thomas CS: Psychiatrists, the public, and confidentiality. Journal of Nervous and Mental Disease 170:319–323, 1982

29. Marshall MF, Menikoff J, Paltrow LM: Perinatal substance abuse and human subjects research: are privacy protections adequate? Mental Retardation and Developmental Disabilities Research Reviews 9:54–59, 2003

30. Mass Shootings at Virginia Tech, April 16, 2007: Report of the Review Panel, Presented to Governor Kaine, Commonwealth of Virginia. Blacksburg, Va, Virginia Tech Review Panel, Aug 2007. Available at www.governor.virginia.gov

31. Smith R: Compilation of State and Federal Privacy Laws. Providence, RI, Privacy Journal Publishers, 2002

32. Woodward B, Hammerschmidt D: Requiring consent vs waiving consent for medical records research: a Minnesota law vs the US (HIPAA) privacy rule. Health Care Analysis 11:207–218, 2003

33. Summary of the HIPAA Privacy Rule: HIPAA Compliance Assistance. Washington, DC, US Department of Health and Human Services, Office of Civil Rights, May 2003. Available at www.hhs.gov/ocr/privacysummary.pdf

34. Administrative Simplification Under HIPAA: National Standards for Transactions, Privacy, and Security. Fact sheet. Washington, DC, US Department of Health and Human Services, 2005. Available at www.hhs.gov/news/press

35. Title 42, Chapter 1, Subchapter A, Part 2: Confidentiality of Alcohol and Drug Abuse Patient Records. Washington, DC, US Department of Health and Human Services, Public Health Service, 2008. Available at ecfr.gpoaccess.gov

36. Behavioral Health Integrated Provider System (BHIPS): Functionality Definition. Austin, Texas Department of State Health Services, 2008. Available at www.dshs.state.tx.us/sa/bhips

37. Yawn BP, Yawn RA, Geier GR, et al: The impact of requiring patient authorization for use of data in medical records research. Journal of Family Practice 47:361–365, 1998

38. Forhan C: Health systems interoperability: lessons learned and planning for change, in Increasing Interoperability in Health Information Systems for Medicaid, Mental Health, and Substance Abuse Treatment: A Compilation of Papers Presented at the Conference, January 24–25, 2007, Washington, DC. Baltimore, Centers for Medicare and Medicaid Services, Rockville, Md, Substance Abuse and Mental Health Services Administration, 2007

39. Petrila J: Some thoughts on HIPAA and cross-system collaboration in increasing interoperability, in Increasing Interoperability in Health Information Systems for Medicaid, Mental Health, and Substance Abuse Treatment: A Compilation of Papers Presented at the Conference, January 24–25, 2007, Washington, DC. Baltimore, Centers for Medicare and Medicaid Services, Rockville, Md, Substance Abuse and Mental Health Services Administration, 2007

40. Coffey RM: Casemix information in the United States: fifteen years of management and clinical experience. Casemix Quarterly 1(1):7–16, 1999

41. American National Standards Institute ASCX: HIPAA EDI Implementation Guides. Bellevue, Wash, Washington Publishing Co, 2003

42. Health Insurance Portability and Accountability Act: Background Information. Fact sheet. Rockville, Md, Substance Abuse and Mental Health Services Administration, 2004. Available at hipaa.samhsa.gov/backgrd.htm

43. Narevic E, Garrity TF, Schoenberg NE, et al: Factors predicting unmet health services needs among incarcerated substance users. Substance Use and Misuse 41:1077–1094, 2006

44. National Plan and Provider Enumeration System (NPPES). Baltimore, Centers for Medicare and Medicaid Services, 2007. Available at https://NPPES.cms.hhs.gov/NPPES

45. Pepitone A: Fostering interoperability with service oriented architectures, in Increasing Interoperability in Health Information Systems for Medicaid, Mental Health, and Substance Abuse Treatment: A Compilation of Papers Presented at the Conference, January 24–25, 2007, Washington, DC. Baltimore, Centers for Medicare and Medicaid Services, Rockville, Md, Substance Abuse and Mental Health Services Administration, 2007

46. Friedman R: A Road map for obtaining federal financial support from CMS for state data sharing projects involving Medicaid, in Increasing Interoperability in Health Information Systems for Medicaid, Mental Health, and Substance Abuse Treatment: A Compilation of Papers Presented at the Conference, January 24–25, 2007, Washington, DC. Baltimore, Centers for Medicare and Medicaid Services, Rockville, Md, Substance Abuse and Mental Health Services Administration, 2007

Delivery of Excellent Mental Health Care and Acceleration of Research: Federal Activities Since the President's Commission Report

Kevin D. Hennessy, Ph.D.
David A. Chambers, Ph.D.

The report of the President's New Freedom Commission set forth six goals and related recommendations to enable adults with serious mental illness and children with serious emotional disturbance to participate fully in their communities. This article focuses on goal 5—"Excellent mental health care is delivered and research is accelerated"—and its four related recommendations. The authors describe federal government activities undertaken since the report was released. To accelerate research, the National Institute of Mental Health (NIMH) has launched initiatives to find ways to interrupt the progress of schizophrenia and to identify interventions for combat veterans with mental health problems. To advance evidence-based practices, the Substance Abuse and Mental Health Services Administration (SAMHSA) has expanded and transformed its National Registry of Evidence-Based Programs and Practices and NIMH has launched a major research initiative to build the knowledge base for dissemination and implementation. To improve and expand the workforce, SAMHSA has published an action plan for workforce development and NIMH has established grants to develop curricula to integrate training in evidence-based practices into clinical training programs. To develop knowledge in understudied areas, NIMH has funded studies to reduce and eliminate disparities and SAMHSA has supported efforts to improve delivery of trauma-informed services, such as the National Child Traumatic Stress Network. Continued advancement in goal 5 areas calls for commitment to working across agency and organizational boundaries to ensure more rapid and widespread dissemination and implementation of research and policies and for further development of ways to promote the participation of all stakeholders. (*Psychiatric Services* 60:433–438, 2009)

In 2002 the President's New Freedom Commission on Mental Health was convened by executive order (1) to report on opportunities to "improve America's mental health service delivery system for individuals with serious mental illness and children with serious emotional disturbances." The commission's 2003 report, *Achieving the Promise: Transforming Mental Health Care in America* (2), contained a series of goals and recommendations designed to enable adults with serious mental illness and children with serious emotional disturbance to "live, work, learn, and participate fully in their communities." When considered alongside other seminal reports, such as the Surgeon General's 1999 report on mental health (3) and the Institute of Medicine's 2006 report on *Improving the Quality of Health Care for Mental and Substance-Use Conditions* (4), the commission's report provides an influential, authoritative, and consistent message regarding the need for dramatic changes in the way individuals with mental illness in this country are treated and cared for.

The conclusion of the Bush Administration is an appropriate time to reflect on the progress that federal agencies have made in achieving the goals outlined in the President's Commission report. A comprehensive overview of federal activities emanating from the commission's recommendations is both beyond our scope and has been presented elsewhere (5). This article seeks to highlight strategic federal government activities that have been specifically developed—or further advanced—to address recommendations included in goal 5 of the report's six overarching goals: "Excellent mental health care is delivered and research is accelerated."

Our current positions within two key federal agencies, the Substance Abuse and Mental Health Services Administration (SAMHSA) and the National Institute of Mental Health (NIMH), as well as the first author's role as a senior policy adviser to the President's Commission, provide us with somewhat unique perspectives on the aftermath of the commission and its report. In many ways, the re-

Dr. Hennessy is with the Office of Policy, Planning, and Budget, Substance Abuse and Mental Health Services Administration, 1 Choke Cherry Rd., Room 8-1017, Rockville, MD 20857 (e-mail: kevin.hennessy@samhsa.hhs.gov). Dr. Chambers is with the Division of Services and Intervention Research, National Institute of Mental Health, Bethesda, Maryland. Originally published in the April 2009 issue of Psychiatric Services.

port's findings—and the commission's very existence—reflect important milestones in our nation's ongoing and collective journey to improve both the condition and the lives of individuals with mental illness. Yet what is particularly compelling—and hopeful—about the commission's report is its emphasis on transformation of the mental health system and the notion that each of us has an important function to fulfill if this transformative effort is to succeed in promoting recovery and full community participation.

With this in mind, we highlight examples of recent SAMHSA and NIMH activities that seek to promote the transformation of mental health systems by ensuring that excellent mental health care is delivered and research is accelerated. What follows are brief descriptions of key federally sponsored activities that underscore how both SAMHSA and NIMH have responded to the four recommendations outlined by the commission for goal 5.

Accelerate research

Recommendation 5.1 of *Achieving the Promise* is "Accelerate research to promote recovery and resilience, and ultimately to cure and prevent mental illness." As the largest scientific organization in the world dedicated to research on the understanding, treatment, and prevention of mental disorders and the promotion of mental health, it can be argued that most of NIMH's annual budget is—directly or indirectly—devoted to carrying out this recommendation. Indeed, the mission statement in the new NIMH Strategic Plan (6) directly addresses this recommendation: "The mission of NIMH is to transform the understanding and treatment of mental illnesses through basic and clinical research, paving the way for prevention, recovery and cure." Rather than discussing the breadth of the NIMH research portfolio, we briefly present several recent activities that highlight the organization's interest in supporting research reflecting this recommendation. Consistent in these initiatives is the desire to ensure that effective interventions fit the needs of populations, community settings, and

service systems, and as the NIMH Advisory Council report, *The Road Ahead* (7), suggests, research includes the partnership of key stakeholders (for example, consumers, families, providers, administrators, and advocates) working in concert to improve the mental health of the United States.

One recent NIMH research initiative—Recovery After an Initial Schizophrenic Episode, or RAISE—seeks to promote the recovery of individuals who have experienced a first psychotic episode and to interrupt the disabling progression of schizophrenia. In a recent request for proposals (8), NIMH called for the development and testing of a "comprehensive and integrated intervention that can be delivered in real world practice settings to promote symptomatic recovery, minimize disability, and maximize social, academic, and vocational functioning." Applications were submitted in August 2008, and after a comprehensive scientific and administrative review, the most competitive applications will receive funding to develop and pilot test the intervention, with a large trial to follow if preliminary results show significant consumer benefit.

A new NIMH request for applications (RFA) focuses on the recovery and resilience of combat veterans returning from Iraq and Afghanistan and calls for research on how services from community-based programs affect outcomes for veterans. The need for such services was documented in a recent RAND study that estimated that as many as a third of veterans returning from combat operations in Iraq and Afghanistan have mental health problems that warrant treatment (9). The RFA is soliciting applications for research funding to assess the impact of state and nonprofit community-based programs on veterans, particularly those who are not receiving services within Department of Defense or Department of Veterans Affairs (VA) programs, such as personnel from the army reserve and national guard and those recently separated from active duty (10). NIMH is interested in building the evidence base on the most effective

ways to help this important population. The RFA set the first submission date in October 2008 and a second one in May 2009. NIMH intends to fund three to six new research grants.

Since the President's Commission report, SAMHSA's Center for Mental Health Services (CMHS) has also provided support to further define and operationalize recovery and resilience in ways that will improve the lives and prospects of persons with mental illness. A CMHS-sponsored national conference in December 2004 brought together more than 100 experts, including consumers, family members, researchers, providers, policy makers, and public officials, to produce a consensus statement outlining key principles necessary to the achievement of mental health recovery (11). Moreover, CMHS provides approximately $2 million annually to fund a network of consumer-support technical assistance centers that are an integral component of disseminating research and other materials related to mental health recovery and the prevention of mental illness (12).

Advance evidence-based practices

Recommendation 5.2 of the President's Commission report challenges the field to "Advance evidence-based practices using dissemination and demonstration projects and create a public-private partnership to guide their implementation." The report further asserts that "The Nation must have a more effective system to identify, disseminate, and apply proven treatments or evidence-based practices (EBPs) to mental health care."

In response to this recommendation, SAMHSA has expanded and transformed its National Registry of Evidence-Based Programs and Practices (NREPP). NREPP was initially developed in the mid-1990s as a registry of substance abuse prevention interventions that documented their efficacy and effectiveness. For this early version of NREPP, well over 1,000 programs were reviewed, and about 150 were selected as worthy of inclusion as a model program on SAMHSA's Web site.

Partly because of the President's

Commission report, NREPP underwent an extensive, multiyear transformation that, among other things, expanded the registry's focus to include interventions to prevent or treat mental illness. Launched in 2007, the redesigned NREPP system and Web site (www.nrepp.samhsa.gov) provides summaries of more than 100 mental health and substance use interventions. The summaries include descriptive information about the intervention and its targeted outcomes, expert ratings of the intervention's quality of research and readiness for dissemination, a list of studies and materials submitted for the experts' review, and contact information for the intervention developer. Users of the NREPP system can customize a searchable database to identify specific interventions on the basis of desired outcomes, target populations, and service settings. Current plans within SAMHSA call for continued expansion of NREPP at the rate of 40 to 50 new intervention summaries per year, with an overarching goal of providing agency constituents with information to inform decisions about selecting evidence-based interventions to address their particular needs and to match their specific capacities and resources.

Although the identification of evidence-based practices is a necessary step in expanding their use in routine clinical and community-based settings, true transformation will require "reframing reimbursement policies to better support and widely implement EBPs" (2). An inherent challenge in determining adequate reimbursement for the types of interventions included in NREPP—as well as reimbursement for interventions in the CMHS-sponsored evidence-based practices toolkits (13)—has been the degree to which the various services that constitute these interventions can be reimbursed through more traditional public purchasers such as Medicaid and Medicare. Although solutions to this and other financing issues have remained somewhat elusive, staff from both SAMHSA and the Centers for Medicare and Medicaid Services (CMS) remain com-

mitted to achieving progress in this area, which is exemplified by a new initiative between SAMHSA and CMS to develop technical assistance for specific evidence-based practices. Moreover, although progress has been made in advancing specific practices, additional work is needed to develop and apply evidence-based (or evidence-informed) approaches to broader issues, such as effective dissemination and implementation strategies, and to systems change and redesign efforts.

For its part, NIMH has also been active in increasing the use of effective, evidence-based interventions. One major initiative has been to build the knowledge base on dissemination and implementation, the processes that most specifically improve the appropriate uptake of effective interventions in clinical and community practice. This area of science intends to bridge the gap between research and practice by developing and testing strategies to improve transmission of scientific findings and embed evidence-based interventions in real-world service systems. An NIMH program announcement in 2002 called for research applications that would "build knowledge on methods, structures, and processes to disseminate and implement mental health information and treatments into practice settings" (14). More recently, NIMH has expanded the scope of the program announcement to include research across multiple disease categories, in recognition of the fact that the facilitators and barriers to dissemination and implementation cut across disease categories. The latest announcements—PAR-07-086, PAR-06-520, and PAR-06-521 (grants.nih.gov/grants/guide/pa-files)—now include participation from the National Cancer Institute; National Institute on Drug Abuse (NIDA); National Institute on Alcoholism and Alcohol Abuse (NIAAA); National Heart, Lung, and Blood Institute; National Institute of Dental and Craniofacial Research; National Institute of Deafness and Communication Disorders; National Institute of Nursing Research; and two National Institutes of Health (NIH) offices—the Office of

Behavioral and Social Sciences Research and the Office of Dietary Supplements. Researchers who apply for these funds are encouraged to build knowledge to address the challenges of embedding complex interventions in service settings and to develop new strategies that overcome attitudinal, financial, and systemic barriers to achieving widespread use of beneficial interventions.

NIMH's current portfolio of dissemination and implementation research grants includes funds for small and large research projects and research centers and career development awards. To improve the dialogue among researchers interested in dissemination and implementation research, the participating NIH institutes have jointly held an annual scientific conference in Bethesda, Maryland, which brings together hundreds of investigators to present research findings, discuss methodological and theoretical challenges, and receive technical assistance from NIH program staff. The first meeting, "Building the Science of Dissemination and Implementation in the Service of Public Health," was held in September 2007 (15). The most recent meeting, "Science of Dissemination and Implementation: Building Research Capacity to Bridge the Gap From Science to Service," was held in January 2009 on the NIH campus (conferences.thehillgroup.com/obssr/di2008/index.html).

Improve and expand the workforce

Recommendation 5.3 seeks to "Improve and expand the workforce providing evidence-based mental health services and supports." Recent surveys of graduate and professional training programs have revealed that few require both didactic and clinical supervision in evidence-based treatments (16,17). Obstacles identified in these surveys included lack of qualified faculty, lack of trainee interest, and substantial research demonstrating that factors other than specific evidence-based approaches are primarily responsible for therapeutic change (18).

Nevertheless, SAMHSA recognizes that a competent and well-trained workforce is essential to providing effective, high-quality, and culturally relevant services to individuals who have mental and substance use disorders or who are at risk of developing them. In 2006 SAMHSA prioritized workforce development issues, which resulted in renewed attention and allocation of resources to this area. In addition, the agency published *An Action Plan for Behavioral Health Workforce Development* in March 2007 (19). Based largely on the pioneering efforts and expertise of the SAMHSA-funded Annapolis Coalition, the report comprehensively details the range of concerns related to workforce development both within behavioral health care and across general medical care and provides the field with wide-ranging and action-oriented recommendations for both improving and expanding the behavioral health workforce.

Of particular note, SAMHSA is nearing the launch of a new Web portal (www.workforce.samhsa.gov) to serve as a central repository for gathering and sharing up-to-date information and resources related to behavioral health workforce development. The Workforce Development Resource Center Web portal will contain searchable databases of educational and training opportunities; discipline- and state-specific licensure and certification requirements; and national, regional, and local job searches. In addition, the portal will house a virtual library of documents on a range of workforce development topics, such as best practices in recruitment and retention and the development of core competencies. By creating an interactive system that creates dynamic connections between individuals and organizations with workforce development needs and educational, training, and professional opportunities and resources, SAMHSA will help create and sustain a behavioral health workforce capable of responding effectively and compassionately to the increasingly complex and diverse needs of consumers and their families.

NIMH has also taken steps to promote workforce training. For example, in April 2007 NIMH sponsored a symposium with the Institute for the Advancement of Social Work, "Partnerships to Integrate Evidence-Based Mental Health Practices Into Social Work Education and Research." The meeting brought together representatives from the research community, social work educators, representatives from national organizations, federal agency staff, and consumers to discuss opportunities to promote the inclusion of training in evidence-based practices in university schools of social work. Presenters discussed existing training programs, state and school perspectives on training in evidence-based practices, and mechanisms to improve the partnership between educational institutions and service agencies (20).

In October 2007 NIMH, along with NIDA, NIAAA, and the NIH Office of Behavioral and Social Sciences Research, released an RFA titled "Programs of Excellence in Scientifically Validated Behavioral Treatments." The RFA offered funds for researchers to develop and test curricula to integrate training in evidence-based practices into university clinical training programs. In issuing the RFA the institutes recognized that although many evidence-based interventions have been demonstrated to be beneficial, few are being delivered by clinicians around the country. To increase the workforce capacity to deliver effective treatments, clinical training programs need courses that comprehensively prepare clinicians to deliver these interventions. Grants were awarded to a number of researchers who have developed the interventions, with the expectation that the investment will result in widespread dissemination of these curricula.

Develop knowledge in understudied areas

Recommendation 5.4 of the commission's report is a call to "Develop the knowledge base in four understudied areas: mental health disparities, the long-term effects of medication, trauma, and acute care." Commissioners agreed that research in these understudied areas is "essential to ultimately improve the quality of mental health treatments and services" (2). These areas of research are represented within the NIMH research portfolio, and the institute has developed specific research opportunities for growth. A few salient examples are noted here.

To reduce health disparities, the NIMH portfolio includes studies that attempt to reduce and ultimately eliminate disparities in prevalence, access, quality of care, and outcomes of treatment. This work cuts across all NIMH divisions, with coordination from the Office of Special Populations. In addition, NIMH has worked to increase involvement of underserved communities in the research process itself through an emphasis on community-based participatory research, which a recent program announcement (PAR-07-004) defines as "scientific inquiry conducted in communities with full partnership status for both community and academic researchers" (21). Mental health grants that use this approach have focused on implementing effective care within underserved communities, improving access to care, and adapting interventions to improve the applicability of treatments to specific populations. Another approach to reducing disparities that NIMH research has pursued is telemedicine. Several grants have used technology to provide services for people in rural and frontier settings. For example, a grant to the University of Arkansas for Medical Sciences is funding a study of the use of telemedicine to provide collaborative care in rural Arkansas.

Similarly, research on the long-term effects of medications, trauma, and acute care has remained an important component of the NIMH research portfolio. The practical clinical trials, such as Sequenced Treatment Alternatives to Relieve Depression (STAR*D), Clinical Antipsychotic Trials of Intervention Effectiveness (CATIE), and Systematic Treatment Enhancement Program for Bipolar Disorder (STEP-BD), have focused on selecting and sequencing the right medications mental following up over time to gauge their longer-term effectiveness. NIMH initiatives in recent years have focused on understanding risk factors and appropriate treatments for posttraumatic stress disorder, including the current RFA on returning combat veterans, and efforts to improve the capacity of first responders to withstand the trauma experience. Finally, the NIMH has participated in several initiatives to improve the provision of acute care. One such program announcement, "Emergency Medical Services for Children," solicits research studies that target the reduction of mortality and morbidity among children seeking services in emergency departments (22). NIMH-funded research has looked at the emergency room as a setting for providing early mental health intervention, primarily through screening, assessment, and referral.

Although primarily a services agency, SAMHSA has also advanced knowledge in other areas. The agency's data strategy calls for collecting and reporting national information on the incidence and prevalence of mental and substance use disorders. Efforts are under way to collect national data on the prevalence of serious mental illness among adults through SAMHSA's National Survey of Drug Use and Health (NSDUH) and to develop prevalence estimates of serious emotional disturbance among children through the National Health Interview Survey of the Centers for Disease Control and Prevention. Recently, the NSDUH has provided estimates of serious psychological distress among various racial and ethnic groups, as well as racial and ethnic differences in use of mental health services and levels of unmet need for services. When examined over time, such data can provide an important tool for assessing the degree of progress in reducing or eliminating mental health disparities.

SAMHSA has also supported efforts to both expand and improve the delivery of trauma-informed services across the country. Since 2001 the agency has sponsored the National Child Traumatic Stress Network (www.nctsn.org), a unique collaboration of academic and community-based service centers. Their mission is to raise the standard of care and increase access to services for trauma-

tized children and their families across the United States by developing and disseminating evidence-based interventions, trauma-informed services, and public and professional education. More recently, CMHS created the National Center for Trauma-Informed Care (www.mentalhealth. samhsa.gov/nctic) to offer technical assistance to stimulate and support interest in and implementation of trauma-informed care in publicly funded systems and programs. Through these and similar efforts, SAMHSA has demonstrated its commitment to using emerging knowledge and research findings to benefit those with or at risk of developing mental illness.

Next steps

The recommendations of the President's Commission on Mental Health reflect a fundamental vision of transformative change that would create a mental health service system that engages, supports, empowers, and strengthens every individual who receives care. As the activities described above suggest, SAMHSA and NIMH have embraced the commission's recommendations, particularly those of goal 5.

It is quite possible that broader forces, such as reductions and restrictions in public funding for health and social services, large numbers of uninsured and underinsured persons, and recent stresses on the domestic and global economies, have adversely affected both federal and state capacities to further achieve needed changes in mental health services and systems, although the effects of such factors are difficult to assess. Admittedly, such constraints force a reevaluation of what is practical and feasible with regard to mental health system transformation. However, as we are beginning to see, they may also provide new and unexpected opportunities to advance long-anticipated objectives related to broader health care reform and system transformation. If that is the case, then the activities of SAMHSA and NIMH described here may provide an important foundation for further progress in accelerating research and delivering excellent mental health care.

From our joint perspectives, continued advancement in goal 5 areas calls for renewed commitments to working across agency and organizational boundaries in ways that will ensure more rapid and widespread dissemination and implementation of key mental health research and policies while further developing and supporting vehicles to promote stakeholder influence in the pursuit and generation of new knowledge to understand and treat—and perhaps ultimately prevent and cure—mental illnesses. And if we fall short of "changing the world," to paraphrase Margaret Mead, at least we may be able to improve it measurably for those with mental illness.

Acknowledgments and disclosures

The views expressed are those of the authors and not necessarily those of SAMHSA, NIMH, or the U.S. Department of Health and Human Services.

The authors report no competing interests.

References

1. Executive Order: President's New Freedom Commission on Mental Health. Washington, DC, White House Office of the Press Secretary, Apr 29, 2002. Available at govinfo.library.unt.edu/mentalhealthcommission/20020429-2.htm

2. Achieving the Promise: Transforming Mental Health Care in America. Pub no SMA-03-3832. Rockville, Md, Department of Health and Human Services, President's New Freedom Commission on Mental Health, 2003

3. Mental Health: A Report of the Surgeon General. Rockville, Md, US Department of Health and Human Services, US Public Health Service, 1999

4. Institute of Medicine: Improving the Quality of Health Care for Mental and Substance-Use Conditions. Washington, DC, National Academies Press, 2006

5. Transforming Mental Health Care in America: Federal Action Agenda: First Steps. DHHS pub no SMA-05-4060. Rockville, Md, Substance Abuse and Mental Health Services Administration, 2005

6. The National Institute of Mental Health Strategic Plan. Bethesda, Md, National Institute of Mental Health. Available at www.nimh.nih.gov/about/strategic-planning-reports/index.shtml

7. National Advisory Mental Health Council: The Road Ahead: Research Partnerships to Transform Services. Bethesda, Md, National Institute of Mental Health, May 12, 2006. Available at www.nimh.nih.gov/about/advisory-boards-and-groups

8. Recovery After an Initial Schizophrenic Episode (RAISE). Bethesda, Md, National Institute of Mental Health, 2008. Available at www.fbo.gov/?s=opportunity&mode=form&id=b036bc88c12dd5fa5740acb30b75b8d1&tab=core&_cview=1

9. Tanielian T, Jaycox LH (eds): Invisible Wounds of War: Psychological and Cognitive Injuries, Their Consequences, and Services to Assist Recovery. Santa Monica, Calif, RAND, 2008

10. Addressing the Mental Health Needs of Returning Combat Veterans in the Community. Bethesda, Md, National Institute of Mental Health, 2008. Available at grants.nih.gov/grants/guide

11. SAMHSA Issues Consensus Statement on Mental Health Recovery. Rockville, Md, Substance Abuse and Mental Health Services Administration, Feb 16, 2006. Available at www.samhsa.gov/news/newsreleases/060215_consumer.htm

12. SAMHSA Congressional Justification and Online Performance Index. Rockville, Md, Substance Abuse and Mental Health Services Administration, 2008. Available at www.samhsa.gov/budget/fy2008/index.aspx

13. McHugo GJ, Drake RE, Whitley R, et al: Fidelity outcomes in the National Implementing Evidence-Based Practice Project. Psychiatric Services 58:1279–1284, 2007

14. Dissemination and Implementation Research in Mental Health. Bethesda, Md, National Institute of Mental Health, July 19, 2002. Available at grants.nih.gov/grants/guide/pa-files/pa-02-131.html

15. NIH Conference on Building the Science of Dissemination and Implementation in the Service of Public Health: Meeting Summary. Bethesda, Md, National Institute of Mental Health, Sept 10–11, 2007. Available at obssr.od.nih.gov/di2007/index.html

16. Weissman MM, Verdeli H, Gameroff MJ, et al: National survey of psychotherapy training in psychiatry, psychology, and social work. Archives of General Psychiatry 63:925–934, 2006

17. Hays KA, Rardin DK, Jarvis PA, et al: An exploratory survey on empirically supported treatments: implications for internship training. Professional Psychology: Research and Practice 33:207–211, 2002

18. Wampold BE: The Great Psychotherapy Debate: Models, Methods and Findings. Mahwah, NJ, Erlbaum, 2001

19. An Action Plan for Behavioral Health Workforce Development. Rockville, Md, Substance Abuse and Mental Health Services Administration, 2007. Available at www.samhsa.gov/workforce/annapolis/workforceactionplan.pdf

20. Partnerships to Integrate Evidence-Based Mental Health Practices Into Social Work Education and Research. Washington, DC, Institute for the Advancement of Social Work Research, Apr 12, 2007. Available at charityadvantage.com/iaswr/evidencebasedpracticesummary.pdf

21. Community-Based Participatory Research at NIMH. Bethesda, Md, National Institutes of Mental Health, 2006. Available at grants1.nih.gov/grants/guide/pa-files/par-07-004.html

22. Research on Emergency Medical Services for Children. Bethesda, Md, National Institute of Mental Health, 2005. Available at grants.nih.gov/grants/guide/pa-files/pa-05-081.html

Transformation of the California Mental Health System: Stakeholder-Driven Planning as a Transformational Activity

Cheryl Cashin, Ph.D.
Richard Scheffler, Ph.D.
Mistique Felton, M.P.H.
Neal Adams, M.D., M.P.H.
Leonard Miller, Ph.D.

Objective: This study describes strategies developed by California counties to transform their mental health systems under the 2004 Mental Health Services Act (MHSA). This voter initiative places a 1% tax on annual incomes over $1 million; tax monies are earmarked to transform county-operated mental health services into systems that are oriented more toward recovery. MHSA implementation itself can be considered "transformational" by balancing greater standardization of mental health service delivery in the state with a locally driven planning process. *Methods:* A qualitative content analysis of the three-year plans submitted by 12 counties to receive funds under MHSA was conducted to identify common themes, as well as innovative approaches. These 12 (out of 58) counties were chosen to represent both small and large counties, as well as geographic diversity, and they represent 62.3% of the state population. *Results:* This analysis showed that the state guidelines and local planning process generated consistency across counties in establishing full-service partnerships with a "whatever it takes" approach to providing goal-directed services and supports to consumers and their families. There was, however, little convergence around the specific strategies to achieve this vision, reflecting both the local planning process and a relative lack of clear policy and guidance on evidence-based practices. *Conclusions:* There are many obstacles to the successful implementation of these ambitious plans. However, the state-guided, but stakeholder-driven, transformation in California appears to generate innovative approaches to recovery-oriented services, involve consumers and family members in service planning and delivery, and build community partnerships that create new opportunities for consumers to meet their recovery goals. (*Psychiatric Services* 59:1107–1114, 2008)

Dr. Cashin, Dr. Scheffler, and Ms. Felton are affiliated with the Nicholas C. Petris Center on Health Care Markets and Consumer Welfare and Dr. Miller is with the School of Social Welfare, University of California, Berkeley. Dr. Adams is with the California Institute for Mental Health, Sacramento. Send correspondence to Dr. Cashin at the Nicholas C. Petris Center on Health Care Markets and Consumer Welfare, 140 Earl Warren Hall, MC7360, Berkeley CA 94720 (e-mail: ccashin@berkeley.edu). An earlier version of this article was presented at the World Psychiatric Association Section on Mental Health Economics meeting, "Investing in Mental Health Policy and Economics Research," March 9–11, 2007, Venice, Italy. Originally published in the October 2008 issue of Psychiatric Services.

California is the nation's largest state with the socioeconomic, demographic, and ethnic diversity of a large country. Efforts to undertake and succeed in a major transformation of its mental health system—as called for in the President's New Freedom Commission report (1) and the Institute of Medicine's report on *Improving the Quality of Care for Mental and Substance-Use Conditions* (2)—face numerous challenges. However, recent events have created a stimulus, if not a mandate, for change. In November 2004, California voters passed Proposition 63, which became the Mental Health Services Act (MHSA) (3,4). This historic legislation places a 1% tax on adjusted gross annual incomes over $1 million and earmarks the tax monies to transform the state's 58 county- and city-operated mental health authorities into more consumer- and family-driven, culturally competent, recovery-oriented systems. Addressing the needs of previously unserved or underserved populations is also a clear priority of the legislation. The MHSA was projected to generate nearly $700 million by fiscal year (FY) 2007, increasing thereafter, but actual funding levels have exceeded projections by more than 30% (5,6). In addition to substantial systemwide investment, the new funds represent about a 10% increase in county mental health budgets (7–19).

MHSA implementation itself can

be considered "transformational" by balancing greater standardization of mental health service delivery in the state with extensive community involvement and stakeholder input. The state issued guidelines to ensure that this major transformation is consistent with the recovery-oriented spirit of the legislation, but the specific approach in each county was defined by a locally driven planning process (20,21).

This article analyzes the content of the plans submitted by 12 counties to transform their child and adult systems of care. The objectives of this descriptive study were to identify the most common and innovative strategies that counties developed to transform their mental health systems and to examine whether MHSA implementation is moving the entire system toward recovery- and resiliency-oriented services, while preserving the flexibility of counties to respond to local needs and priorities.

Context and values of MHSA

MHSA grew out of successful experience with innovative models implemented in California, including a recovery-oriented program targeted to homeless consumers with mental illness, known as "AB2034," which was recognized as a model program by the President's New Freedom Commission (3). The experience with these models created the expectation that the state's mental health system can and should promote recovery for adults with serious mental illness and resilience for children and adolescents with serious emotional disturbances. Services funded by MHSA are required to promote the concepts of recovery and resilience, as well as support consumer-operated services, reflect the diversity of mental health consumers, and plan for each consumer's individual needs (3,22).

The first funding was made available in FY 2006 for the community services and supports (CSS) component of MHSA (other components include workforce education and training, capital facilities and technology investment, prevention and early intervention, housing, and innovative programs). Each county was required

to submit a three-year plan to transform child and adult systems of care, subject to guidelines of and approval by the Department of Mental Health (DMH) (5,20,22,23). DMH also provided guidelines and a small amount of funding for the county-level planning processes. The planning guidelines specified that consumers and family members must be included in the process, particularly those from groups that were previously unserved or underserved. The counties also were required to include representatives from relevant agencies, including law enforcement, education, and social services (23). The stakeholder process involved topic-specific workgroups, the development of publicly available discussion documents, and general stakeholder meetings. It is estimated that over 100,000 stakeholders participated across the state (24). As of May 2008 all 58 California counties had submitted plans, and 57 of those had been approved by DMH (20).

DMH guidelines mandated that new and expanded services be provided through full-service partnerships (FSPs). FSPs, which are rooted in the assertive community treatment and wraparound services models (25), use a team approach to provide comprehensive, community-based psychiatric treatment, rehabilitation, and support for "whatever it takes" to move toward recovery and resilience for target populations. FSPs may provide housing, employment, and other services necessary to meet individual recovery goals (5). Each county's CSS allocation could be applied to a combination of FSP, system development to improve core services, and outreach and engagement to identify and reach populations currently unserved or underserved. The DMH specified that at least 51% of CSS funds must be used for FSP programs.

Methods

A qualitative content analysis was conducted of the three-year CSS plans submitted by 12 of California's counties. The study was conducted from November 2006 to November 2007. Although the information used was publicly available, and therefore

informed consent was not required, approval by the University of California, Berkeley, Institutional Review Board for a broader study of MHSA implementation also covered this study.

The sample of counties was selected to represent both small and large counties and geographic diversity (for example, north or south and interior or coastal). The willingness of local leadership to participate was also a factor. No county that was asked to participate refused, and the sample counties represent 62.3% of the state population.

The unit of analysis is an individual program within the county plans (N=141 programs in 12 county plans). The plans were structured around programs, which we define as an integrated set of services, providers, outreach strategies, and treatment approaches designed to meet the specific needs and recovery and resilience goals of a target population. Counties could propose to initiate or expand multiple programs within their plans in the three categories (FSP, system development, and outreach and engagement), and the number of programs per county ranged from four to 31, with an average of 12.

We analyzed the CSS plans by using established qualitative content analysis methods. We used directed content analysis to examine the array of services planned as part of FSP programs based on the American Association of Community Psychiatrists (AACP) guidelines for recovery-oriented services (26,27). Directed content analysis involves coding the content into predefined categories based on existing theory, research, or well-accepted criteria (28). A set of eight service categories was defined before analysis through an iterative process reflecting the AACP guidelines, DMH guidelines, and the actual description of services given in the plans. The defined service categories include therapeutic and rehabilitative services, services for co-occurring disorders or substance abuse, case management, peer support, outreach, employment and education services, housing, and other supports.

Categories could not be identified

before analysis of the strategies that counties developed for client- and family-driven systems, cultural competence, and community collaboration. Therefore, we conducted conventional content analysis; in this type of analysis, coding categories are derived inductively from the content (28). The content of the programs was coded into the categories and compiled to analyze the range of strategies and whether there was concentration in any of the categories.

Results

Array of planned FSP services

Of the 86 programs that were identified as FSPs, 63% (N=54) planned to provide services in six of the eight categories. Thirty percent (N=26) planned services in all eight categories. The most frequent services were in the therapeutic and rehabilitative category, with 94% of FSP programs specifying these services (Table 1). In the housing category, 85% of programs planned to directly provide, contract for, or facilitate linkages to housing services. The emphasis on housing is an important aspect of recovery-oriented services, but it may also reflect the concern of California voters about the local consequences of unserved homeless residents with mental illness (29).

Employment and education were included in 77% of the programs and peer support in 72%. Only 76% of the programs specifically identified case management services. Because case management is a core element of the FSP model, it may be that counties assumed that this feature of the program did not need to be stated explicitly. If this is not the case, programs without case management could not be expected to achieve the objectives of FSP. Efforts to better integrate mental health and substance abuse services were explicitly planned in 66% of the programs across all age groups, in 65% of programs targeted to adults (26 of 40 programs), and in 61% of programs targeted to transition-aged youths (20 of 33 programs).

In addition to the evidence-based assertive community treatment model that formed the basis for FSP, DMH encouraged counties to use more evidence-based and emerging best practices. This was a challenge for counties, because DMH did not provide criteria for levels of evidence or fidelity scales, and disagreement remains about defining evidence-based mental health practices (30). The counties responded by identifying 24 models that can be considered evidence-based or emerging best practices (Table 2) (27). The most common practices included integrated systems of care for co-occurring disorders and mobile service teams providing outreach, crisis response, assessment, and short-term treatment. There was a particular focus on expanding evidence-based interventions for children, including multidimensional family therapy and therapeutic foster care.

Planned housing services included residential treatment, supportive housing, permanent and transitional housing subsidies and support, master leases, and emergency housing. Employment services focused on vocational training and support, skills development, and job readiness training. The range of supportive services varied, and the most frequent was assistance with benefits and entitlements, provided by 17% of FSP programs (15 of 86 programs). Several FSP programs (six of 86 programs, or 7%) planned to complement their service arrays with a "recovery curriculum" developed and run by community-based organizations.

Strategies for system transformation

To analyze the strategies for transformation and changing the culture of the system to be more client and family centered, improve cultural competency, and increase community collaboration, we examined all 141 programs in the three program categories. The most common and innovative approaches are summarized below.

Client- and family-driven mental health system. DMH program requirements emphasize that the needs and preferences of consumers and family members must drive the policies, programs, and services in the system. To achieve this goal, a significant share of the new positions created in the programs was allocated to consumers and family members. Several programs also specified a role for consumers and family members on policy boards and cultural competency committees and provided opportunities for them to be part of program planning and management.

Peer support services are a key element of recovery-oriented programs and an important way to involve consumers and family members in service planning, outreach, and delivery. The range of peer support services planned is presented in Figure 1. Peer recovery support and peer recovery advocates (in 41% of programs) and peer-run and family-run support groups (22%) were the most common strategies. Including peer specialists on multidisciplinary teams is planned in 11% of programs. Wellness centers are being developed or expanded to create a supportive, peer-run environment for consumers in 9% of programs. Other approaches to bringing the voices of consumers

Table 1

Array of services planned within 86 full-service partnership programs under the Mental Health Services Act in 12 California counties

Service category	N	%
Therapeutic and rehabilitative services	81	94
Housing	73	85
Employment and education	66	77
Case management or coordination	65	76
Peer support	62	72
Co-occurring disorders or substance abuse	57	66
Outreach or community education	55	64
Other supports	52	60

Table 2

Number of programs (N=141) in 12 California counties planning on providing services based on evidence-based or emerging best practices under the Mental Health Services Act[a]

Evidence-based or emerging best practice	Programs for			
	Children, youths, and family	Transition-aged youths	Adults	Older adults
Comprehensive, continuous, integrated system of care for co-occurring disorders	6	8	4	3
Mobile response, assessment, or service teams	2	3	2	8
12-step program for substance abuse	1	4	3	2
Cognitive-behavioral therapy	4	3	2	1
Integrated Dual Disorders Treatment or Illness Management and Recovery	1	1	3	1
Dialectical behavior therapy	3	1	1	1
Functional family therapy	4	2	—	—
Multidimensional treatment foster care	3	2	—	—
Aggression replacement training	3	1	—	—
Incredible-years model	4	—	—	—
Transition-to-independence model	—	4	—	—
Parent-child interaction therapy	2	—	—	—
Evidence-based parenting training	2	—	—	—
Law enforcement crisis intervention training	—	—	2	—
Improving Mood Promoting Access to Collaborative Treatment (IMPACT) model	—	—	—	1
Supported employment	—	—	1	—
Geriatric field screening	—	—	—	1
Multidimensional treatment family therapy	1	1	—	—
Medication management approach to psychiatry	—	1	—	—
Brief strategic family therapy	1	—	—	—
Infant mental health	1	—	—	—
Multisystemic therapy	1	—	—	—
Massachusetts Youth Screening Instrument (MAYSI-2)	1	—	—	—
Family preservation crisis intervention	1	—	—	—
Total	41	31	18	18

[a] The programs are not mutually exclusive; some programs cover more than one age group.

and family members to the community included a "speaker's bureau" (N=1, or 1%) and a radio show (N=1, or 1%) that will include consumers and family members as featured guests.

Cultural competency. Throughout the MHSA legislation and DMH guidelines, there has been an emphasis on improving the cultural competency of county mental health services to reduce the current racial and ethnic disparities in access to services (20,31). Increasing the number of bilingual and bicultural staff, consumers, and family members to deliver services is planned in 57% of programs (Figure 2).

The ability to recruit, hire, and retain bilingual and bicultural staff has been a challenge for many of California's counties. Several programs included strategies for increasing their capacity to integrate bilingual and bi-

cultural service providers, such as collaborating or contracting with ethnic-specific community-based organizations, co-locating services in ethnically based health clinics, or engaging consumers, family members, or community workers from different ethnic communities to provide outreach or supportive services. Other strategies included training for staff and collaborating organizations, developing culturally and linguistically appropriate policies and procedures, and using interventions that have demonstrated efficacy in the populations and communities being served.

Community collaboration. All counties expressed the need to better collaborate with other government agencies, community-based organizations, primary care providers, and other stakeholders to provide mental health services that are holistic and integrat-

ed with other services that consumers may be receiving. Specific strategies for working more closely with community stakeholders are shown in Figure 3.

The most common strategies included contracting or collaborating with community-based organizations to operate the program, extending the hours of operation, or providing supportive services (28% of programs), as well as collaborating with educational institutions and businesses to create vocational and employment opportunities (17% of programs). Several programs identified contracting with community-based organizations as a way to achieve other goals, such as reaching underserved ethnic communities, increasing the number of bilingual and bicultural service providers, or hiring consumers and family members when

Figure 1

Strategies for increasing peer support services under the Mental Health Services Act among 141 programs in 12 California counties

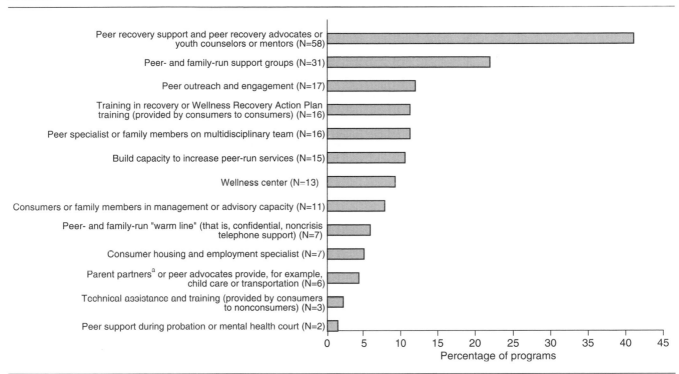

a Defined as primary caregivers of children or youths who are or have in the past received public mental health services

Figure 2

Strategies to improve the cultural competency of mental health services under the Mental Health Services Act among 141 programs in 12 California counties

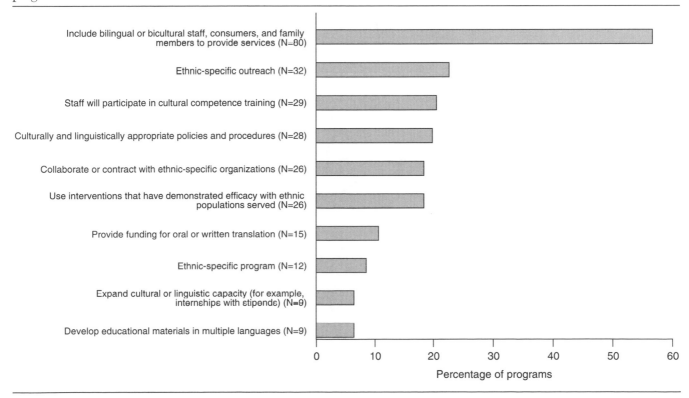

Figure 3

Strategies to improve community collaboration under the Mental Health Services Act among 141 programs in 12 California counties

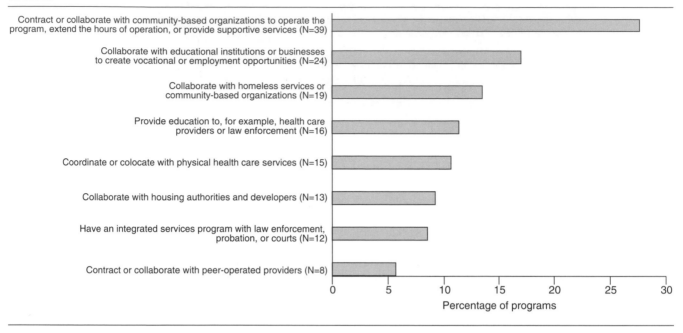

county policies and procedures pose excessive barriers. Several programs, particularly for older adults, planned to educate and collaborate with primary health care providers, and others planned to colocate services in primary health care clinics.

All counties identified improved collaboration with law enforcement and the criminal justice system as a priority, and 30% of all programs are specifically targeted to offenders with mental illness. Strategies included placing clinicians in courts, probation offices, and juvenile halls, as well as including probation officers on the multidisciplinary FSP teams. Several programs planned to strengthen relationships and understanding within the criminal justice system about mental illness through education programs for law enforcement professionals, including evidence-based crisis intervention training.

Discussion

This study used qualitative content analysis to describe the plans of 12 diverse California counties for transforming the state's mental health system. Identifying categories of services and strategies to describe such a large transformation initiative was a chal-

lenge. The AACP guidelines for recovery-oriented services were a useful framework, but they failed to capture the subtlety of different strategies the counties are using to reach out to unserved and underserved mental health consumers and to serve them in a different way. An important outcome of MHSA implementation may be a deeper understanding of not only the types of services needed to promote recovery and resilience but also attributes of the services and how they are delivered, which would facilitate future attempts to characterize and describe such a transformation.

Within the constraints of the analytical framework, this study showed that California's approach to implementing MHSA, blending broad principles with specific local strategies, is clearly reflected in the county plans. The analysis demonstrated that there is considerable consistency across counties in planning FSP programs that provide a full range of services to do "whatever it takes" to partner with consumers and support their individual recovery goals.

The strategies and approaches for transforming the culture of their systems into more consumer- and family-driven, culturally competent sys-

tems with strong community collaboration are as varied and diverse as the counties themselves. New approaches to involving consumers and family members in service planning and delivery are evident throughout the plans. Creative partnerships have been proposed with other government agencies and institutions, such as law enforcement and the criminal justice system, physical health care providers, educational institutions, and the private sector. The diversity in strategies also may reflect different starting points of system development and a lack of evidence about "what it takes" to achieve recovery and resilience.

Several weaknesses in the plans also were identified, and some of these are indicative of gaps in the state-level guidelines. For example, an important weakness is the lack of guidance on evidence-based practices. The result is that other than the FSP model based on assertive community treatment, evidence-based practices are infrequently specified in the plans. The plans are also relatively limited regarding concrete strategies for improving cultural competency and strengthening community collaboration.

Conclusions

Driven by a new funding initiative, California has approached a major transformation of its mental health system by creating a synergy between a state-level framework of overarching principles and goals and community-based stakeholder planning for local implementation. This process itself may be transformational, generating county plans that reflect a consensus on local concerns and values that should drive the state mental health system while responding to the tremendous diversity in needs, priorities, and cultural values among California's mental health consumers, family members, and communities.

This analysis focused on the planning process, so it is not possible to draw conclusions about the quality or fidelity of the programs, their effectiveness, or whether they will spark the intended mental health system transformation. The challenge will be to ensure that implementation achieves the stated goals of the legislation to promote recovery and reduce the negative consequences of untreated mental illness, including suicide, incarcerations, school failure or dropout, unemployment, prolonged suffering, homelessness, and removal of children from their homes. The legislation calls for the establishment of the Mental Health Services Oversight and Accountability Commission to guide and monitor MHSA implementation. A basic statewide data system is now in place to track the progress of individual FSPs toward reducing adverse events among enrolled individuals. Evaluating the implementation of the county plans and holding counties accountable for outcomes will be a future step. However, the state and counties need time to gain experience and set realistic expectations for this monumental effort at transformation.

There are many obstacles to the successful implementation of these ambitious county plans. Maintaining the participatory approach and open dialogue of the planning process through program implementation could prove to be a challenge. Program success also will depend on the counties' ability to recruit, hire, train, and retain qualified staff, consumers, and family members who reflect the cultural and linguistic diversity of the consumers and are committed to integrating recovery principles into all aspects of program implementation. Although the counties are clear in their intention to improve the cultural competency of their systems and strengthen community collaboration, the concrete steps required are not fully developed in the plans. Counties may have been waiting for the workforce education and training portion of MHSA funds to become available to strengthen cultural competency, which raises the issue of the appropriate sequencing of implementation of the legislation.

In addition, the relative lack of clear policy and guidance on evidence-based practices leaves much uncertainty about the potential effectiveness of the strategies adopted by the counties. These weaknesses may have been overcome if the state had been more structured and directive in its policy, but the approach that was taken needs to be considered in light of California's diversity and history. There is a long-standing tradition in California of decentralization in the mental health system, and the state works to find the most constructive balance between defining system-level principles and facilitating locally driven policies and practices.

Despite these challenges, the vision of the legislation and the DMH, together with the comprehensive, broad-based county planning processes, gives the counties clear roadmaps to proceed with implementation and make adjustments in programs and strategies to achieve the goal of promoting recovery and resiliency for the state's residents served by the county mental health systems.

Acknowledgments and disclosures

This research was funded by the California HealthCare Foundation (award number 04-1618). The authors thank Stephen Mayberg, Ph.D., for his review and comments on the article. The authors also thank Sukari Ivester, Ph.D., Timothy Brown, Ph.D., Jennifer Rice, M.P.H., and Tracy Finlayson, Ph.D., for their contribution to the qualitative analysis and comments on earlier drafts and Candy Pareja, B.A., Bonnie Li, B.A., Jennifer Rice, M.P.H., Sukari Ivester, Ph.D., and Tracy Finlayson, Ph.D., for contributing to the coding of the content of the county plans.

The authors report no competing interests.

References

1. Achieving the Promise: Transforming Mental Health Care in America. Pub no SMA-03-3832. Rockville, Md, Department of Health and Human Services, President's New Freedom Commission on Mental Health, 2003

2. Improving the Quality of Health Care for Mental and Substance-Use Conditions. Washington, DC, Committee on Crossing the Quality Chasm: Adaptation to Mental Health and Addictive Disorders, Institute of Medicine, 2006

3. Mental Health Services Act. Sacramento, State of California, 2004. Available at www.dmh.cahwnet.gov/prop63/mhsa/docs/mentalhealth servicesactfulltext.pdf

4. Initial Statement of Reasons: California Code of Regulations: Title 9: Rehabilitative and Developmental Services: Division 1: Department of Mental Health: Chapter 14: Mental Health Services Act. Sacramento, State of California, 2005 Available at www.dmh.cahwnet.gov/LawsandRegulations/docs/REGSDec29final.pdf

5. Mental Health Services Act Expenditure Report Fiscal Year 2005–2006: Addendum: A Report to the Legislature in Response to AB 131 Omnibus Health Budget Trailer Bill, Chapter 80, Statutes of 2005. Sacramento, State of California, Department of Mental Health, 2006. Available at www.healthvote.org/uploads/pdf/MHSAExpenditureReport.pdf

6. Mental Health Services Act Expenditure Report Fiscal Year 2006–2007: Addendum: A Report to the Legislature in Response to AB 131 Omnibus Health Budget Trailer Bill, Chapter 80, Statutes of 2005. Sacramento, State of California, Department of Mental Health, 2007. Available at www.dmh.cahwnet.gov/prop63/mhsa/docs/resourcelistings/final-mhsalegrptmay 20075-17-07.pdf

7. Counties Annual Report Fiscal Year 2004/05. Sacramento, State of California Controller, May 10, 2007. Available at www.sco.ca.gov/ard/local/locrep/counties/reports/0405counties. pdf

8. Alameda County: Mental Health Services Act: Community Services and Supports: Three-Year Program and Expenditure Plan. Oakland, Calif, Alameda County Behavioral Health Care Services, Jan 17, 2006

9. Fresno County: Mental Health Services Act: Community Services and Supports: Three-Year Program and Expenditure Plan. Fresno, Calif, Fresno County Department of Behavioral Health, Sept 25, 2005

10. Kern County: Mental Health Services Act: Community Services and Supports: Three-Year Program and Expenditure Plan, Kern County Department of Mental Health, 2006. Available at www.co.kern.ca.us/kcmh/mhsa/mhsacsssubmittedplan.asp

11. Los Angeles County: Mental Health Services Act: Community Services and Supports: Three-Year Program and Expenditure Plan. Los Angeles, Department of Mental Health, County of Los Angeles, Oct 2006. Available at dmh.lacounty.info/stp/cssplansummary.cfm

12. Mental Health Services Act (MHSA) Three-Year Program and Expenditure Plan: Community Services And Supports: Fiscal Years 2005–06, 2006–07, and 2007–08. Salinas, Calif, Monterey County Department of Health, Behavioral Health Division, Oct 2005. Available at www.co.monterey.ca.us/health/behavioralhealth/pdf/cssplanbudget.pdf

13. Placer County: Mental Health Services Act: Community Services and Supports: Three-Year Program and Expenditure Plan. Auburn, Calif, Placer County Health and Human Services Department, Nov 2, 2005

14. Riverside County: Mental Health Services Act: Community Services and Supports: Three-Year Program and Expenditure Plan. Riverside, Calif, Riverside Department of Mental Health, Dec 30, 2005. Available at mentalhealth.co.riverside.ca.us/opencms/english/mhsa/RevisedPlan11006pdf1.pdf

15. San Bernardino County: Mental Health Services Act: Three-Year Program and Expenditure Plan: Community Services and Supports: Fiscal Years 2005–06, 2006–07, 2007–08. San Bernardino, Calif, San Bernardino Department of Mental Health, Feb 7, 2006. Available at www.co.san-bernardino.ca.us/dbh/mhsa/prop63/sanbernardinocountymhsacssfinal.pdf

16. San Diego County: Mental Health Services Act: Community Services and Supports: Three-Year Program and Expenditure Plan. San Diego, Calif, San Diego County Health and Human Services Agency, Dec 31, 2005

17. San Francisco County: Mental Health Services Act: Community Services and Supports: Three-Year Program and Expenditure Plan. San Francisco, San Francisco Department of Mental Health, 2007. Available at www.sfdph.org/dph/comupg/oservices/mentalhlth/mhsa/commsvcsspts/default.asp

18. San Joaquin County: Mental Health Services Act: Community Services and Supports: Three-Year Program and Expenditure Plan. Available at www.sjmhsa.net/documents/plan section b/css plan 1.pdf

19. San Mateo County: Mental Health Services Act: Three-Year Program and Expenditure Plan: Community Services and Supports: Fiscal Years 2005–06, 2006–07, 2007–08. Stockton, Calif, San Joaquin County Behavioral Health Services, June 2006. Available at sanmateo.networkofcare.org/mh/home/smprop63/mhsacommunityservicesandsupportsplan2.pdf

20. Mental Health Services Act Home Page. State of California, Department of Mental Health. Available at www.dmh.ca.gov/prop63/mhsa/default.asp

21. Scheffler R, Smith R: The impact of government decentralization on health spending for uninsured in California. International Journal of Health Care Finance and Economics 6:237–258, 2006

22. Three-Year Program and Expenditure Plan Requirements: Fiscal Years 2005–06, 2006–07, 2007–08. Sacramento, State of California, Department of Mental Health, Aug 1, 2005. Available at www.dmh.ca.gov/dmhdocs/docs/letters05/05-05css.pdf

23. County Funding Request for Mental Health Services Act (MHSA) Community Program Planning. Letter No. 05-01. Sacramento, State of California, Department of Mental Health, Jan 18, 2005. Available at www.dmh.ca.gov/dmhdocs/docs/letters05/05-01.pdf

24. Fact Sheet: Mental Health Services Act (Prop 63). Sacramento, State of California, Department of Mental Health, Oct 2007. Available at www.cahpf.org/godocuserfiles/423 mhsa fact sheet october 2007.pdf

25. Assertive Community Treatment Association. Available at www.actassociation.org/actModel

26. Sowers W: Transforming systems of care: the American Association of Community Psychiatrists Guidelines for Recovery Oriented Services. Community Mental Health Journal 41:757–774, 2005

27. Farkas M, Gagne C, Anthony W, et al: Implementing recovery oriented evidence based programs: identifying critical dimensions. Community Mental Health Journal 41:141–158, 2005

28. Hsieh H, Shannon S: Three approaches to qualitative content analysis. Qualitative Health Research 15:1277–1288, 2005

29. Scheffler R, Adams N: Millionaires and mental health: Proposition 63 in California. Health Affairs (suppl Web Exclusives):W5-212–W5-224, Jan–June 2005

30. Tanenbaum S: Evidence-based practice as mental health policy: three controversies and a caveat. Health Affairs 24:163–173, 2005

31. Mental Health Services Act: System Transformation: Community Services and Supports: Considerations for Embedding Cultural Competency. Sacramento, State of California, Department of Mental Health, 2005. Available at www.sbcounty.gov/dbh/mhsa/15%20feb%2005%20-%20considerations%20for%20cultural%20competence.pdf

"We Never Used to Do Things This Way": Behavioral Health Care Reform in New Mexico

Cathleen E. Willging, Ph.D.
Leslie Tremaine, Ed.D.
Richard L. Hough, Ph.D.
Jill S. Reichman, Ph.D.
Steven Adelsheim, M.D.
Karen Meador, J.D.
Elizabeth A. Downes, Ph.D.

This column describes the first year of efforts in New Mexico to reform the behavioral health system. The process, guided by principles of cultural exchange theory, seeks to establish a "collaborative culture" among all stakeholders involved, including state agencies, consumers, families, advocates, and providers. Challenges have included inadequate system funding; insufficient development of skill sets among state personnel; underestimation of time and labor needed to address complex tasks; varying federal statutory and funder requirements for individual agencies; lack of a solid infrastructure for data collection, management, and dissemination; and clear definitions of the roles and relationships of local stakeholders to the state leadership group. (*Psychiatric Services* 58:1529–1531, 2007)

Dr. Willging, Dr. Hough, and Dr. Reichman are affiliated with the Pacific Institute for Research and Evaluation, 612 Encino Pl., N.E., Albuquerque, NM 87106 (e-mail: cwillging@bhrcs.org). Dr. Willging and Dr. Hough are also with the Department of Psychiatry, University of New Mexico, Albuquerque, where Dr. Adelsheim is affiliated. Dr. Tremaine is with the County of Santa Cruz (California) Health Services Agency. Ms. Meador and Dr. Downes are with the Behavioral Health Services Division, New Mexico Human Services Department, Santa Fe. Fred C. Osher, M.D., is editor of this column. Originally published in the December 2007 issue of Psychiatric Services.

In July 2005 New Mexico began a planned five-year process of restructuring its entire public behavioral health care system. The 17 state agencies and offices that finance mental health and substance abuse services were convened into a behavioral health purchasing collaborative ("the Collaborative") that contracted with a single managed care organization (ValueOptions) to administer these services (1,2).

The first year of the restructuring was conceptualized as a period of "do no harm" in which the daily provision of services within community settings was to remain undisrupted while the Collaborative focused on "nuts and bolts" issues, such as instituting new processes for enrollment, billing, and governance within the public sector. In particular, initial reform efforts centered on the development of mechanisms for interdepartmental oversight and collaboration and for involvement of consumers and providers in the restructured system. During this first year, the Collaborative also obtained a section 1915(b) waiver from the federal government to facilitate the carve-out of behavioral health services on a statewide basis. In addition, a Mental Health Transformation State Incentive Grant was obtained from the Substance Abuse and Mental Health Services Administration to aid in the overall transformation process.

Set in motion through legislative action, the Collaborative aspires to advance partnerships at the highest levels of state government and with community stakeholders in order to achieve the long-term goals of streamlining service delivery, reducing administrative expenses, boosting the quality of oversight capacity, and decreasing duplicative and costly paperwork demands for providers within the state's fragmented and beleaguered behavioral health system.

We have come together as state officials, providers, and researchers to consider the groundwork put in place thus far to promote and sustain a systemwide ethos of collaboration, an accepted precondition for successful behavioral health reform in New Mexico. In this column we highlight issues that policy makers in other settings might consider as they undertake similar reforms. We offer a reflective account of the cultural exchange process underlying the reform, identifying the challenges that have affected collaboration among multiple stakeholder groups.

Cultural exchange and integration across state agencies

We have found that cultural exchange theory enhances our understanding of critical issues affecting this initiative. The theory emphasizes processes of communication, compromise, and negotiation of attitudes, knowledge, and practices among stakeholders from diverse "cultural" environments (in this case, state agencies and local communities) (3–5). Stakeholders' motivations and behaviors are shaped by the experiences, values, and assumptions of colleagues and peers immersed in these environments. Stakeholders must step outside of their traditional settings, explore and adopt new ways of interacting and cooperating with others, and collectively produce a "collaborative culture" to effect comprehensive system change.

The theory proposes the following processes for successful exchanges between stakeholder groups and the formation of a collaborative culture capable of supporting transformation of a large service system:

♦ Establish precedents for effective collaboration at the top

♦ Identify change agents who can communicate to different stakeholder groups by virtue of their experience or role within those groups

♦ Create a common language across stakeholder groups

♦ Provide forums in which these groups can convene, articulate their values and visions, share ideas, and identify areas of compromise and agreement.

State leadership considers interagency collaboration to be vital to the development of an effective and efficient administrative infrastructure for public service delivery. From the cultural exchange perspective, the achievement of reform goals will necessitate the emergence of a collaborative culture among all agencies involved in transition processes. Indeed, anticipating resistance to change, the leadership has fostered conditions for communication, compromise, and consensus building within state government. They organized relevant state agencies into the Collaborative to coordinate policy, service financing, and legislative priorities, while allowing each to maintain its mission and build on its strengths. Collaborative members have included cabinet secretaries and agency directors.

The state's largest purchasers of behavioral health care—the Human Services Department, the Department of Health, and the Children, Youth and Families Department— might easily have dominated collaborative efforts. However, agencies specializing in labor, vocational rehabilitation, education, housing, corrections, and special populations were enlisted as full partners with equal voting privileges in the Collaborative, regardless of how much funding they could commit to behavioral health care. The Collaborative's monthly meetings became a forum for cultural exchange between previously disparate delivery systems and provided the precedent for and modeling of partnerships to other stakeholders. Collaborative members also reached consensus on overarching values and how reform efforts could target specific outcomes, such as lower suicide rates, increased services for special populations, and workforce development.

Another cultural exchange principle—identification of change agents —was addressed through the establishment of cross-agency teams. These teams, which typically comprised agency deputies, met more frequently than the Collaborative to hammer out reform implementation details. Their membership, roles, and responsibilities were defined in such a way as to steer clear of instituting new bureaucratic lines of authority and to instead accommodate candid communication about implementation issues, maximize potential for collaboration, and improve overall system responsiveness and performance. Prominent linkages were in data management and information systems, planning, performance measurement, evaluation, workforce development, licensing and certification, financing, contracting, and purchasing. Care was taken to identify relationships and functions of state personnel working on reform-related projects, opportunities for blending extant knowledge and skills across agencies, and areas in which staff training and greater cultural exchange were warranted. These efforts supported the emer-

gence of a collaborative culture within state government.

Challenges to integration

The process of arriving at productive cultural exchanges between state agencies and consensus about common values and goals is far from a straightforward undertaking. We contend that it requires open appraisals of the "real world" considerations shaping the work of state personnel involved in system change.

Several challenges to interagency integration within New Mexico—and, we suspect, within other large state systems of care—have been encountered. Inadequate funding for the behavioral health system has hindered hiring of additional state personnel to aid reform initiatives. Insufficient development of skill sets among state personnel to work in new areas, such as cross-system planning, financing, evaluation and performance measurement, has also been problematic. Although changing work demands create opportunities for employee growth and advancement, they are also stressful in the absence of systematic skill development. Another challenge has been underestimation of time and labor needed to allow cross-agency teams to struggle with complex tasks, such as defining and implementing common service definitions and standards and monitoring the ValueOptions contract. Attempts to explicate key contributions of member agencies have led to occasional turf battles within teams.

In addition, federal statutory and funder requirements and the politically defined accountability under which individual state agencies must continue to operate complicate attempts to create a consolidated system for oversight and responsibility within state government. Reflections of this tension are reports that cross-agency teams feel limited in decision making in areas where cabinet secretaries retain final authority.

Lack of a solid infrastructure for data collection, management, and dissemination has impeded interagency collaboration efforts. A stronger infrastructure is needed to share evaluation reports, information, and updates with stakeholder groups in "real time." Also, some state agencies with priorities outside the scope of behavioral health care will most likely require incentives to allocate funds and personnel to advance reform initiatives over time. Finally, despite the Collaborative's relative success in speaking as one, how its messages are circulated and interpreted among agency leadership and personnel has varied, sometimes causing confusion in agencies and in their communications with the public.

The Collaborative is attempting to address such challenges while tempering expectations and accepting that the reform process is not a "quick fix" to endemic problems of fragmentation.

Cultural exchange with community stakeholders

The engagement of community stakeholders as partners in system transformation efforts is a significant, albeit particularly demanding, component of effective cultural exchange in the public sector. From the outset, state officials sought to establish mechanisms for cultural exchange between themselves and community stakeholders. First, they embedded the Behavioral Health Planning Council—a governor-appointed statewide advisory committee of consumers, families, advocates, and providers—into the enabling legislation for the Collaborative. Second, they created a statewide network of local collaboratives (LCs) to function as "the voice of the people" within specific geographic areas. Because the council's linkages to this burgeoning LC network were not clear, each LC now nominates individuals to serve on the council.

Although a great deal of energy and enthusiasm was devoted to the development of the LC network, the facilitation of meaningful cultural exchange between LCs and the Collaborative was not easy. New Mexico could not build on established stakeholder systems and lacked other viable mechanisms to systematically solicit and act upon input from various communities within the state (6). This deficient infrastructure made the identification of appropriate local representation in the LCs prob-

lematic. Protracted and tense negotiations ensued over the definition of "consumer" and the appropriate balance of consumer-family and provider-agency members in each LC. Many community members also remained unaware or skeptical of the LC initiative.

The Collaborative also wrestled with what types of decisions should be made at the state level versus the community level, how to distinguish which specific stakeholder groups possess power to influence and act upon such decisions, and how to adjust to their new role of supporting community voices across formerly distinct behavioral health and human service systems.

It was difficult to establish the forums that cultural exchange theory suggests are essential for community stakeholder groups to articulate values and priorities, identify areas for compromise, and forge collaborative cultures. Major problems such as distances that rural stakeholders must travel, time and financial resources required to attend meetings, and differential social capital of community and state agency representatives stymied the communication of local perspectives in meetings. Some community stakeholders—especially those removed from urban areas where most reform-related events were held—remained pessimistic that their voices mattered and confused about the roles of the Collaborative and the cross-agency teams. In their eyes, ValueOptions was the most recognizable face of the reform, and some harbored suspicions that a for-profit partner such as ValueOptions would actually prioritize the improvement of behavioral health service delivery.

Conclusions

Research on innovation diffusion has shown that "adoption of new ideas or technology is often hampered when the stakeholders . . . share similar values but organize them differently" (3). Conflicting notions about stakeholders' roles and relationships pose barriers to system-level change. Such barriers were present in New Mexico before the recent reform. However,

state officials have recognized the need to introduce a collaborative culture to effect systemwide transformation.

Ongoing efforts to agree on definitions of stakeholder roles and to treat stakeholders as equal partners are intrinsic to this effort. Although power differentials remain—that is, between higher- and lower-ranking state personnel, between agencies with large and small behavioral health budgets, and between these agencies and the Collaborative, the Council, and the LCs—this endeavor to change state bureaucracy from within through the institutionalization of a partnership approach portends favorably for the transformation process. Lessons learned in the first year of New Mexico's attempt to nurture collaborative culture offer important insights for other states that wish to pursue cross-agency work and community engagement to enhance systems of care.

Acknowledgments and disclosures

This work was supported by grant R01-MH-076084 from the National Institute of Mental Health.

The authors report no competing interests.

References

1. Willging CE, Semansky R: Another chance to do it right: redesigning public behavioral health care in New Mexico. Psychiatric Services 55:974–976, 2004

2. Hyde PS: A unique approach to designing a comprehensive behavioral health system in New Mexico. Psychiatric Services 55:983–985, 2004

3. Brekke JS, Ell K, Palinkas LA: Translational science at the National Institute of Mental Health: can social work take its rightful place? Research on Social Work Practice 17:1–11, 2007

4. Bailey FG: Debate and Compromise: The Politics of Innovation. Totowa, NJ, Rowan and Littlefield, 1973

5. Palinkas LA, Allred CA, Landsverk JA: Models of research-operational collaboration for behavioral health in space. Aviation, Space, and Environmental Medicine 76: B52–B60, 2005

6. Willging CE, Semansky R, Waitzkin H: New Mexico's Medicaid managed care waiver: organizing input from mental health consumers and advocates. Psychiatric Services 54:289–291, 2003

Mental Health Transformation: Moving Toward a Public Health, Early-Intervention Approach in Texas

Vijay Ganju, Ph.D.

This column describes a mental health system transformation initiative in Texas that aims to fully integrate mental health as a component of public health and early-intervention efforts. The process has included a formal needs assessment initiative and a broad-based interagency Transformation Workgroup made up of executive-level agency staff, consumers and family members, and representatives of the legislature and governor's office. Community collaboratives have been formed to instigate transformation at the local level. Major objectives include development of consumer and family networks, workforce development and training, and an improved data and technology infrastructure. (*Psychiatric Services* 59:17–20, 2008)

I n various ways the President's New Freedom Commission on Mental Health described the mental health system in the United States as fragmented, inadequate, and inefficient (1). The national picture is reflected in the Texas mental health system.

Paradoxically, this situation has developed nationally—and in Texas—as a result of the successful development of a community-based mental health system. Over the past three decades, an increasing number of

Dr. Ganju is project director of the Texas Mental Health Transformation State Incentive Grant. Send correspondence to him at 909 W. 45th, Austin, TX 78751 (e-mail: vijay.ganju@dshs.state.tx.us). Fred C. Osher, M.D., is editor of this column. Originally published in the January 2008 issue of Psychiatric Services.

persons needing mental health care have received services in their home communities. As more people have remained in the community, a multitude of programs and services, including those related to housing, employment, criminal justice, child welfare, and education, have developed to meet the needs of adults and children with mental health disorders. The different eligibility criteria, standards of care, funding sources, reporting requirements, and regulations, along with a lack of coordination among the various federal, state, and local agencies involved, have resulted in the fragmented and disjointed nature of the mental health system. This column reports on efforts in Texas to overcome fragmentation and fully incorporate mental health as an integral component of public health and early-intervention efforts.

Transformation in Texas
The need for transformation
A project that matched data from multiple agencies in Texas determined that youths in the child welfare system who eventually became involved with the juvenile justice system had significantly more behavior problems, substance abuse issues, and family members with a criminal history (2). In addition, youths in the child welfare system with behavior problems had significantly higher levels of earlier school discipline problems than other youths in the child welfare system. Other data indicated that 46% of all emergency room visits in Texas involved behavioral health as a primary or contributing factor (3). In addition, 26% of all hospital admissions were found to be related to behavioral health issues.

These data begin to suggest the nature of the larger, fragmented, multiagency mental health system. Texas essentially has a "back end" mental health system, in which persons must be increasingly dysfunctional to gain access to and receive services, putting pressure on social services, education, and justice systems and highlighting the need for mental health services in these systems. When coupled with demographic projections for the state, these data suggest huge increases in future costs for the juvenile justice, child welfare, and criminal justice systems. The inability to identify at-risk youths and intervene early creates a potentially enormous burden on the Texas economy if current rates of institutionalization and incarceration continue (4).

This perspective is buttressed by formal needs assessment initiatives that involved consumers and family members, local stakeholders, and state agency personnel (5). Some of the key areas identified were early identification; intervention and easier access; resources for safe and affordable housing; increased "voice" for consumers and family members; improved interagency coordination; a lack of mental health professionals, especially in rural areas; a lack of adequate training supports; and a need for better data sharing and information exchange across agencies.

Approach to transformation
To address these needs Texas has embarked on an ambitious mental health transformation initiative to fully incorporate mental health as an integral component of public health and early-intervention efforts. Although

many aspects of transformation were under way before the publication of the President's New Freedom Commission report, these activities now receive additional support through a Transformation State Incentive Grant from the Substance Abuse and Mental Health Services Administration (SAMHSA). Texas is one of nine states to receive such a grant.

The initiative has a vision for transformation: within a public health framework, all Texans will have quick and easy access to early intervention and mental health services and supports of high quality. To move forward with transformation, and in line with federal grant requirements, the governor has designated a broad-based interagency Transformation Workgroup. Members are executive-level staff of state agencies, four consumers and family members, and representatives of the Texas legislature and the governor's office. This workgroup essentially serves as the "board" for the transformation effort and is supported by an implementation team of staff and contractors. Several multiagency teams have been formed to address key priority areas: consumer and family member initiatives, workforce development, data and technology, housing, employment, criminal and juvenile justice, children and adolescents, and older adults.

The logic model for transformation in Texas essentially consists of building a sustainable infrastructure that results in a culture of partnership and "systemness" across agencies at both state and local levels and of developing adequate resources, both fiscal and human, to provide a wide array of high-quality services consistent with a recovery and resilience orientation. This public health and early-intervention framework represents a radical shift given that current eligibility criteria have a narrow focus on populations that are the most dysfunctional.

How will such transformation occur? Experts who have studied transformation across a range of industries and organizations have identified some general principles that constitute the knowledge base and the best thinking about transformation (6–8).

In general, three distinct but overlapping components are needed: building consensus about the need, urgency, and vision for transformation; promoting and learning from the implementation of innovative structures and practices; and sustaining and disseminating the innovations that are key components of the envisioned system. Commitment of leadership, buy-in of stakeholders, and communication are critical initial aspects; demonstrable, measurable successes that result from innovation are equally important; and plans to sustain such success systemwide are the last stage of transformation.

In a state as diverse as Texas, transformation presents a formidable challenge. But the broad approach is to build on current strengths and initiatives, address pivotal needs and priorities, implement innovations through demonstration projects or community projects that will serve as learning experiences, and document "successes" and "wins" in terms of measurable outcomes and benefits. A basic assumption of this approach is that transformation has to occur at both state and local levels. Activities at the state level will not result in improved access or outcomes for consumers unless transformation also occurs at the local level. Focusing on certain key activities is necessary, and the role of consumers and family members is paramount in defining, advancing, and sustaining transformation.

Context for transformation

Fortunately, Texas has several strengths on which to build its transformation initiative. Through a historical capacity to develop partnerships with universities, the state has supported a research agenda incorporating results and lessons learned into practice. The Texas Medications Algorithm Project (9,10), which has been the basis of initiatives in other states as well, is an example of such a partnership.

More recently, the state has restructured health and human services agencies so that public health, mental health, and substance abuse are part of the same agency. This organiza-

tional merger has also fostered interagency initiatives that involve criminal justice, juvenile justice, rehabilitation services, and early intervention. Various sites within the state that are implementing systems-of-care initiatives funded by SAMHSA's Center for Mental Health Services also provide models for interagency initiatives at the community level. In addition, as a result of a legislative mandate, the specialty mental health system has implemented a Resiliency and Disease Management System, which promotes evidence-based practices for both adults and youths on a statewide basis.

Texas has also developed a Web-based electronic health record system—the Behavioral Health Integrated Provider System (BHIPS)—which recently won the prestigious Davies Award for innovative uses of information technology in health care. The system supports both clinical treatment and billing for the state's addiction providers and is a model that is being disseminated nationally (11). This system is being expanded and piloted to include mental health services.

Transformation initiatives

Building on these strengths, the state has identified key initiatives to establish a multipronged approach to transformation. These include community collaboratives to instigate transformation at the local community level, development of consumer and family member networks, workforce development, use of data and technology, policy and legislative change, and special interagency programmatic initiatives proposed by the Transformation Workgroup related to peer support, housing, employment, school-based services, and older adults.

Community collaboratives for transformation

Eight communities have been selected through a competitive process to move forward with transformation at the local level. Major objectives of these community collaboratives are to address mental health transformation priorities at the local level and to develop models and tools for community collaborative development in other parts of the state.

Requests for application were sent to county judges, with the expectation that existing or newly created broad-based community coalitions consisting of consumers and family members, elected officials, providers, and leaders from businesses and philanthropic organizations would respond through county commissioners' courts. Communities with history and experience in such partnerships were given preference.

Selected communities will receive technical assistance and support to advance their transformation initiatives. Each community will receive resources for information technology innovations; however, for the most part, the transformation initiatives will be supported through community resources. The eight communities that were selected represent the broad diversity of the state and include urban–metropolitan areas, rural areas (including a rural "frontier" area) and the Texas Mexico border area. These different areas were defined as part of the application process so that each could be represented in the transformation initiative.

The eight communities will work together as part of a transformation learning collaborative. Also, the other 12 communities that applied will be part of a larger group of communities that will participate together in the transformation effort. As part of the plan to go to scale on a statewide basis, these eight communities represent the first wave of transformation at the local level. This experience will then be the basis for broader diffusion and dissemination.

Consumer and family member "voice"

Consumer and family member leaders in the state-level Transformation Workgroup have identified several priority areas: communication and consensus building across consumer and family member organizations, promotion of a recovery and resilience orientation, development of peer support services, and develop-

ment of consumer and family member networks. In initial meetings, consumers and family members of all the state agencies on the Transformation Workgroup (including 12 state agencies and the Department of Veterans Affairs) have been represented. A major objective is the development of consumer networks in areas served by the community collaboratives.

Workforce development and training

Transformation depends on the ability of the system to expand the capacity to provide more and higher-quality services. In an early-intervention framework, this includes the capacities of other systems beyond the traditional specialty mental health system—for example, the school system and the criminal and juvenile justice systems.

Two major initiatives in Texas are occurring in this area. First, through an amalgam of funding sources, health specialists are being placed in all 20 of the state's regional education service centers. The specialists, in turn, provide training and technical assistance to school districts in the geographic area for which they are responsible. Each health specialist will receive specific mental health training and additional support as the specialist works with school health personnel and teachers in the school districts. As part of this activity, a mental health component is being integrated into the mandatory health curricula.

Second, in collaboration with the Hogg Foundation for Mental Health, a Texas Mental Health Training Institute is being established to provide a centralized locus for training initiatives and workforce development initiatives. The major focus of this collaboration is to develop a sustainable training infrastructure in the state that will build needed competencies in the existing and emergent workforce.

Dialogue is also occurring with university and community college personnel related to preservice training, but the potential of having an impact on college curricula or licensing standards is seen as a long-term strategy.

Data and technology

Data and technology infrastructure are key areas that support transformation through three mechanisms: enhancing connectivity and coordination of mental health care across both state and local agencies in real time; supporting infrastructure development, such as training initiatives and the creation of consumer networks; and providing data to document transformation successes and outcomes in a quality improvement framework.

At both the state and local levels, systems to increase connectivity and integration are under development. At the same time, the expansion of the state's BHIPS system is being piloted to include mental health components. In certain communities, instant messaging systems have been used to coordinate services across mental health and jail systems. Such innovative initiatives are also being explored through the community collaboratives component.

Policy and legislation

A major strategy of the transformation effort is to develop products and deliverables in appropriate time frames to inform policy related to mental health transformation in legislative sessions.

At the request of the Texas Senate Committee on Health and Human Services, the Transformation Workgroup developed and submitted recommendations for the future mental health system in Texas. These recommendations became the basis of an omnibus mental health transformation bill that was considered during the most recent Texas legislative session but did not pass, primarily because of competing priorities rather than any objections at a policy level. However, several bills related to transformation on data sharing did pass. Building on this experience, the core transformation components (an orientation to recovery and resilience, early detection, data sharing, and standardized metrics and outcomes) will be the basis of proposals developed for the next legislative session.

Special services initiatives

On the basis of various needs assessment activities, priorities have been identified for housing, employment, children and adolescents, older adults, and the criminal justice and juvenile justice systems. Implementation initiatives developed by interagency workgroups are under way for each of these priority areas.

Challenges

Mental health transformation presents a tremendous opportunity for a quantum jump to address the issues of organizational schisms and the lack of adequate infrastructure and resources that have plagued the specialty public mental health system. At the same time, there is a certain degree of hubris to think that mental health issues will be the driver of major reform in the functioning of multiple agencies across federal, state, and local government.

A major challenge is to integrate new initiatives with their own logic and imperatives under a transformation rubric. For example, as a result of efforts by a broad-based coalition of policy makers, providers, consumers, and advocates, the Texas legislature recently appropriated $82 million for mental health crisis redesign. Similarly, over $500 million related to behavioral health services was appropriated to other state agencies. Planning efforts are focusing on how to relate

transformation principles and objectives to these initiatives. Inherent in such initiatives is the recognition that a federal grant that constitutes .1% of the public health agency's annual budget is not going to result in transformation. The grant can leverage change, but it is incumbent on the system to direct new and existing resources in transformative ways.

Although integration of mental health with public health and a multiagency approach has obvious benefits, the explicit broadening of such a perspective requires buy-in and commitment of organizations and groups with diverse missions where the link to mental health is often seen as tenuous. A major aspect of transformation is to shape and define the belief that benefits are perceived as "wins," at least in some measure, by all involved.

Acknowledgments and disclosures

The author reports no competing interests.

References

1. Achieving the Promise: Transforming Mental Health Care in America. Pub no SMA-03-3832. Rockville, Md, Department of Health and Human Services, President's New Freedom Commission on Mental Health, 2003

2. Texas Department of State Health Services: Behavioral health issues and juvenile justice involvement: a vicious cycle? Behavioral

Health News Brief, vol 2, no 1, Dec 2006, pp 2–3. Available at www.dshs.state.tx.us/sa/bhnewsbriefvolume2issue1120306.pdf

3. Wells K: Texas Hospital Discharges in 2005 With a Mental Health or Substance Abuse Diagnosis. Austin, Texas Department of State Health Services, June 2007

4. Mental Health Transformation Comprehensive Plan. Austin, Texas Department of State Health Services, Sept 2006

5. Voices Transforming Texas: Texas Assessment of Mental Health Needs and Resources. Austin, Texas Department of State Health Services. Sept 2006

6. Kotter J: Leading Change: Why transformation efforts fail. Harvard Business Review, March–Apr, 1995, pp 59–67

7. Mazade N: Concepts of "Transformation." Alexandria, Va, National Association of State Mental Health Program Directors Research Institute, Jan 2005

8. Cebrowski A: Transcript of Admiral Cebrowski's presentation at the National Association of State Mental Health Program Director's Research Institute workshop on change management. Alexandria, Va, NASMHPD Research Institute, Oct 2004

9. Rush AJ, Rago WV, Crismon ML, et al: Medication treatment for the severely and persistently mentally ill: the Texas Medication Algorithm Project. Journal of Clinical Psychiatry 60:284–291, 1999

10. Miller AL, Crismon ML, Rush AJ, et al: The Texas Medication Algorithm Project (TMAP): clinical results for patients with schizophrenia. Schizophrenia Bulletin 30: 627–647, 2004

11. Enos G: Technology that informs treatment. Behavioral Healthcare 27(2):36–38, 2007

Developing Statewide Consumer Networks

LaVerne D. Miller
Latrease R. Moore, M.A.

Statewide consumer networks (SCNs) that provide direct services, advocacy, and technical assistance to smaller consumer-operated services have emerged over the past 15 years. As states seek to include the "consumer voice" in systems transformation and to support consumer-operated services, the expertise, community-organizing, and advocacy skills offered by networks are assets to all stakeholders. This column examines models currently in use by SCNs in six states. It compares their developmental histories and organizational, leadership, and decision-making models to provide guidance to other states that wish to develop strategies for organizing, supporting, and sustaining SCNs. (*Psychiatric Services* 60:291–293, 2009)

The President's New Freedom Commission report challenged states to create recovery-oriented systems and made recommendations for ensuring that mental health care is consumer and family driven. One mechanism proposed was for consumers to play an active role in state and federal mental health policy reform. The commission concluded that when consumers are actively involved in developing the policies that shape mental health services, they are more likely to continue in recovery; to take a dynamic role in managing their services, treatment, and support; and to build meaningful and healing relationships with service providers.

Although there is limited empirical

Ms. Miller and Ms. Moore are affiliated with Policy Research Associates, Inc., 345 Delaware Ave., Delmar, NY 12054 (e-mail: lmiller@prainc.com). Henry J. Steadman, Ph.D., served as editor for this column. Originally published in the March 2009 issue of Psychiatric Services.

evidence to guide states in enhancing their transformation goals via consumer involvement, examples of successful models of incorporating consumer and family activities into state initiatives exist. One mechanism many states are developing is statewide consumer networks (SCNs).

Why statewide consumer networks?

An SCN is a group of affiliated consumers and family members, advocacy groups, and organizations that support states in the development of policies and quality assurance activities related to mental health services. These networks also have a substantial influence in strengthening organizational relationships and developing leadership and business management skills among consumers. SCNs have an impact on laws governing mental health practice by providing a consumer voice, which is a fundamental step in ensuring that mental health care is consumer and family driven. Networks also provide consumers with leading roles in transforming service provision, developing and implementing training and research, and putting policies into practice. Incorporating consumers into these roles has a direct effect, not only improving service provision but also reducing the reluctance of people with mental illnesses to seek help.

The Substance Abuse and Mental Health Services Administration has provided descriptions of some of the many activities of networks (mental health.samhsa.gov/cmhs/community support). They include teaching the public that mental health care is essential to overall health, promoting consumer- and family-driven care through training, writing position papers for mental health councils and state administrators, eliminating disparities in mental health systems through regional partnerships, developing media and

training materials, promoting recovery and resilience through self-help models, promoting use of technology to access information and mental health care by creating interactive Web sites for consumer information exchange, and implementing technological advances to disseminate information statewide and nationwide.

Several states have successfully supported the creation of SCNs, and their experiences provide valuable lessons on initiation and sustainability. In this column we compare the developmental histories and organizational, leadership, and decision-making models of statewide networks in six states—Alabama, Alaska, California, Maryland, Oregon, and Wisconsin. These states were selected because of their regional diversity as well as their willingness to share their experiences with consumers and state partners. Each network and its leadership continue to provide ongoing technical assistance and support to emergent networks in other states.

In spring 2008 executive directors in each state were sent surveys via e-mail to gather information on the developmental process and organizational structure of the network. Responses were received and follow-up calls were made to gather additional details on network sustainability. Responses indicated that networks encountered initial difficulties in organizing and sustaining themselves and that forming an SCN was accomplished through strong leadership and partnership. This column describes methods used by states that were cited by network executive directors as contributing to the successful continuation of their SCN.

State partnership

The conventional wisdom is that state involvement in the development of SCNs is minimal, unwelcome, and rare. However, for some of the networks surveyed, the state played an active role in identifying and articulating the need for a statewide network, funding the network's activities, and providing ongoing technical assistance to the network and its staff and leadership.

State agencies have been actively involved in initiating and facilitating the development of consumer networks. For example, in California the State Mental Health Agency supported the creation of an independent SCN. The network is 25 years old, and ten years ago state leadership was instrumental in the network's transition from a grassroots organization, which operated more or less like a collective, to an independent not-for-profit organization. Although incorporation as a not-for-profit entity allows the state to contract with the network and the network to contract or subcontract with other statewide organizations, such as the National Alliance on Mental Illness (NAMI), many advocates and activists believe that incorporation has changed the networks' culture and focus. This perspective has frequently led to the development of working boards on which consumers serve as gatekeepers of the values of the consumer movement and its history.

In Wisconsin the first step in the emergence of an SCN was taken when the State Mental Health Agency used NAMI as a fiscal pass-through to fund consumer-run organizations and projects. In response to fiscal concerns, the State Mental Health Agency reached out to consumer leaders with a proposal to start a network. Consumer leaders, in collaboration with the state, played an important role in helping consumer organizations reconstitute themselves into consumer-run and consumer-driven not-for-profit organizations in which 90% of all board members and 100% of staff are consumers.

Even in states where consumers have independently organized themselves into a network or coalition, state government actions have indirectly raised awareness of the need for a network. In Alaska executive-level staff of five local or regional organizations formed a consortium in response to a statewide request for proposals. The goal of the consortium was to mitigate or eliminate the competition among consumer organizations for scarce resources and create a network that would receive and distribute these funds to consumer organizations. This group has grown to include 18 organizations, with representation covering most of Alaska's regions.

In 1985 Maryland's network began as a steering committee of representatives from four local consumer groups that was created to take positions on policy issues affecting the statewide mental health system. At the time, there were only four consumer groups in four jurisdictions in Maryland. Other groups developed over the years, and in 1992 On Our Own received a Service System Improvement grant from the National Institute of Mental Health's Community Support Program to officially start a statewide consumer group. On Our Own of Maryland was incorporated in October 1992; it is one of the oldest and largest SCNs, with membership consumer organizations in every Maryland county.

Finally, Oregon's network represents what can occur when consumers who share concerns over issues such as seclusion and restraint and disaster preparedness evolve into an SCN without funding or institutional support. This network consists largely of consumers who have no formal affiliations to agencies or projects, although many are involved in other statewide initiatives.

Lessons learned

State involvement in the development and nurturing of an SCN is not in itself an indicator of future success or failure. Rather, the most reliable indicators of future success are the organizational, leadership, and decision-making models that are adopted and implemented through a consensus of consumer leaders and supporters. In this section we describe how these models were used by the states to make a lasting impact on the development and sustainability of SCNs.

Organizational models

Networks in the six states surveyed all developed organizational models that were designed to support the overall function of the network. Networks that serve as a fiscal pass-through for smaller organizations or discrete projects that receive direct funding from the state have developed more formal organizational models that promote fiscal and leadership accountability. Maryland, Wisconsin, and California fall into this category. Each network is a not-for-profit organization that directly contracts with the state and other organizations for the delivery of services. These deliverables are clearly defined in contracts; advocacy, peer-support services, and training are some of the direct services that they provide. However, virtually all of the networks' resources are spent providing technical assistance and support to the organizations that they fund.

In contrast, neither Oregon's network nor Alaska's consortium have direct oversight over other consumer organizations. Alaska's consortium is a "fellowship," denoting the personal commitment that members have to each other as well as the transparency of their business dealings. Networks in Maryland, California, and Wisconsin emphasize advocacy and represent the interests of their organizational membership.

It is clear that one size does not fit all and that the model that has emerged in each state has been shaped by the network's function. However, it is also important to note that although state governments had some impact on moving things forward, consumers and their supporters ultimately decided which model best met the needs of consumers, their organizations, and funding sources. Some tension continues to exist in moving from informal and more loosely affiliated individuals and organizations to more formal "business" entities. More than anything else, the personality and leadership style of network management have the greatest impact on balancing often-conflicting interests.

Leadership models

All the networks that are membership organizations have boards consisting of representatives from these organizations. California and Alabama have "at large" seats on their boards. California's at-large seats were added to promote diversity. Most boards are required through either bylaws or articles of incorporation to strive for regional representation on the board. Alabama's board consists of 13 members (currently all consumers), who represent 12 regions and one at-large member. Similarly, Maryland's board is primarily composed of representatives of the various consumer-run programs across Maryland.

In contrast, Alaska's model is innovative and probably endures because of the motivating factors that brought the group together. The consortium began operating as somewhat of a business monopoly, or oligarchy, that the state had to recognize. Once the consumer organizations began collaborating and stopped bidding against each other, the state was "forced" to work with the consortium. Alaska's network came together with concrete purposes. The network members decided to divide up the money and not compete with each other. Key leadership features were transparency, financial disclosure, and leaders' concerted efforts to "give away their power."

Decision-making models

Most executive directors who responded to the survey were clear about the roles and responsibilities of board members compared with those of staff. However, some observed that an inherent conflict exists when a board sees itself more as a working board as opposed to a governing body. In practice, all the boards have more involvement in day-to-day activities than one would find in more traditional not-for-profit organizations. Most organizations have reached an accommodation with their boards, which makes it possible to operate effectively as an organization. Alaska's consortium does not take official votes and rules by consensus. When consensus is not reached immediately, the issue is tabled and discussed at a later date. In the end, a network's official structure is not always indicative of how decisions are ultimately reached. It is apparent that the consensus-building model used in Alaska actually operates in an informal way within other

networks. Most successful organizations seem to maintain some balance between the two decision-making models discussed here.

Discussion

States have an array of organizational, leadership, and decision-making processes to choose from as they move forward. These decisions should be made during a process that is driven largely by consumers with the support of the state. It is not essential to have unanimity in the consumer community or among its leaders to begin the process of bringing a diverse cross-section of stakeholders together for what may be best characterized as the first step in the process of supporting the development of an SCN.

All the networks, with the exception of Oregon's, which emphasized recruitment and engagement of pioneers and other advocates, experienced tensions with advocates and activists during their creation. It is difficult to explain the roots of many of these tensions. However, the states recognized that engaging pioneers was important to the growth and stability of the network. Most have benefited from identifying and engaging "boundary spanners" (1) within the consumer community. These boundary spanners are frequently pioneers who have their feet in both grassroots and larger, more formal organizations.

Consumers should be part of the planning process for the initial planning meeting. Technology can be used to increase the involvement of organizations and individuals. It is also important for the state to have reasonable expectations for the initial stages of this process. Strong and visionary leadership by a core group of consumers and their partners is a stronger predictor of success and sustainability than how quickly the network comes together and a lack of dissent. The key is to set a strong foundation for growth, with the understanding that setting and achieving more modest objectives may lead to attaining loftier goals.

States that do not have consumer

networks should take advantage of technical assistance and support from states that do and decide what role the Office of Consumer Affairs can and should play. Most of the networks surveyed reported that state support and technical assistance were helpful in the formative stages of network development. Some states have used statewide or local not-for-profit technical assistance organizations. All agree that strategic planning and mentoring by older, more established networks were essential to the survival of the nascent networks.

Clarity and transparency in regard to emerging network interests and short- and long-term involvement of consumers in the planning process are needed to avoid the attribution of negative motives to the endeavor. Such an approach also sets the tone for future collaborations between the state and consumer organizations. The dependence of most networks on the state government for operational funds and the manner in which funds are distributed to member organizations frequently create tensions between the network and state agencies. The trend toward state support may compromise the appearance of the independence of networks. Therefore, it is strongly recommended that network founders diversify the funding base of the emergent network.

As states embark on the process of supporting development of a consumer network, the SCNs surveyed for this report provide guidance on how states should move forward and what steps can be formalized to enhance the likelihood of success in creating and sustaining SCNs.

Acknowledgments and disclosures

This research was supported by grant 283-07-3600 from SAMHSA's Center for Mental Health Services. The points of view expressed are those of the authors and do not necessarily represent the official position or policies of SAMHSA.

The authors report no competing interests.

Reference

1. Steadman H: Boundary spanners: a key for the effective interactions of the justice and mental health systems. Law and Human Behavior 16:75–87, 1992

Mending Missouri's Safety Net: Transforming Systems of Care by Integrating Primary and Behavioral Health Care

Dorn Schuffman, M.A.
Benjamin G. Druss, M.D., M.P.H.
Joseph J. Parks, M.D.

Missouri has begun a three-year pilot program across the state to integrate the primary care services provided by federally qualified health centers (FQHCs) and the behavioral health services provided by community mental health centers (CMHCs). This column describes the integration initiative, in which start-up funds were provided in 2008 to seven FQHC-CMHC partnerships (a total of $700,000 to each pair over 3.5 years). It reviews lessons learned during the first year of the project in bringing these two very different public systems of care together to mend the public health safety net. (*Psychiatric Services* 60:585–588, 2009)

Missouri's Department of Mental Health (DMH) has taken up the challenge of goal 1 of the President's New Freedom Commission (1), "Americans understand that men-

Mr. Schuffman is senior consultant, Missouri Behavioral Health/Primary Care Integration Initiative, and Dr. Parks is director of the Missouri Department of Mental Health, Jefferson City. Dr. Druss is Rosalynn Carter Chair in Mental Health, Rollins School of Public Health, Emory University, Atlanta. Send correspondence to Dr. Druss at the Department of Health Policy and Management, Rollins School of Public Health, Emory University, 1518 Clifton Rd. NE, Room 606, Atlanta GA 30322 (e-mail: bdruss@emory. edu). Fred C. Osher, M.D., is editor of this column. Originally published in the May 2009 issue of Psychiatric Services.

tal health is essential to overall health," by working across state agency lines to transform the public mental health system in Missouri. As a result of the department's work in 2005 with the Missouri Medicaid state agency, the legislative Missouri Medicaid Reform Commission acknowledged that Medicaid reform must take place in the context of the public mental health system transformation being led by DMH. This provided a unique opportunity for Missouri to develop a pilot program for integrating care between the state's federally qualified health centers (FQHCs), the most important group of public-sector primary care providers, and its community mental health centers (CMHCs), which serve as the entry point for the public mental health system in Missouri. Together, the primary care system of the FQHCs and the behavioral health system of the CMHCs form the foundation of Missouri's public health safety net.

However, one system often treated primary care needs as though mental health issues did not affect other physical health problems, and the other acted as though mental health problems could be adequately addressed without addressing issues related to general medical care. In other cases, these systems were duplicating services and fighting over scarce resources, instead of looking for ways to improve efficiency through collaboration. Consequently, DMH secured new state funding to promote collaboration between FQHCs and CMHCs and mend the safety net

through the integration of primary and behavioral health care at seven sites in Missouri involving FQHC-CMHC collaborations.

Integration has often meant introducing behavioral health professionals into a primary care team. However, the Missouri initiative was also designed to address the findings of a report by the National Association of State Mental Health Program Directors (2) that documented that individuals with serious mental illness are dying 25 years earlier than the general population "largely due to treatable medical conditions that are caused by modifiable risk factors such as smoking, obesity, substance abuse, and inadequate access to medical care." Therefore, the Missouri initiative, while requiring the more typical integration of behavioral health professionals into primary care settings, also requires bringing primary care directly into CMHC settings to ensure that individuals with serious mental illness have ready access to primary care that is integrated with their comprehensive behavioral health care. It is expected that this bidirectional approach will also help to build a robust collaboration between medical and mental health providers in support of sustainability.

Design of the Missouri initiative

In September 2007 DMH invited FQHCs and CMHCs to collaboratively submit proposals for funding of integration initiatives that addressed the following requirements: location of FQHC primary care clinics at CMHC treatment sites and integration of behavioral health professionals employed by the CMHCs into FQHC primary care teams; full documentation in the on-site client records of the care provided; appropriate adoption of evidence-based, best, and promising practices and care management technologies; and receptivity to consumer-driven services, person-centered planning, and consumer empowerment. DMH encouraged applicants to use the four-quadrant model developed by the National Council for Community Behavioral Healthcare (3) to describe their proposals and the populations to be served. Although the integration initiative was developed by DMH's Division of Comprehensive Psychiatric Services, screening for and treatment of alcohol and drug use disorders or referral for screening and treatment were also required.

Successful applicants were awarded $100,000 for the period January 1, 2008, to June 30, 2008, and $200,000 a year for the three succeeding fiscal years to be shared equally by the FQHC and CMHC partners each year. A panel of independent reviewers selected seven sites from among the 13 applications received. One-time planning grants ($30,000 each) were awarded to the six applicants that were not selected for full funding to allow them to lay the groundwork to apply for full funding in subsequent years.

Each of the fully funded sites proposed to integrate one or more behavioral health professionals employed by the CMHC (licensed social worker, licensed professional counselor, psychiatric nurse practitioner, or psychiatrist) into one or more FQHC clinics and to establish an FQHC primary care clinic staffed by one or more primary care professionals within a CMHC facility (registered nurse, licensed practical nurse, advanced practice nurse, or physician). The successful applicants include collaborative initiatives from urban, suburban, and rural communities. One successful applicant is a CMHC that is also an FQHC located in one of the state's fastest growing suburban areas. The six sites that received planning grants also represent urban and more rural areas.

Technical assistance

DMH and the professional associations representing the CMHCs and FQHCs collaborated to create a technical assistance team to assist the local partners in addressing the many changes in policies, procedures, understandings, and attitudes required for successful implementation and to help identify and address needed changes in state policies and procedures to ensure the sustainability of the initiative. The three-member technical assistance team provides centralized training and on-site consultation for the behavioral health professionals who are making the transition to a primary care setting. The team also provides consultation and training for the primary care staff at the FQHC sites to help them understand how they can best utilize the newly integrated behavioral health professionals. The team members are committed to the initiative on a half-time basis.

A grant from the Missouri Foundation for Health supports the team, which is composed of a senior administrator with significant experience in Missouri's public mental health system, the clinical program manager from the FQHC professional association, and a clinical psychologist with experience in providing behavioral health services in primary care settings.

Preliminary lessons learned

During the first year of the initiative we learned, or were reminded of, a number of lessons that may be helpful to others who are interested in transforming systems of care, promoting collaboration between FQHCs and CMHCs, integrating primary and behavioral health care, and improving access to care for individuals with serious mental illness.

Project management

Major system transformation initiatives of this magnitude require a project management capacity that includes both the experience and the time to successfully implement and monitor the program. In practice, the technical assistance team has served as a project management team. This was possible because the team includes both a senior administrator, who served for many years in DMH, as well as the clinical program manager for the FQHCs professional association, who transferred some of her existing duties to other staff in order to devote considerable time to the initiative. This enabled the team not only to provide individual consultation to the sites but also to help design the evaluation of the initiative, collect performance data, develop contracts, and work with state and federal authorities to coordinate oversight responsibilities and with the state's Medicaid authority to ensure that DMH start-up funding for the FQHCs is handled in a manner consistent with Medicaid reimbursement rules.

Site visits are conducted every two or three months. During key development stages, some sites have monthly visits or teleconference meetings.

Start-up funding

Upfront funding is important to address the concerns of capital-strapped CMHCs and FQHCs regarding the cost of start-up and of care for the uninsured, as well as to free partners to focus on establishing a strong collaboration without being stymied by turf and resource issues.

Concerns over a lack of capital have limited the development of collaborative efforts to integrate care in Missouri, and the availability of start-up funding was important in getting interested parties to commit to collaboration. The seed funding has been critical in motivating sites to work through the many logistical details and challenges involved in implementing this initiative, especially where the partners had no history of collaboration.

The volume of clients in need of care at a given site appears to be an important factor determining the financial viability of these new clinics. It remains to be seen whether there is adequate volume to financially sustain the new services, particularly for the new satellite FQHCs that have opened in CMHCs.

Myths, misunderstandings, and real differences

Many myths and misunderstandings exist within the public health and public mental health systems regarding the advantages enjoyed and constraints faced by their sister system. It is important to recognize and dispel these myths and misunderstandings early in the transformation process, while acknowledging the real differences between the systems that need to be addressed.

CMHCs and FQHCs generally do not understand the complexities of each other's funding sources and financing mechanisms. In Missouri, some CMHCs erroneously believed that FQHCs did not have to worry about "the bottom line" because of the Medicaid cost-based reimbursement they receive, and some FQHCs mistakenly believed that CMHCs were required to serve everyone who met certain diagnostic criteria because the CMHCs received DMH funding. Misunderstandings about the constraints under which each system operates also led some representatives from both systems to harbor feelings that their sister agency was guilty of "dumping" patients on them.

Among the real differences between the two systems that require attention are their approaches to consumer financial participation. In Missouri, Medicaid clients are charged a copayment by FQHCs but not by CMHCs, and each FQHC establishes its own sliding fee scale, whereas CMHCs use a DMH sliding fee scale. Therefore, individuals who receive service from both an FQHC and a CMHC as part of the integration initiative could be subject to different copayment and sliding fee approaches.

"All politics is local"

Even with a shared goal, there will be different problems, solutions, and levels of progress and success at each site. Local conditions dictate nearly every aspect of the actual form, progress, and success of implementation. Each site is different. In some cases, the FQHC and CMHC have worked together successfully before, in other cases they

have come to the collaboration with some suspicion based on their history, and in still others the collaboration represents the first time their staff members have met one another. Each site has different resources that it is able to commit to the initiative. Each site proposed a somewhat different model for integration and had a somewhat different understanding of the challenges it would face in implementation.

The technical assistance team works to ensure some consistency across the sites. The team provided each site with an orientation to the integration model that is promoted by the DMH as well as in-depth training of clinical staff regarding what integration looks like in the clinical setting and the key skills needed to be successful in an integrated setting.

Nevertheless, each site retains the flexibility to structure its initiative to address local conditions and needs, and these factors affect the pace of implementation. One site, which began seeing consumers within four months of receiving start-up funds, would have had an even quicker start-up if it had not experienced information system connectivity problems. Other sites were slower to initiate integration, often because of the need to recruit and train staff. One site was delayed by the fact that both partners were moving into new facilities. At two other sites, changes were made in the staff originally selected for integration. Most sites were able to begin some integration of staff by the sixth month. Two sites were still in the initial stages of integration after nine months. No site has yet developed full caseloads.

Collaboration and culture

The hard work of team building should not be ignored or underestimated, both at the level of creating a successful collaboration between two agencies and of successfully integrating new clinical staff into a treatment team. FQHCs and CMHCs have distinct organizational cultures and operational environments. When two agencies have little or no experience working together—and may have misconceptions or even suspicions

about each other—it is important to consciously attend to clarifying roles and responsibilities, understanding each other's cultures and environments, and creating trust (4).

Behavioral health professionals who are introduced into a primary care setting for the first time often have to make a number of adjustments to their accustomed ways of working. Primary care settings are faster paced, call for interventions of shorter duration, and require more flexibility in availability than most behavioral health professionals are used to. At the same time, primary care staff often do not recognize the ways in which behavioral health professionals can be helpful in augmenting the care they provide.

Financing

The most critical issues for sustainability appear to be securing Medicaid reimbursement for behavioral health services provided to assist individuals in managing chronic illnesses, such as diabetes, and to develop appropriate mechanisms for covering the cost of services to the uninsured. Many people who do not have a behavioral health diagnosis but who have chronic general medical problems require behavioral health services and supports to effectively manage their illnesses. However, these services are not currently reimbursable through the Missouri Medicaid program. Although the Medicaid agency acknowledges the importance of these services, it remains a challenge to devise a cost-effective approach to introducing reimbursement for them at a time of state budget shortfalls.

Being able to appropriately meet the needs of individuals without insurance is also a critical factor for sustainability. Both FQHCs and CMHCs have limited resources to address these needs, and yet the integration initiative is likely to increase the demand on each system. A major objective of the initiative is to determine to what extent existing funds can be leveraged to meet the anticipated increase in demand and to what extent the additional funding that has been provided to the sites by DMH for the initiative will continue to be required.

Momentum

Sustainability will be a function of the ability to maintain momentum for the initiative despite changes in leadership and management at the state and local levels. At the time of this writing, Missouri state government is in transition from a Republican gubernatorial administration to a Democratic administration. In addition, like many other states, Missouri is likely to face budgetary challenges. Therefore, although the executive leadership of the DMH does not automatically change with a new administration, the new governor will have significant influence over the policies and initiatives of DMH, including the extent to which funding for the integration initiative is supported, expanded, or curtailed. (Although the DMH director is a member of the governor's cabinet, DMH is one of a handful of state agencies with a commission that has responsibility for appointing and removing the director.)

Likewise, changes in leadership at the local sites or in budgetary realities could challenge the sustainability of the initiative. Although there have, in fact, been some changes in leadership at the local level since the initiative began, the new leadership has maintained the level of commitment.

Conclusions

The Missouri Initiative is still in the early stages of implementation, and data collection by an independent evaluator has just begun. The evaluation will assess primary care and behavioral health care performance measures, staff attitudes, consumer experiences of integrated care, and the impact of the pilot program on access to and cost of care.

Although co-location of staff has been initiated at all sites, caseloads remain low at most sites, and changes in staffing at some sites have meant what has amounted to starting over. Many issues remain to be resolved to ensure sustainability, including making certain that integration becomes part of the culture of each organization, weathering challenging budget times, and developing secure sources of reimbursement for integrated services. Over the next two years we will be learning new lessons that should help other states and stakeholders better understand the value of, and the most successful strategies for, strengthening the public health–mental health safety net by promoting collaboration between FQHCs and CMHCs, integrating primary and behavioral health care, and improving access to primary care for individuals with serious mental illness.

Acknowledgments and disclosures

Dr. Druss's work on this initiative is supported in part by grant K24MH075867 from the National Institute of Mental Health.

The authors report no competing interests.

References

1. Achieving the Promise: Transforming Mental Health Care in America. Pub no SMA-03-3832. Rockville, Md, Department of Health and Human Services, President's New Freedom Commission on Mental Health, 2003
2. Parks J, Svendsen D, Singer P, et al: Morbidity and Mortality in People With Serious Mental Illness. Alexandria, Va, National Association of State Mental Health Program Directors, Oct 2006
3. Mauer B, Druss B: Mind and Body Reunited: Improving Care at the Behavioral and Primary Healthcare Interface. Albuquerque, NM, American College of Mental Health Administration, Mar 2007. Available at www.acmha.org/summit/pre_summit_paper_021907.pdf
4. Covey SMR: The Speed of Trust: The One Thing That Changes Everything. New York, Free Press, 2006

Mental Health Policy and Services Five Years After the President's Commission Report: An Interview With Michael F. Hogan

Lloyd I. Sederer, M.D.

Editor's Note: As the nation awaits a new administration and as states face budget cuts and increasing demand for health and human services, *Psychiatric Services* asked Dr. Hogan to offer his thoughts about the past, present, and future of mental health policy and services through a series of questions posed by Dr. Sederer.— *Howard H. Goldman, M.D., Ph.D.*

Dr. Sederer: I'd like to begin by asking you about the President's New Freedom Commission on Mental Health. It has been five years since the commission's report was published. What were the overarching conclusions of that report?

Dr. Hogan: The report speaks for itself. I would say that the first thing we learned was that mental health is and must be a bipartisan matter. Policy ideas that emerged in the work of the Carter Commission 25 years earlier were implemented incrementally in successive administrations, including the conservative Reagan administration. Our commission, appointed by President Bush, built on work done during the Clinton administration—largely the efforts of Surgeon General David Satcher.

A second lesson is that mental health problems are pervasive and have profound consequences for people's lives and health and often lead to disability. The prevalence of untreat-

ed mental health problems leads to enormous economic costs yet support for mental health care is not commensurate with this impact.

Another fundamental lesson is that recovery from mental illness is a reality and must be a goal of our mental health care system. Although the phenomenon of recovery was mentioned in the Surgeon General's report on mental health in 1999, it was substantially elevated by the work of the New Freedom Commission. In turn, our understanding of the significance of recovery was greatly enhanced by former First Lady Rosalynn Carter. When she met with the commission, Mrs. Carter stated that the greatest change in the field in the 25 years since the Carter Commission "is that we now understand that it is possible for anyone with mental illness to recover." The fundamental conclusion here is one of hope.

LIS: Is there an enduring message from the New Freedom Commission's work?

MFH: Perhaps it is that for us to succeed with our mission of recovery we will need ongoing policy changes and leadership across a spectrum of programs and settings—not just in specialty settings and state mental health systems. We will need to be engaged in health and school reform, disability policy, affordable housing, criminal justice, and all the other places where adults and youths with mental disorders appear in our health and human services systems. And we know that advancing this work by having a commission every 25 years is not going to be sufficient.

Recovery and transformation

LIS: Earlier this year my colleagues and I published in this journal an arti-

cle that aimed to define recovery (1). How do you understand recovery, and why has it gained the status that it has?

MFH: There are different ways to see recovery. There is the reality now established in long-term studies, from Eugen Bleuler to Courtney Harding, of the outcomes of people with schizophrenia. Good outcomes are far more possible than we had imagined. Following people over decades, not just years, was what proved this point. Recovery is also the appreciation that it is possible to have a good life despite what can often be a crushing and catastrophic illness. This message has been articulated by people who have lived it, like Ed Knight and Pat Deegan. And finally there is the meaning of recovery as hope.

LIS: "Transformation" sounds like a bit of a religious or revolutionary happening. How do you define it? What does it take to make it happen?

MFH: Transformation as a concept emerged organically for the commission. "Reform" seemed like a stale idea. Transformation resonated with members' beliefs that change is deeper than what happens from the "top down" and with structural change. Transformation reflects a more nuanced but also a more realistic view whereby subtle changes in processes can over time deeply affect how people and organizations behave. It is a view of change that can begin anywhere and may initially seem small and incremental but its effects are, well, transformative. Because no one is in charge of the complex and fragmented mental health system, we have no one person or authority to orchestrate change. In this sense, transformation as a process of change is like recovery; expert guidance and leader-

Michael F. Hogan, Ph.D., is commissioner of the New York State Office of Mental Health (NYSOMH). He served as the chair of the President's New Freedom Commission on Mental Health. Dr. Sederer is the medical director of NYSOMH. Originally published in the November 2008 issue of Psychiatric Services.

ship are required, but lasting change is achieved by the people involved.

LIS: How is it that the United States spends so much money on mental health care and yet it seems as if we have such a low "return on investment" when we consider the suffering, disability, and death (from suicide and physical illnesses) that mental illnesses produce?

MFH: Drs. Richard Frank and Sherry Glied published a remarkable analysis of 50 years of the history of health economics and mental health, *Better but Not Well* (2). They found that although health care spending overall has increased two- to threefold after accounting for inflation, mental health spending as a proportion of the gross domestic product has been essentially flat. Yet access has dramatically increased; quality is much improved, as measured by the proportion of care that is consistent with effectiveness research (though we have still far to go); and the well-being of people with mental illness is generally better. It is important to emphasize that improvements in well-being are largely due to improvements in mainstream programs: Social Security, Medicaid, Medicare, and health insurance. Those with the most severe impairments, however, still face many challenges. But considering that people are in sum better off, while mental health spending is flat, we can say that mental health care is a great buy!

LIS: Can we do better?

MFH: We are faced with the combined challenges of complexity, fragmentation, and absence of a national health care system or set of policies. Responsibility for mental health care has dissipated over time to multiple federal, state, and local settings. This is especially a result of the "Medicaiding" of services. In terms of access to and quality of care, the state Medicaid director is perhaps more important than the state mental health director. But the state Medicaid director may not appreciate the nuances of mental health and mental illness. Thus we face the problem of how to organize and deliver services in a dissipated and fragmented system of care where no one is in charge and complex solutions are not likely to take root.

If we are to meet the needs of our constituents, we will need action at community, state, and national levels. How might we proceed to improve the integration, continuity, and quality of care? At the community level we could adopt the idea of a "clinical home" for people with mental illnesses. This locus of responsibility may be in primary care for some people, especially those with nonpsychotic illnesses such as depression and anxiety disorders, and in the mental health specialty sector (for example, a mental health center) for people with severe and persistent illnesses. Providing a full range of health care services over time in one setting can improve quality, comprehensiveness, continuity, and integration of care. As we know better than ever, co-occurring conditions are the rule, not the exception, so health and mental health services—as well as mental health and chemical dependency services—need to be readily accessible and integrated.

At the state or regional level we need to rediscover the core concept of a system of care. States have lost that concept with the dominance of Medicaid and health maintenance organizations. I don't imagine a singular model for a system of care, but we need leadership to root it in mental health centers, county governments, and primary care plans.

Finally, leadership is dearly needed at the federal level. Although the Center for Mental Health Services [CMHS] of SAMHSA has the point responsibility for programmatic leadership, we have seen the mental health block grant diminish to 1%–2% of state mental health expenditures. CMHS simply does not have enough leverage or clout. Frank and Glied suggested in their book that the President might try appointing a "mental health czar"—someone with a White House office. I don't know what the solution is, but we need a new approach. Perhaps we might achieve this with a new federal administration representing either political party.

Change

LIS: Surgeon General Satcher's work demonstrated that there are highly effective treatments but that the problem is the gap between what we

know and what we do. What do we need to do to close that gap?

MFH: We know from the change literature that it takes 15 or more years for new practices to be incorporated into everyday settings. Although we are getting smarter about how to support adoption of evidence-based practices, the message here is to stay with it. We also know that organizations that have experience with change are better able to accommodate new change. We need to help provider organizations achieve some stability and also have some success with change so that they can become self-adapting change organizations.

For change to take root there is a clear need for leadership at the state and federal levels. But most change is change that people initiate themselves. Leaders create the circumstances that allow for communities and providers to do the right thing. Lao Tse, the great Chinese warrior-philosopher, said you can tell a great leader from a good one (and a bad one) because the people say, "We accomplished great things together."

LIS: You have led public services in four states over three decades. What observations do you have about leading processes of change?

MFH: One lesson is to work in places where people are about to do great things. I have been fortunate in that regard. It is also possible to build the capacity of organizations and even systems to be what Margaret Wheatley, an expert on organizational behavior, has termed "leader-ful."

What can we do now?

LIS: You have emphasized that fragmentation of services with too little accountability is at the heart of why good people and the dedication of precious resources do not succeed. Where do we begin?

MFH: As I mentioned earlier, the idea of a clinical home with dedicated clinicians being accountable to a recipient and family is something we can do now. As we try to stabilize, improve, and expand care in mental health clinics in New York State, the quality standards that you developed for the state support this approach. We are also focused on how best to support the adoption of evidence-based practices and have created child and adult EBP centers at the New York State Psychiatric Institute.

LIS: Our good friend and colleague Dr. Bob Drake has shown that among people with a severe mental illness and a co-occurring substance use disorder, 50% get no care, 45% get poor treatment, and 5% get evidence-based practice. Yet we keep focusing on improving the care of the 5%!

MFH: Exactly. This turns our attention to how we can become more consumer oriented in order to better engage and retain people in care. When people stay with treatment, these treatments have a chance to work. We must make our clinics and programs more receptive in terms of making people feel comfortable, having hours of operation that accommodate their needs, and conveying a sense to the recipient and family that we are here to help, 24 hours a day. Settings that include people in recovery as staff and that offer programs run by consumers also help normalize the experience of coming in for care. We have also learned that sending people with co-occurring disorders to multiple sites of service doesn't work very well—"sequential" care is often futile. If we can engage people and provide integrated mental health and substance use services, a tall order, that is precisely what people need. That is what we are doing here in New York, in conjunction with our sister agency the State Office of Alcoholism and Substance Abuse Services.

LIS: On a related matter regarding integrated treatment, the disturbing eight-state study by National Association of State Mental Health Program Directors [NASMHPD] demonstrated that adults in the public mental health care system get physically ill sooner and more severely and die 25 years earlier than their age counterparts—from chronic diseases like diabetes, heart and lung diseases, and cancer. Where do we start here?

MFH: Everywhere. The SPAN program developed by our agency is an example. It is about health and wellness that is consumer focused and calls for consumers to take responsibility, with our assistance, for S (smoking cessation), P (prevention,

including knowing your numbers such as BMI, blood pressure, and glucose), A (activity), and N (nutrition). Doing this in state hospitals will be difficult, but where it really needs to be done (and where it will provide a bigger lift) is throughout community-based services, integrating primary care and mental health services. We are working on that, and it is now a focus for the NASMHPD medical directors. Consumers are our best allies in this endeavor, because they know better that we do that getting better mentally doesn't help that much if your body is falling apart.

LIS: People with mental disorders and substance use disorders can never stabilize or recover without safe and secure housing. Yet there is no way that enough supportive housing can be funded, built, or rented for the numbers of disabled people in need for generations to come. What would an effective housing policy look like at the federal and state levels?

MFH: At the federal level today there is an 80% reduction in investment in affordable housing compared with 30 years ago. It is as if affordable housing has been deleted from the federal agenda. Yet great breakthroughs have occurred, such as the Housing Trust Fund. Maybe we will see some change with the next administration. At the state level, mental health agencies need to partner with other state agencies charged with housing development and promote set-asides, increase attention to people with disabilities, assist provider and development organizations to access capital financing and tax credits, and enlist private-equity developers into the affordable housing market.

Howard Goldman, editor of *Psychiatric Services*, published an article in 2003 in *Health Affairs*—"How Do You Pay Your Rent?" He reminds us of the grassroots effort that is also needed to make housing part of the conversation, since a person's housing status is a critical-path matter, especially for people with serious mental illness.

Closing thoughts

LIS: The economy is tanking, state and federal budgets are in desperate conditions, and too many promises

about community mental health have gone unmet. Yet I know you have hope and that we all need hope—our consumers, their families, and we professionals alike. Where do we find hope? How do we nurture it?

MFH: It might be said that we are at the worst of times: fragmentation, stigma, frozen budgets. But there are rational reasons for hope. We are still in the first decade after the Surgeon General's report on mental health. Our scientific understanding of mental illness continues to blossom, and we can claim substantial effectiveness for our treatments—when clients get them. We have cause for rational optimism, and we need to carry it into the next decade.

The next generation of mental health professionals and the services they provide need to move well beyond the confines of mental health. Our field and its leaders and practitioners must embrace many other sectors, such as schools, primary care (for adults and youths), the courts, juvenile and adult correctional systems, and wherever else our clients' paths cross. There is a growing awareness and receptivity in these settings that we are all working with many of the same people, only at different moments in their lives—and that if we work together we will surely do better than we are now. Reflecting this awareness, the *American Journal of Psychiatry* is publishing a series of papers on mental health in the mainstream of public policy.

Rational optimism says that there has not been a better time to be hopeful. Change is occurring. Because we live in the day-to-day we may be among the last to recognize it. The ground is shifting toward a new, more recovery-oriented and integrated approach to mental health care. We are on the right path and need to stay the course.

LIS: Thank you for your insights.

References

1. Lieberman JA, Drake RE, Sederer LI, et al: Science and recovery in schizophrenia. Psychiatric Services 59:487–496, 2008

2. Frank RG, Glied SA: Better but Not Well: Mental Health Policy in the United States Since 1950. Baltimore, Johns Hopkins University Press, 2006

A Public Health Model of Mental Health for the 21st Century

A. Kathryn Power, M.Ed.

In 2003 the President's New Freedom Commission called for the transformation of the public mental health system to one that is person centered, recovery focused, evidence based, and quality driven. In this column the director of the Center for Mental Health Services describes progress made by the center over the past five years as well as challenges and opportunities. She presents a strategic forecast, based on stakeholder input, to guide policy formulation and resource allocation. Central to the forecast is the concept of a public health model of mental health that takes a community approach to prevention, treatment, and promotion of well-being. (*Psychiatric Services* 60:580–584, 2009)

There is no health without mental health. This simple yet profound statement is at the heart of transformation not only of the mental health system in the United States but of health care itself. At a time when the new Administration is seeking pragmatic and progressive solutions to health care reform, the Center for Mental Health Services (CMHS), part of the Substance Abuse and Mental Health Services Administration (SAMHSA) in the U.S. Department of Health and Human Services (DHHS), has both the opportunity and the responsibility to play a leading role in health care policy, financ-

Ms. Power is director of the Center for Mental Health Services, Substance Abuse and Mental Health Services Administration, 5600 Fishers Ln., Room 17-99, Rockville MD 20857 (e-mail: kpower@samhsa.gov). Originally published in the May 2009 issue of Psychiatric Services.

ing, and services. We are in the business of building resilience and facilitating recovery for all Americans. The time to do so is now.

External events are shaping discussions about mental health services and health reform. Passage in October 2008 of mental health parity legislation has ushered in a new era of opportunity for the integration of mental health care and general medical care. The current economic downturn places stress on individuals, provider systems, and states and communities. And a number of groups have called for an increased focus on public health and prevention to promote the well being of individuals, families, and communities and to strengthen U.S. competitiveness and national security.

CMHS is well positioned to implement a public health approach to mental health. Several major reports—including those by the Surgeon General, Institute of Medicine, and the President's New Freedom Commission on Mental Health—have called for fundamental transformation of the nation's mental health system. In response, CMHS has led the effort to advance a recovery-oriented, person-centered approach to mental health recovery and state mental health systems transformation. This effort anticipates the development of a defined strategy for mental health care for the nation as a whole.

Together with mental health care consumers and family members and key stakeholders at the federal, state, national, and local levels, CMHS has initiated dialogue and begun to implement change in a number of critical areas. Most notably, CMHS has helped develop programs and services that are person centered, recovery

focused, evidence based, quality driven, and outcomes oriented.

In the coming years, the sense of what it means to improve the nation's health will continue to evolve. Increasingly, the focus will move from illness to health. New practice models will integrate mental health with general health care. Electronic medical records will improve efficiency and reduce medical errors, and personal health records will put tools for recovery and wellness in the hands of consumers. CMHS is ready to help guide these changes.

To help us do so, I asked staff, consultants, and key stakeholders to reflect with me on the progress CMHS has made vis-à-vis mental health transformation over the past five years and the challenges and opportunities it faces in the next five years. We conducted a comprehensive literature review and formal constituent input process. The result is a strategic forecast to guide the center's work in formulating policy and directing resources. We are in the process of finalizing the forecast, which will serve as the basis for more formal strategic action.

Information gathering

Clearly, no assessment of how the mental health field has evolved in recent years would be complete without a review of the key documents that have both influenced and reflected change. *Mental Health: A Report of the Surgeon General* (1) established the historic and scientific base for the existence and treatment of mental health conditions. *Achieving the Promise: Transforming Mental Health Care in America* (2) and the subsequent Federal Action Agenda (3) specified the need for a consumer- and family-driven system of mental health care that embraces recovery. *Improving the Quality of Health Care for Mental and Substance-Use Conditions* (4), part of the Institute of Medicine's Quality Chasm Series, outlined the evidence base for quality mental health care and the need for services to be person centered and coordinated across all systems of care.

These seminal reports provided a platform for more recent analyses about the ways in which changing market forces—including the predominance of Medicaid as a funder of public mental health services—have affected public and political discourse about mental health and mental illnesses in this country (5,6). Together with scientific findings that reveal significant disparities in health and health care delivery for people with serious mental illnesses, these policy documents point toward a future in which mental health is regarded as essential for overall health.

Findings in the scientific literature were corroborated and amplified by the voices of individuals who make policy, provide services, and have experienced mental illnesses and recovery. CMHS consulted its staff, key constituents, and leading experts in the field, including members of the CMHS National Advisory Council and its Subcommittee on Consumer/ Survivor Issues. Respondents were asked to examine CMHS accomplishments vis-à-vis mental health transformation and suggest areas for future investment. They made it very clear that the time for study and reflection are over; now is the time for concerted, focused, and deliberate action.

In particular, these individuals made some important observations. Many respondents pointed out that mental health care and general medical care services need to be better coordinated and integrated. There was a great deal of discussion about recovery from mental illnesses and the tools and resources needed to promote it. Respondents encouraged CMHS to build on its recovery focus and develop tools and financial incentives to support the development of recovery-oriented systems of care. Most respondents raised

concerns about future funding for public mental health systems. Financing issues include both the allocation of resources and the scope of coverage. Some respondents expressed the need for a defined national mental health policy that reflects and guides the U.S. global position on mental health and mental illness. Respondents also expressed concern about the size, quality, and aging of the mental health workforce. Some respondents stressed the fact that data can be a powerful tool in quality improvement, and outcomes need to be standardized to promote their use. They also noted opportunities for expanded use of technology in data collection, as well as in support of direct services, health promotion, and wellness. Finally, most respondents believe that transformation of the mental health system will continue to evolve in the coming years.

On the basis of our literature review and key informant input, we developed a framework for our strategic forecast that includes a vision, values, priorities, and strategies, coupled with basic core functions. Taken together, these key elements assisted us in creating a template that both guides our work and serves as a pulse check on our progress.

Vision, values, and priorities
The CMHS vision is grounded in and inclusive of the SAMHSA vision of "a life in the community for everyone." We advance our vision as both a signpost of where the nation must head and a benchmark for the use of CMHS resources.

CMHS envisions a nation in which mental health is regarded as essential for overall health and in which all individuals have access to the community opportunities and health and social supports that will help them excel in a complex and competitive society. To achieve this vision of a preferred future, our work must be grounded in a set of values that guide the programs CMHS supports, the services that these programs provide, and the infrastructures that support them. In our preferred future:

♦ Recovery is the expected out-

come. All mental health services and supports are driven by the primary goal of recovery, and all providers acknowledge and offer the hope of recovery. Consumer-operated services and programs are implemented as an evidence-based approach to promote recovery.

♦ Service recipients direct their own care. Consumers of mental health services have full access to and make informed use of effective services and tools that allow them to take charge of their recovery and their lives.

♦ Services are evidence based. Routine mental health care is grounded in evidence-based practice and practice-based evidence and is coordinated across all medical and social systems of care.

♦ Performance management drives quality improvement. Process and outcome measures support evolving cycles of change, and performance goals are tied to specific outcomes.

These values form the basis for and are embedded in our key priorities. In the next few years, every service, program, or activity we support must adhere to, advance, and promote the following five priorities.

First and foremost, CMHS will embrace the concept and practice of a public health model of health care. The public health model is a community approach to preventing and treating illnesses and promoting well-being. It addresses treatment for individuals across the lifespan while developing interventions for the entire population. As steward of the nation's mental health, together with our SAMHSA partners in substance abuse treatment and prevention, CMHS informs and educates individuals about mental health and well-being; develops policies and mobilizes public-private partnerships that support individual and community health efforts; ensures a competent workforce; and evaluates the effectiveness, accessibility, and quality of our services, programs, and activities. Each of these is considered an essential public health service, and all are reflected in our principal strategies, highlighted below.

Second, we will use the tools of

public health to advance holistic, person-centered health care. A holistic approach is grounded in the knowledge that health is a function of the complex interplay between body, mind, spirit, and community. Person-centered care is respectful and responsive to the needs and values of individuals and honors and supports recovery and wellness. All of our programs, services, and activities must meet this standard.

Third, we know that in the spirit of public health, which considers both the health of individuals and the health of the community, we must attend to the broad determinants of health. These include the personal, social, economic, and environmental factors that influence health, well-being, and wellness. For people with mental illnesses this means focusing on such issues as poverty; widespread unemployment; inequitable distribution of health care resources; and the discrimination, fear, and bias that keep people with mental health problems at the margins of society. Without access to housing, health care, employment, and social support, individuals are excluded from all that it means to be healthy in today's society.

Fourth, the public health approach demands that prevention, early intervention, and treatment services be delivered by a customer-focused workforce. Practicing in a 21st century health care environment demands a competent, capable, sustainable, and culturally diverse workforce. Members of this workforce—including mental health consumers—must be recruited, educated, trained, and supported to practice whole-health, person-centered health care.

Finally, health care that is inclusive of individual, community, and social factors must demonstrate its value as measured by both short- and long-term outcomes—hence our focus on continuous quality improvement. Evaluating the effectiveness, accessibility, and quality of personal and population-based health services is a key tenet of the public health approach. We must assess not only the programs, services, and activities we support but also the way in which our decisions are made.

Principal strategies

Creating whole-health, person-centered health care, achieved through a public health approach that addresses the broad determinants of health, demands attention to strategic change in several important spheres of influence. CMHS is well positioned and prepared to address the following three key areas, with specific actions and policies.

Building the information base

Information is the foundation on which a public health approach is built. Four specific actions are included in this area. First, CMHS will review, disseminate, and provide technical assistance on effective mental health promotion and mental illness prevention strategies. Promoting mental health and preventing mental illnesses are the essence of a public health approach to health care. The concepts of mental health promotion and mental illness prevention rest on the knowledge that mental health exists on a continuum, with neither health nor illness existing in pure isolation from one another. The recently released Institute of Medicine report on prevention, supported by SAMHSA, has some exciting findings about our ability to promote mental health and prevent mental health problems, particularly among our nation's youth (7). CMHS can promote these strategies to preclude the onset of mental disorders, lessen their impact, and forestall comorbid conditions and long-term disability.

Second, CMHS will help develop, disseminate, and measure the broad determinants of mental health. Without action to address the broader social, economic, political, and environmental factors that have an impact on health and well-being, both individual and community health suffer. This is evidenced by the fact that individuals with serious mental illnesses die, on average, 25 years earlier than the general population. They die from treatable medical conditions that are caused by modifiable risk factors, including smoking, obesity, substance abuse, and inadequate access to medical care (8). CMHS can ensure that such disparities will be addressed.

Third, CMHS will promote the dissemination of evidence-based practice and practice-based evidence. In its broadest sense, inequality in health care is driven by social, economic, and political factors. Inequality also results, particularly in mental health treatment, when providers rely on outdated science rather than on the best available evidence-based interventions. Many communities lack the financial or technological resources required to keep abreast of the latest developments in science and service. To address these gaps, CMHS can ensure that resources for the development and use of evidence-based practice and practice-based evidence are made available to those who need this help the most.

Fourth, CMHS will harness communications technology to promote involvement in treatment, services, and policy. Informing, educating, and empowering people about health issues are considered essential public health services. Electronic communication can promote health literacy, disseminate public health messages, support healthy behaviors, and create virtual learning communities. Internet-based and other interactive tools, including social networking, put information and decision-making technology that supports recovery directly into the hands of consumers. CMHS can use these powerful tools to foster peer support, convene national policy discussions, and promote online learning about person-centered care and recovery.

Providing national mental health policy leadership

Information is ineffective without policies that support its use. Two specific actions are included in this area. First, CMHS will emphasize and coordinate the role of mental health in evolving health reform, including the development of a national mental health policy. Public health is a population-based approach that supports the development of whole-health, person-centered health care. This requires that the mental health community be intimately involved in any and all discussions of health care policy at

Table 1

Core functions of the Center for Mental Health Services and associated steps

Core function	Description	Specific steps
Initiate	Identify a need	Assess existing and emerging issues
		Evaluate opportunities for broader impact
		Track trends that define the problem
		Develop ways to address identified need
Facilitate	Take action	Identify and convene potential partners
		Develop a range of solutions and products
		Determine the appropriate change agents
		Support and fund services, programs, and activities
		Follow up to ensure accountability
Disseminate	Distribute findings	Review results of services, programs, and activities
		Develop tools for individuals and systems
		Enhance existing tools for new situations
		Use multiple communication channels
		Provide technical assistance
Measure	Evaluate outcomes	Measure services, programs, and activities
		Evaluate results against goals
		Use data for quality improvement

the federal, state, and local levels. As a leading voice for mental health promotion, mental illness prevention, recovery, and treatment, CMHS can lead discussions with key stakeholders about evolving health policy and the role for mental health.

Second, CMHS will cultivate leaders in the public and private sector who are informed about all aspects of mental health financing. As several observers have noted, financing policies were the principal driver of system change in mental health in the latter half of the 20th century. Medicaid policy in many ways is synonymous with mental health policy; managed care also shapes the delivery of mental health services. In addition, passage of mental health parity will have an impact on employer-sponsored health insurance coverage and, by extension, on private and public systems of care. CMHS can help create shared objectives for public and private payers for mental health services to promote whole-health, person-centered health care.

Providing leadership to the field

Finally, information and policy are two components of our approach to public health. The third is field leadership. Four specific actions are included in this area. First, CMHS will help states and communities adopt whole-health, person-centered health care. Many states and communities have made great strides in this area, but others lag behind. By definition, all sectors that have an impact on the lives of people with mental health problems must be involved and invested in transforming mental health services. These sectors include, but are not limited to, health care, housing, transportation, employment, education, social services, services for veterans, criminal and juvenile justice, and child welfare. CMHS can play a leading role in promoting and supporting the level of collaboration required to have an impact on the financing, delivery, and evaluation of mental health and general health care services.

Second, CMHS will help educate, train, and support a 21st century health care workforce. Mental health and general medical treatment and services are only as good as the workforce that delivers care. The practice of mental health care and general medical care must include assessment of the full range of health-related issues, treatment planning that takes each of these factors into account, and support for the whole person. Such services must be offered in both mental health and general medical settings by practitioners and providers who can practice in a cul-turally diverse, multidisciplinary, high-tech health care environment. CMHS can play a leadership role in educating, training, and supporting the modern health care workforce.

Third, CMHS will help empower and mobilize the individuals who will lead the mental health and general health care fields. Significant change in accepted practice—represented by the adoption of whole-health, person-centered health care—requires transformational leaders. Consumers and family members who have experiences with mental illnesses must be empowered and mobilized to shape, inform, and provide leadership to the mental health care and general medical care fields. Likewise, practitioners and providers must become leaders capable of engaging with consumers and family members and of embracing the technological tools and resources that support a public health approach. CMHS will continue to define key leadership skills and provide the training and technical assistance to advance them.

Fourth, CMHS will develop a performance management culture that uses data to make financing and programmatic decisions. Programs that use public funds to provide health care services must be held accountable for producing results. CMHS uses a variety of tools to collect and report process and performance data on its services, programs, and activities. These data must become the centerpiece of performance management tools and processes that provide timely, relevant, and actionable information. Performance improvement activities based on the judicious use of data will ensure that all CMHS-funded services, programs, and activities promote person-centered, recovery-focused, evidence-based, quality-driven, and outcome-oriented health care.

CMHS core functions

Each of the strategies enumerated above can be realized by using a set of public health tools and processes that CMHS calls its "core functions." These core functions reflect the center's legislative and congressional mandates and provide a standard by which any potential service, program, or activity can be judged and implemented.

Most resources under CMHS stewardship are responsive to congressionally mandated programs. These include the Mental Health Block Grant, Children's Mental Health Initiative, Protection and Advocacy for Individuals With Mental Illness, and Projects for Assistance in Transition From Homelessness. A set of discretionary activities, called Programs of Regional and National Significance, focuses on new and emerging priorities. These include such areas as reducing and eliminating the use of seclusion and restraint, developing trauma-informed services and systems, and addressing the overrepresentation of individuals with mental illnesses in the criminal justice system.

To ensure that both its congressionally mandated and discretionary programs are designed to create and sustain a public health model, CMHS uses the tools highlighted in Table 1. Each of these tools or core functions is one element in an overarching framework for change that ensures accountability, transparency, and alignment with available resources. Taken together, they are part of an iterative and continuous process that provides a framework for current and future action.

Next steps

The development of this strategic forecast is not the end point in a process of change; instead, it is a critical step toward achieving the vision of a preferred future. The task going forward is to ensure that every current and planned service, program, and activity is grounded in the values and emerging priorities of DHHS and SAMHSA and implemented according to the core public health functions. In order for a strategic forecast to have lasting value, there must also be an ongoing process of review, measurement and accountability, and process improvement. As we finalize our work on the strategic forecast, we will create a formal vehicle for performance management to ensure that our work is person centered, recovery focused, evidence based, and quality driven. The individuals we serve deserve nothing less.

Acknowledgments and disclosures

The author reports no competing interests.

References

1. Mental Health: A Report of the Surgeon General. Rockville, Md, US Department of Health and Human Services, US Public Health Service, 1999

2. Achieving the Promise: Transforming Mental Health Care in America. Pub no SMA-03-3832. Rockville, Md, Department of Health and Human Services, President's New Freedom Commission on Mental Health, 2003

3. Transforming Mental Health Care in America: The Federal Action Agenda: First Steps. Rockville, Md, Substance Abuse and Mental Health Services Administration, 2005

4. Improving the Quality of Health Care for Mental and Substance-Use Conditions: Institute of Medicine Quality Chasm Series. Washington, DC, National Academics Press, 2006

5. Grob GN, Goldman HH: The Dilemma of Federal Mental Health Policy: Radical Reform or Incremental Change? New Brunswick, NJ, Rutgers University Press, 2006

6. Frank RG, Glied SA: Mental Health Policy in the United States Since 1950: Better but Not Well. Baltimore, Md, Johns Hopkins University Press, 2006

7. O'Connell ME, Boat T, Warner KE (eds): Preventing Mental, Emotional, and Behavioral Disorders Among Young People: Progress and Possibilities. Washington, DC, National Academies Press, 2009

8. Parks J, Svendsen D, Singer P, et al (eds): Morbidity and Mortality in People With Serious Mental Illness. Alexandria, Va, National Association of State Mental Health Program Directors Medical Directors Council, 2006